SHIFTING THE FRONTIERS

SHIFTING THE FRONTIERS

FRONTIERS

An Action Framework for the Future of the Caribbean

Edited by
WINSTON DOOKERAN AND CARLOS ELIAS

IAN RANDLE PUBLISHERS
Kingston • Miami

UWI
ST. AUGUSTINE
CAMPUS

Published in collaboration with the of the Office
of the Principal, The University of the West Indies,
St. Augustine Campus, Trinidad

First published in Jamaica, 2016 by
Ian Randle Publishers
16 Herb McKenley Drive
Box 686
Kingston 6
www.ianrandlepublishers.com

© 2016, The University of the West Indies
ISBN: 978-976-637-919-3 (hbk)
ISBN: 978-976-637-937-7 (pbk)

A CIP catalogue record for this book is available from
the National Library of Jamaica

Book Design by Ian Randle Publishers
Printed and Bound in the United States of America

Table of Contents

List of Figures

List of Tables

Professor Clement Sankat

Preface

Professor Clement Sankat
Pro Vice-Chancellor and Campus Principal,
The University of the West Indies, St. Augustine, Trinidad

The Caribbean region is enduring a crisis of protracted development as the second decade of the twenty-first century comes to an end. This reality is reflected in several persistent challenges which the Caribbean region continues to face, including slow growth rates, high debt burdens, weak governance structures and institutions, escalating crime and violence, high youth unemployment and a stalled regional integration process, just to name a few. To effect change at this juncture in the history of the Caribbean region, what is needed is a dispensation of new ideas, new thinking, new actions, new paradigms, new models and mechanisms for execution, that challenge the status quo of traditional Caribbean development for the benefit of its people. The region must find a way to translate individual smallness and fragmentation into opportunities for the whole that are of an immense multiplying magnitude compared to the future of single, small island-states with their inherent limitations.

Cognizant of this reality, UWI St. Augustine Campus and by extension the regional University of the West Indies partnered with the Ministry of Foreign Affairs, Trinidad and Tobago led by the Honourable Winston Dookeran and the United Nations System in Trinidad and Tobago, led by Mr. Richard Blewitt along with many other international development partners, including—CARICOM, the Commonwealth, the Association of Caribbean States (ACS), Corporacion Andinade Fomento (CAF), and the Organization of American States (OAS) among others, to host the *Forum on the Future of the Caribbean* on May 5–7, 2015. This Forum, aptly entitled, *Disruptive Thinking. Bold Action. Practical Outcomes* was intentionally designed to be a mould-breaking and transformative medium for discussion, debate and dialogue to help the region re-position itself and be acknowledged as an important player on the international stage and secure sustainable development in an ever-evolving and competitive world system.

This highly anticipated Forum made good on its promise and certainly did not disappoint. It brought together a large cross-section of passionate participants including Prime Ministers, Ministers of

Government, members of the Diplomatic Corps, representatives of international and regional organizations, captains of industry, academics, policy makers, practitioners, members of civil society, trade unions and young professionals. Participants came from all walks of life, from professionals with letters to ordinary citizens, not only from the English-speaking Caribbean but also from the wider Spanish, French and Dutch-speaking Caribbean, and extra-regionally. I must give special mention to the many young people, including our distinctive UWI students who presented and made very relevant contributions. I was also heartened by the comments and questions that came from the audience which were very thought provoking and sometimes even unsettling, but always kept the discussion focused and had the the best interest of the people of our region in mind.

As I reflected upon this unique Forum, I therefore could not help but think that this is the type of forthright, open and inclusive discussion/discourse our region needs to have on an ongoing basis. This must be the new normal for our conferences; forums that take us out of our comfort zones and force us to think independently, creatively and outside the box. As I opined at the opening ceremony, 'bold solutions to our present challenges will not reside in past thinking…bold thinking must no longer be on the periphery, it must now be at the centre!' It was Dr. Antonio Prado who said on the first day of the Forum that, 'we need disruptive thinking for a disruptive age'. This is an indispensable environment for the progress and advancement of our Caribbean civilization and therefore I submit that the Forum on the Future of the Caribbean was an extraordinary event in the history of the countries of the wider Caribbean region and by extension the people of the Western Hemisphere and the Global South.

This publication, a collaborative effort and output from the Forum on the Future of the Caribbean aims to preserve the thoughtful, valuable and significant contributions made by the various presenters and participants. It not only serves as an institutional memory for the Forum, but we also hope that it will set the stage for translating concepts into action. Indeed, a plethora of fresh ideas and perspectives were shared by a wide range of participants which are brilliantly captured within the pages of this publication. To this end, the articles, presentations and speeches presented throughout this book address a range of important topics for Caribbean development including the concept and importance of Convergence; building resilience in Small Island Developing States (SIDS); the need for better data and better measurement which will result in better decision making; new thinking for new times; pillars for sustainability, poverty and inequality, governance, education, health, transportation, energy, food security, regional disaster preparation, and gender; the role of the private sector, climate change, financing solutions and global diplomacy in the Caribbean region among many others. The diversity and breadth of knowledge, experience and youth of the participants have produced a truly intellectually stimulating, creative and seminal publication. I therefore would like to commend all the presenters and participants for their contributions, and I extend special thanks to Dr. Carlos Elias and his team for spearheading the organization of this publication. Notwithstanding the wide gamut of issues captured, I must note that the common thread throughout this publication is *A CALL FOR ACTION AND EXECUTION TOWARDS A WIDER CARIBBEAN INTEGRATION AND CONVERGENCE.* My hope is, therefore, that this relevant and timely publication, will not be stored on a shelf in the libraries of our various institutions; rather, it will find itself on the desks and agendas of regional and national leaders, and that it will serve as a guide to move the countries of our region forward in unison.

I firmly believe that as we go forward, we as a people must not lose the bold spirit of radical thinking, nor the momentum that this Forum has uniquely created for a time such as this. We must press forward with disruptive thinking and bold actions remembering the revolutionary words of Dr. Martin Luther King Jr, who said that, 'change does not roll in on the wheels of inevitability…it comes through continuous struggle'. We as a Caribbean people must therefore be resolute and unyielding in our commitment to see change if we truly desire a better future for our Caribbean people. Together, we must stimulate radical ideas and rethink the future of the Caribbean. This calls for creative, critical and independent thinking and imagination to be at the centre. When I addressed the audience on May 5, 2015, I took this very same approach and shared some of my own ideas for the future of the Caribbean region. I asked the audience to be imaginative and to consider several possibilities:

What if…we removed every barrier to trade for manufactured and agricultural goods within the Caribbean region that have been certified by their States of origin? What if…we ensured the free movement of people within the Caribbean region and created a Union of Caribbean States? What if…we brought together the resources of the Caribbean including capital, technology, labour, energy, manufacturing, production and distribution knowledge, our land and marine assets to build a robust production capability within the region?.... What if the regional UWI introduces a liberal fee regime that opens itself up to the wider world, including the West Indian Diaspora?.... What if...all State funded higher education institutions, universities, colleges and technical institutes are brought together to form one Regional Collegiate System?.... What if all countries of the Caribbean implemented legislation with structured funding for research at 1% of their GDP, or University funding was guaranteed and enshrined in the constitutions of our countries as a percentage of GDP?.... Or... what if...the countries of our region developed and implemented a Caribbean Future Vision that will guide long-term capital development projects that cannot be changed with political election cycles of individual states, apart from exceptional circumstances?

These and several other 'doable' proposals from our participants are articulately captured in this outstanding publication. I would like to commend Mr. Winston Dookeran for his tremendous foresight and passion in bringing this conference to fruition, and also the entire Steering Committee, and the other supporting agencies for their steadfastness in compiling such a relevant and useful publication. I also wish to thank them for allowing the UWI to play such a prominent role in this endeavour as it bears witness to our role as the intellectual centre and leader in the region.

As Pro Vice-Chancellor and Principal of the St. Augustine Campus of The University of the West Indies, it is truly my pleasure and privilege to commend this publication to the people of our wider Caribbean region. Together, let us endeavor to enter a new chapter of Caribbean development; one that envisages a much enlarged Caribbean space creating new and unimaginable opportunities for our people, and one that taps into our creativity, collective strengths, diversity and richness. Let us rethink our concept of individual sovereignty to support such a vision and re-chart our course to economic growth and social empowerment, with a bold spirit of radical thinking and resolve. Failure is not an option.

December, 2015

List of Contributors

Amitav Acharya

Dr. Amitav Acharya is Professor of International Relations at the School of International Service, American University, Washington, DC, and Chair of the University's ASEAN Studies Centre. He has held professorships at several other universities including the University of Bristol, UK Professor, Nanyang Technological University, Singapore, and York University, Toronto, Canada in addition to being a Fellow of the Harvard University Asia Centre, and the Harvard John F. Kennedy School of Government. Professor Acharya's publications number over 20 books and 200 journal and magazine articles. His most recent book is entitled *Whose Ideas Matter: Agency and Power in Asian Regionalism* (Cornell, 2009). He has published in journals including *International Organization*, *International Security*, *World Politics*, *Journal of Peace Research*, *Pacific Affairs*, and *Washington Quarterly*.

David Anyanwu

David Anyanwu is the Founder and Lead at GoDev Consulting, a Trinidad and Tobago based development consulting firm. A graduate of the University of the West Indies, he completed a PhD in International Relations from its Institute of International Relations in 2013. Dr. Anyanwu served as a Consultant in the Ministry of Foreign Affairs for the Caribbean Future Forum. His experience extends to working in the non-profit sector and lecturing in international relations in the Faculty of Social Sciences of The University of the West Indies, St. Augustine Campus. His research interests cover civil society, armed violence reduction, regionalism, technical barriers to trade with a specific emphasis on the impact of food standards and regulations on SME exports. He has consulted for ILO, UNDP and COMSEC.

Sir Hilary Beckles

Professor Sir Hilary Beckles is Vice Chancellor of The University of the West Indies. He is a distinguished University administrator, an internationally reputed economic historian and a specialist in higher education and development thinking and practice. Sir Hilary has received numerous awards including Honorary Doctor of Letters from the University of Glasgow, University of Hull, and the Kwame Nkrumah University of Science and Technology, Ghana, in recognition of his major contribution to academic research into transatlantic slavery, popular culture, and sport. He is an editor of the UNESCO General History of Africa series and Chair of the CARICOM Commission on Reparations. Professor Beckles has written extensively on the history and development of West Indies cricket. Among his numerous publications are *Britain's Black Debt: Reparations for Slavery in the Caribbean; The History of Barbados;* and *Centering Woman: Gender Discourses in Caribbean Slave Society*

Miguel Carrillo

Miguel Carrillo is Executive Director and Professor of Strategy of the Arthur Lok Jack Graduate School of Business at The University of the West Indies St. Augustine campus. He is one of the most sought-after experts in the area of Strategy and Innovation across all continents, and for a range of institutions and multilateral agencies including the World Bank, the Inter-American Development Bank and private sector organisations such as Ernst and Young, Coca Cola, CEMEX, Volkswagen and Novartis. He has published in several international journals and has been the lead researcher of the Global Entrepreneurship Monitor Project in Chile, Trinidad and Tobago, Guyana and Suriname. He is the pioneer or champion of other nova research for the region in the area of Business Analytics, Cluster Mapping, Sustainable Innovation and Governance.

Sylvia Dohnert

Dr. Sylvia Dohnert is a private sector Lead Specialist at the Competitiveness, Technology and Innovation Division of the Inter-American Development Bank, and Compete Caribbean Executive Director from November 2012. Dr. Dohnert has a PhD. in Economic Development and Regional Planning from the Massachusetts Institute of Technology (MIT), and ample experience on economic development issues throughout the Latin American and Caribbean region. She has worked on the design and implementation of projects that support private sector development and competitiveness in Bolivia, Brazil, Chile, Paraguay, Uruguay, Venezuela, and the CARIFORUM region. Her interests include government economic development policy, global supply chains, clusters and SME development. During her time at Compete Caribbean, the program has gained a solid reputation for delivering catalytic technical to stimulate private sector development, productivity and innovation. Some of the completed Compete projects have already contributed to 3000 jobs region-wide. Sylvia is based in Bridgetown, Barbados.

Winston Dookeran

Winston Dookeran is a former cabinet minister in the government of Trinidad and Tobago serving in the posts of Minister of Finance as well as Planning and latterly as Minister of Foreign Affairs from 2010 to 2015. His public service career also includes a stint as Governor of the Central Bank of Trinidad and Tobago. Mr. Dookeran was a Visiting Scholar at the Centre for International Affairs at Harvard University, and a Visiting Scholar at the World Institute for Development Economics Research of the United Nations University. He served as the Senior Economist at the United Nations Economic Commission for Latin America and the Caribbean and as a lecturer at the University of the West Indies Department of Economics. Mr. Dookeran's recent books are focused on Caribbean issues, and include *Power, Politics and Performance: A Partnership Approach for the Development* and *Leadership and Governance in Small States: Getting Development Right*. He is a graduate of the London School of Economics and Political Science and the recipient of an honorary doctorate from the University of Manitoba

Carlos Elias

Dr. Carlos Elias has more than 20 years experience working in international development, mostly in the Caribbean. He provides consulting services to several multilateral institutions and previously worked on staff at the World Bank and the Inter-American Development Bank. Dr. Elias specializes in economic development with an emphasis on the selection of investment priorities at the national and sub-national levels, which requires expertise in macroeconomic analysis, analysis of private sector issues, and experience in evaluation of programs and projects using cost benefit analysis and other methodologies. Dr. Elias also teaches economics at Radford University and is a Senior Research Associate at Virginia Technical Institute.

Kayla Grant

Kayla Grant is a consultant in the Competitiveness and Innovation Division of the Inter-American Development Bank and the Compete Caribbean Program. She holds a Master's Degree in International Trade Policy from The University of the West Indies and a Bachelor's degree in International Business and Economics.

Philomen Harrison

Dr. Philomen Harrison is currently the Project Director, Regional Statistics, Caribbean Community (CARICOM) Secretariat. At the CARICOM Secretariat she has been engaged in the process of strengthening the range and quality of statistics in the Region in collaboration with the Standing Committee of Caribbean Statisticians, the CARICOM Advisory Group on Statistics and many regional and international organizations. She has worked for several years in the area of statistics and has spent the past eleven years at the CARICOM Secretariat. Prior to joining the CARICOM Secretariat she worked on Population, Household and Establishment Surveys as well as in the National Accounts Division of the Central Statistical Office, Trinidad and Tobago.

Preeya Mohan

Preeya Mohan served as the Academic and Policy Coordinator for the Caribbean Future Forum. She played a key role in shaping the Forum's academic and policy content, topics and sessions as well as the selection of speakers. She graduated with a PhD in Economic Development Policy (high commendation) from the Sir Arthur Lewis Institute of Social and Economic Studies (SALISES), University of the West Indies (UWI), St. Augustine, for which she was awarded the Eric Williams Memorial Scholarship. Dr. Mohan has worked on a wide range of topics focused around Caribbean growth and development including diversification, natural disasters, extractive industries, Caribbean economic history, firm competitiveness and innovation, value chains and clusters. She is currently a pPost-doctoral research fellow at SALISES.

Clement Sankat

Professor Clement Sankat is a member of the Executive Management Team of The University of the West Indies (UWI) and is currently Pro-Vice-Chancellor and Campus Principal of the St. Augustine Campus, Trinidad. As Campus Principal since 2008, he is focused on building the capacity, quality, sustainability and reach of the St. Augustine Campus of the UWI. He is a senior member of the academic staff of the Department of Mechanical and Manufacturing Engineering of the Faculty of Engineering, UWI, St. Augustine Campus and is a registered professional Mechanical/Agricultural Engineer with the Board of Engineering of Trinidad and Tobago. For more than thirty years, Professor Sankat has been engaged in Departmental, Faculty, Campus and University administration and leadership at the UWI. He is a former Head, Department of Mechanical Engineering, Assistant Dean, and Dean of the Faculty of Engineering (2000–2007), Campus Coordinator for Graduate Studies and Research at St. Augustine, Pro-Vice-Chancellor for Graduate Studies and since January 1, 2008, the Campus Principal, UWI, St. Augustine.

Iwan Sewberath-Misser

Iwan Sewberath-Misser is an experienced international development finance specialist with a strong academic (economic planning) background. He began his career in Suriname as head of the Department of International Finance and Technical Cooperation before serving in several senior staff and management positions at the Inter-American Development Bank in Washington, DC. He built an extensive network in the Caribbean region and is very well respected by many policy makers. He currently serves as Director/Representative of the Development Bank of Latin America (CAF) in Trinidad and Tobago.

The Honourable Winston Dookeran and Professor Clement Sankat

Acknowledgements

We wish to acknowledge the role played by The University of the West Indies, St. Augustine campus through its Principal, Prof Clement Sankat in facilitating this conference both as hosts and as participants through members of its faculty. Our special thanks go to the Government of Mexico as well as the Corporacion Andina de Fomento (CAF) for providing financial support and to UNDP for logistical support. Our gratitude also goes to the Government of Trinidad and Tobago through its Ministry of Foreign Affairs and to the many regional and international development partners including CARICOM, the Commonwealth, the Association of Caribbean States (ACS) the OAS among others. We would like to thank all the people that provided direct and indirect inputs to the organization of the Forum and the preparation of this book, in particular to Dr. Preeya Mohan and Dr. David Anyanwu, who were instrumental to the success of these efforts; and to Ms. Melissa Lauro, for outstanding suggestions, editing and proofreading contributions to this publication. Finally, we thank the presenters for making the Forum the rich and energizing exercise that it was and to all those who worked behind the scenes to make the planning and execution of the Forum a success.

Editors' Introduction

This publication comes at a time when the world is recognizing that something special is happening. In January 2016, world leaders met in Davos, Switzerland, to discuss these events. The following quote is appropriate to set the stage for the publication in a contemporary setting, one that will influence the future of the Caribbean. In January 2016, Mr. Enrique Pena Nieto, President of Mexico, wrote:

> The current era of innovation, in which cutting-edge technologies are disrupting entire economic sectors at a breathtaking rate, has been called the Fourth Industrial Revolution. It is also the theme of the World Economic Forum's annual meeting this week in Davos, Switzerland – and rightly so. In the coming years, the scope and pace of innovation will transform how we produce, distribute, and consume. To maximize the benefits, we must take steps now to prepare our economies and societies, with a focus on three key areas: education, the business environment, and connectivity. Facing the fourth industrial revolution. https://www.project-syndicate. org/commentary/mexico-fourth-industrial-revolution-response-by-enrique-pena-nieto-2016-01

Editing this publication during our continuously evolving world context has been extremely rewarding. The forum, held on May 5, 2015 on the St Augustine campus of The University of the West Indies (UWI), and on May 6 and 7 at the Hyatt Regency Hotel, Port of Spain, Trinidad, was attended by over 400 delegates and provided the perfect format for discussing, formally and informally, the future of the Caribbean. It is worth quoting in its entirety the introduction to the Forum as presented in the original programme (which has been included as an appendix to this publication):

> Welcome to what we believe will be a mould-breaking gathering of progressive Caribbean policy-makers, thinkers, business and civil society leaders. We have ensured that this will be a Forum that amplifies the voices of dynamic young leaders willing to challenge the status quo and champion new solutions. We have worked hard

to develop an innovative and ambitious forum designed specifically to catalyse disruptive thought, research and action needed to build a transformed and sustainable future for the Caribbean.

OUR KEY THEMES WILL BE:

1. Capturing the ambitions of the region
2. Embracing Caribbean convergence
3. Tackling poverty and inequality
4. Advocating innovative financing solutions
5. Shaping a new Global Compact through diplomacy

The goal of inducing disruptive thought and discussions was achieved. The first section of this publication presents three proposals that challenge our current views of the region and beyond. Winston Dookeran emphasizes the imperative for convergence, shifting the frontiers, as he puts it, for the Caribbean to continue evolving into the future. Sir Hilary Beckles calls for a rekindling of the revolution, one that historically achieved so much for Caribbean countries. Professor Amitav Acharya introduces us to a multiplex view, one in which the Caribbean as a whole could have a large impact acting together as a region. These three outstanding pieces highlight the need for a new vision for the future of the region.

From there, we kept the format of the publication close to the daily format of the Forum. Section 2 presents summaries of discussions held during the first day of the Forum under the theme *Stimulating Radical Ideas*. We chose to summarize discussions in four chapters: on Convergence, Vulnerabilities, Climate Change, and Sustainable Development.

Section 3 presents summaries of discussions held during the second day of the Forum. The theme was *Rethinking the Caribbean Future*. We had a very difficult time summarizing what happened when the leaders of the region generously offered their views and engaged in dialogue with the audience about common issues of interest. Fortunately for us, the session was taped and transcribed, and is available on the Internet website of the Forum at http://caribbeanfutureforum.com/. We encourage our readers to follow up by listening to the outstanding presentations of Prime Minister Dr. Ralph Gonsalves of St. Vincent and the Grenadines and Dr. Kenny Anthony of St. Lucia, as well as other members of the panel and comments made by Forum attendees. The section also includes discussions held on private sector issues and on the heightened role that it should play in the future, alone and in the context of private–public partnerships. The section ends with the significant contribution made by the Commonwealth Secretariat on building resilience by developing a vision of the Caribbean in 2050. We thank the Commonwealth Secretariat for allowing us to include the summary of their work in this publication, and kindly note that a full version will be published separately. We encourage our readers to read the full report when it becomes available.

Finally, section 4 presents summaries of discussions held during the third and last day of the Forum: *Taking Action for Sustainable Outcomes*. Participants delivered a clear message to the leaders of the region: more action, less talking. Participants shared their frustration and hinted at a region in which the people felt like one, but their governments behaved like many. Three chapters are included in this final section. The first one is a call for filling the information gaps that are necessary for the design and implementation of programmes and projects in the region. The second chapter highlights the central role that diplomacy needs to play in energizing the integration/convergence process. And the final chapter provides suggestions on the development agenda consistent with the outcomes of the Forum.

The publication also includes in the appendices sections, the full version of speeches delivered during the Forum, a reproduction of the full Forum agenda, and a selection of photographs capturing scenes from the three days of discussions.

We want to recognize the excellent work of Dr. Preeya Mohan and Dr. David Anyanwu both of whom were instrumental in organising the Forum and whose participation was invaluable during the Forum itself. After the Forum, they led the process of summarising results. This publication would not be possible without their contributions.

To end this note, we clarify that the Forum should be framed within a process in motion, not as a one-time event. Participants clamoured for action, but as the publication makes clear, action on so many fronts requires leadership to define priorities, and leadership to act now. We hope that this publication will provide a stepping stone in that direction.

Carlos Elias and Winston Dookeran
January 2016

Minister Vasant Bharath and Professor Sir Hilary Beckles

PART ONE
SHIFTING THE FRONTIERS

The Honourable Winston Dookeran

CHAPTER 1
Shifting the Frontiers: Defining the Imperative of Caribbean Convergence in the Twenty-first Century

Winston Dookeran

DEFINING THE INSPIRATIONAL MOMENT

The Forum on the Future of the Caribbean marked the start of an exciting new chapter in the development of the Caribbean. It was a moment of true possibility—one that we must grasp. It is now incumbent upon those of us who attended and participated in the event to free ourselves from both the constraints of traditional thinking and the limits imposed by entrenched views that suggest 'it's just not done that way'.[1]

My inspiration to have this forum was influenced by the changing global and economic landscape in which the Caribbean is strategically positioned, and it is in this regard that the idea came to me to have a forum to address the growing concerns among Caribbean nations. The opportunity to take a leadership role comes at a time when the Caribbean Community (CARICOM) is said to have stalled and perhaps run its course in addressing these issues and, therefore, now requires a different approach.

Fazal Karim, Minister of Tertiary Education and Skills Training in Trinidad and Tobago, aptly said, 'leadership is about delivering results.'[2] This Forum is itself an act of assuming leadership responsibility to ensure the frontiers of future generations are as good as, or indeed better than, those of the present. Convergence, therefore, plays a central role which requires a realignment of political and economic logic with the realities of contemporary Caribbean economic problematique. I offer a full exposition of this in my new book *Crisis and Promise in the Caribbean: Politics and Convergence.*[3]

In the forty years since its birth, the Caribbean integration movement has achieved much but may have reached its limits.[4] Consequently, there exists an urgent need to respond to the current realities and emerging global trends which require greater engagement from the public, students, academics and policy makers in moving CARICOM towards a new trajectory of Caribbean convergence. The immediate concern is to design ways to improve the convergence process among the Latin American and Caribbean countries. This convergence process must also be sensitive to the current and emerging global dynamics.

The emerging trade and economic structure is rapidly changing—in both its dynamics and the architecture. For example, the articulations of global groups such as the Brazil, Russian, India and China (BRICS), and the regional convergence as in the case of the Association of East Asian Nations (ASEAN), are some examples of alternative ways of dealing with global development. It is important to note that emerging markets have become economic power houses in the current global economy. They have become the major consumers with increasing national savings and growing capital markets. It is interesting that the South–South and North–South trade is overtaking the traditional North–North trade metrics. This emerging trade architecture is supported by a growth and expansion of multinationals from the emerging markets. In addition, emerging market economies hold almost three-quarters of sovereign wealth funds.[5]

The global financial architecture in the twenty-first century has also undergone dramatic changes. This emerging financial architecture is multipolar with the yuan asserting its role alongside the dollar and the euro. Sovereign wealth funds from emerging markets are fuelling outward foreign direct investments and growth in bilateral investment treaties. Furthermore, significant changes have occurred in the governance structure of the global financial system of the Basel III where a number of rulemaking institutions have extended membership to BRICS. In this way, all G20 countries were included as members in the Basel committee[6] and Goldman Sachs's *Dreaming with BRICS: The Path To 2050* predicts that BRICS 'could be larger than the G6 by 2039'.[7]

Public–private partnerships provide necessary breathing room to countries with limited fiscal capacity to fund infrastructure and other investments in the region. The role of the private sector and private institutions in economic growth has become pivotal to the forging of convergence. It calls for innovative forms of partnerships between states and the private sector, and for global and regional development finance institutions in integrated production. In short, the emerging public–private partnership demonstrates the trend towards a more inclusive political economy.

The world has also moved from multilateral to multitrack diplomacy. We live in a different world today. The number of players has increased markedly, and similarly, the web of interests and influence has become significantly more complex and interrelated. In Trinidad and Tobago, we have deliberately begun to search for a new method for reinforcing multilateralism, and we recognize that we must operate on a multitrack policy of diplomacy. But at this point in time, the choices are not clear. What is clear is that to protect our vital interest, we must be engaged in moving away from a diplomacy of protection to one of engagement. A multitrack diplomacy is really what we have been engaged in, whether it is at the United Nations, in our bilateral relationships with countries, or in our relationship with the emerging order globally; at all times, the fundamental objective is to ensure that we now move towards a diplomacy of engagement. Specifically, we have begun to open our doors to Latin American institutions. Trinidad and Tobago now enjoys full membership in the Latin American Development Bank (CAF), which is significant because we now see the integration of Latin America and the Caribbean being funded by sources and resources from Latin America and the Caribbean. This policy choice is a remarkable departure from our reliance on the traditional multilateral institutions such as the World Bank and the IDB.

SET THE ARCHITECTURAL FRAMEWORK/KEY IDEAS/IN CONTEXT OF REALITY

For a new Caribbean economic space to become a reality, it must be based on new models of intervention which can position both CARICOM countries and the wider Caribbean to engage in this convergence in order to seize the opportunities that the global market provides. The international political economy has changed from what it used to be, when CARICOM countries first became independent nations, and thus requires a different approach to its economic development.

Sachs notes that convergence 'occurs when the per capita income of the poorer regions rises more rapidly in percentage terms than the per capita income of the richer region, so that the ratio of per capita incomes of the poorer regions to richer regions rises toward one, that is, the same standard of living'.[8] Sachs, like other economists, believes this 'catch-up effect' is taking place with the rise of the global middle class, bringing an unprecedented convergence of perceptions, ideas and nuances signaling that a new global order has already arrived, and requires that the Caribbean region create a new framework (going beyond the old inherited structural arrangements) that is better suited to the region's needs. With this convergence, relations can deepen to create the kinds of incisive institutions which can deal with today's challenges.

Figure 1.1: Convergence framework[11]

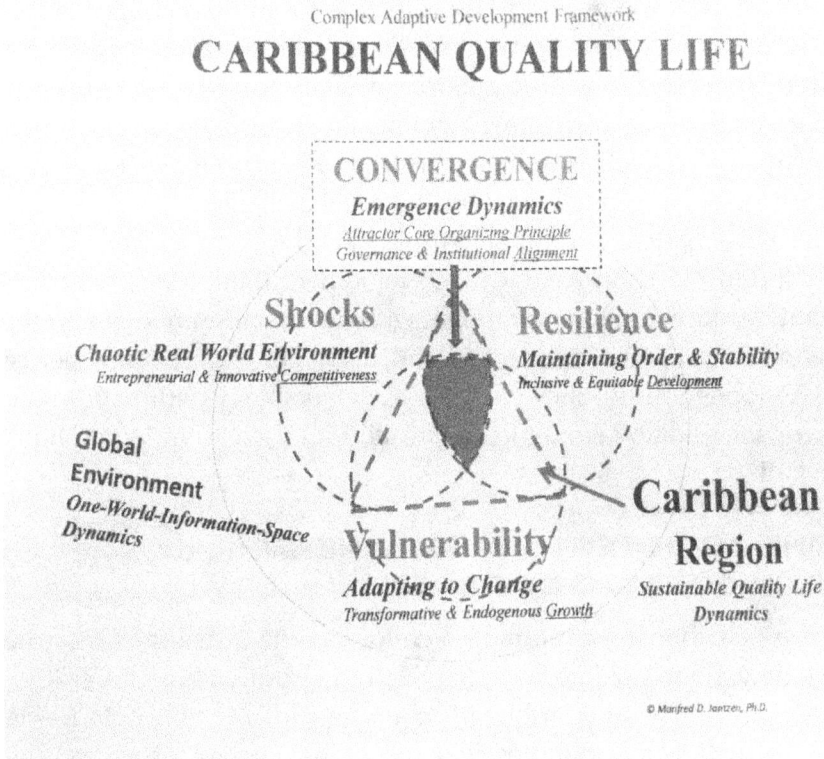

Complex Adaptive Development Framework

CARIBBEAN QUALITY LIFE

CONVERGENCE

Emergence Dynamics

Attractor Core Organizing Principle
Governance & Institutional Alignment

Shocks   **Resilience**

Chaotic Real World Environment   *Maintaining Order & Stability*
Entrepreneurial & Innovative Competitiveness   *Inclusive & Equitable Development*

Global
Environment
One-World-Information-Space
Dynamics   **Caribbean**

Vulnerability   **Region**

Adapting to Change   *Sustainable Quality Life*
Transformative & Endogenous Growth *Dynamics*

© Manfred D. Jantzen, Ph.D.

Dierdre McCloskey warns, correctly, that conditional convergence is not inevitable.[9] Countries must transform themselves to adapt to new conditions and to be prepared to take advantage of opportunities. As the history of Trinidad and Tobago shows, it is possible for real income per capita to be cut in half during an economic downturn, and then to rapidly double again during an economic boom. Why is volatility such a key characteristic of the Caribbean? In Trinidad and Tobago, and also in other countries in the region, socioeconomic performance depends on many factors, such as designing appropriate or wrong policies, high or low prices of Caribbean exports, and good or bad luck among more. As the region moves forward, governments and stakeholders should be aware of these issues that transcend temporary political cycles.

In the first chapter of this publication, I put forward my thinking on the meaning of convergence.[10] This is well depicted in a framework diagram by Manfred Janzen and his team on the Caribbean Future Initiative. See figure 1.1.

CONVERGENCE

We know that the nature and characteristics of small Caribbean economies make them extremely sensitive to global trends. The success of these economies is dependent on how well they adapt and adjust to changing global conditions. We can glimpse some of the future in current discussions from the Economic Commission for Latin America and the Caribbean (ECLAC)12 to the emerging post-2015 development framework.[13] There will be a greater role for public–private partnerships driven by non-state entities.[14]

There are definite gains made by using convergence as a response to emerging global changes. Expanding the economic space provides the scope for leverage in production and competitiveness. Caribbean convergence is the strategy to move the Caribbean integration process towards fuller and more complete integration, within the Caribbean and beyond. The rationale behind the new 'Caribbean integration' strategy is striving towards a convergence of economies of scale with capital. The strategy draws upon the new convergence framework that transcends borders of integration both regionally and globally. Therefore convergence of 'economic spaces' is a response to the limitations of the CARICOM integration process and opening of new spaces for confronting the development challenges ahead. Accordingly, convergence is a shift from a physically limited plane to an 'open economic space'.[15]

In the first instance, convergence is about the addition of new institutions which allow the Dominican Republic, the Dutch and French islands and French Guiana to be engaged. Convergence is *not* about creating something new, nor is it opposed to CARICOM integration. Rather, it is about bringing new political and economic dynamics to the process of Caribbean integration by reworking the existing frameworks in 'innovative' and 'flexible' ways (logic of politics) to cope with changing global realities, and redefining the modalities of execution.

What is innovative in this convergence framework is a new form of public–private partnership within an 'economy of the Caribbean Sea' with a focus on production integration, distribution and competitiveness (the logic of economics) as supporting trade and markets. Convergence is about adding future value to the workings of the integration process, and supporting the structures built over the last 40 years. This is in line with the call for building regional capacity to address global challenges.[16]

Convergence strategies and partnership go together. The discussions on 'Regional Economic Integration Caribbean Convergence and Competitiveness' in the Caribbean Growth Forum launch event (2012) has, in a way, set the tone for action and change. Two important issues were recognized: the 'political imperative of convergence' and the need for 'appropriate correcting mechanisms' that align the needs of the local with the regional. It was also noted that the problem with Caribbean integration is in its 'failure of implementation.' The larger Caribbean space is heterogeneous with contrasting economic differences that are politically sensitive. The discussions concluded that the genesis for convergence (integration without borders) should first of all be political, requiring a political will and advocacy. Creating the Caribbean Sea economy is first a politics-driven process.

The new structures must aim at production integration, competitiveness and distribution across this economic space (i.e. the economic logic), in addition to trade and markets. It must allow for economies of scale and space. According to this economic logic, convergence is not just about enlargement of markets and trade, it is about making the region resilient and globally competitive to capture opportunities in the future. The partnership approach is a stakeholder approach that provides us with a practical way forward as we align national strategy with a regional one. Central to this regional space is aligning the logic of politics (e.g. inclusiveness, cooperation) with the logic of economics (e.g. production integration, competitiveness and distribution).

A careful review of the various ideas and solutions put forth so far identify four broad convergence strategies to support the pillars of the Caribbean Sea economy: Finance, Clustering, Infrastructure and Production. These strategies are mutually interdependent and therefore need to be addressed together. The whole convergence process rests on executing these strategies. While these may appear as broad regional strategies, the specifics will be closely studied and spelled out by research and policy groups that are proposed in the policy imperatives. They are outlined in greater detail in the final chapter of this publication on the Caribbean Future Initiative.[17]

Finance Strategy

The economic convergence process will have to confront political challenges and redesign the economic and financial architecture. Finance and liquidity are the lifeblood of any economic system (national, regional or global). The task is to shore up sufficient regional finance to ensure there is enough liquidity to support convergence. There are four ways to achieve this financial strategy: buffers, capital mobility, regional stock market and development finance.

The buffers we are alluding to are those that are internally generated and shored up as sovereign wealth funds and international reserves. The other form of buffer is that which externally supports small states and exists in terms of international institutions. These forms of regional and national buffers provide the necessary flexibility to adjust to a new frontier of Caribbean convergence. The requirement for national buffers will also act as a disciplining tool for the fiscal policy of the Caribbean Sea's respective economies. Furthermore, these economies should also look at engaging other Latin American countries and the emerging markets in efforts to find new buffers.[18]

The creation of a regional stock exchange is an added advantage of expanding regional production, trade and equity markets. There must be a fully integrated capital market, free flow of capital, open investment strategies, accompanied by a review of double taxation treaties.[19] We will need to review and harmonize rules that facilitate movement of capital in the economy of the Caribbean Sea. The financial sector in the Caribbean has a size of 350 per cent of GDP and yet the region is in major deficit or public financing.[20] Therefore, convergence will also require redefining the role of development finance institutions that must respond to the needs for a new convergence process. It will require the 'bring[ing] together [of] development finance institutions to redefine the role of development finance that is sensitive and supportive to regional needs and the convergence process'.[21]

Resource Clustering Strategy

Clustering is a regional grouping of firms and institutions. They include an array of collaborating and competing services and providers that create a specialized infrastructure supporting the industries and businesses.

Typically, clustering draws upon a shared talent pool of specialized skills and/or resources. Clustering represents a synergy and dynamic relationship among companies, stakeholders, institutions and economies in the region.[22] They contribute to developing regional networking, and through public–private partnerships.

Regional clusters have the ability to offer local goods and services, knowledge and linkups that cannot be matched by outside rivals. In this way, clustering can contribute to innovative competitiveness and transformative endogenous growth. Clustering also relates to production integration that will enhance regional competitiveness and value-added manufacturing and services. It means the clustering of regional resources to consolidate growth, innovation and competitiveness. For instance, regional 'branding' of products and multidestination tourism are ways of clustering. Another example is the mix between the resources of bauxite, energy and finance proposals to establish a global entity which will facilitate a global clustering process.

Clustering would also mean a regional strategy for capital mobility and foreign direct investment (FDI), and it would facilitate the regional transfer of knowledge, skills and technology, regionally based and owned investments for promoting innovation, and a regional strategy for information and communications technology (ICT) and information exchange. Synergies also occur in clustering universities and technical institutions in the region—for example, partnering for innovation and competitiveness. Clustering is about complementarities in convergence in the Caribbean Sea economic space. Pooling of resources could precipitate faster and more sustained growth which could then spill over to affect all other countries. It could also imply Caribbean convergence of capital with resource-rich countries driving the process.

Infrastructure Strategy

The infrastructure for the new frontier of Caribbean convergence includes terrestrial transport linkages, aerial linkages and communications technology with cross-border capabilities, border management and security and regulation of the movement of people. Improved and low cost regional transport (e.g. freeing and encouraging regionally based/owned low cost carriers to compete with one another) is absolutely critical for facilitating greater movement of goods and people within the region. Endogenous growth should also improve labour productivity, especially through targeting youth and addressing equality and equity that benefit all stakeholders. Improving infrastructure facilitates quicker and cheaper movement of goods, services and people.

Regionally owned (private and/or public) low cost air carriers operating in the economy of the Caribbean Sea will boost trade, production and multiple tourist destinations. This in itself will promote entrepreneurship and business opportunities across the economic space—a kind of spread effect that will lock in the private sector. There is tremendous scope for public–private partnerships in developing the region's infrastructure (universities, R&D centres, hospitals, air and sea transportation networks, telecommunications network).

Industry and Production Strategy

A strategy of production integration is central to all the pillars of the economy of the Caribbean Sea.[23] The emphasis is on production integration led by the private sector. The important issue here is to design appropriate modalities to stimulate private sector response. These modalities need to be incorporated in the partnership approach. The private sector would be invigorated if it were included as stakeholders in the new public–private partnership.

A new role for the private sector to share risks and reap rewards of partnering with the public sector needs to be accompanied by a Caribbean investment programme designed to foster production distribution and integration across the convergence space. This will stimulate subcontracting and outsourcing of manufacturing and services which will in turn reinforce entrepreneurship and competitiveness across the Caribbean Sea economic space.

Production integration buttressed by capital mobility and regional equity markets will unleash a whole new regional economic dynamism in creating a new frontier of Caribbean convergence. It has been noted that encouraging regional value chains would link the internationalization decisions of the leading economic players within the convergence process.[24] The strategy should focus on reducing transaction costs,[25] coordinating the supply of regional public goods and generating regional value chains.[26]

It is in this context that the Forum on the Future of the Caribbean provided a platform for disruptive thinking, bold actions towards practical outcomes. The purpose of the Forum was to provide a broader discussion drawn from a historical perspective of economic growth and development in the region. This Forum purports to raise the political awareness and ambition for the region and the need to act more and talk less. In my opening speech, I said, 'The Caribbean is in search of a new space in this global order'.[27] This space I am referring to is the convergence process which would require an 'equilibrium between economic logic and political logic as we recalibrate our reform strategies for political and economic development'.[28]

Thus, the Forum On the Future of The Caribbean was intended to fully explain the economic benefits to be derived from convergence within the Caribbean and to the greater Caribbean and beyond. In addition, it sought to energize the process to modernize institutions, establishing them as rules of the game or as the incentive framework that determine how decisions are made. Likewise, the Forum's theme, 'disruptive thinking, bold action, practical outcomes' was not a place to 'listen to listen' but 'listen to act' which was the 'real' disruptive thought that came out of the Forum. The biggest surprise was not the emergence of an unexpected proposal, but the realization of a deeply rooted frustration among participants about the inability of the region to act and behave as one. Participants noted that the convergence process—cultural, social— among the people was real and strong, but it was not followed up by the leadership of the region and its governments.

IMPERATIVES FOR FUTURE ACTION: A LEADERSHIP CHALLENGE FOR SHIFTING THE FRONTIERS FOR CARIBBEAN DEVELOPMENT

Getting the politics of development right requires solving the alignment gap between the logic of politics and the logic of economics. International, regional and local politics may well be the most significant obstacles to development. It would also appear to be the single largest hurdle in finding solutions to the current global crisis. Getting the politics of development right requires cooperation and coordination of priorities, policies and action at all levels.

A new leadership with a global mind-set must engage the various communities of interest to find more durable solutions in a volatile global environment.

This new international leadership must find the right mix of power, politics and economics to achieve the necessary performance level for sustainable regional and global economic growth and ultimately development benefitting the citizens of all Caribbean nations.

The politics of this nation is at a turning point, and it is this generation, in this twenty-first century, that begins to turn the corner, and we must not hold back growth and development; instead we must break the anti-growth coalition that has dominated Caribbean societies. The time has come for a new leadership to search for a new paradigm for development—one that will identify political and economic logic; one that would construct new measures for financial sustainability; and one that will design a strategy for basic development that puts enquiry at the centre.[30] We must do so within the framework of a democratic system functioning at its best.

The previous notes provide what I hope will become the beginning of a new awakening for Caribbean development.

But, as noted during the Forum, Caribbean citizens also need to see actions taken in the direction of convergence, leading to higher growth and development in the region. A six-point action proposal for Caribbean convergence is a call for action now (see box 1.1).

We will also need to realign assisting delivery instruments to adapt to the convergence process. Therefore, we briefly examine existing institutions and organizations that can serve as modalities of execution towards a new frontier of Caribbean convergence (see box 1.2).

Box 1.1: Framework Actions[29]

Expanding the economic and political space
Set up a high-level, action-oriented body to pursue the widening of an active economic space
Developing a Caribbean Sea Convergence integrated transport logistics
Establishing a Caribbean Sea Convergence Capital Mobility Policy
Develop Caribbean Sea Convergence Energy and Food Security Policies
Redefining the role of development finance institutions

Fittingly, I conclude this opening chapter with an opinion editorial that was prepared ahead of the Forum on the Future of the Caribbean which lays out the imperatives for the future.

Box 1.2: The institutional actions that must be addressed for implementation[31]

CARICOM Secretariat
Caribbean Development Fund
Latin America and Caribbean economic system (SELA)
Association of Caribbean States (ACS)
Caribbean Sea Commission
The Economic Commission for Latin America and the Caribbean (ECLAC)
Council for Trade and Economic Development (COTED)
Council for Foreign and Community Relations (COFCOR)
Caribbean Growth Forum

Opinion Editorial

Throughout my academic and political life, I have sought constantly—in the interests of Caribbean progress and development—to challenge the status quo. It has long been my view that existing and often lazy orthodoxies will never solve the complex political, social and cultural challenges faced by this great and diverse region.

In my new book, *Crisis and Promise in the Caribbean: Politics and Convergence*, I express what I believe to be the 'political imperative of convergence'—the need for 'appropriate correcting mechanisms' that align the needs of the local with the regional, and that create a common and synchronizing logic between our economic aspirations and our political actions.

Our need for a change in strategy has never been stronger. The discredited and fragmented politics of the past must, in my view, give way to an ambitious new agenda—one that not only recognizes the economic, social and cultural benefits of convergence across our region, but one that actually breaks down the barriers to progress in what is a complex, enigmatic region, characterized by great diversity in size, population, geography, history, language, religion, race and politics.

The Forum on the Future of the Caribbean marked the start of an exciting new chapter in the development of the Caribbean. It was a moment of true possibility and one that we must grasp. The inaugural Forum brought together a ground-breaking gathering of progressive Caribbean policy makers, thinkers, business heads and civil society leaders. The event was innovative and ambitious. It was designed specifically to catalyze the disruptive thought, bold action and practical outcomes that are required to create a dynamic legacy for a better, convergent Caribbean future.

Our sincere desire was that by triggering transformative academic research and by setting public policy and sustainable development priorities (and by establishing the actions required to address them), the Forum would define a shared manifesto for us all, the implementation of which would create a resilient, home-grown yet international Caribbean future. In that process, we would generate the public appetite and scrutiny to drive the programme forward to success.

The Forum for the Future of the Caribbean promised much. The United Nations Development Programme (UNDP), along with its partners from CARICOM and the Commonwealth Secretariat, are to be congratulated for their collaboration, ambition and energy in making the event happen— and to have made it happen so quickly and with such clear purpose. It is now incumbent upon those of us who attended and participated in the event to free ourselves from both the constraints of traditional thinking and the limits imposed by entrenched views that suggest 'it's just not done that way'.

This Caribbean region of ours has vast reserves of economic, social and cultural potential; it is our job to unlock it.

APPENDIX 1

Box 1. Framework Actions

1. Expand the political and economic space.

2. Support and approve the expansion of CARICOM to the economy of the Caribbean Sea. Set up a high-level, action-oriented body to pursue the widening of an active economic space beyond CARICOM to include the Dominican Republic, Cuba, the Dutch and French Caribbean Islands and French Guyana.

3. Develop a Caribbean Sea Convergence integrated transport logistics. Reiterate that transport and logistics are critical to achieving transformative endogenous growth and competitiveness in the economy of the Caribbean Sea.

   a. Propose a ministerial meeting to take place calling all airlines operating in the region to look at how the logistics of transport could be rationalized and improved to provide better interconnection and networking;

   b. Propose this meeting to look at low cost air carriers involving the region's private sector, and/or public–private partnership to this end;

   c. Establish a regional research group to look at sea transportation and make recommendations for providing a system of sea transportation within the economy of the Caribbean Sea.

4. Establish a Caribbean Sea Convergence Capital Mobility Policy. Endorse finance and capital mobility as the backbone for sustaining the pillars of convergence of the economy of the Caribbean Sea. Reiterate that there must be a fully integrated capital market and free flow of capital.

   a. Propose that a single capital market should be established. Therefore, all stock exchanges in the region are mandated to meet and work out the modalities in a time frame;

   b. Recommend all members of the economy of the Caribbean Sea to create national sovereign wealth funds and regional buffers as a measure to offset external shocks;

   c. Set up a regional committee to review and harmonize mechanisms to facilitate intraregional investments. Organize a regional meeting of all private sector organizations to identify areas and strategies of production integration and public–private partnerships.

5. Develop Caribbean Sea Convergence Energy and Food Security Policies.

   Reaffirm that energy and food security are essential for the convergence of the economy of the Caribbean Sea.

   a. Set up a policy group to look at developing a common energy security plan to clearly define the rules for complementarities in the use and clustering of regional energy and natural resources for a new frontier of Caribbean convergence. Ensure that regional resources will be utilized for strengthening production integration and competitiveness;

   b. Set up a policy group to examine a common policy on self-sufficiency in food.

   c. Implement a Caribbean Sea Convergence Finance Policy.

6. Agree that development finance institutions are isolated and compartmentalized into public sector and private sector in their modus operandi.

   a. Propose that all the development finance institutions in the region (CDB, IDB, TAFF, CAE and others) should meet to redesign their lending paradigm in the region to deal with the current problems and support the convergence process;

   b. Bring together development finance institutions to redefine the role of development finance that is sensitive and supportive to regional needs and the convergence process.

We will need to realign existing delivery instruments to adapt to the convergence process. Therefore we briefly examine existing institutions and organizations that can serve as modalities of execution toward a new frontier of Caribbean convergence.

APPENDIX 2

Box 2. The institutional actions that need to be addressed for implementation

1. The CARICOM secretariat is the principle administrative organ of CARICOM. The new ambassador to CARICOM, Clarence Henry, has indicated that there is need for CARICOM through its secretariat to 'devise a Marshall-like strategic development plan to propel economic recovery'.

2. The Revised Treaty of Chaguaramas (2001) has led to the creation of a regional fund (Caribbean development fund) to provide technical and financial assistance to address the issue of regional asymmetries among CARICOM members.

3. The Latin America and Caribbean economic system (SELA) was established in 1994 and provides consultation and coordination for the adoption of common positions and strategies to foster cooperation and integration among countries in Latin America and the Caribbean.

4. The Association of Caribbean States (ACS) is an organization established in 1994 to strengthen regional cooperation and integration process with a view of creating an enhanced economic space in the region.

5. The Caribbean Sea Commission was established in 2008 under the auspices of ACS. Its purpose is to share information, provide advice and build consensus among partners in the wider Caribbean region over ocean governance.

6. The Economic Commission for Latin America and the Caribbean (ECLAC) the Caribbean was included in 1984. It is the central entity on issues of the region as a whole and for policy.

7. The Council for Trade and Economic Development (COTED) was established under the auspices of CARICOM secretariat to promote issues of trade and economic development in the region.

8. The Council for Foreign and Community Relations (COFCOR) was created for greater foreign coordination and to advance a new Caribbean diplomacy.

9. The Caribbean Growth Forum was launched in 2012 as an initiative to facilitate a platform for public–private dialogue around the growth challenge. It engages a broad group of stakeholders and critical players including the private sector and civil society.

NOTES

1. Winston Dookeran. 'Forum looks to set new strategy for the Caribbean.' Opinion Editorial, www.caribbeanfutureforum.com, 2015.
2. Fazal Karim. 'Karim: Good leadership is about delivering results.' http://www.news.gov.tt/content/karim-good-leadership-about-delivering-results#. VeX_nha5u2l, 2015. Accessed September 1, 2015.
3. Winston Dookeran. *Crisis and Promise in the Caribbean: Politics and Convergence* (England: Ashgate Publishing Limited, and USA: Ashgate Publishing Company, 2015).
4. The CARICOM region recently celebrated 40 years of signing the Treaty of Chaguaramas on July 4, 2013.
5. For more on emerging markets and global political economy, see World Bank, 'The 34 Role of Emerging Market Economy Demand during the Post-2005 Boom,' Contribution from the World Bank to the G20 Commodity Markets Sub Working Group 71266, April 2012; World Bank, Multipolarity The New Global Economy (World Bank, 2011); Gordon Hanson, 'The Rise of Middle Kingdoms: Emerging Economies in Global Trade, NBER Working Paper 17961, March 2012. Accessed September 2, 2014, http://www.nber.org/ papers/w 1796 l; Gaston Fornes, 'Emerging Markets: The Markets of the Future,' MPRA Paper No. 42315, September 2012. Accessed September 2, 2014, hnp://mpra.ub.uni-muenchen.de/42315/; Joshua Aizenrnan (2007), "Large hoarding of international reserves and the emerging global economic architecture," Working Papers No. 07–08 2007, Santa Cruz Center for International Economics. Accessed September 2, 2014, hnp://hdl.handlenet/10419/64101; Robert B. Zoellick, 'After the Crisis,' Development Outreach, World Bank Institute, December 2009.
6. See Stephany Griffith-Jones, 'Perspectives on the Governance of Global Financial Regulation.' Paper presented at the Commonwealth Finance Ministers Meeting, Limmasol, Cyprus, September 30 through October 3, 2009. The Commonwealth Secretariat.
7. For more on BRICS, see Goldman Sachs Report 'Dreaming with BRICs: The Path 35 to 2050,' Global Economics Paper No. 99 (October 2003 and Sandra Lawson, 'Dreaming with BRICs: The Path to 2050.' CEO Confidential (October 2003/12). In the article by Sujay Mehdudia, 'The Way Forward From Policy discussions to delivering tangible benefits, BRJCs nations plan on wider cooperation' published online in The Hindu on the February 21, 2013, which speaks clearly to the need for action by moving from 'policy discussions to delivering tangible benefits,' http://www.thehindu.com/news/cities/Delhi/the-way-forward/article4435519.ece.
8. Sachs, Jeffrey. *Common Wealth: Economics for a Crowded Planet.* (New York: The Penguin Press, 2008).
9. McCloskey, Deirdre. 2010,122. *Bourgeois Dignity, why economics can't explain the modern world.* The University of Chicago Press.
10. Winston C. Dookeran, "New Frontier for Caribbean Convergence: Integration without Borders." Presented at the Headquarters of the United Nations Economic Commission for Latin America and the Caribbean (UN

ECLAC) during the official visit of the Honourable Winston Dookeran, Minister of Foreign Affairs of the Republic of Trinidad and Tobago, to the Republic Of Chile, Santiago, Chile, April 9, 2013.

Winton C. Dookeran's work on convergence has been published and reprinted in Mandarin and Spanish. See *Una nueva frontera para la convergencia del Caribe: la integración sin fronteras*. Comisión económica para America Latina y el Caribe (CEPAL). Santiago Chile: 2013 and Dookeran, Winston. 'A new frontier for Caribbean convergence,' *Trans. Fudan International Studies Review*, August 2014 *(translated in mandarin)*.

11. Sourced from Jantzen, N; Saha, G; Nicholson, M; Curling, A; Kacal, E; Lewis, D and Bodrham; T. 'Caribbean Future Initiative: In the Context of the Caribbean Future Forum'. Paper prepared for Winston Dookeran, Minister of Foreign Affairs, August 2015.

12. ECLAC, Opportunities for Convergence and Regional Cooperation: High level Summit of Latin America and the Caribbean. February 21–23, 2010, Cancun, Mexico.

ECLAC, 'The politics of global financial regulation rulemaking.' ECLAC Brief 2012, Washington Office.

13. ECLAC, 'The Caribbean Forum: Shaping a Sustainable Development Agenda to Address the Caribbean Reality in the Twenty-first Century' (Draft Report), Bogota, March 5–6, 2013. Adam Moe Fejerskov and Niels Keijzer, Practice Makes Perfect? The European Union's Engagement in Negotiations on a Post 2015 Framework for Development. DIIS Report 2013:04.

14. L.B. Andonova, 'Globalization, Agency, and Institutional Innovation: The Rise of Public-Private Partnerships in Global Governance' (Goldfarb Center Working Paper No. 2006–2004).

15. Winston C. Dookeran (ed) *Crisis and Promise in the Caribbean: Politics and Convergence* (Ashgate Publishing Ltd, 2015), 200.

16. ECLAC, Opportunities for Convergence and Regional Cooperation: High Level Summit of Latin America and the Caribbean, February 21–23, 2010, Cancun, Mexico.

17. Jantzen, M; Saha, G; Nicholson, M; Curling, A; Kacal, E; Lewis, D and Bodrham; T. 'Caribbean Future Initiative: In the Context of the Caribbean Future Forum.' Paper prepared for Winston Dookeran, Minister of Foreign Affairs, August 2015.

18. Anthony P. Gonzales, 'Assessment of the Convergence Model of Integrated Production.' Symposium to discuss the paper: 'Introduction to the Convergence Model of Integrated Production.' ECLAC Sub regional Headquarters for the Caribbean, Trinidad and Tobago, May 9, 2013.

19. Winston C. Dookeran, 'Introducing the Convergence Model of Integrated Production'. Concept paper presented a Meeting of Regional Integration Bodies in the Margins of the UNECLAC, March 2013, Bogota, Colombia.

Winston C. Dookeran, Address at the Trinidad and Tobago Manufacturer's Association 57th Anniversary Celebrations, April 2013.

20. Winston C. Dookeran, Address at the Conference on Global Governance and Reform of the International Financial System: Impact on the Americas, OAS, Washington DC, April 22, 2013.
21. Winston C. Dookeran, "New Frontier for Caribbean Convergence: Integration without Borders." Presented at the Headquarters of the United Nations Economic Commission for Latin America and the Caribbean (UN ECLAC) during the official visit of the Honourable Winston Dookeran, Minister of Foreign Affairs of the Republic Of Trinidad and Tobago, to the Republic Of Chile, Santiago, Chile, April 9, 2013.
22. Michael Porter, 'Cluster and the New Economics of Competition,' *Harvard Business Review* (November–December, 1998).
23. Winston C. Dookeran, 'Introducing the Convergence Model of Integrated Production.' Concept Paper presented at the Meeting of Regional Integration Bodies in the Margins of the UNECLAC, March 7–9, 2013, Bogota, Colombia.

    Winston C. Dookeran, Address at the Trinidad and Tobago Manufacturers' Association 57th Anniversary Celebrations. April 2013.
24. ECLAC, Opportunities for Convergence and Regional Cooperation: High Level Summit of Latin America and the Caribbean. February 21–23, 2010, Cancun, Mexico.
26. SELA, Productive development and industrialization in Latina America and the Caribbean. Permanent Secretariat of SELA, Caracas, Venezuela, July 2012, SP/Di No. 18–12.
27. Winston Dookeran, 2015: *Emerging Caribbean Space In The Global Setting of Our Times, Will the Caribbean Miss This Opportunity.* Opening Speech at the Forum on the Future of the Caribbean, Hyatt, Port of Spain, May 6, 2015
28. Winston Dookeran, 'Crisis and Promise in the Caribbean, Politics and Convergence.' Weatherhead Center for International Affairs, Harvard University, (Ashgate Publishing Ltd, 2015).
29. For a more detailed list, see Appendix 1.
30. Drawn from Winston C. Dookeran and Manfred Jantzen 'A New Leadership Challenge,' in *Power Politics and Performance: A Partnership Approach for the Development* (Kingston: Ian Randle Publishers, 2012), 233.
31. For a more detailed list see Appendix 2.

CHAPTER 2
Rekindling the Revolution

Sir Hilary Beckles

This is an expanded version of the opening statement delivered by Sir Hilary Beckles on the second day of the Forum on the Future of the Caribbean, May 5–7, 2015, Port of Spain, Trinidad and Tobago.

Honourable Ministers of Government, distinguished guests, a very good morning to everyone. I wish to begin by thanking our host, Minister Winston Dookeran, for extending the invitation to address this forum. Minister Dookeran is arguably the most dangerous man in the Caribbean this day simply because he has called for radical and critical thinking in order to drive forward our civilization. In the not very distant past such a call would have incurred the wrath of the powers and principalities responsible for our governance. But times have changed.

The future now calls for a deliberate detachment from many conservative and reactionary aspects of our traditions. The Minister has brought us here to plan this revolutionary departure. I have read his remit and my understanding of it is that it beckons us to complete the detachment of our Caribbean world from its colonial scaffold. The assumption is that the Caribbean is fixed to inhibiting structures while the world is rapidly evolving and moving on. This circumstance has assured our economic dependency and social backwardness. It is a matter of common sense, one is urged to conclude, that the rocket cannot be launched unless from the scaffold.

In the Caribbean we have been seeking to do just this for over three hundred years. The uprooting of slavery was a critical nineteenth century development which was followed by the rejection of indenture and the rise of nationhood in the twentieth century. In all of this we have sought to propel the region into a matured sense of social integrity and economic legitimacy.

Critically, we have been in flight from the legacies of the imperial crimes that have been associated with our modern origins.

Taken collectively, these actions suggest that Caribbean people have been among the most revolutionary people in the world. We have placed the mental states of social justice, cultural tolerance, political freedom, and economic self-determinism at the centre of our existential being. This morning we are gathered to pay respect to this liberating and uplifting legacy, and to call for a return to our philosophical source. We are here, today, ladies and gentlemen, to rekindle the revolution.

There is a strong perception within our region that many of our development failures and limitations can be accounted for in terms of the stalling of the revolutionary momentum. There is also a belief that we have gone adrift because our compass is no longer fixed on that which matters most: *the liberation of the potential of our people.* The colonial scaffold is keeping us attached to backward economic structures and reactionary political relationships, obsolete economic thinking and oppressive governance models, and critically, the untrue conclusion that the intellect and cultures we carry in our heads and hearts are not the riches of the region but the wealth that lies beneath our feet.

In response to the Minister's invocation, the call I wish to make this morning is for the rekindling of the Caribbean revolution. I wish to draw attention to the need to re-energize our thrust and to refocus our agenda for transformative development. I am not worried that some of you may very well respond by suggesting that I am asking for us to swim against the tide. This has long been our history. Swimming against the tide has been the logic of the Caribbean revolution. It has been an integral and ancestral part of the desire of the colonised to pursue the 'American dream.' Colony by colony we have come awake from the Columbus nightmare. Colony by colony we have realised the importance of loading the Admiral back on to the Santa Maria and sending him back to Spain from whence he came.

On my way here last night, I was sharing my thoughts for this presentation with a passenger on the plane. He listened carefully, and then responded with the sobering question: "Hilary, do you believe in God? Why are you proposing such ungodly actions?" The

Caribbean, he insisted, is the most fragmented and fractured place in the world. Then he made his final declaration. "Dr Eric Williams was right when he said what God has put asunder let no man put together." "The Caribbean", he continued, "is a world united by fish and divided by folks."

My academic discipline is economic history, not theology. I chose this discipline as a young man, a teenager in fact, because I was occupied, maybe obsessed, with the matter of development. I was driven to find an understanding of economic transformation as an instrument for the uprooting of abject poverty. I knew then what we all know and want now. We wish to see the Caribbean world develop more aggressively in its material dimensions; we wish to see systems of governance and political relations that are rooted in the Caribbean philosophy of justice 'as a must' and freedom 'as a fact'. We wish cultural and ethnic tolerance and respect. We wish for inner and outer respect for our evolving Caribbean identity. That is, we wish for a validation of the Caribbean revolution.

We must fully understand this if we wish to be advocates for the unlocking, the unchaining, of our Caribbean potential. We must return forcefully to the historical source to find the energy we will need for the future. To historicise who we are is a prerequisite for creatively imagining what we must do in order to achieve what we desire. The notion that the Caribbean is at a crossroad, for example, conceals more than it reveals. It is an incomplete conception. The truth is more evident in the notion that the Caribbean is a crossroad, and has always been.

The Indigenous people knew this. The Caribbean, for them, was the crossroad that linked the north and south of the hemisphere to a centre. Then came the crushing moment of modernity's madness; in it we saw generations lost to genocide. This was followed by the importation of millions of enchained Africans and indentured Indians. The project was to accumulate wealth and build prestige for Europeans without limits upon human costs. This project was the origin of the 'West', a transatlantic economy and cultural ecology with its vortex in the Caribbean.

The 'West', then, began in the Caribbean. It was an economic civilization centred upon the Caribbean. The business of buying and selling African bodies was the world's leading commodity trade. The

Caribbean was the principal market. The world's shipping, finance, banking, insurance, brokerage, and entrepreneurial energy turned to the Caribbean and created the most dynamic centre of global capitalism. But this 'West' has now relegated mother Caribbean to the 'south'. We are now faced with an immoral outcome, an unacceptable geopolitic, in which the Caribbean as cultural centre finds itself in the economic south. This is the heart of the crisis we face. History, it seems, has dealt us a hard blow. We are seeking to return to the centre without the legacies of unfree labour. This is the reason we are gathered here this morning. The Caribbean revolution has sought to move the region from the economic south to the centre of our 'West'. It is this unification of history and economics that haunts every conscious moment of our being.

The Caribbean, then, is at once a crossroad and a cradle of the modern world. We are the world's first global village. We are the most globalized people on God's earth. Just look around and see in our faces what we really are! We are the migrant progeny of Africans, Asians and Europeans, inhabiting a world long integrated by our surviving indigenous hosts. We are also their admixtures, the inescapable triumph of humanity over ideology; the search for love within the hate culture of labour; a determination to find peace in the war zone that was the plantation.

No one can therefore tell us about the features and forces of globalization. No one is qualified to lecture us about the economics and politics of globalization. We are the owners of the brand. We are the homeland of the brand. We know of it as a double-edged sword. We know of its genocide, chattel slavery, and its deceptive indenture. We also know of its wealth created by trade; its fortunes forged in the financing of production; and the institutions through which foreign nations networked our region for their domestic preparations to dominate the world. Modern imperial Europe matured in the Caribbean. The modern 'United States' began its journey as a colonial system serving as an appendix of what it now calls the 'the islands'. Modernity was made in the Caribbean. It owes the Caribbean respect.

For three hundred years the finest minds of women and men in the region have been dedicated to detaching it from the colonial scaffold in order to liberate the potential of its people. They have insisted upon the internal unity of the descendants of genocide, slavery and indenture. These crimes against humanity have been declared as three acts of a single play performed in a theatre of imperial warfare and colonial mayhem. More blood has been shed on the Caribbean stage than any other. No one can tell us about globalization. We know of it because we have it within our blood. We are globalization in every intelligent use of the concept.

We have to understand this; we have to begin by believing in this. This truth must inform the philosophical and economic basis of our detachment. The first step we must take is to believe, once again, in the moral integrity of the Caribbean's rightness to respected nationhood. The development of the region cannot be based upon a parley with pirates. Citizens must insist upon a meaningful possession of their space and to the right to define its organization by popular engagement and action. The legacies of piracy must be placed firmly and irretrievably behind us. All those who have committed crimes against humanity within our homeland in order to extract and extort wealth should be held accountable. Reparatory justice must be a part of the healing and development process and a critical aspect of the definition and defence of citizenship. Economic models rooted in the colonial dispensation cannot be legitimised as sustainable.

In order to indigenize our economic thinking we must accept that we are crafting a revolutionary reversal of these historical trends. Let us take for example the concept of nation building. Building nations out of this historical experience is in itself revolutionary. The rooting of the project in the philosophy of freedom with material development is also in itself revolutionary because our bodily bondage and economic backwardness were grounded in the inhumanity and barbarism of chattel slavery, deceptive indenture and native genocide. Economic development and political freedom, therefore, are revolutionary in this context.

The notion that the production and equitable distribution of wealth in this region is for the benefit and advancement of its people is revolutionary. It is contrary to historical models in which the production of goods and services and wealth accumulation were primarily for the benefits of societies beyond our shores.

The development of our democratic sensibility is also revolutionary against this context. Contemporary Euro-American civilization locates its ideological roots and political centre of gravity in the value systems of ancient Rome and Greece—societies that embraced and celebrated slavery and imperialism as development models. This was the cosmology brought to the Caribbean by Admiral Columbus. He unpacked this world view and unleashed hell upon the region. This is why I have said, time and time again, that until this region repatriates the Columbus mentality to mainland Spain, we will be harvesting his seeds for generations to come.

The Caribbean is the antithesis of the ontology of the European. From the beginning it was the site of resistance and creation of the new modernity. Europe's Enlightenment was fraudulent from a Caribbean perspective because it led to genocide and slavery. The English celebrated the great scientist Sir Isaac Newton at home and sent the infamous John Newton, slave trader, to the Caribbean. The French celebrated 'Liberty and Fraternity' at home and sent the *Code Noir* to the Caribbean.

We have to recognize and accept that in our Caribbean world the philosophical seeds of justice and freedom, of equality and citizenship, were sown not in Rome or Athens but in Port-au-Prince. It is on the battlefields and in the legislature of Haiti that this region first breathed the fresh air of humanity: free at last. The Americans fought for their independence against imperial Britain. They won, but kept slavery as the basis of nation building. This was because their revolution was rooted in the ideas of Athens and Rome. These ideas meant that the new nation was forced back unto the battlefield a century later to fight the world's bloodiest civil war in order to clean up the mess that resided in a basic truth: that slavery, racial oppression, and democratic freedom cannot coexist as the basis of a free nation. The Haitian founders drafted laws that declared slavery a crime against humanity. They also declared all inhabitants equal citizens. This is where in our region and hemisphere, for the first time, ordinary people were able to mobilize to bring a democratic sensibility into their society. This is where we took our first step in claiming Caribbean leadership of the modern world. This truth has been a source of fuel for two hundred years. From Haiti, every Caribbean community aspired to nationhood and citizenship. Today, 80% of our people are living as free citizens. Colonies exist still, standing in oppositions to the Caribbean revolution and the Haitian declaration.

The Caribbean Revolution has not failed. It cannot fail. It has been pushed back, driven on the defensive. Counter-forces surround us and have made their local recruits. But we must be clear in our thoughts and focussed in our actions. It is not that we have failed in our development agenda. It is that our progress has stalled. It is that we have been driven off target and our commitment to ideals weakened. With reduced self-awareness our actions have strengthened the hand of the counter-culture. Many of the ideas with which we still conceive our development came with the *Santa Maria*, and hence our drift away from the ideas of Port-au-Prince.

Let us look at the significance of all of this. Caribbean peoples were able to overthrow the most oppressive regimes ever created in human history and to establish our democratic sensibility. To do these things required tremendous confidence and self-belief. From L'Ouverture to Rodney, from Garvey to Bishop, imagining and attaining the democratic Caribbean required tremendous confidence and self-belief. We should recognise that counter-forces are seeking to dismantle this mental construct and to replace it with mendicancy and mediocrity. These forces seek also to assure that we lose faith in the legitimacy and the logic of a Caribbean world that finds existential energy in our sense of self-reliance. If the Caribbean revolution is defeated, they imagine, the people will turn inwards upon themselves, against themselves, and in a cannibalistic fashion, devour their young.

I cannot accept the success of this train of thought any more than I can accept an inevitable defeat of Caribbean freedom and development. We Caribbean people have no historical reason to have doubt or to lose our self-confidence. The world is what it is. We are who we are. We have made much of the modern world, and it is for us to continue its remaking. We are at the centre and must behave as if we are. In our journey from the 'South' of our 'West' to its centre we have suffered many setbacks. But a setback is not a defeat. It is not a derailment. It is what it is: a retreat in order to advance. It is a physical step that knows within its biomechanics the irresistible and inevitable urge to step forward.

So we are gathered at this forum to speak about rekindling the revolution. In order to do so we must recognise the need to restore our confidence and self-belief by returning to the philosophical vision that drives our engines. Put simply, we cannot stay within the decayed and crumbling scaffold of colonialism. We cannot believe that these ancient, imperial relations will save us from the aggression of globalization. We cannot believe that within these old relations are seeds for our salvation. Within these relations we have seen the subversion of our agricultural regimes, the weakening of our financial services industries, and the creation of new challenges to our tourism sectors.

Simply put then, the Caribbean must leave the plantation great house and navigate its journey across those open lawns into the twenty-first century. We have to stop seeing ourselves as extensions and appendices of other power systems. We have to leave this dependency mentality at the back door of the twentieth century and learn the art of forging new alliances with a new agenda. In our Caribbean world we have sources of energy from India, Africa, China, Brazil, and beyond. These are our indigenous energy sources that have been marginalised by Europe's domination of our world. We must turn over this upside down world of relations and rebuild from the bottom.

With these new energy sources activated we must then complete the development discourse by foregrounding the need for closure in respect of reparatory justice for this region. Reparatory justice for the crimes that have been committed in this region is critical to rebuilding our self-respect as a people. It is critical to the maturity of our sense of citizenship; it is critical for our sense of ownership of the Caribbean. I repeat. This is our home and those who have committed crimes within it must be held accountable. Only within this process will the lion and the lamb find peace.

It is often forgotten, even as we embrace our great son, Sir Arthur Lewis, whose centenary we celebrate this year, that in his 1938 little book, *Labour in the West Indies*, he argued the case for reparations. The crime of slavery, he noted, the two hundred years of unpaid labour, have to be accounted for. Until it is accounted for the Caribbean will not reach its political maturity. Reparatory justice in every instance begins with the capacity of the victim to assert a claim. Not to do so is to sustain the disrespect of the criminal beneficiary. No one wins in this scenario. No one is freed. The crime festers.

The suppression of this truth resides at the core of our contemporary acceptance of the widespread, abject, inhumane poverty in our midst. If the poverty-stricken naive 'Carib', African and Indian are deemed undeserving of reparatory justice because they are the wretched of the earth, the scum of the society, then the slums in which they wallow are legitimised as their just entitlement. How much longer can we surrender our citizens to the vulgarity of such reasoning?

There is too much poverty in our Caribbean. While we accept our responsibility to remove as much of it as we can, we must insist that those primarily responsible must return to the table and participate in cleaning up the mess. This Caribbean was designed to create and sustain the mass impoverishment of our peoples. That was its overriding philosophy and economy. We must commit to uprooting the mentality that accepts this poverty as normal. It cannot be the basis of a modern Caribbean citizenship.

Let us look at the role of the State in all of this. We are being told that in modern systems of political governance the state must remove itself to the margins of the development model. To this I say, back up just a moment. If you examine the economic development model of any successful nation, not one is based upon the marginalization of the state. All are based on the assertion that the state has a core responsibility not only to create and sustain environments, but to be a major player within these ecologies. The state urges and empowers individuals and organizations to act and creatively react in bringing enhanced values to their communities. It is also expected to be a role model within the model.

The State must pass laws and create legal infrastructure that empower entrepreneurship, particularly in balancing public and private capital in order to create public goods and accumulate private property. The State is the custodian of the wealth of society, and must redirect that wealth for the development of the many. If in the Caribbean it retreats at this moment into the margins of economic thinking and action, it will render citizens even more vulnerable than they have been in the past. We must reject this external economic dogma that seeks to impose upon us a language and literature that is inconsistent with our historical experience and contemporary reality.

Let us now look at the issue of building entrepreneurship. All of us have been critical of the role of imperial entrepreneurship in our civilization. All of us have been calling for an indigenous entrepreneurship that takes upon itself responsibility for the creation and redistribution of wealth that will benefit our communities. To be critical of our relationships to foreign capital while being dependent upon it is merely to recognize the need for public accountability and responsibility. I believe that this is important and necessary. In recent decades our economies have competed at only two of the three necessary levels. If you examine our economic history you will find that we have successfully competed at the level of price; that we have successfully competed at the level of quality; but today we are failing in our competition at the level of creative innovation. This is where we are trapped at this moment. Logic suggests, then, that this is the moment for unleashing our creativity in respect of innovation for competition. There is no other key that will unlock our potential.

To do this we have to focus upon education, research, and the commercialization of our ideas. There is still in the Caribbean a crippling mutual suspicion in the relationship between industry and academia. We do not have a highly developed research culture but we are not going to achieve innovative creativity for competitiveness without respect for research and the application of funding to value creation. Our universities are still not effectively aligned to this process.

When we enter into Asia, for example, and we see the remarkable development projects and models, what we find at their core is an alignment of research, academia, entrepreneurship and innovation. Universities and industries are articulated into a process of value creation and the redistribution of the wealth of that innovation. In the Caribbean we are disjointed in our development thinking. Private capital has not warmly embraced education and innovation as the salvation of entrepreneurship and development. The suspicion of new knowledge and critical thinkers still resonates negatively in our political cultures. It is now a threat. It is counter-revolutionary. CARICOM officials are being crucified; but they have committed no crime. The evidence that drives the accusation is not with them; it is with us, the citizens and our leaders. We should begin at the beginning. Each Caribbean community still sees itself as a nation that desires to be larger than the whole. We imagine ourselves as discrete nations when in fact we are just communities within the nation.

The political logic of the last fifty years has been that the parts are seeking to be greater than the whole. These are fragments to be unified. But we still experience them as shards cutting apart our minds. The madness of myopia is now endemic. Trapped in our spaces we curse the geo-politics of insularity. We ran from the plantation into a prison. We want to be free. The 1805 constitution of Haiti declared that all native and enslaved people of the region who arrive on its shores will be declared free and a citizen. We need in 2015 to reconnect to the thinking of 1805.

There are two hundred million people who can rightly claim the Caribbean as home. From Mexico through the islands, to the coast of Colombia and into Caracas, the Caribbean world beckons to be functionally unified. We are not going to find the strength of our collective consciousness upon the notions of nations built with two hundred thousand people. It is counter-revolutionary to think and to act that way in the context of Caribbean history. Nothing that is sustainable can be achieved with these sub-systems of myopic thought. They have reached the end of their absurdity. We need to follow the native trail. The indigenous people travelled the Caribbean north-south and east-west. We must allow history to teach us economics, politics and sociology. If we follow the native trail we shall find water. They saw the Caribbean as one survival space. Our archaeological researchers have found their commercial and domestic goods that were made in Mexico, Belize and Guatemala in Barbados and Trinidad and elsewhere in the islands.

Upon this ancestral perception of the Caribbean as one survival place, we have imposed the absurdity of insularity. We have to wake up from this imperial divisive dream. We are a common civilization made up of dozens of languages, many of them inherited from our colonial legacies, but we do not speak the languages of our neighbours. We have maintained an educational system that does not make it mandatory for every child to speak Spanish and English. What kind of future are we imagining in this Caribbean world if our children are lost before translation? How can we imagine a Caribbean economic future without the fundamental of effective communication?

We have to invest much more in the education of our young people. At the moment we are faced with a tragic circumstance. In our hemisphere, from Alaska to Argentina, the Caribbean has the lowest enrolment of the youth (age cohort 18 to 30 years) at the tertiary level. Furthermore, it appears that numbers are shrinking in some communities. It is particularly disturbing when you realize that a society's potential for economic development and social transformation—read sophistication—is a function of the number of people within it who have been exposed to formal training and higher education. The successful development models we have examined have emphasized the same fundamental point. Citizens must be exposed at the higher level of education with technical and philosophical content if their societies and economies are to develop.

Minister Dookeran, I wish to say this. At the moment the Republic of Trinidad and Tobago has established the most expansive investment in tertiary education in the region. This has to be celebrated; this has to be seen as the model for the future.

In Barbados we have seen a disastrous 30 per cent collapse of nationals enrolled in university education in the last two years. The country is struggling to achieve 1 per cent growth in the economy within the context of a widening fiscal deficit. The country opted to reduce the investment in higher education as a response to this circumstance, but it is now evident that the roll back will weaken other critical macroeconomic variables necessary for development.

The tertiary sector is simply not a site of expenditure but an investment platform on which development is launched. There is no logical separation of learning for self and society. They insist upon cross fertilization. Furthermore, the principal drag upon Caribbean economic development at this time is not a shortage of capital, but a chronic shortage of relevant skills and critical areas. We have a human resource crisis, not a capital crisis. Investments follow skills and consciousness. The Caribbean needs to be sharpened up and made aggressively investment-ready. In addition to the acquisition of technical skills and knowledge those countries that have achieved phenomenal economic development in the last thirty years found national mobilization in the desire to reverse the legacy of disrespect citizens had experienced in the colonial period. They were motivated by the need to turn around their diminished reputation, and to chart a path of dignified existence within the world. The United States of America was driven by this imperative in the nineteenth century, as were the colonised countries of Asia and Africa in the twentieth. We in the Caribbean must continue to use our historical experience as a source of energy. To drive our peoples out of a state of doubt and despair will require these understandings.

We must therefore rekindle the Caribbean revolution. This is the mandate of this post-recessionary circumstance. Self-reliance must never be alienated from our thinking. We must detach from the colonial scaffold, and forge new global relationships based upon our historical and cultural experiences. The deepening of our democratic sensibility, both within the economy and in public governance, will redound to the benefit of the youth in whose name we act.

An assault upon the hardened poverty that surrounds us must be attached to the demand for reparatory justice for historical crimes. Education, health, and cultural institution reside within this framework. Also, the regional integration movement is not simply about economic institutions and political governance. It is about ethnic relations, gender equality, and cultural interaction. On this emerging leg of our journey there is no place for race. No space in society for class bigotry. The arrogance of ethnicity is counter-productive and must be rejected as contrary to the collective community sense of self and sensibility.

We are the world's first global village. We must resolve to teach the world how to demand and pursue economic growth with social justice, peace, tolerance, and the display of dignity. Our world was founded in the mayhem of imperial greed and the system expression of man's inhumanity to man. We, the Caribbean world, are the carriers, the custodians of the antithesis of these inhumanities. It is within these contexts that we will see good reason to rekindle the Caribbean revolution as both vehicle and vision for our global world.

CHAPTER 3
The View from a Multiplex World

Professor Amitav Acharya

It is my great honour to be with you today to speak at the Forum on the Future of the Caribbean. Although you have chosen me to be the keynote speaker, I may be the least knowledgeable person in this room when it comes to Caribbean affairs. I bring in an outsider's perspective. As a student of global affairs and the author of a recent book on the changing world order, which seems to be doing rather well around the world, I am here to offer some reflections on where the Caribbean fits in and how it can position itself in a rapidly and fundamentally changing world situation.

The unipolar moment dominated by the US is over. The international order which gave the US a position of hegemony, what I call the American World Order is fading. The emerging world order is not a multipolar world, as many describe it. I would call it a Multiplex World, very different from multipolar world like Europe before World War II. A Multiplex World has four features:

- First, the Multiplex World is like a multiplex cinema. Instead of showing one movie, it shows several with different scripts, actors, producers, directors. The audience has a choice. In today's world, instead of just one superpower, or a handful of great powers calling the shots (as during European multipolarity), a multiplex world has multiple actors. Order is shaped by not just the great powers or even states, but also international organizations, non-governmental organizations, transnational social movements, multinational corporations, and even terrorist networks, such as ISIS and Al Qaeda.

- Second, a Multiplex World is marked by complex global interdependence. This interdependence is based not only on trade, but also finance, production networks, environment, disease, human rights, social media, etc. Such issues link countries in different parts of the world in a way and to a degree never seen before in human history, including in the age of empires.

- Third, a Multiplex World has multiple layers of governance: global, inter-regional, regional, domestic, cities, etc. I would especially highlight the role of regionalism and regional governance.
- Finally, a Multiplex World is a decentered world. It's non-hegemonic. For the first time in 200 years, there will be no global hegemon, like the UK and the US. In fact, we may never have a world with a single hegemonic power. It's a world where, to use the language of Star Trek, "no one has gone before".

In a Multiplex World, power will increasingly shift from the West to the Rest. We have already seen plenty signs of this. According to UNDP's Human Development Report, 2013, aptly titled: *The Rise of the South: Human Progress in a Diverse World,* the combined GDP of China, Brazil and India—the three leading economies of the developing world—now about equals the combined GDP of the six major industrial nations of the West—US, Germany, UK, France, Canada, and Italy.

The US government (Department of Agriculture) estimates that by 2030, using conventional methods of calculating GDP at current prices, China and India will become the second and third largest economies of the world. The US will be barely ahead of China. But using purchasing power parity (PPP) calculations, China may have already become the world's largest economy. According to a recent OECD survey, China and India could account for 46% of the world's GDP by 2060, more than all the current OECD members combined.

What is more interesting is that there is also evidence of a more general 'rise of the South'. According to the UNDP Human Development Report 2013, the South has increased its share of the global output from one-third in 1990 to about half now. Developing countries increased their share of world merchandise trade from 25% in 1980 to 47% in 2010. And South-South trade has jumped from less than 8% of world merchandise trade in 1980 to over 26% in 2011. There has also been a marked success in extreme poverty reduction (below $1.25 per day): Brazil from 17.2% to 6.1% in 2009, China from 60.2% in 1990 to 13.1% in 2008, India from 49.4% in 1990 to 32.7% in 2010.

Is the Caribbean positioning itself to adjust and respond to these profound global shifts? I am not so sure. The idea of Caribbean Convergence proposed by the Foreign Minister of Trinidad and Tobago is a very timely idea, and its realization is possible, but it needs to address the new realities of the world.

You have asked me to be disruptive. But disruptive thinking does not mean impractical thinking. Communism was the most disruptive ideology of the past two centuries. But it failed because it could not provide practical solutions to our problems.

So the ideas I am going to put forward are both disruptive and practical in the Caribbean context. Please forgive me if some of them disturb you or challenge prevailing wisdom and policies too much, because that is precisely what I have been asked to do.

With this, let me present a number of ideas.

The first idea is moving beyond the small state mindset and embracing the developmental state model.

Until now, the Caribbean countries have positioned themselves as small states and emphasized the twin concepts of vulnerability and resilience. These remain important but they should move beyond the small state mindset. The small state discourse came about when people lived in the world or predatory great powers, such as Europe before World War II, or the Cold War. State sovereignty is a firmly established principle now, and the only way small states can collapse is through internal mis-governance. On the other hand, the Multiplex World offer many opportunities for small states to become smart developmental states.

The idea of developmental state initially emerged in East Asia. But it is now applied to others, including some states in Africa. Such a state gives priority to sustainable economic development, rather than rent-seeking. Through careful regulation and planning, industrial policy, partnership with the private sector, a state takes policy measures to develop the economy. It does not mean giving unlimited license to domestic or foreign corporations to exploit the people, but regulating them to adhere to nationally determined standards for wages, labour conditions, and taxes. It places strong emphasis on technical education. A developmental state embraces performance legitimacy.

A developmental state need not be an authoritarian state, as in the case of the initial Asian tiger economies. As the case of South Korea, Taiwan, and now Indonesia and the Philippines shows, democracy and development can go hand in hand. So the leaders and peoples of the Caribbean democracies need not be afraid of the developmental state. Trinidad and Tobago has all the markings of a nascent developmental state, but it is also a vibrant democracy.

A second idea is enhancing economic interdependence through production networks and developmental regionalism.

Most people associate regional integration with trade liberalization. This is a narrow view. Another approach to regional integration, one pioneered in East Asia, is production networks. A production network does not imply one company from a Caribbean nation setting up factories in other Caribbean countries. It also means encouraging corporations to locate the production of a single product in several Caribbean locations.

East Asia has the most extensive phenomenon of production networks. According to an Asian Development Bank study, in 2006/07, exports within production networks accounted for over 60.3% of total manufacturing trade in East Asia, and production network exports accounted for 66% of total manufacturing exports in ASEAN. The East Asian experience shows that international production networks differ from simple hosting of exporting multinationals and that such networks gradually lead to involvement of local firms and entrepreneurs.

Another form of regional economic cooperation is developmental regionalism. This involves the creation of better development opportunities through joint infrastructure development, better transport and communications links. Developmental regionalism also involves undertaking selective and staggered market integration policies that allows less developed members of a group more time to protect and develop specific national industries to achieve better competitiveness before they become fully part of a free trade area.

The Caribbean nations should broaden their approach to regionalism by adopting policies to create regional production networks and practice developmental regionalism.

The Caribbean should also explore multilateral trade and investment agreements with the emerging powers, especially China. According to a 2012 Report by the Economic Commission for Latin America and the Caribbean, China could displace the European Union as the region's second largest trading partner in the middle of the coming decade. The report also notes that China helped to bolster the region's exports during the financial crisis. As the Report says, 'the region's rapid recovery from the crisis were due to its increasing links with the Asia and the Pacific region, and China in particular'. 'China's great importance in world trade and its (still) low level of trade with Latin America and the Caribbean represent challenges and, at the same time, major opportunities for the region.' A multilateral agreement will allow Caribbean nations to both stimulate Chinese trade and investments in the region, but also to regulate some of its problematic aspects.

A third idea is Cooperative Security.

Traditionally, small states have chosen from two main foreign policy orientations. One is alignment with a big power. The other is non-alignment. In a Multiplex World, the best foreign policy for most countries is multi-alignment.

A world of established and emerging powers requires a foreign policy of inclusiveness. Such an approach is also known as cooperative security, which is founded upon the principle of 'security with', rather than 'security against', of inclusion rather than exclusion.

In the Caribbean context, a policy of cooperative security with the big powers must be based on a new initiative over and above the CARICOM or the ACS. This would involve the development of a forum, to be called the Caribbean Global Forum that includes all the Caribbean countries and all the main players of the international system, including the US, EU, China, Japan, India, Brazil and Russia.

The Caribbean Global Forum should include the Dominican Republic and Cuba. The reasons are too obvious. Caribbean countries should draw strength from the Dominican Republic and proactively prepare for the opening up of Cuba. The time for doing this is now.

Such a forum could meet annually at the foreign ministers' level and it should meet only in the Caribbean, not in Washington, Beijing or Brussels. The agenda of this meeting should be set by the Caribbean countries. The Forum is to be conceived as a dialogue, rather than as an institution in the formal sense. Its key goal would be reduce uncertainty and create predictability at a time of profound regional and global change. The first sitting of the Caribbean Global Forum should be here in Trinidad and Tobago, which should not shy away from assuming a leadership role in developing this forum.

What might be the issues to be covered by this meeting? The key objective would be to discuss the impact of global changes on the Caribbean and the response of the Caribbean to the changing global environment. What are the implications of the global power shift for the Caribbean? Some of these changes with potentially serious consequences (and opportunities) for the Caribbean include the emergence of new trade blocs, the Trans-

Pacific Partnership, Transatlantic Trade and Investment Partnership and the Pacific Alliance at a time of continuing impasse at the WTO. Also important are the emergence of parallel global and regional institutions like the BRICS Bank and the Asian Infrastructure Investment Bank. The forum should also discuss the regional and global implications such as the potential opening up of Cuba, and non-traditional security issues such as transnational crime, terrorism and the security implications of climate change (including its impact on natural disasters). Another important issue would be improving connectivity within the Caribbean and between the Caribbean and rest of the world.

A Caribbean Global Forum will allow the countries of the region to position themselves collectively on the world stage, avoid getting caught up in the rivalries among the big powers, or side with one against the other. It will be consistent with, and step towards, the idea of Caribbean Convergence put forward by Trinidad and Tobago.

A fourth idea concerns reform and strengthening of Caribbean regional institutions.

Until now, the European Union has been regarded as the ideal type of all successful efforts at regional integration. In other words, to be judged successful, regional groups in other parts of the world must look and operate like the way the EU does. This myth has been perpetuated by the EU itself, whose inter-regional partnership agreements often try, directly or indirectly, to impose the EU model and pathway to regional integration.

I have not found many places where the EU or its predecessors' EEC' model actually fits the local context. In exporting its regionalism through development partnerships, the EU often adopts a one-size-fits-all approach—a linear, teleological view that integration is best advanced through functional and political spill-over. This has unintended consequences: new supranational institutions are created that simply do not work. The EU is a highly legalistic institution and its model lacks flexibility in advancing regional integration in different parts of the world. Excessive dependence on EU aid may also harm the Caribbean's own plans for regional integration. Moreover, the EU model is facing serious crisis within Europe itself.

In the meantime, alternative pathways to the EU model have emerged, especially in East and Southeast Asia, where regionalism is more informal, market-driven and anchored on production networks. For example, the

EU has a budget of about 140 billion euros and a diplomatic corps of its own. ASEAN has a budget of 16 million and a Secretariat staff less than 200. While the Caribbean nations have signed an Economic Partnership Agreement with the EU, and the OECS has created some institutions that have some autonomy and ability to take the initiative in some areas of policy, the Caribbean countries should not blindly copy the EU's institutional model, but look to these other forms, such as ASEAN.

Some alternative to EU-style bureaucratic and supranational institutions is 'networked regionalism', which involves deeper and continuous communication and coordination between national and regional agencies. The Caribbean and CARICOM should give more consideration to networked secretariats of its regional bodies. Another concept is participatory regionalism which calls for engagement of NGOs and civil society networks in developing regional cooperation projects. This would make Caribbean regionalism less elitist and top-down, and increase support for its key initiatives and projects.

A fifth idea is to nurture a common regional identity and shared leadership.

Many studies have shown that successful regionalism requires a common identity. Does the Caribbean have a common identity? Is the Caribbean actually a region? Identity and regionness are not simply a matter of geographic location or socio-cultural similarities. Like national identity, regional Identity is not a given, but can be constructed. Regions, like nations, are 'imagined communities'. A common identity involves developing a 'we feeling' in the region.

A regional identity can be civilizational, based on affinities in culture, religion, language, ethnicity, etc. Non-Western countries often develop a postcolonial identity, based on shared histories and legacies of colonialism.

The Prime Minister of St. Vincent and the Grenadines, Dr. Ralph Gonsalves, has spoken about a Caribbean civilization. Let me propose an extension of this idea. The Caribbean is a civilization of civilizations. It includes indigenous pre-Colombian civilizations, elements of the Greco-Roman civilization that came with the European colonial powers, Indian and Chinese and African civilizations, as well as the Islamic civilization, the true founder of economic globalization. What is more striking is that there is no better place in the world than the Caribbean to comprehensively debunk Samuel Huntington's clash of civilizations. Even a cursory look at Caribbean culture, music and cuisine would suggest that far from being a clash of civilizations, it is a feast and melody of civilizations.

Last, but not the least, is the idea of regional leadership. Does the Caribbean have a natural leader? If it has, who might it be? Will he or she stand up? I suspect no Caribbean nation wants to play the role of leader.

In resolving this issue, one should keep in mind that power, especially physical power is not the same as leadership. And leadership need not be singular, but plural. Leadership can be shared. In ASEAN, which is considered to be one of the more successful examples of regionalism in the non-Western world, there is no single leader. Indonesia, the largest country, usually leads in the political-security arena. Singapore, the richest economy, leads on issues of regional economic cooperation. The Philippines, a democracy with a strong domestic civil society, leads on issues of socio-cultural cooperation. In reality though, any member country can lead ASEAN depending on the issue and context. So countries of the Caribbean should not be afraid to lead, they should lead in different areas. Leadership can be shared between stronger and weaker nations, between rich and poorer countries.

A CARIBBEAN HUMAN SECURITY CENTRE

The success of regional organizations is often spurred by a common threat. But this need not be an external military threat. The danger of inter-state war or external aggression against a Caribbean nation is too minimal although this does not mean they should abolish their armed forces. Rather the key threats to the region are non-traditional security threats or threats to human security, which can also spur regional cooperation. Many threats today are 'intermestic': they affect both domestic and external security of countries.

Human Security is not a new concept in the Caribbean. What is often not realized is that the concept of human security is not something that the West is imposing on the Rest. The idea did not originate come from the West. It came from the Global South, from the unlikely combination of a Pakistani, Mahbub ul Haq and an Indian Amartya Sen, both economists. Human security involves both freedom from fear and freedom from want. It involves reducing poverty, enhancing capacity in education and health, as well as reducing threats such as crime, drug trafficking, money laundering, terrorism, people-smuggling. The UNDP's *Caribbean Human*

Development Report, 2012 offers an excellent survey of the range of human security threats facing the region, which should become the basis of both national responses and regional cooperation.

The UNDP Report noted that 48% of respondents to the Citizen Security Survey 2010 had worried at some time about becoming victims of crime. The report has clearly articulated the relationship between crime and underdevelopment. As it puts it:

> Crime, particularly violent crime...erodes confidence in the future development of countries, reduces the competitiveness of existing industries and services by, for example, imposing burdensome security costs, and may negatively alter the investment climate.

There is already a good deal of progress in regional cooperation against such threats, especially against crime and disaster management. Similar agencies could be created in other areas such as pandemics, and maritime threats. The creation of a regional human security monitoring and implementation center could be a useful step in this direction. Ultimately, the goal of the Caribbean countries should be to create a Caribbean Security Community where not only inter-state conflicts are 'unthinkable', but also where transnational threats met with a firm and collective response.

I have now outlined a few ideas for reinventing Caribbean regionalism. Some of them are more disruptive than others. But all are eminently doable, or practical given the region's current resources. We need further elaboration of each of these areas to have a proper discussion and debate. But I am confident that these ideas, if pursued seriously, will lead to the successful reinvention and strengthening of Caribbean regionalism and Caribbean regional identity.

Professors Clement Sankat and Patrick Watson

PART TWO
STIMULATING RADICAL IDEAS

CHAPTER 4
Convergence of Ideas and Ideals

David Anyanwu

A strong focus on social equity and responsibility as well as a robust approach to gender inequality can represent new pathways for sustainable development in the Caribbean. Similarly, by embracing bold and radical ideas with little or no dependence on foreign models, the region must move away from its preoccupation with short-term thinking and quick-fix solutions which often do not lead to sustainable goals. A transformation is needed—both in thinking and in policy—to stymie these 'institutional redundancies' to which Winston Dookeran has referred. Of course this view is consistent with the arguments forwarded during the Forum for more bold, radical and long-term visioning. This lines up with Daron Acemoglu and James Robinson's view that governments should forge societies that create incentives, reward innovation and allow everyone to participate in economic opportunities.[1] Amitav Acharya goes further with the approach that small states such as those in the Caribbean should become smart developmental states, taking the right policy measures to develop the economy within the framework of performance legitimacy.[2]

SITUATING THE CARIBBEAN IN THE GLOBAL POLITICAL ECONOMY

The view that the region is at a critical juncture in its history is now commonplace as a plethora of Caribbean leaders and scholars have in the past sought to highlight the need for a concerted, powerful, effort to tackle myriad and daunting economic and social challenges that confront the region.[3] Similarly, its institutions, notably the Caribbean Community (CARICOM), is facing unprecedented questions about its adequacy to respond to the challenges besetting the region's economies in this new global political and economic climate. Forty-two years after the establishment of CARICOM, and nearly fifteen years after the signing of the Revised Treaty, questions are still asked about whether the institution is well positioned to steer the Caribbean ship into this new economy in which countries unable to produce high-quality goods and services at competitive values through the benefit of regional and global value chains stand little if any chance of prosperity.

The ability of the Caribbean to position itself to adjust and respond to the global shifts that are taking place, particularly in a new convergence, will require the modernization of its key institutions to reflect the realities of the new world. The region will also need to 'synthesize the political and economic logic'[4] because, as Acemoglu and Robinson observed, 'it is man-made political and economic institutions that underline economic success or the lack of it'. In essence, it is the politics that will create completely different institutional trajectories to spur economic success.[5]

As the world evolves, it is expected that regional institutions must adjust and be able to respond to the internal and external demands of the environment in which they operate. In fact, Dookeran, in his capacity as Foreign Minister of Trinidad and Tobago, has said in many public engagements that while the geopolitical context has changed over the years, global and regional institutions have not—in neither process nor structure. From this perspective, institutions represent not only structures and entities but also the processes and rules of the game of the incentive framework that ultimately shape decision making, as emphasized by the work of Douglas North and James Buchanan.[6] CARICOM and its constituents confront the same dilemma. Member states in particular, are faced with two distinct but equally challenging choices: to basically maintain CARICOM as a 'toothless regional bureaucraticachinery' or to modernize this institution and develop a long-term adaptation strategy that would enable it to become a relevant body for accelerating Caribbean-wide economic convergence.

Dookeran notes that the imperative for a Caribbean convergence model is predicated on the notion that the integration models based on trades and markets do not capture the full scope of the development challenge that is linked to production and distribution.[7] Prior to this, Norman Girvan also argued for a new way of thinking about a satisfactory model on which the practice of integration might be based—one that goes beyond the limitations of Caribbean Single Market and Economy (CSME) implementation and addresses the underlying constraints of regional development including competitiveness, critical mass, human capital, knowledge and resource endowments, yet capable of practical implementation.[8] Similarly, the Economic Commission for Latin America and the Caribbean (ECLAC) called for 'greater regional policy coordination in the context of an increasingly complex global agenda'.[9]

There is perhaps no doubt that Caribbean institutions have become redundant and the entrenched rules and current processes that shape the region's engagement with the rest of the world are no longer effective for survival in this new economy in which knowledge and technologies are transforming traditional practices in international political economy.[10] Dani Rodrik argued that 'the rate at which lagging economies catch up [with advanced economies] is determined by their ability to absorb ideas and knowledge from the technology frontier'.[11] This was very clearly articulated in several presentations delivered at the Forum on the Future of the Caribbean. The palpable participation of Caribbean people in the Forum reflect their belief in the integration project and also their frustration that government action has not formalized this aspiration. While a history of inaction has dashed the expectations of the peoples of the region and partly rendered CARICOM ineffective, it has not made it irrelevant to support the steering of the region in this new economy. Thus, a clarion call was made for the modernization of Caribbean institutions to reflect the realignment of global economic and political forces.

The region's need for economic growth and development calls for a new kind of engagement—one that prioritizes measures facilitating cross-border business activities within a wider Caribbean context. The various presentations and speeches given at the Forum bolstered the view that the requirements of this new global economy demand an acceleration of the process of convergence to create a seamless accumulation of production in the Caribbean. Convergence as proposed by Dookeran and based on discussions in the Forum on the Future of the Caribbean is a process already in motion. The question is, however, whether CARICOM countries and their institutions will wait to be naturally forced into this process and as such suffer the consequences of late decision-making as we have seen in the case of the lack of proactive action before the end of the EU preferential arrangements for both bananas and sugar. Or whether we will choose to commandeer our own destiny and accelerate this process to our advantage.

Given these seismic changes that are reshaping the global economic and financial architectures, changes in the region's integration process may no longer be in the hands of regional leaders. Globally, we see the emergence of new challenges, new actors and the increasing shift of power from the West to the East. Driven by the preconditions for global efficiency, we see new configurations of countries in self-serving networks such as the Pacific Alliance, Pacific Basin Forum and the Trans-Pacific Economic Cooperation. What they all have in common is the pursuit of more flexible yet sustained forms of integration which can afford them the leverage to reframe the terms of their engagement with the rest of the world.[12] Similarly, the emergence of parallel global and regional institutions like the BRICS Bank and the Asian Infrastructure Investment Bank also represent important shifts in the global environment. These, in addition to steadily growing relations between the United States and Cuba, present challenges as well as opportunities for the Caribbean.

Even within the English-speaking Caribbean, countries are making adjustments although without a coordinated regional approach. Trinidad and Tobago has also already taken steps to engage the Latin American region as an observer in the Pacific Alliance,[13] a full member of the Development Bank of Latin America and a member of the Brazilian constituency in both the IMF and World Bank. As Belize assiduously pursues closer ties in Central America, Guyana and Suriname are repositioning their hemispheric and regional interests as they become more South American than Caribbean. These actions by governments reflect their recognition of the need for action and their understanding that it is only through good government and bold political and economic actions, particularly in creating more investment opportunities, that they can chart the path of their countries to prosperity in this new economy.

CONVERGENCE IN CRISIS

Convergence as presented here is more than the mere facilitation of production integration which normally would enable countries to import intermediate goods from within the bloc while satisfying rules of origin requirements.[14] It will also drive regional logistics and infrastructure development, resolve the challenges associated with regional financing and financial integration, and facilitate movement of skilled labour across sectors; moreover, it constitutes a regional energy strategy as well as more coordinated regional strategies for exploring the vast but mostly untapped resources in blue and space economies. Even the multiplex world which Acharya described in the Forum has as one of its features multiple layers of governance including a pivotal role of regionalism and regional governance.[15] In this context, can the growth levels in countries such as

Suriname and Guyana be sustained in this new economy, or can the misfortunes of the highly indebted services economies of the Caribbean be turned if the region remains largely fragmented and separated by sovereignty?

David Anyanwu defines convergence as a response to global requirements for efficiency. CARICOM countries must be ready and willing to explore newer platforms for economic, political and diplomatic cooperation, or they will be left behind.[16] In fact, Mathew Bishop observed that the Caribbean is already 'excluded from the processes of change' due to the region's preoccupation with 'interminable and fearful parochial debates about pooling sovereignty'.[17] He agrees that unlike the Caribbean region, the rest of Latin America is already responding to these global demands for efficiency through their participation in some of these new processes of regional integration and newly emerging patterns of economic growth and development. There is no doubt that Caribbean countries, particularly CARICOM states, need to strengthen their economic engagement with each other in this convergence.

Caribbean convergence as a new form of engagement with the rest of the Caribbean and a pathway to development is predicated on three key points: (a) a new approach to regionalism that focuses on the wider hemisphere; (b) an emphasis on capability building through cooperation and not just a focus on trade and markets; (c) and a strong focus on production integration, competitiveness and equity of the Caribbean economies in the global economy. Convergence does not also seek to supplant existing structures and processes, but rather focuses on 'getting things done' in a transformative manner through greater policy coordination beyond the framework of existing integration structures.[18] This is really where the added value resides for the region given the call by CARICOM citizens for action towards a better and more secure future. It is about bringing new political and economic dynamics to the process of regional integration by recapturing existing frameworks in innovative, flexible ways to cope with changing global realities; it is about redefining the modalities of execution in a new economy.[19]

The concept of convergence energises the political and economic efforts of Caribbean integration and must be pursued with the goal of overcoming the political difficulties which are real and formidable. Norman Manley observed and noted that the 'old ways in politics are no longer equal to the new needs', and that the challenge for 'today's political leaders is to sweep aside the impediments...mobilizing their societies to understand that action is not further to a regional dream but represents the very price of survival in today's world'. Given that inaction at the national level and the powerlessness of the regional institutions to compel states have frustrated regional initiatives, politics should not be allowed to become a deterrent for the advancement of the Caribbean region, instead it must be equal and responsive to the demands for an accelerated convergence.

The independent sovereignty of CARICOM member states has meant that the original objectives of CARICOM, as articulated when it was set up in 1973, have been pursued with limited success. Although cooperation in areas of security has achieved some results, particularly in combating the illicit trafficking of drugs and small arms as well as in education, much remains to be done in key areas of energy, agriculture, transport, logistics and finance to name a few. Economic integration has not progressed as anticipated by the founding fathers of integration, and with the 'pausing' of the single economy process, the prospects for deepened engagement is not promising. Similarly, foreign policy harmonization has suffered because of its dependence on successful and deepened integration. These shortcomings cast shadows on the abilities of most countries in the region —particularly the less developed countries (LDCs)[20] and Haiti[21] which are emerging from what is fast becoming a vicious cycle of persistent low growth, high GDP-to-debt ratios, sizeable fiscal challenges and high unemployment. As a process already in motion, the acceleration of Caribbean convergence by Caribbean states is a positive step which can only help quicken the growth process and support the realization of the original objectives of the Caribbean integration project.

CONVERGENCE, GOVERNANCE AND ECONOMIC GROWTH IN THE CARIBBEAN

Charting the pathway for growth and development in a convergence must be based on reliable data and measurements. As gathered from Lino Briguglio's presentation at the Forum, the combination of multiple indicators to measure the performance of Caribbean states is imperative for development planning. His research used multiple indicators related to economic, political and social governance (the Worldwide Governance Indications, the Macroeconomic Stability sub-index of the Economic Resilience Index, and the non-income component of the Human Development Index) to assess the state of governance in the Caribbean.

Although the study focusing on thirteen Caribbean Small States (CSS)[22] found a positive correlation between governance scores and GDP per capita, it did not show a positive correlation between governance scores in CSS with economic growth.

In highlighting the similarities among the CSS surveyed, Briguglio noted the macroeconomic challenges that beset CSS, which included high debt, negative current account balances[23] and their vulnerability to external shocks. According to him, such vulnerability is linked to high levels of trade openness, export concentration, dependence on strategic imports and process to natural disasters in these countries.[24] It must be stated however, that Caribbean scholars—particularly Dookeran—have argued against the use by mainstream financial institutions of openness and vulnerability to predicate the mode of their engagement with these countries as this cannot help in the development of meaningful and sustainable strategies for the region. Hence the need to develop 'internally generated and externally supported' policy buffers as well the development of indicators that better reflect the multidimensional vulnerabilities of CSS.

In fact Dookeran noted that:

> economic shocks are not a temporary phenomenon for the Caribbean region; they are also not the exception to the steady state, they are the norm. Indeed, we have always been negotiating how we respond in our entire economic history to economic shocks. This contrasts the approach of international financial institutions that have predicated there windows of support on the basis that economic shocks as if these are a temporary phenomenon that can be dealt with by cash flow injections. It has not worked and therefore the time has come for us to redefine those windows of support on the basis of the new premises and the new realisation about our economic challenges. The issue of searching for economic space as one of the basis upon which we can ensure that we have the wear it all in order to capture the opportunities that the world offers.[25]

As predicted by economic growth theory, the countries with the lowest GDP per capita grew the fastest, with the exception of Jamaica which did not record positive growth (see table 4.1). This is also consistent with the economic convergence literature[26] grounded in the neoclassical model of economic growth,[27] as well as with findings of studies examining its relationship between this variable. Biguglio explained that a possible reason is that commodity-exporting CSS were less likely exposed to external shocks than tourism and financial dependent CSS, and thus they tended to grow faster. The study also showed that GDP growth was likely to be negatively correlated with governance indicators in CSS compared to GDP per capita which was likely to be positively correlated. A simple average of Briguglio's three indicators showed that Guyana, Jamaica and Trinidad and Tobago received the lowest governance scores compared to the Bahamas and Barbados which received the highest (see table 4.2).

Table 4.1: GDP per capita and Real GDP Growth in CSS[28]

Country	GDP Per Capita	Growth (r) 2010–2013	Growth (r) 2003–2013
Antigua & Barbuda	13,838	−1.24	1.986
Bahamas	24,489	1.08	0.435
Barbados	15,373	0.18	1.063
Belize	4,602	2.47	3.354
Dominica	7,034	0.26	2.566
Grenada	7,697	−0.02	1.680
Guyana	3,729	4.96	3.296
Jamaica	5,134	−0.08	0.513
St. Kitts & Nevis	13,115	−0.69	1.322
St. Lucia	7,801	−0.61	1.768
St. Vincent & the Grenadines	6,563	0.45	2.119
Suriname	9,240	4.60	4.986
Trinidad & Tobago	20,611	0.12	4.187

Sources: IMF (2014)

The study also showed that high-income CSS such as Bahamas and Trinidad and Tobago registered lower governance scores in three governance indicators when compared to the average of their rest-of-the-world counterparts. The overall average governance score for twelve CSS (excluding Guyana) was lower than the overall average of their counterparts. Debt was singled out as the most important source of instability in the CSS using the STB-ERI index.[30]

The main conclusions of Briguglio et al. are two-fold. In the first instance, and with regards to the relationship between governance and GDP per capita, their research found that high political, economic and social scores correlated with GDP per capita, thus suggesting a positive relationship between good governance and economic prosperity. The authors were, however, cautious in drawing conclusions given the argument that economic development 'may enable the country to better afford governance institutions and not vice-versa' or that both could be simultaneously generated.

Table 4.2: Governance Scores and Rankings for CSS[29]

Country	WGI		ERI		HDI		AVERAGE	
	Score	Rank	Score	Rank	Score	Rank	Score	Rank
Antigua & Barbuda	0.783	6	0.348	8	0.870	3	0.667	3
Bahamas	0.802	5	0.810	2	0.933	2	0.848	2
Barbados	1.000	1	0.701	3	1.000	1	0.900	1
Belize	0.235	11	0.565	5	0.773	5	0525	8
Dominica	0.746	7	0.464	6	0.769	6	0.660	4
Grenada	0.524	8	0.297	9	0.790	4	0.537	7
Guyana	0.000	13	0.377	7	0.000	13	0.126	13
Jamaica	0.272	10	0.000	13	0.689	7	0.321	12
St. Kitts & Nevis	0.815	3	0.037	12	0.601	9	0.484	10
St. Lucia	0.839	2	0.064	11	0.660	8	0.521	9
St. Vincent & the Grenadines	0.802	4	0.231	10	0.584	10	0.539	6
Suriname	0.222	12	0.664	4	0.307	12	0.398	11
Trinidad & Tobago	0.320	9	1.000	1	0.571	11	0.631	5

Sources: World Bank (2014) for WGI, Briguglio (2014) for STB-ERI, UNDP (2014) for NY-HDI

Table 4.3: CSS Correlations between Governance indicators, GDP per Capita and Growth[31]

	Variable	Correlation with WGI	Correlation with ERI	Correlation with HDI	Correlation with AVG
	GDP PC	0.4.8n	0.616*	0.281n	0.694*
Caribbean Small States	Real Growth 03–13	−0.603*	0.437n	−0.463n	−0.360n
	Real Growth 10–13	−0.679*	−0.339n	−0.468n	-0.45n

Sources: IMF (2004)

Conversely, and as table 4.3 shows, the analysis does not reveal a positive correlation between the governance indicators and economic growth in the thirteen countries surveyed. Both tables 4.1 and 4.2 show that commodity exporting CSS—mainly Guyana and Suriname, which did not score very high on the governance indicators—have the highest growth rates among the CSS. This is compared to the tourist and financial service–oriented economies of Barbados and the Bahamas, although with relatively high governance scores are some of the slowest growing CSS.

Briguglio et al. conclude that the negative correlation between good governance and growth could be due to what they call 'diminishing marginal good governance'—the difficulty which a country is likely to face in improving governance 'if it reaches or almost reaches a peak when compared to a country which has considerable room for improvement.'[32] They note that chances of growth are still likely to be improved by good governance and as such, the negative correlation should not be interpreted as an indication of the incompatibility of good governance and economic growth and hence the unimportance of the former. Instead, the very high standards of living in some of the best governed countries should be seen as an indication of the benefits of well-governed economies.

As a process already in motion, convergence of Caribbean economies will accelerate deepened and sustained engagement between countries of the Caribbean and beyond in an 'economic space' that includes CARICOM states as well as the Dominican Republic, Cuba, the Dutch and French Islands and French Guyana. This will create a market of 40,000,000 people that will drive economic activity and development in the productive sectors of resource-rich CARICOM countries such as Guyana, Suriname and Trinidad and Tobago.[33] Dookeran further noted that capturing the region's economic space by new models of intervention within a new convergence of the Caribbean region will allow the English-speaking CARICOM region and Haiti to move from a gross domestic product (GDP) of around $70 billion to operating in a wider Caribbean Sea economy with a GDP of about $350 billion.[34] The numbers are significant and can propel unprecedented levels of development in the smaller economies. However, without action and the commitment to purpose at the political level, nothing can happen. Bishop notes that if CARICOM member states cannot implement directives under the Revised Treaty after twenty-five years, then their chances of meaningfully participating in an economic convergence, which will entail sustained engagement at a wider level and with more disparate countries, is therefore unfathomable.[35]

TOWARDS A SUSTAINABLE CARIBBEAN

Viktor Sukup notes that Caribbean integration is a crucial necessity given the inability and impossibility of any single country in the region, regardless of its size or endowment in resources, to unilaterally be a 'real economic' power. Caribbean countries including its microstates will face enormous challenges in defending their vital interests against more powerful states and multinationals. Therefore, in a global economic environment marked by steep competition not only based on price and size, but also on quality, innovation, application of new knowledge as well as food and health technologies, priorities to be enacted especially in the context of Caribbean convergence are a common industrial policy in addition to common regional policies on energy, transport, environment, agriculture and food production, tourism and disaster prevention. The region will also need a convergence in fiscal policies and treatment of the challenges to the free movement of capital.[36]

In his presentation to the Forum, Sukup drew on examples from integration models and experiences in Europe and elsewhere to show how building regional markets can reduce intra-regional development gaps. He identified some key instruments for successful regional integration, which included a clear regional community preference as well as 'coherent industrial energy, transport, research and development policies, common policies in areas such as fiscal policy and a framework for engaging multinational enterprises (MNES)[37] as well as a consistent common political will.[38] Compared to the other regions he studied, Sukup found the greatest imperative for deepened integration in the Caribbean region. This therefore suggests that the strong historical, cultural and political linkages which Caribbean countries share present the basis and incentive to accelerate the ongoing convergence process.

For example, improving US–Cuba relations presents opportunities and challenges for the rest of the Caribbean primarily because of new fronts of competition particularly in the tourism. This foreseeable challenge can also be harnessed into an opportunity in a Caribbean convergence if countries are able to embark on joint and collective tourism projects. Anyanwu notes that 'opportunities for cooperation especially in tourism investment towards strengthening businesses and developing multidestination tourism and sports tourism can be advanced through public-private partnerships (PPPs) within the framework of a Caribbean Sea convergence'.[39] He further notes that convergence will set the stage for a new group of tourists and tourism activities and create new ways to scale up the quality and value of tourism activities offered in the region through integration of provider-activities.[40] This of course will depend on successes in other areas—particularly a regional transport policy which can provide the framework for reducing the cost of intra-regional travel which at the moment is extremely uncompetitive compared to destinations beyond the region.

Sukup however also argued that the integration discourse should be reanalysed in light of the challenges of the European integration, and he favoured a balance between neoliberal and development state market approaches in driving regional economic development. Situating his contributions in the broader convergence debate, he argued for a regional approach to fiscal, industrial, energy, transport and research and development policies. He adds that the integration project would run into difficulties like the ones in the European case if adequate tools are not in place to secure equitable and efficient distribution of the costs and benefits among states.[41]

Both Dookeran and Anyanwu have articulated this view in other papers on convergence. In fact, Dookeran identified inclusive and equitable development as one of the pillars of Caribbean convergence—others being endogenous growth, entrepreneurial competitiveness and adaptive and realigned institutions.[42] Similarly, Anyanwu noted that since Small and Medium Enterprises (SMEs)[43] will be the engine to drive growth in this convergence, their capacities should be strategically improved to meet the technical demands of cross-border activities of a new economic space. This would entail the creation of conditions that provide the right macroeconomic environment including access to credit, foreign exchange, important inputs and fair taxation as well as the provision of effective labour laws and regulations to raise the quality of employments in SMEs.[44]

Sukup observed that there is a 'considerable trade-off between the desirable, and even very necessary distributive justice inside any (regional) group and maximum economic efficiency for the entire group, which tends to produce acute political tensions between the relative or absolute 'haves' and 'have-nots'. Consequently, the richer countries tend to often lack the necessary attitude of solidarity with the poorer ones, while those can then, in turn, easily lose their initial enthusiasm for the regional project.[45] While the ongoing crisis in Greece has greatly polarized

Europeans given the large policy mistakes of the Greek government and their unwillingness to make difficult but necessary adjustments to meet the terms of their bail arrangements (conditions far more lenient than many developing countries including those in the Caribbean had to ensure under their IMF mandated structural adjustment programmes), the European Union's solidarity with Greece in avoiding their exit from the Euro does not completely support Sukup's thesis. It is therefore important, in accelerating convergence, that a sense of solidarity is supported especially by the leading economies to avoid a 'winner-takes-all' approach to cooperation and integration.

In considering the costs of adjustment for the less developed economies of the region and how to prevent further marginalization in an arrangement which can provide a new kind of competition, it is important that the right political and macroeconomic imperatives exist to ensure that the benefits of convergence can actually trickle down to smaller businesses and the process does not become the domain for larger firms including national and regional conglomerates. SMEs remain the bedrock of development in the region, and no industry or economy can lay claim to survival and prosperity without a viable and competitive SME base. There is the need therefore for adequate SME frameworks to ensure that the process does weaken the competitiveness of SMEs but rather provides the scope for building their capacities to take advantage of new market opportunities, technology and value chains as well as meet process and product standards and regulations. With the acceleration of the convergence process, it is possible that firms from larger countries may capture large parts of the smaller countries' markets. It is important therefore to ensure that the cost of adjustment for countries, particularly the smaller economies can be balanced by gains in the economic space.

The 'political imperative for convergence' and the need for 'appropriate correcting mechanisms' must be confronted with as much dexterity as the economic challenges. While acknowledging the steps taken in the past forty years towards cooperation, some of the political challenges he identified which have impacted CARICOM integration over the years and which have implications for convergence include competing relations with China and Taiwan,[46] and the Petro-Caribe arrangement which he finds not only to be beneficial for non-oil rich countries of the region (vital for oil imports), but also to breed a new kind of dependency which is likely to hurt these economies if cash-strapped Venezuela under a new leadership decides to cut its aid to the Caribbean. He also notes the ideological challenges of balancing a perpetual US supervision of the region with interests in Venezuelan-Cuba sponsored 'socialist' grouping such as ALBA, as well as the complex challenges of the Haiti (a CARICOM member state)—Dominican Republic (an aspirant member). The political logic of convergence is to foster cooperation among like-minded states over common interests. This must be reconciled with the economies of convergence and the reality of Caribbean political economy, if the process is to be successful.

These are real challenges and these countries, regardless of size, have very strong positions on these issues. The Dominican Republic—Haiti dispute has been one of those contentious issues that the region has had to deal with both at the regional and hemispheric levels and which has seriously tested the political 'unity' of CARICOM leaders. The current issue is the new Dominican citizenship rules which came into effect after a 2013 court ruling[47] that stripped citizenship from children born to undocumented immigrants, the vast majority of whom are Haitian, and that threaten to force many who have been living here for years to leave. The Dominican Republic, like other countries in the region, has a long history of discriminating against Haitians. After all, Haiti is still the only CARICOM member state that still requires a visa to visit several islands in the region. It is not uncommon for Haitians attending regional meetings or, while on personal trips, to travel all the way to Miami for a connection yet still be unable to travel to their destinations in the Caribbean. It is also not unusual for Haitians travelling on personal trips to be subjected to vast scrutiny at points of entry, with a significant number often unable to gain entry due to a range of trumped-up issues.

Nevertheless, it was in the Forum that Prime Minister Ralph Gonsalves of St. Vincent and the Grenadines, commenting on the Dominican Republic—Haiti dispute, unequivocally stated that his country would secede from CARICOM if other member states brought in the Dominican Republic 'through the back door' without resolving the current divisive migration issue. This reaction from Prime Minister Gonsalves was a further expression of a key outcome of the forum—the sense of 'oneness' which Caribbean people share and which also is one of the strengths of the region, even if its governments fail to act accordingly.

Political challenges are not unexpected, and they truly deserve proper analysis for the greater good. Hence, Dookeran has argued that this new paradigm of economic cooperation and governance in the Caribbean and beyond will call for bold political and economic decision-making, new and innovative ideas, and integrated interests towards win-win outcomes. Despite the challenges, countries must expand their political horizons.

Given that countries of the region must respond to this global demand for efficiency, 'the management by countries of the politics of a Caribbean Sea economy would be critical for convergence in terms of reconciling alliances, competing ideologies, historical and linguistic differences with their economic realities'.[48] CARICOM states 'may not necessarily have to damage a relationship to gain one or vice versa. This quest however calls for a level of pragmatism in the strategy employed. In the long run, the economic benefits are likely to outweigh the political differences given the orientation towards getting business going and getting the economy right'.[49]

In presenting convergence as the best approach for the future development of the Caribbean, Henry sought to make the case for sustainable development as a pathway to secure the future the region wants. Sustainability, she noted, 'is based on the premise that people and their communities are made of social, economic and environmental systems which are in constant interaction and must be kept in harmony or balance if the community is to continue to function to the benefit of its inhabitants now and in the future'.[50] Her presentation identified several pathways to sustainable development, including the creation of new urban centres and urbanization of rural areas, income redistribution and the dual roles of agriculture and sports. She also identified the challenges which hinder the development process such as absence of long-term strategies, globalization, the inequitable distribution of resources, gender inequality and poverty.

On the role of agriculture, she highlighted the region's endowment in several unique crops that could be harnessed within a regional approach and in a new convergence to increase food security and sustainability for the region. She also noted that the region's extremely high food import bill would be significantly reduced if people were socialized to eat more of what is regionally produced. This could be supported through improving the capacity of farmers, particularly in sustainable farming and in the marketing of their produce. Thus, sustainable practices by regional governments can bring effective and efficient measures for food security and sustainability. There is also the need for political action and economic initiatives to address the challenges of social inequality, which if left unattended, stand to derail social sustainability at the national and regional levels. Henry observed the need for a diversification of investments in sport, admonishing regional governments to not just focus on track and field despite excellence in that core area, but also incorporate a variety of sports.

Dookeran has argued that the acceleration of convergence will facilitate the development of globally competitive cross-border productive enterprise. Through public–private partnerships, the competitive advantage of the region's economies will not be predicated on countries' resource endowments but rather on their improved capabilities to finance new activities and upgrade existing ones as well as transition to knowledge-based industries, which can only come through integrated private decision-making in investment and production. Going forward, the focus has to be on the long-term sustainable transformation of Caribbean economies, including the development of knowledge and skills as well as adaptation to new technologies—all prerequisites for competitiveness in this new economy. The region needs transformative leadership and its institutions need to be modernized. It must move away from quick-fix and politically expedient politics and policies to long-term initiatives for which implementation must now commence.

NOTES

1. Acemoglu, Daron, and James A. Robinson. 2013. *Why nations fail; the origins of power, prosperity and poverty.* New York: Crown Business.
2. Acharya, Amitav. 2015. Keynote address delivered at the Forum on the Future of the Caribbean, in Port of Spain, Trinidad and Tobago on May 6, 2015.
3. Linden Lewis (2003) argued in that: 'The Caribbean is at a critical juncture of its history and development. The economic and social challenges facing the region are daunting to say the least. The region faces a future without any guarantees'. Prior to this, former Prime Minister of Trinidad and Tobago, Hon Basdeo Panday in a speech at the Heads of Government meeting in 1999 noted that the need to 'ensure [that] the appropriate institutional arrangements are strengthened and that decisions taken are speedily implemented' as part of the process of responding challenges the region is faced with at that critical juncture in its history.
4. Dookeran, Winston. 2015. 'Emerging Caribbean space in the global setting of our times—will the Caribbean miss this opportunity?' Introductory keynote address delivered on Day Two of the Forum on the Future of the Caribbean, May 6, 2015.

5. Acemoglu, Daron, and James A. Robinson. 2013. *Why nations fail*, op cit.

6. The seminal work of Douglas North emphasizes understanding institutions as rules of the game, for example in 'Institutions, Institutional Change and Economic Performance' published in 1990. The seminal work of James Buchanan takes a complementary approach by using economic analysis for politics in what is known as the Public Choice School, best presented in the book *The Calculus of Consent* written by Buchanan and Gordon Tullock, originally published in 1962.

7. Dookeran, Winston (2012). 'Caribbean convergence: revisiting Caribbean integration'. Caribbean Development Bank Roundtable. May 2012.

8. Girvan, Norman (2010). 'CARICOM's elusive quest for integration'. Caribbean Development Bank. April 2010.

9. Economic Commission for Latin America and the Caribbean, 2010. Options for Regional Convergence.

10. O'Brien and Williams (2013) identified three ways in which this transformation is happening including: the way we work; our consumption patterns; as well as in food and health technologies.

11. Rodrik, Dani (2011). 'The future of economic convergence'. Paper prepared for the 2011 Jackson Hole Symposium of the Federal Reserve Bank of Kansas City, August 25–27, 2011. https://www.sss.ias.edu/files/pdfs/Rodrik/Research/future-economic-convergence.pdf

12. Anyanwu, David. 2015. 'Caribbean convergence: an essay'. Paper commissioned by ILO for the Forum on the Future of the Caribbean. May 2015.

13. The Pacific Alliance is a mechanism for the economic and commercial integration of Chile, Colombia, Mexico and Peru, formally established via the Framework Agreement of June 6, 2012. The Alliance also establishes an important commitment to cooperation in the matter of flexible migration.

14. Estevadeordal, Antoni (2012) "Economic integration in the Americas: an unfinished agenda." The Road to Hemispheric Cooperation: Beyond the Cartagena Summit of the Americas. The Brookings Institution. Latin America Initiative

15. Acharya, Amitav. 2015. Op cit.

16. Anyanwu, David. 2015. Op cit.

17. Bishop, Mathew. 2014. "Editorial: The Caribbean amidst new regional and global dynamics." *Caribbean Journal of International Relations & Diplomacy.* Vol.2, No, 4, December 2014: p4.

18. Anyanwu, David. 2015. Op cit.

19. Dookeran, Winston. 2014. Opening statement to the 19th Ordinary Meeting of the Ministerial Council of the Association of Caribbean States (ACS). February 14, 2014.

20. CARICOM LDCs include OECS Member States as well as Belize.

21. Technically, Haiti is not classified as a LDC in the Revised Treaty but is seen as such by the United Nations. Its treatment as a LDC in CARICOM as with several other issues has very unclearly defined.

22. Antigua and Barbuda, Barbados, the Bahamas, Belize, Dominica, Grenada, Guyana, Jamaica, St. Kitts and Nevis, St. Lucia, St. Vincent and the Grenadines, Suriname and Trinidad and Tobago.
23. Suriname and Trinidad and Tobago being the exceptions in this regard
24. Briguglio, Lino, Carmen Saliba and Melchior Vella, 2015. 'Governance in the Caribbean small states – evidence from three global indicators'. Islands and Small States Institute, University of Malta. Paper presented on Day 1 of the Forum on the Future of the Caribbean, St. Augustine, Trinidad and Tobago, May 5, 2015.
25. Dookeran, Winston. 2015. 'Emerging Caribbean space in the global setting of our times – will the Caribbean miss this opportunity?' op cit
26. Ricardo Hausmann. 2014. 'In Search of Convergence'. Project Syndicate, August 20, 2014
27. For more see Dani Rodrik (2011) and Ricardo Hausmann and Dani Rodrik (2003).
28. Taken from Briguglio et al. 2015.
29. Ibid.
30. Ibid.
31. Ibid.
32. Ibid.
33. Anyanwu, David. 2015. 'Caribbean convergence: an essay' op cit
34. Dookeran, Winston. 2015. 'Emerging Caribbean space in the global setting of our times—will the Caribbean miss this opportunity?' op cit
35. Bishop, Mathew. 2014. Editorial: 'The Caribbean amidst new regional and global dynamics.' *Caribbean Journal of International Relations & Diplomacy.* Vol.2, No, 4, December 2014: p5.
36. Sukup, Viktor. 2015. 'Regional integration and cooperation as one of the crucial elements of Caribbean development – some lessons from European and worldwide experiences.' Paper prepared for the Forum on the Future of the Caribbean, May 2015.
37. The need for a region-wide framework for the operation of MNEs. The ILO through its Tripartite Declaration of Principles Concerning Multinational Enterprises and Social Policy (also known as the MNE Declaration) can provide the framework for sustainable engagement by regional MNEs especially towards minimizing the economic cost and promoting the economic benefits of economic convergence. It will encourage positive contribution by MNEs to economic and social progress in Caribbean countries.
38. Sukup, Viktor. 2015. Op cit
39. Anyanwu, David. 2015. Op cit
40. Ibid
41. Sukup, Viktor. 2015. Op cit
42. Dookeran, Winston. 2013. "A new frontier for Caribbean convergence." *Journal of International Relations & Diplomacy.* Vol. 1, no, 2, pp. 5–20 June 2013.
43. Anyanwu has argued that the economic development of Caribbean economies as well as the successful diversification of their national

economies cannot be attained through the reliance on a few large firms such as Angostura, Grace, Carib Exports etc. The role of SMEs in the growth and economic development strategy of Caribbean economies is significant because they are a major source of foreign exchange, employment, as well as contribute to the reduction of each country' food import bill. For more on SMEs see David Anyanwu (2014).

44. Anyanwu, David. 2015. Op cit
45. Sukup, Viktor. 2015. Op cit
46. The 'one china policy' presents challenges for the region. Several countries in the Caribbean, among them the Dominican Republic, Haiti and St. Kitts and Nevis maintain diplomatic relations with Taiwan. In the last decade, Dominica and St. Lucia have switched between both states.
47. https://www.opensocietyfoundations.org/press-releases/dominican-republic-court-ruling-raises-mass-statelessness-threat
48. Anyanwu, David. 2015. Op cit
49. Ibid.
50. Henry, Sustainable Development. Presentation made at the Forum on the Future of the Caribbean, May 5, 2015.

CHAPTER 5
Caribbean Common Vulnerability Requires Regional Solutions

Carlos Elias

In spite of common history, language, and government systems and traditions, Caribbean countries' economic performances vary widely.[1] But this chapter also shows that the region faces a common set of threats: exposure to weather events, smallness and openness, unemployment and strong linkages to business cycles of large economies in North America and Europe. These common vulnerabilities also call for a regional approach that is designed to address common threats. For these reasons, this chapter concludes with the suggestion that policy designed to facilitate growth and development from a regional perspective should be framed within a dual objective framework: (i) a country-specific set of policies and programs that respond to individual needs and realities, but with interconnections with supplemental regional coordination; and (ii) a region-specific set of policies and programs designed to lower common vulnerability. This chapter focuses on economic issues; however, the suggested framework applies more generally to social, health, education, security and more.

APPARENT SIMILARITIES BUT VERY DIFFERENT OUTCOMES

It is easy to be confused by the obvious similarities of countries in the region and to extrapolate from those similarities to economic systems and performance. This is a mistake. Table 1 presents a summary of key economic performance indicators for Caribbean countries and Latin America for the period 2000–2014. The table presents information on the level of GDP per capita on the last year of data available, which for most countries is 2014; the real growth rate of GDP per capita comparing 2014 to 2000; the coefficient of variation of real GDP per capita growth; the levels of youth and total unemployment; and finally the average annual inflation for the period 2010–2014.[2] The table presents the countries ranked by the growth rate from 2000 to 2014, the second column in the table.

The table offers the opportunity to highlight the large differences in economic performance among countries of the Caribbean. The following list summarizes them:

- Income per capita varies widely, from over US$30,000 in Trinidad and Tobago to less than US$2,000 in Haiti.

- About 30% of Caribbean countries are wealthier than the Latin American average—The Bahamas, St. Vincent and the Grenadines, St. Kitts and Nevis, Antigua and Barbuda, Suriname and Trinidad and Tobago. Trinidad and Tobago's income per capita is the highest in Latin America.

- In spite of the wealth of the region, most countries are growing slowly and some have shrunk since 2000. The Bahamas, Barbados, Haiti and St. Lucia in 2014 had real income lower than in 2000. From 2000 to 2014, the per capita income in Jamaica, St. Vincent and the Grenadines, St. Kitts and Nevis, and Belize grew less than 1% per year; and Grenada and Dominica less than 2%. Only the per capita income in Guyana, Antigua and Barbuda, Suriname and Trinidad and Tobago grew faster than Latin American. Only Suriname and Trinidad and Tobago grew faster than 3%, which is high by Latin American standards but low when considering that it would take either country more than twenty years to double real income per capita.[3] Real growth rates in the Caribbean are too low which calls for a regional comprehensive effort to design and implement new policies: a new modern framework for Caribbean Growth and Development.

- Except for Suriname and Trinidad and Tobago, Caribbean countries' growth rates are significantly more volatile than Latin American. Ignoring St. Lucia's result which is an outlier, see note 5: the most volatile countries measured are Haiti, Antigua and Barbuda, Barbados and St. Kitts and Nevis. In general, volatility is a problem for all countries in the region, which reinforces the issue of common vulnerabilities even when country performance varies widely. In other words, because of large vulnerability to common factors, economic performance in the region shows high volatility regardless of relatively high wealth.

- Unemployment is a serious problem in the Caribbean, greater than it is in Latin America. Of the countries in the region, only Trinidad and Tobago has lower youth and total unemployment than Latin America. All the other countries have significantly higher unemployment rates.
- Youth unemployment is a problem for all countries in the region. Almost one-third of young people in The Bahamas, Barbados, Jamaica and Belize cannot find jobs. Close to one-fifth of the young in Haiti, Guyana and Suriname cannot find jobs. The consequences of these facts may be severe, and policies to lower youth unemployment should be prioritized. Moreover, the long-term negative impact of youth unemployment on long-term income stream and its links to violence and drug-related crime calls for a focus on regional youth unemployment within a more comprehensive plan to increase employment in the region.[4]
- Compared to Latin America, total unemployment is a problem for all countries except for Haiti, Suriname and Trinidad and Tobago. In general, total unemployment is about half of youth unemployment.
- With few exceptions, monetary policy appears to be adequate to maintain low inflation levels throughout the region. Most Caribbean countries have lower inflation rates than Latin America, with the exception of Haiti, Jamaica, Guyana, Suriname and Trinidad and Tobago. In these countries, however, inflation rates may be explained by localized events, such as food shortages or temporary pass-through exchange rate fluctuations.

A closer look at the growth performance since 2000 is presented in figure 5.1. The figure shows two panels: the left panel shows Caribbean countries from table 5.1 that have a growth performance lower than the Latin America average, and the panel on the right shows countries with a better performance than the Latin America average. What is striking is the poor performance of the countries in the left panel. These countries show low annual growth rates, stagnation and, worse, negative growth rates. Compared to Latin America, which exhibits an upward trend, these countries exhibit flat or decreasing trends. The panel on the right shows, by contrast, the dynamism of Trinidad and Tobago, Suriname, and Guyana, and the long business cycles reflected in the performance of Antigua and Barbuda.

Table 5.1: Economic performance of Caribbean countries 2000–2014[5]

	GDP per capita (i)	Real per capita growth rate GDP 2000–2014 (ii)	Annual real growth coefficient of variation (iii)	Unemployment, youth total (% of total labour force ages 15–24) (iv)	Unemployment, total (% of total labour force) (iv)	Inflation, consumer prices 2010–2014 (v)
Bahamas, The (1)	23,491	−13.3%	(2.1)	28.9%	13.6%	1.7%
Barbados (1)	13,575	−10.9%	(7.0)	27.0%	12.2%	1.7%
Haiti (1)	1,732	−5.0%	(9.3)	17.4%	7.0%	6.2%
St. Lucia (1) (3)	10,393	-0.6%	284.82[6]	NA	22.2%	3.0%
Jamaica (1) (2)	8,893	5.8%	(5.4)	35.5%	15.0%	8.9%
St. Vincent and the Grenadines	22,669	13.3%	1.5	NA	NA	2.2%
St. Kitts and Nevis	22,669	13.3%	4.2	NA	NA	2.2%
Belize (1) (2)	8,184	13.8%	2.1	29.7%	14.6%	1.0%
Grenada	11,944	18.1%	4.0	NA	NA	1.6%
Dominica	10,699	26.1%	1.9	NA	NA	1.5%
Latin America & Caribbean (all income levels) (1)	15,534	29.9%	1.2	13.4%	6.2%	3.8%
Guyana (1)	7,218	35.4%	1.4	23.9%	11.1%	6.2%
Antigua and Barbuda	21,800	42.4%	9.0	NA	NA	2.5%
Suriname (1) (2)	16,247	63.5%	0.5	22.5%	7.8%	7.0%
Trinidad and Tobago (1) (2)	30,285	65.4%	1.0	13.2%	5.8%	7.2%

Source: Data from database: World Development Indicators, last updated 11/12/2015

Notes: (i) PPP (current international $); 2014 unless indicated.
(ii) PPP (constant 2011 international $).
(iii) Calculated on annual real values of per capita growth, PPP constant 2011 international $.
(iv) Modelled ILO estimate.
(v) Annual average 2010–2014.

(1) Unemployment data for 2013.

(2) GDP per capita for 2013; GDP per capita growth rate for 2000–2013.

(3) Unemployment is a national estimate (not ILO methodology).

The positive impact of investments in the exploitation and transformation of gas, and the related industrialization, explains the success of Trinidad and Tobago. Guyana and Suriname benefit from the extraction and export of minerals, especially gold, and to a lesser extent agriculture commodities. Antigua and Barbuda shows a common characteristic of the Caribbean: business cycles tend to be very long. This is a serious problem because it takes a long time for countries in the region to recover from downturns, amplifying the costs of the recovery.[7]

Figure 5.1: Growth performance 2000–2014 (PPP, real GDP per capita, constant 2011 international $)

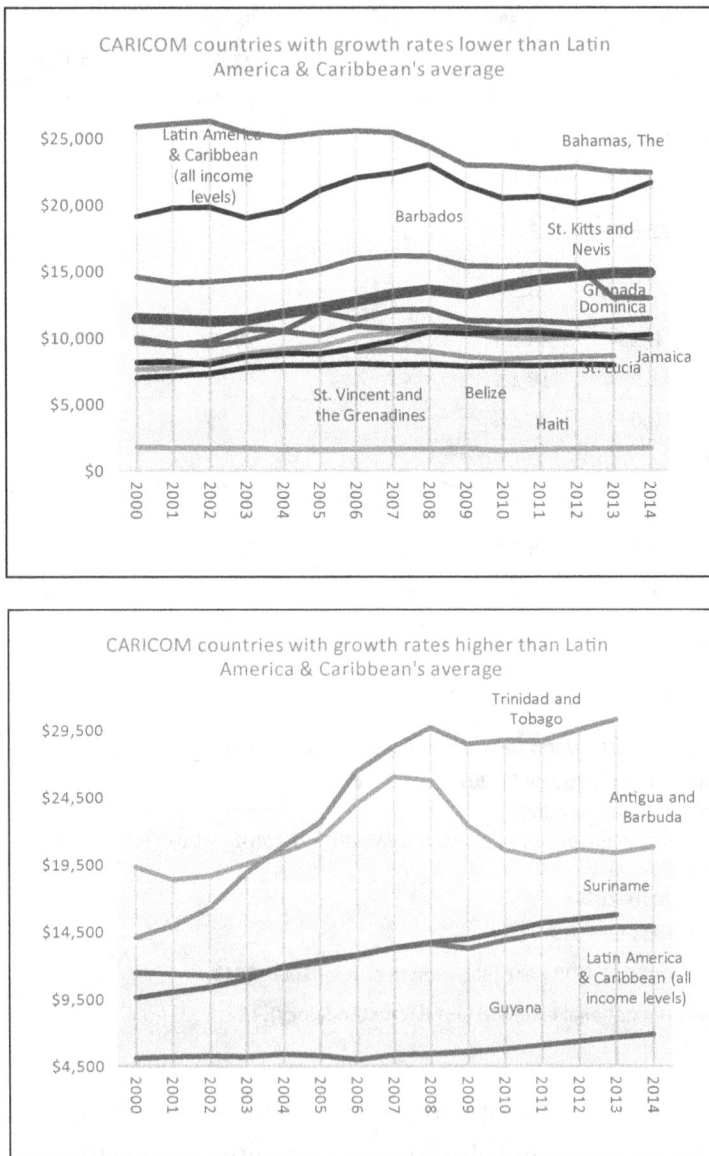

Source: Data from database: World Development Indicators, last updated 11/12/2015

Unfortunately, data limits the analysis of the large divergence of economic performance in the Caribbean. Limited information allows for a superficial analysis of the main contributors to growth in Barbados, Jamaica, St. Lucia and Trinidad and Tobago. Table 5.2 shows the average contribution to growth from labour, capital and total factor productivity (TFP). The table highlights the differences between three countries that show sluggish performance and Trinidad and Tobago, as noted by the average growth rates, with Trinidad and Tobago outperforming the rest by a factor that ranges between 3 and 5. The contribution of labour and capital to growth is comparable across the board: labour contribution to growth is almost the same for all Caribbean countries with the exception of Barbados, and capital contribution to growth is similar for all countries with the exception of St. Lucia, which shows greater contribution, and Trinidad and Tobago, that shows less. Economic theory predicts that TFP is the discriminating factor separating growth performance. This is the case because the growth drivers are innovation and creation, ideas and new ways to increase productivity. This is the case for the Caribbean, where Trinidad and Tobago's TFP shows the highest TFP in the region.[8]

Table 5.2: 2000–2014 average contribution to growth by factor

	Barbados	Jamaica	St. Lucia (1) (2)	Trinidad and Tobago (2)	Latin America (3)
Growth of GDP	0.8	1.5	1.0	4.2	3.1
Contribution related to labour quality	0.2	0.0	NA	0.1	NA
Contribution related labour quantity	−0.1	0.5	0.4	0.5	NA
Contribution related to capital services (ICT)	NA	0.4	NA	NA	NA
Contribution related to capital services (non-ICT)	0.7	0.3	1.8	0.2	NA
TFP growth	0.2	0.5	−1.1	3.4	-0.5

Notes: (1) Labour contribution to growth is not disaggregated between quality and quantity.
(2) Capital services contribution to growth is not disaggregated between ICT and non-ICT.
(3) TED does not present Latin America contribution to growth from labour and capital, only TFP.

Source: The Conference Board. 2015. The Conference Board Total Economy Database™, May 2015, http://www.conference-board.org/data/economydatabase/.

Figure 5.2 shows TFP for Barbados, Jamaica, St. Lucia, Trinidad and Tobago and Latin America. The figure highlights the large contribution of TFP to growth in Trinidad and Tobago. In particular, the increases for 2002–2008 are linked to large investments in the energy sector, with the construction of LNG plants and industries that use energy. Importantly, the main driver of TFP during this period is the emergence of a number of small and medium enterprises (SMEs) in the energy sector that develop services provided to multinational corporations in the country and abroad. These SMEs are expanding their presence and production share in Trinidad, and also in selling services and investing abroad. Since 2014, Trinidadian companies are aggressively participating in exploration and related investments in the energy sector in Suriname and other neighbouring countries. The figure highlights the relevance of focusing on TFP to augment growth in the Caribbean. Lack of information precludes a deeper analysis of the underlying factors that explain growth in the region, an issue that is recurrent throughout this publication and also presented as recommendations in a chapter in the last section.

Figure 5.2: Total Factor Productivity 3-year moving average

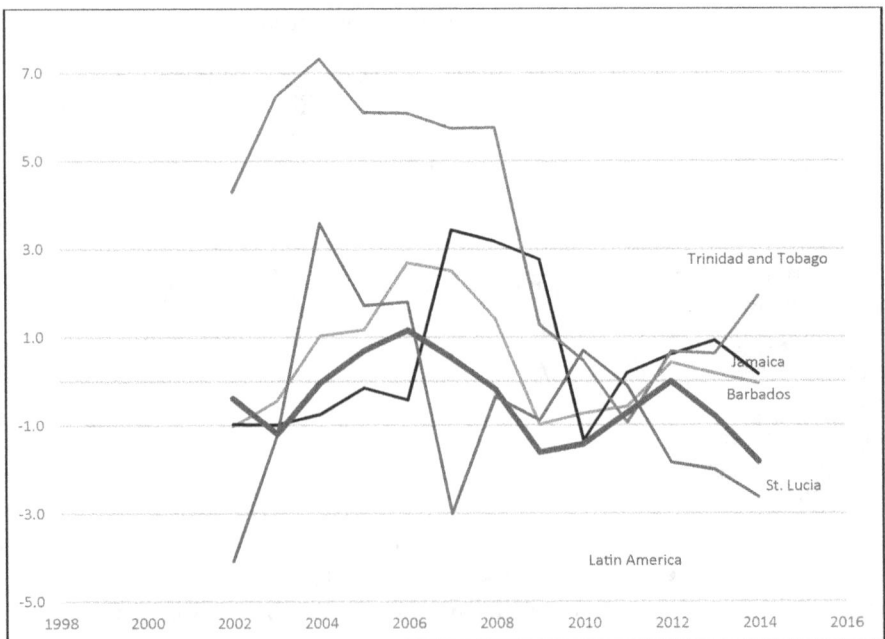

Source: The Conference Board. 2015. The Conference Board Total Economy Database™, May 2015, http://www.conference-board.org/data/economydatabase/.

But are there structural characteristics of small states that predetermine economic outcomes? Previous work debunks commonly held beliefs of the challenges and performances of small states. William Easterly and Aart Kray in 1999 presented the results of extensive analysis of a ten-year panel data from 157 countries, including 33 small states—defined as countries with a population fewer than 1 million.[9] Economic theory provides ample rationale for assuming that small states are challenged due to size-related issues: economies of scale cannot be achieved, and in some cases it may lead to increasing returns; fiscal institutions tend to be weak due to small size and exposure; diversification is difficult given narrow factors assets; politics and interlocking of interests and actors; and exposure to weather events, among others. Because of this, Easterly notes that analysis of small states is littered with dramatic titles including phrases such as 'problems', 'vulnerability', 'small is dangerous', and 'paradise lost', not to mention the title to the present chapter in this publication. The evidence shows that the common held belief of smallness as a problem is exaggerated.

Easterly's analysis focuses on testing whether small states are on average less developed and grow slower than non-small states. The evidence strongly suggests that this hypothesis should be rejected. The analysis shows that, after controlling for many factors, small states have on average higher income and productivity levels than the rest, and that they do not grow less. Such as the evidence presented previously in this chapter, Easterly also points to higher volatility due to exposure to openness and weather. However, openness is also an advantage as it allows small states to benefit from positive changes in terms of trade. Easterly's analysis is dated and not Caribbean specific; however, the evidence available for the region supports the main findings. As for recommendations, the Easterly analysis points to increasing openness to capital markets to build financial buffers that may shield the inevitable, and unpredictable, downturns that characterize small states.

In line with the work of Easterly, during the conference Inder Ruprah presented results of his work analysing growth and competitiveness in the Caribbean.[10] The analysis focuses on comparing Caribbean performance to other small economies in the world, termed ROSE for the 'rest of small economies'. Ruprah finds the Caribbean economies do not compare well to ROSE. In particular, the analysis shows that size, as suggested in Easterly's work, does not necessarily imply negative outcomes, especially when ROSE comparators (which face similar characteristics) are doing better than the Caribbean. The answer, according to Ruprah, is related to the 'sclerosis hypothesis is that special interest groups devote their resources to unproductive rent-seeking to redistribute social wealth. By enlarging their slice of the pie (real GDP), these interest groups reduce the enlargement (economic growth) of the total pie, which in turn reduces total social gains. This happens by influencing policy. Small and politically stable societies like those in the Caribbean foster the development and institutionalisation of growth-retarding special interest groups, which are then better able to influence policy to redistribute resources in their favour. Large discretionary tax expenditure (taxes waived), often used under the banner of industrial policy, could be interpreted as returns to these groups'.[11]

The previous paragraphs provide an overview of growth performance in the Caribbean. The rest of this chapter draws on discussions during the Forum. This chapter presents Sebastian Auguste's work measuring Caribbean vulnerabilities. The paper estimates vulnerability factors for the region, and in particular the probability of a growth crisis. The estimations show that a few variables can successfully predict growth crises, and that this is due to the undiversified structure of Caribbean economies, and that the variables that can trigger a growth crisis are foreign shocks. An important factor related to vulnerability is the short-term impact of extreme weather on inflation, an issue that was presented by Eric Strobl.

This chapter complements Auguste's paper with the work of Dorian Noel on financial issues in the Caribbean, and the paper on fiscal rules by Anthony Birchwood. These two papers noted that financial and fiscal vulnerability is lower for the region as a whole instead of for individual countries. The analysis of bank spreads shows that spreads are higher in the Caribbean than in other regions of the world, and that operation costs and non-performing loans are the key factors in explaining spreads. The analysis of fiscal rules notes that they make sense but that they depend on the level of debt in each economy.

To address vulnerability, it is important to identify sources of financing. In this chapter, the issue of financing development is presented from two perspectives: domestic and international. Domestically, the issue of financing investments is related to allowing the free flow of capital in the region. Some markets have excess reserves in the financial system, whereas other markets have excess demand for credit. Moreover, the depth of domestic markets varies significantly across the region, with some sophisticated products that exist in off-shore financial sectors. The financial knowhow available may be used to prepare a better-coordinated, deeper regional financial system that would increase the efficient provision of financial services.

The international perspective is related to the mismatch between the income per capita levels of the region and its vulnerability. Because of the mismatch, Caribbean countries do not have access to concessional lending from multilateral and bilateral institutions. The cost of lending, therefore, is high and compares to private sector and official sources of lending.

Caribbean vulnerability

Auguste presented results of a probit model using data from Barbados, Belize, Jamaica and Trinidad and Tobago on the probability of being affected by several factors commonly defined as affecting Caribbean economies.[12] According to Auguste, the definition of vulnerability is the risk of a country seeing its development hampered by a natural disaster or external shocks, similar to the concept used in finance of value at risk. The literature on the impact of external shocks highlights its asymmetric impact: negative shocks tend to have a long-term negative impact on performance; positive shocks have short-term minor positive impact on performance.

The analysis involves extensive econometric testing focusing on the following variables as predictors of a crisis: changes in commodity prices; occurrence of natural disasters; total cost; US growth; interest rates in the United States; changes in exchange rates; number of visitors to the country and how long they stay; changes in terms of trade; debt; government spending; fiscal deficits; changes in levels of international reserves; and inflation.

The general findings of Auguste's analysis reveal: (i) few variables explain the probability of a Caribbean country being in a crisis; (ii) crisis are path dependent, that is, the same shock would have a different impact on a country depending on which section of the economic cycle it is at the time of the shock; and (iii) external shocks dominate the outcome, although local conditions may amplify or dampen the final outcome.

Country results follow expected trends. Trinidad and Tobago's probability of a crisis increases when oil prices drop, when the immediate past performance is bad, and when international interest rates increase. Jamaica's probability of a crisis increases when the immediate past performance is bad, when growth in the United States decreases, and when the country suffers from a natural disaster. Barbados' probability of a crisis increases when immediate past performance is bad, when government spends too much, or when US growth decreases. Finally, Belize's probability of a crisis increases when oil prices drop, when debt is high, and when US growth decreases. Figure 5.3 summarises the result of the analysis, and it is important to note that the figure shows the probability of a crisis by country, with Jamaica being the most vulnerable, followed by Trinidad and Tobago, Barbados and Belize.

Figure 5.3: Predicted probabilities of a crisis in the Caribbean according to the Auguste analysis

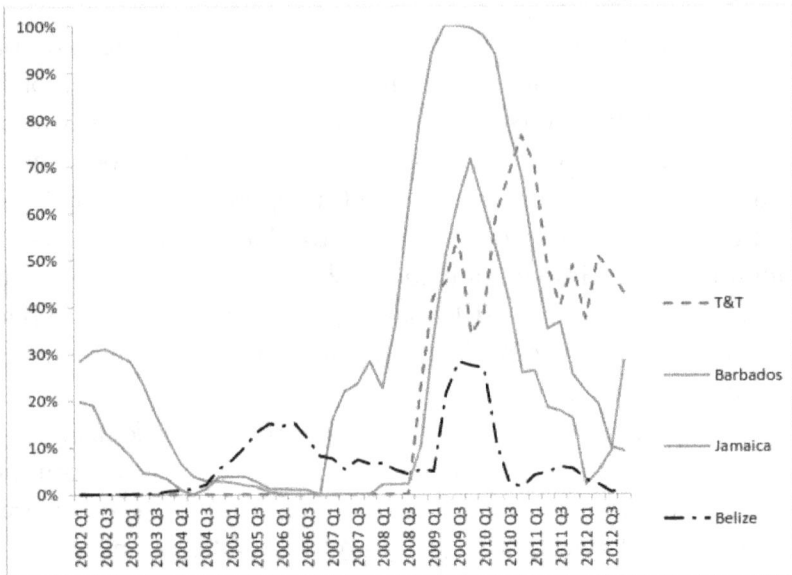

Note: predicted probabilities for the simple probit model based on the best fit model estimated according to Table 6.

Source: Auguste and Cornejo (2015)

INFLATION AND EXTREME WEATHER

During the Forum, Eric Strobl presented on the impact of extreme weather on inflation in the Caribbean.[13] He noted that extreme weather is responsible for over US$3 trillion in damages worldwide over the past 35 years, and that climate change may accelerate the frequency of such events. Most of the literature focuses on the impact of these events on economic performance, but very little focuses on the transmission mechanisms of extreme weather events through prices. The Caribbean's exposure to such events, and the intrinsic logistical challenges result in short-term shortages for goods, which trigger increases in prices, and in some cases result in persistent high inflation. The analysis presented by Strobl provides the framework for the design of fiscal and monetary policies that could be implemented after a country has suffered a weather event, aiming at lowering the additional negative impact on inflation and facilitating the recovery. For example the Philippines implements policies designed to lower prices of goods and services, especially food and housing, during and immediately after an extreme weather event hitting that country. The Caribbean Catastrophe Risk Insurance Facility also considers the inflationary impact of extreme weather on inflation and provides support in case of need.

HOW TO ADDRESS VULNERABILITY ISSUES FISCAL RULES

Anthony Birchwood analyses the impact and usefulness of fiscal rules in the Caribbean. Some countries in the region exhibit persistent large fiscal deficits and debt, and large negative external current account balances. The analysis is based on a dataset of 25 small economies for the period 2007–2011. Using as a benchmark the fiscal rules embedded in the EU Maastricht Treaty that limit the fiscal deficit to 3% and debt to 60% of GDP, the analysis tested whether these benchmarks might improve overall macroeconomic balances. The results are promising because for those countries within the benchmark, domestic balances improve when foreign direct investment is promoted and external balances are sustainable. Importantly, the results also show that growth has a positive effect on domestic balances, but only when debt is low. Birchwood notes that there is non-linear relationship between growth and domestic balances, and the nonlinearity is defined by the debt level – in this case 60% of the GDP.

Flexibility for monetary and fiscal policies is, arguably, an important characteristic of macroeconomic management in the region. However, flexibility may result in difficult implementation of counter cyclical policies that require discipline and austerity when economies are doing well. From this perspective, a regional facility to focus on counter cyclical policies, such as insurance, may work well in the Caribbean.

Fiscal rules designed to maintain domestic balances, control inflation, lower debt and ultimately attempt to lower exposure to necessary foreign savings may be appropriate for the Caribbean. The role played by the IMF and other multilateral institutions is important in this context because they have the financial strength to provide short-term funding when needed. Funding, in this context, would be contingent upon agreements between Caribbean countries and multilateral institutions, which may be strengthened if there is transparency in macroeconomic management if countries also agree to a set of fiscal rules – such as rules on balancing the budget, limiting debt and spending.

FINANCING DEVELOPMENT

Dorian Noel focuses on the impact of liberalising the banking sector on bank spreads in the region.[14] Domestic financing is the most important source of funding for the private sector. For this reason, an efficient banking sector would facilitate investments, lowering vulnerability as economies strengthened and diversified. The analysis uses a dataset on bank-level consolidated financial statements for the period 1998–2012. Banks included are active in nineteen Caribbean and eight Latin American countries and include 314 banks that jointly held over US$47 billion in assets, roughly 12% of the combined GDP.[15]

Figure 5.4: Spread in the Caribbean region

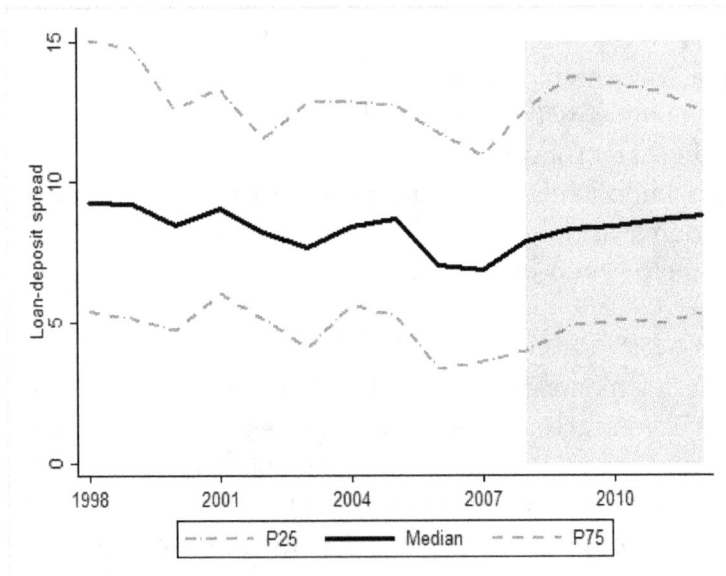

Source: Noel, Dorian, Michael Brei, and Anthony Birchwood. 2015. 'Bank spreads in the Caribbean and Latin America'. Mimeo presented in the Forum of the Future of the Caribbean, Port of Spain, May 2015.

Figure 4.4 presents the spread, loan minus deposit interest rate, for the Caribbean region from 1998 to 2012. The shaded area notes the international financial crisis that started in 2007 but whose impact was felt throughout the region from 2008. The figure highlights a problem for domestic financing in the region: spreads are too wide and are increasing. Because of this fact, funding investment is expensive and limited for private sector projects. To some extent, this figure also notes great financial friction in the region compared to other Latin American economies that have lower spreads and the trend shows narrowing the spread instead of the enlarging trend recorded for the Caribbean.

The major drivers of bank spreads are administrative costs and non-performing loan portfolios. Moreover, as noted in the previous paragraph, spreads are increasing, in part because of the impact of the global financial crisis that resulted in spread increases of over 1%. There is a difference between locally owned and foreign banks, with higher spreads identified in domestic banks—the difference is small, only 0.6%. Liquidity also appears to impact spreads: higher liquidity is correlated to higher spreads.

From a policy perspective, the results point to an area for improvement: lowering administrative costs and increasing operational efficiency would have an impact on reducing spreads and real interest rates on loans. Such as for other issues, additional research and data collection is needed to design policies that would accelerate financial intermediation in the region.

Funding may also come from international sources, for private and public projects. Importantly, closing the current account balance for countries in the region requires a healthy flow of foreign direct investment and access to international capital markets. The problems that the region faces are related to both limited foreign direct investment opportunities and also limited access to voluntary international markets. These twin constraints need to be examined more closely by collecting data and measuring the impact of limited access to funding on growth and development.

Ex ante, however, Forum participants noted the urgent need to focus on short-term funding problems for countries in the region that have high debt, experience slow growth, and face external imbalances. These countries are also characterized by relatively high income levels, which in some cases disqualify them from concessional lending from multilateral and bilateral donors. Lack of access to concessional lending may have a large negative impact because, in many cases, these countries cannot access alternative sources of funding, and when they do, the cost of funding may be high. For these reasons, Forum participants requested of decision makers a review of funding policies regarding access to concessional lending.

CONCLUSION AND RECOMMENDATIONS

The information presented during the Forum leads to recognizing vulnerabilities in the region and a comprehensive effort to its identification, measurement and early detection. A regional approach is necessary to lower risk and insure the region from the negative impact of common vulnerabilities.

But the region is also heterogeneous, with countries that are similar in many respects though different in terms of economic performance. Recognizing the need for countries in the region to act together in lowering common risk, therefore, also requires recognition of differences. Regional policies, therefore, should meet the dual objective of mapping out actions designed for each Caribbean country complemented with mapping out actions designed for the region as a whole. This approach is challenging but necessary to successfully lower risk across the region.

The following recommendations may set the stage for a common understanding on how to lower risk in the Caribbean:

- The region needs an early warning system capable of identifying an increased risk at the country and regional levels. The system should be able to objectively measure and assess risk.
- Country specific policies should be in place to be implemented when country risk increases. These policies would require regional coordination and supplemental support from other countries in the region.
- Regional policies should be in place to be implemented when regional risk increases.
- Funding for these policies may be thought of as macroeconomic insurance against risk events. Funding should come from Caribbean countries' savings supplemented with multilateral and bilateral lines of credit. The financial engineering of this fund may be similar to the Heritage and Stabilisation Fund of Trinidad and Tobago, but for the region, the purpose would be solely to stabilise economies by maintaining macroeconomic balances.

- Fiscal or other rules may strengthen the functioning of a regional facility to lower risk. The rules would provide transparency and guide common regional goals of stability and growth.
- Banking regulations and supervision would be more effective if presented from a regional perspective. The purpose would be to increase financial intermediation and to lower financial friction throughout the region. Importantly, the main indicator of success of such a policy would be the increase in lending to the private sector for investment.

NOTES

1. Caribbean countries are those countries that are members of CARICOM: Antigua and Barbuda, The Bahamas, Barbados, Belize, Dominica, Grenada, Guyana, Haiti, Jamaica, Montserrat, St. Lucia, Sr. Kitts and Nevis, St. Vincent and the Grenadines, Suriname and Trinidad and Tobago.
2. The source of this information is the World Bank dataset as noted in the table. The coefficient of variation is calculated as the ration of the standard deviation to the average, and provides a proxy for volatility of real GDP growth rates. Unfortunately the dataset does not include poverty estimates.
3. Assuming the implied annual growth rate of 2000–2014. Using the same estimation, the number of years it would take to double income: 187 for Jamaica; 84 for St. Vincent and the Grenadines and St. Kitts and Nevis; 81 for Belize; 63 for Grenada; and 45 for Dominica.
4. The literature is large in presenting the negative impact of youth unemployment in long-term job and wage performance throughout life. A brief literature review may be found in 'The joint impact of labour policies and the "Great Recession" on unemployment in Europe' Dal Bianco, Silvia, Randolph L. Bruno and Marcello Signorelli. *Economic Systems*, Volume 39, Issue 1, March 2015, Pages 3–26.
5. The World Bank dataset does not include data on Montserrat; all other CARICOM countries are included in the table.
6. The annual average growth rate for St. Lucia between 2014 and 2000 is close to zero, for this reason this ratio is very large, reflecting this fact more than volatility per se.
7. See an analysis of long business cycles for Trinidad and Tobago in: Rojas-Suarez, Liliana and Carlos Elias (Editors). *From Growth to Prosperity: Policy Perspectives for Trinidad and Tobago*. 2006. IDB Special Publications on Development. Inter -American Development Bank, Washington DC.
8. Trinidad and Tobago exhibit large TFP contributions to growth from 2002 to 2007, especially in 2003 TFP was 10.9% and in 2006 10.8%. In part this may be attributed to data limitations and errors in measuring labour and capital contribution to growth. In spite of these probable measurement errors, investments in the gas industry and the expansion of private sector

activities in the service energy sector confirm the large impact of innovation on growth.

9.   Easterly, William, and Aart Kray. 1999. 'Small States, Small Problems?' World Bank Policy Research Paper 2139. The World Bank Development Research Group, Macroeconomics and Growth.

10. Ruprah, Inder, Karl Melgarejo, and Ricardo Sierra. 2014. 'Is there a Caribbean sclerosis?: stagnating economic growth in the Caribbean'. IDB monograph, Washington D.C.

11. Ibid. Page 75.

12. Auguste, Sebastian, and Magdalena Cornejo. 2015. 'Vulnerability in small island economies. The case of the Caribbean'. Mimeo presented in the Forum of the Future of the Caribbean, Port of Spain, May 2015.

13. Strobl, Eric, Andreas Heinen, and Jeetendra Khadan. 2015. 'The inflationary costs of extreme weather'. Mimeo presented in the Forum of the Future of the Caribbean, Port of Spain, May 2015.

14. Noel, Dorian, Michael Brei, and Anthony Birchwood. 2015. 'Bank spreads in the Caribbean and Latin America'. Mimeo presented in the Forum of the Future of the Caribbean, Port of Spain, May 2015.

15. Caribbean countries include Antigua and Barbuda, Anguilla, Aruba, Barbados, Bahamas, Bermuda, British Virgin Islands, Cuba, Curacao, Dominica, Grenada, Haiti, Jamaica, Saint Kitts and Nevis, Cayman Islands, Saint Lucia, Saint Vincent and Trinidad and Tobago, Belize, Costa Rica, El Salvador, Guatemala, Guyana, Honduras, Panama and Suriname.

CHAPTER 6
How Do We Address Climate Change?

Preeya Mohan

INTRODUCTION

The countries of the Caribbean are on the front lines of vulnerability to climate change. Warmer temperatures, sea-level rise and increased hurricane frequency and intensity threaten economic development and livelihoods throughout the region. Rising sea levels can lead to more salt water intrusions into aquifers that supply fresh water[1], a resource in short supply on some islands, especially in the Eastern Caribbean. This brings with it soil salination which can negatively affect agricultural crops and, consequently, income, employment and food security. Although Caribbean countries are highly dependent on imported food, there is still a significant amount of domestic consumption of agricultural products, and given the impact of climate change which can result in droughts and floods, this can lead to higher food prices in the future. Warmer sea waters create stronger hurricanes,—for a region that is already classified as the most disaster-prone in the world because of the frequency of hurricane strikes it has experienced. Hurricanes have cause widespread economic and social damage including loss of lives, property and livelihoods in the region on an almost annual basis. Since 1970, hurricane damage equivalent to more than 2% of GDP can be expected every 2.5 years in the region.[2] It takes years for the islands to recover from a single hurricane's impact. Moreover, populations and property in the region are largely concentrated in coastal areas and may not be able to withstand stronger winds, deeper incursions from more forceful ocean surges and heavier rains.[3]

Climate change may cause greater precipitation during storms and contribute to landslides and flooding which would negatively affect infrastructure, homes and agriculture. As infrastructure for disposal and treatment of sewage in the Caribbean is underdeveloped, mere flooding can promote waterborne disease.[4] Climate change will also accelerate the erosion of coastal beaches and protective mangroves. Coastal houses, hotels and other buildings, along with roads and other infrastructure are vulnerable along with beaches, which can negatively affect tourism on which the region is highly dependent. The fishing sector is also at risk because coral reef habitats are stressed by warmer oceans, and coral bleaching negatively affects coral reefs, which are vital for the region as they provide fishing grounds, coastal protection and tourism opportunities. More frequent and longer droughts can also be expected. This can lead to greater health risks including greater heat stress for vulnerable populations, poorer sanitation conditions from limited water supplies, contaminated water from floods and conditions that can favour the spread of water and vector-borne diseases, such as dengue fever, malaria and diarrhoea. This would put a strain on public health services. Higher temperatures can also negatively impact agriculture and ecosystems. Finally, climate change can negatively affect energy prices in the region. All Caribbean islands except Trinidad and Tobago are net hydrocarbon importers. As temperatures increase in a region that is already hot for most of the year, electricity consumption for air conditioning may increase, raising the demand and possibly the price for energy.[5]

These devastating impacts may occur regardless of the fact that the Caribbean has marginally contributed to the release of greenhouse gases that drive climate change compared with large developed and developing countries. Table 1 shows the potential costs of inaction for the region if greenhouse gas emissions continue to increase. There is a great deal of savings possible from acting now to prevent the negative consequences of climate change, and so the cost of inaction should be seriously considered. The projections are not comprehensive but are based on three categories of climate change effects: 1) hurricane damages, 2) tourism losses and 3) infrastructure damages due to sea-level rise. Hurricane damages are extrapolated from the average annual hurricane damages in the recent past; tourism losses are assumed to be proportional to the current share of tourism in each economy; and infrastructure damages are due to sea-level rise yet exclusive of hurricane damages, which are projected as a constant cost per affected household. For the three categories, the region's cost of inaction is projected to total US $22 billion annually by 2050 and US $46 billion by 2100. These costs represent 10% and 22%, respectively, of the current Caribbean economy.[6] While the regional average is large, there is considerable variation around this average where the smaller islands would bear higher costs. For instance, the projected cost of inaction reaches 75% of GDP or more by 2100 in Dominica, Grenada, Haiti, St. Kitts and Nevis and Turks and Caicos.

Table 6.1: Caribbean Region-Cost of Inaction (US$ billions)

	2025	2050	2075	2100
Cost of inaction ($ US billion)				
Hurricanes	1.1	2.8	4.9	7.9
Tourism	1.6	3.2	4.8	6.4
Infrastructure	8.0	15.9	23.9	31.0
Total	10.7	21.9	33.7	46.2
Total Cost as a per cent of GDP (%)	5.0	10.3	15.9	21.7

Source: Bueno et al. (2008).[7]

Scarce resources in the region that could be used for poverty alleviation and other social services and sustainable development will have to be diverted to cover these costs of climate change, which threaten sustainable development in the region. In mitigating the costs of climate change, appropriate data and vulnerability measures are critical to inform policy making and strategic planning. This chapter outlines two examples on how to address environmental vulnerability in the Caribbean which were presented at the Forum: 1) measuring vulnerability by observing SMEs infrastructure investments; and 2) designing and implementing integrated coastal zone management techniques.

These issues are summarised in the rest of this chapter. Section 2 summarizes the work of Asad Mohammed and Perry Polar entitled 'Small and Medium Enterprises as indicators of resilience to climate change in the Caribbean'. The paper proposes a series of practical indicators to measure the vulnerability, resilience and adaptive capacity using Small and Medium Size enterprises (SMEs) from which inferences can be made about their host communities. Section 3 outlines the work of Rahanna Juman and Khalil Hassanali, 'Integrating Climate Change Adaptation into Coastal Zone Management'. The study proposes integrated coastal zone management (ICZM) as the best approach for achieving balance between economic development and conservation in fighting climate change by managing human activity within coastal zones, and addressing conflicts amongst different resource users and uses.

SMES AS INDICATORS OF RESILIENCE TO CLIMATE CHANGE IN THE CARIBBEAN

SMEs play an important role in the functioning of a community and will support communities to better prepare for, adapt to and mitigate climate hazards.[8] Caribbean governments need to have a better understanding of vulnerability and the extent to which interventions will improve resilience and the adaptive capacity to justify policy interventions and investments. SMEs are a practical force in the development of a vulnerability indicator system. SMEs are discrete enumerable entities, they have a range of internal processes which are also measurable, they normally conduct risk management as part of their daily operations, they are impacted by small and large scale external interventions of any nature and their survival is linked to the well-being of their host community. Also, the private sector in the Caribbean is largely composed of SMEs. The World Bank Enterprise Surveys of Latin America and the Caribbean determined that 91% of enterprises in the Caribbean were SMEs.[9] The region has a severe data collection problem; however, data on SMEs is often collected by national agencies and are accessible. Assessments of the parameters associated with SMEs can be collected pre-intervention, during the life cycle of the intervention and post intervention, where an intervention is a large infrastructural project that is expected to reduce vulnerability. Hence, the impact of an intervention can be determined. The results still apply and can be generalized to the whole.

SMEs' Vulnerability Indicators

The data required for the SMEs indicators include secondary data, structured/semi-structured interviews, focused interviews and general observations. Eight SMEs' indicators are used to determine the vulnerability level of SMEs categorised as very high vulnerability (5), high vulnerability (4), moderate vulnerability (3), low vulnerability (2) and very low vulnerability (1). The indicators combine to estimate a mean score of vulnerability. Also, the pre-project assessment scores can be compared with post project assessment scores. A composite value based on the sum of means can be calculated to give an estimated vulnerability score pre and post project implementation to indicate the impact of the project. Areas with 'very high vulnerability' and 'high vulnerability' should be prioritized for interventions to reduce their vulnerability. Areas with 'moderate', 'low vulnerability' or 'very low vulnerability' should be monitored for changes. The indicators used to determine estimates of vulnerability are as follows:

1. **SMEs per area**: Because SMEs are responsive to risk as part of their normal operations, they are likely to employ asset adaptation

strategies which make their business and area of operation more resilient to the negative impacts of climate change. Areas, which have large numbers of businesses, are also more likely to be able to collectively lobby for infrastructural improvements which can increase resilience. Generally, the larger the number of SMEs per area, the greater the possibility of improved resilience to climate change. SMEs can be classified according to the number of employees based on the national classifications for SME (i.e. < 50 employees). The number of SMEs in each sample area can be determined and divided by the area (km^2) which corresponds to the geographic area of activities of the project. Data on informal enterprises can also be collected, and cumulative and disaggregated totals are presented in the analysis.

Because some areas, such as urban areas, will have higher concentrations of SMEs than others, such as rural areas, the density indicator could be highly skewed. Hence, the appropriate range to correlate SME per area (i.e. km^2) to vulnerability may have to be non-symmetrical. The methodology proposes a density indicator of SMEs in the project area as a good indicator of the relationship between the SMEs' population and the general population of the area. The higher the density of the SMEs, the stronger the relationship to the host community. Density can be classified based on variations from the national average using a square root scale. This will contribute to the understanding of the host community's vulnerability. For example:

a.　0 to the national average for Trinidad and Tobago, the range will be 0–16 = Very high vulnerability (5)

b.　National average +1 to ($\sqrt{}$ national average)^3 for Trinidad and Tobago, the range will be 17–64 = High vulnerability (4)

c.　($\sqrt{}$ national average)^3 +1 to ($\sqrt{}$ national average)^4 for Trinidad and Tobago, the range will be 65–256 = Moderate vulnerability (3)

d.　($\sqrt{}$ national average)^4 +1 to ($\sqrt{}$ national average)^5 for Trinidad and Tobago, the range will be 257–1024 = Low vulnerability (2)

e.　> ($\sqrt{}$ national average)^5 for Trinidad and Tobago, the range will be >258 = Very low vulnerability (1)

2. **Type of Industry**: In the case of localised disasters, businesses which are highly dependent on the local community are more vulnerable

than businesses which service a wider geographical range. Thus, if the adaptive capacity of the community is high, then the business is likely to survive the disaster and, conversely, if the community has a low adaptive capacity, then the business will suffer.

3. The Central Statistical Office (CSO) in Trinidad and Tobago classifies industries in the following categories: Sugar; Petroleum industries; Food Processers and Drink; Textiles, Garments, Footwear and Headwear; Printing, Publishing and Paper converters; Wood and Related Products; Chemical and Non-Metallic Minerals; Assembly-type and related industries; Miscellaneous Manufacturing; Construction; Distribution; Hotels and Guesthouses; Transportation, Communication and Storage; Finance, Insurance, Real Estate and Business Services; Educational and Cultural Community Services; Personal Services. This categorization of enterprises, which is similar across the region, does not lend itself to an understanding of linkages within the community. Based upon field data assessments, interviews and the focus group discussions, this general typology of the activities carried out by SMEs can be adapted and classified as the following:

   • Very high linkage (Retailing of food and other personal products) – items which are purchased in day-to-day operations due to proximity to community (small shops, vendors etc.) = Very high vulnerability (5)

   • High linkage (Services) – Services which are utilized due to proximity to community (hair dressers, car repair garages etc.) = High vulnerability (4)

   • Moderate linkage (Large retail and Light manufacturing) – Business which may be established in a community but service a wider market (e.g. supermarkets, large clothing shops etc.) = Moderate vulnerability (3)

   • Linked (Construction) – SMEs involved in construction can repair other business premises after a climate change induced disaster hence their presence builds adaptive capacity (Wedawatta and Jones 2008) = Low vulnerability (2)

   • Low linkage (Other) – SMEs which are connected to the national economic sector such as those in Sugar; Petroleum industries; Chemical and Non-Metallic Minerals; manufacturing etc. have larger markets and are aware of international adaptation practices and are less likely to be affected by localized disasters affecting the community = Very low vulnerability (1)

Both the percentages of each type of industry in a project area and an average vulnerability rating can be calculated.

3. **Registration status of business**: Registration is an effective way of separating formal and informal enterprises with the latter normally outnumbering the former. Registered SMEs pay taxes and legally access services (electricity, water etc.); they have filing systems and access to credit and insurance coverage, and as such are likely to be more established and hence more resilient than informal enterprises. An increasing proportion of registered businesses to informal businesses will give an indication of formal growth in the area and its increasing resilience.

Formal SMEs are registered with the state through a legal mechanism such as the Companies Act in Jamaica and Trinidad and Tobago. However, a challenge is that businesses may be registered with the Companies Registrar but not be currently operational. Although the Board of Inland Revenue (BIR) may be a more suitable source of secondary data, there is a challenge with accessibility. Formal businesses are required to display Value Added Tax (VAT) certificates or Articles of Incorporation, which will assist in verification in a primary data gathering process.

The percentage of registered SMEs relative to informal SMEs in a project area can be calculated using the formula (Registered SMEs/Informal SMEs) x 100. Businesses can be classified as the following:

a.   Very low registration (0–20%) = Very high vulnerability (5)

b.   Low registration (21–40%) = High vulnerability (4)

c.   Moderate registration (41–60%) = Moderate vulnerability (3)

d.   High registration (61–80%) = Low vulnerability (2)

e.   Very high registration (81–100%) = Very low vulnerability (1)

4. **Tenure Status**: In the Caribbean, tenure status for SMEs can generally be classified on a continuum from informal to formal development, with a range of intermediate tenure types and perceptions of security. SMEs may be established on land with tenure status other than freehold or leasehold (which are the most formal and secure tenure types), squatting, family land, traditional land and rented land. Documentation of tenure status is also a challenge, which may

limit control over legal infrastructural improvements. Generally, there tends to be a correlation between increasing levels of tenure security and the level of formal planning of settlements. This factor, more than the actual tenure status, would affect the vulnerability of SMEs to climate change. Given the limited enforcement abilities of national agencies, SMEs on informal tenure will often operate with the confidence of those with formal tenure, and will make adaptation strategies.

The assessment of this indicator is partly paradoxical. If there is ownership of the premises, the vulnerability level can be higher if both the premises and business are affected. Nevertheless, when the premises are owned the vulnerability level decreases as there is a higher probability the property would be improved to reduce hazards (e.g. presence of a solid building structure, drainage, etc.). SMEs which rent have less control over infrastructural improvements. It should be noted that data may not be up to date from secondary sources as property may change hands. Even though data is becoming available from agencies dealing with regularisation of informal settlements this data will most likely need to be collected from primary sources.

The tenure status of SMEs can be classified according to the following:

- Informal tenure (squatting) = Very high vulnerability (5)
- Traditional holdings/family lands = High vulnerability (4)
- Rented premises = Moderate vulnerability (3)
- Formal tenure without documentation = Low vulnerability (2)
- Formal tenure with documentation = Very low vulnerability (1)
- The percentage of each category can be calculated and an average score determined.

5. **Insurance:** The existence of personal (e.g. life, health, etc.) or business insurance (e.g. fire, public liability, business interruption, goods in transit, workmen's compensation ect.) can allow for financial resources to be available post disaster if the business was damaged, or there was injury or loss of life by the owner or employees. The Insurance status can be classified according to the following:

- No personal or business insurance = Very high vulnerability (5)
- Personal but no business insurance = High vulnerability (4)
- Single protection business insurance = Moderate vulnerability (3)
- Multiple protection business insurance = Low vulnerability (2)
- Both personal and multiple protection business insurance = Very low vulnerability (1)

The percentage of businesses/owners in each category can be calculated and an average score determined.

6. **Type and location of data storage**: Business information (e.g. accounts, employee information, supplier information, contracts etc.) are useful for the proper functioning of business and for taxation purposes, and will be necessary for post disaster recovery. Information stored on premises without backup are at greater risk than information stored off-site. Paper files may pose more of a risk than electronic files if not copied. A trend where persons utilized their mobile phones to store business information was noted in Jamaica. The type and location of data storage status can be classified according to the following:

- No data storage = Very high vulnerability (5)
- Data on mobile device = High vulnerability (4)
- Single copy paper and electronic files on premises only = Moderate vulnerability (3)
- Paper and electronic files off premises = Low vulnerability (2)
- Paper and/or electronic files backed up in multiple locations = Very low vulnerability (1)

The percentage of SMEs in each category can be calculated and an average score determined.

7. **Organisation membership:** Some businesses are part of larger business organizations. Businesses in internationally linked Business Associations (e.g. American Chamber of Commerce of Trinidad and Tobago) are more likely to conform to environmental standards than locally formed Associations (e.g. Chamber of Commerce). The former is likely to threaten environmental issues alongside financial issues while the latter may deal with it as a 'special' topic. SMEs are more likely to be linked to locally formed associations which offer

business support (financing and training) rather than those focusing on networking.

The organisation membership status can be classified according to the following:

- No organisation membership or links to training and networking opportunities = Very high vulnerability (5)
- No organisation membership but access to training and networking opportunities = High vulnerability (4)
- Membership in a locally formed Association = Moderate vulnerability (3)
- Membership in an internationally linked Association = Low vulnerability (2)
- Membership in internationally linked and local Associations = Very low vulnerability (1)

The percentage of SMEs in each category can be calculated and an average score determined.

8. **Topography and environmental conditions**: The topographical and environmental conditions determine the internal bio-vulnerability of SMEs. This generally would not change drastically unless hard engineering adaptation solutions were given, for example those associated with large infrastructural projects. Based on multi-hazard datasets and datasets on location of businesses, an internal biophysical vulnerability score can be calculated for SMEs. Given the strong relationship between informal economic activities and SMEs in the Caribbean, the maps allow for visualization of the risk present and illustrate the higher risk along the coast.

The values for risk can be assigned as follows: 'Very High Vulnerability' (5), 'High Vulnerability' (4), 'Moderate Vulnerability' (3), 'Low Vulnerability' (2), and 'Very Low Vulnerability' (1).

A mean score can be calculated based on aggregate scores for SMEs.

Table 6.2 summarises the vulnerability rating system based on the indicators which all range from 1-5.

Table 6.2: Parameters for Composite Index of SME vulnerability

	Very Low Vulnerability (1)	Low Vulnerability (2)	Medium Vulnerability (3)	High Vulnerability (4)	Very High Vulnerability (5)	Weighting
SMEs per area	> (V national average)[5]	(V national average)[4] +1 to (V national average)[5]	(V national average)[3] +1 to (V national average)[4]	national average +1 to (V national average)[3]	0 to national average	0.15
Type of Enterprise	Other	Construction	Large retail/ manufacturing	Services	Food and personal items	0.2
Registration status of business	81-100 % Formal SMEs /Informal SMEs	61-80 % Formal SMEs /Informal SMEs	41-60 % Formal SMEs /Informal SMEs	21-40 % Formal SMEs /Informal SMEs	0-20% Formal SMEs / Informal SMEs	0.1
Tenure Status	Formal tenure with documentation	Formal tenure without documentation	Rented premises	Traditional holdings/ family lands	Informal	0.1
Insurance status	No personal or business insurance	Personal but no business insurance	Single protection business insurance	Multiple protection business insurance	Both personal and multiple protection business insurance	0.1
Type and location of data storage	No data storage	Data on mobile device	Single copy paper and electronic files on premises only	Paper and electronic files off premises	Electronic files backed up in multiple locations	0.05
Organisational membership	No organisation membership or links to training and networking opportunities	No organisation membership but access to training and networking opportunities	Membership in a locally formed Associations	Membership in a internationally linked Association	Membership in internationally linked and local Associations	0.05
Topographical and Environmental conditions	Composite score	Composite score	Composite score	Composite score	Composite score	0.25

Source: Mohammed and Polar (2015).[10]

The paper randomly assigns weights to the various factors making up the index. Given that Topographical and Environmental conditions have a heavy influence on total vulnerability, this indicator is given a weighting of 0.25. The type of Industry indicator is given a weighting of 0.2, while SMEs per area, registration, tenure status and insurance status are each given a weighting of 0.1. Type and location of data storage and organisation membership are each given a weighting of 0.05. A final composite score can be calculated based on the sum of the means, pre and post project. To properly assign weights, however, the robustness of the results must be tested by changing the weights systematically and determining the impact on the index. Alternatively, if sufficient data are available, a regression equation can be used.

Final SMEs Beneficiaries, that is, SMEs that are in the geographic area of the project and are likely to benefit directly from infrastructural improvements, are the most appropriate targets for targeted questionnaires. They can be identified from visual inspection in the sampling area culled from project documents and assess pre-intervention, during the project life and post the project life. Their presence can be contextualized in terms of socioeconomic data on the area.

Associated SMEs beneficiaries, that is, those benefiting financially from the projects through providing goods and services, are not practical for targeting because they can only be identified well into the project life from procurement lists. As some successful companies may subcontract by other companies, the number of Associated SMEs beneficiaries may be large. It may be useful to interview post project to determine if their association with the project resulted in the use of "greener" technologies or higher standards of operation, and if these were translated to other local projects, which could reduce community and/or national vulnerability.

Conclusion

There is a growing need to build the adaptive capacity/resilience of communities and collect information that helps to understand that such capacity is required for short, medium and long term planning. SMEs are a relevant bottom-up unit of analysis which can provide information and data, which support a more complete understanding of climate change on a local level. Due to the heterogeneous nature of SMEs, they may give a broader understanding of adaptive capacity in communities than aggregated data. The methodology proposed is robust yet simple enough to allow for urban practitioners, Non-Governmental Organisations (NGOs), business associations, communities and individuals to participate in data gathering, calculating the index and understanding the results. In the identification of the eight indicators, there was balance between factors intrinsic to the resilience and adaptive capacity of the SMEs and the impact of collective SMEs on an area. Along with a better understanding of the role SMEs play in the community, and a means to determine a vulnerability score for external shocks and stresses based on multihazard risk, the proposed methodology should be able to allow comparison of the resilience of communities.

INTEGRATING CLIMATE CHANGE ADAPTATION INTO COASTAL ZONE MANAGEMENT

The paper argues that ICZM is the best approach to achieve balance between economic development and conservation by managing human activities within the coastal zone and addressing conflicts amongst different resource users and uses. It uses a case study of Tobago which can be applied to other inlands in the region. Climate change and its accompanying negative effects can exacerbate problems associated with many stakeholders and interests competing for limited coastal space. ICZM is a strategy to adapt to climate change impacts and to reduce vulnerability to coastal hazards by sustainably managing a country's coastal and ocean space, resources and activities. It is a participatory process that requires discourse, co-ordination and harmonization among governments, the private sector, local communities and others. It endeavours to improve governance so that conflict is alleviated and sustainable development is fostered. Trinidad and Tobago's economy, similar to other countries of the region, has always been supported by coastal and marine resources, primarily oil and gas, tourism and fishing. It is inevitable that conflicts would arise where several human activities occur in the same area and depend on the same natural resources. The multiplicity of laws and policies impacting coastal areas creates problems such as overlapping jurisdiction and a lack of proper coordination amongst enforcement and management agencies. Public education programmes are limited and sporadic, and have generally failed to transform attitudes towards sustainable development in coastal areas. These problems have led to unsustainable utilization of the coastal resources. In April 2012, the Cabinet of Trinidad and Tobago appointed a multi-sectoral Steering

Committee to develop an ICZM Policy Framework, Strategies and Action Plan. To assist with the development of a policy that incorporates climate change considerations, the IDB funded a Technical Cooperation entitled 'Piloting the integration of climate change adaptation and coastal zone management in Southwest Tobago'. Southwest Tobago was selected because it is low-lying and vulnerable to impacts of climate change; it is the most populated and developed part of Tobago; and it is home to some of the most diverse and sensitive ecosystems in the country; there are data available for analysis. This paper describes the lessons learnt from the technical cooperation and provides insights into how they could inform the national ICZM policy framework, strategies and action plan not only for Trinidad and Tobago but for the wider Caribbean region.

Coastal Vulnerability and Risk Assessment for South West Tobago

A vulnerability and risk assessment was conducted for Southwest Tobago based on climate change scenarios. Two climate scenarios were adopted: Representative Concentration Pathways (RCPs) 8.5 and 4.5, in addition to present day conditions.[11] The RCPs are greenhouse gas concentration (not emissions) trajectories adopted by the IPCC for its Fifth Assessment Report (AR5). RCP8.5 'high' is the highest of the RCPs and with high climate sensitivity represents the greatest level of climate risk, and RCP4.5 'mid' sensitivity is selected to represent a middle level of the RCPs which has the largest number of Global Climate Model simulations.[12] The study focused on vulnerabilities related to coastal flooding and erosion. Consequently, the climate change variables of interest, in relation to potentially changing coastal processes that drive these hazards, are: mean sea-level rise (SLR) and extreme water level events (incorporating changes in sea level and wind parameters). The assessment was then used to develop a methodology to formulate a Coastal Vulnerability Index (CVI) which identified areas that are at risk to erosion and/or permanent or temporary inundation and their potential impacts to human and economic activities. One major hindrance to the scenario modelling is the lack of accurate, long-term data. The study produced a number of GIS maps showing tidal inundation, flood extent and erosion extent under the different RCPs and risk maps for human and economic activities.

With regards to the National ICZM, the CVI approach clearly identifies and prioritises locations that require future climate change adaptation planning within the ICZM process. A key lesson from the pilot study was that consistent, complete datasets are not available for many of the key features required to be defined for the full CVI analyses. These include tidal, wave, topography, bathymetry, beach profile, aerial photography and land use data. Another key lesson is the relative lack of transparency of data existence/availability. It is therefore recommended that relevant government agencies coordinate to identify existing available datasets, and define metadata related to source, resolution, date and format.

Ecosystem based approach (EbA) to Climate Change Adaptation (CCA) and ICZM

EbA aims to avoid poorly planned engineering solutions for CCA that could work against nature by constraining regular ecological cycles, which may lead to mal-adaptation and increased social vulnerability.[13] ICZM represents a public planning process for achieving the goals of the EbA with increased efficiency through rational and objective spatial planning for future sustainable uses. ICZM and EbA provide a robust framework to determine strategies and measures for climate resilience. In the pilot study area, the aim was to apply an EbA to CCA and ICZM. To do this, a climate change response plan was developed that recommended seven adaptation responses (Table 6.3).

Table 6.3: Climate change adaptation response[14]

Adaptation Response	Description
Maintain/restore wetlands	Protection for existing wetlands and mangroves in SW Tobago from development, pollution and habitat changes that may be exacerbated by sea-level rise. Developing/enforcing legislation or modifying land use rules (e.g., zoning) to facilitate wetland migration inland. Prohibitions on shoreline hardening.
Maintain Sediment Transport	Adaptation options that maintain sediment transport in order to reverse changes that have already occurred or changes that will continue to occur. Combined with other actions, these adaptation options may work to prevent loss of coastal habitats and enable habitats (reliant on sediment supply such as mangroves) to accrete at a rate consistent with sea-level rise.

Preserve coastal land/ development (including infrastructure)	Adaptation options that focus on land use planning and management, land exchange and acquisition programs, and retrofitting infrastructure. These adaptation options primarily aim to preserve coastal land on which development is planned or already exists.
Maintain shorelines utilizing "soft" measures	Approaches for maintaining shorelines in the face of sea-level rise include both "soft" measures and "hard" measures. Each of these approaches or some combination of them may be appropriate depending on the characteristics of a particular location (e.g., shore protection costs, property values, the environmental importance of habitat, the feasibility of protecting shores without harming the habitat.
Maintain shorelines utilizing "hard" measures	Shoreline protection through hardening techniques such as constructing bulkheads, seawalls, revetments and breakwaters, or reinforcing dikes and headlands. Adaptation options that use hardening techniques are often preserving existing development (e.g., homes and businesses) and infrastructure (e.g., sewage systems, roads), or protecting land available for future development or infrastructure.
Preserve Habitat for Vulnerable Species	Adaptation options that involve actively increasing coastal ecosystem boundaries or removing barriers that prevent habitat expansion or migration. Actions to increase ecosystem boundaries could include purchasing upland development or property rights and expanding the planning horizons of land use planning to incorporate longer-term climate predictions.
Maintain water quality	Sea-level rise and changes in the timing and intensity of precipitation can affect the water quality of coastal receiving waters. Protecting existing infrastructure and planning for impacts to new infrastructure can help reduce vulnerability to these impacts (e.g., sizing drainage and sewer treatment systems to accommodate changes in flow). Other options for maintaining water quality of mangroves and wetlands include preventing or limiting groundwater extraction from shallow aquifers and protecting land subject to flooding by plugging canals.

Based on the erosion rates identified by IMA (Figure 6.1), the potential erosion rates (Figure 6.2) and flood inundation risk (Figure 6.3) under the various climate change scenarios modelled, the coast was divided into six coastal behaviour units (Figure 6.4). The climate change scenarios were modelled by the Halcrow Group Trinidad and Tobago Limited.[15]

Figure 6.1: Beach profile volatility in Southwest Tobago

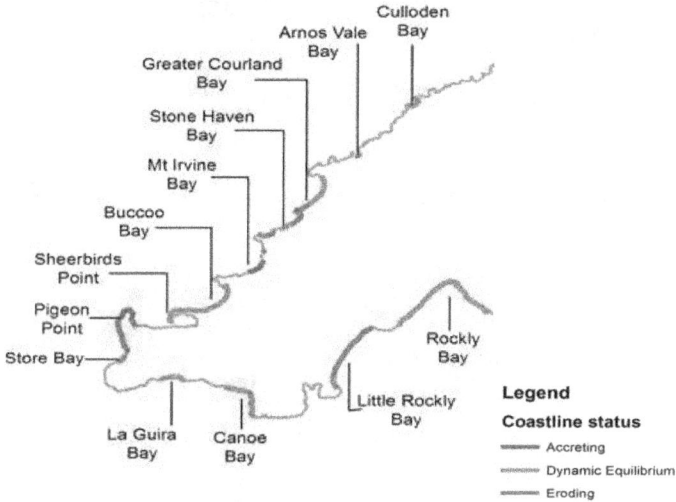

Figure 6.2: Erosion potential in the SW Tobago based on different climate change scenario[16]

Figure 6.3: Flood inundation risk to the pilot area under various climate change scenarios[17]

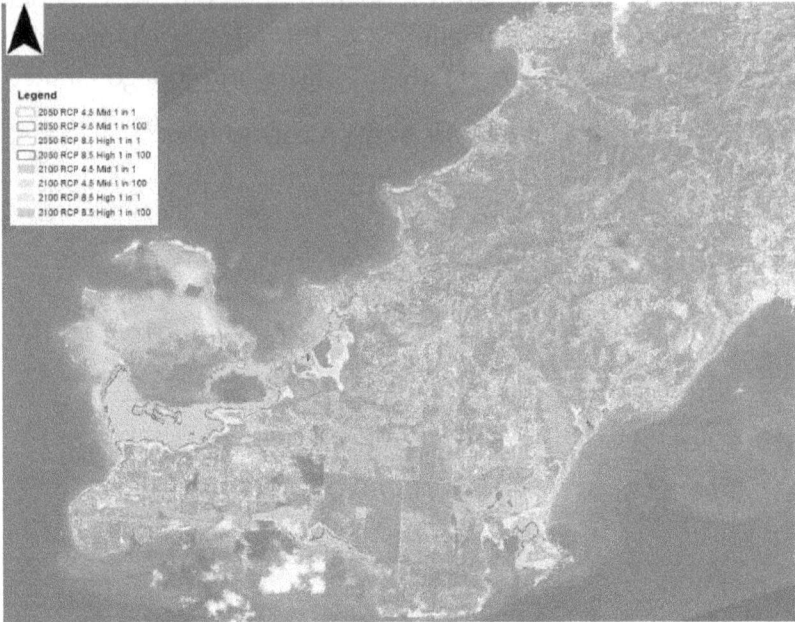

Figure 6.4: Indicative limits of Coastal Behaviour Units in Southwest Tobago

Figure 6.4: Legend

- Coastal Behaviour Unit A–Great Courland Bay to Rocky Point;
- Coastal Behaviour Unit B–Rocky Point to Pigeon Point;
- Coastal Behaviour Unit C–Pigeon Point to Crown Point;
- Coastal Behaviour Unit D–Crown Point to Canoe Bay;
- Coastal Behaviour Unit E–Canoe Bay to Lowlands (Petit Trou Lagoon);
- Coastal Behaviour Unit F–Lowlands to Rocky Bay.

Using the options elicited in the climate change response plan, the best adaptation course of action for coastal behaviour units in Southwest Tobago were considered for two realistic and meaningful time periods: 0–5 years (short term to urgent action required) and 5–25 years (longer term planning). The appropriate adaptation response was determined by answering five EbA questions, which reveal how vulnerability and risk impact due to climate change affect ecosystems and social and economic features of the coastline.

The EbA questions were as follows:

1. Who are the main stakeholders and ecosystems, and what are the relationships between them?
2. What is the structure and function of the ecosystems, and what means are in place to manage and monitor them?
3. What are the important economic issues that will affect the ecosystem and its inhabitants?
4. What are the likely impacts of the ecosystem on adjacent ecosystems?
5. What are the long-term goals and have flexible way of reaching them been determined?

An assessment is presented for Coastal Behaviour Unit B: Rockly Point to Pigeon Point (Table 6.4 and 6.5).

Table 6.4: EbA Analysis – Rocky Point to Pigeon Point

2.2.2 Coastal Behaviour Unit B – Rocky Point to Pigeon Point:

	Coastal Behaviour Unit B – Rocky Point to Pigeon Point	
Guideline EbA "Questions"	Discussion Points (Observations)	Climate Change Vulnerability Adaptation Response Need (H/M
Who are the main stakeholders and ecosystems, and what are the relationships between them?	Mt Irvine beach facility and golf club users, surfers, Grange Bay recreational users, Buccoo community residents (and visitors/guests houses etc). Relationship between them is the importance of a healthy coastal environment to continually attract tourists to the CBU to ensure economic livelihoods. Topographic low areas add flood risk management needs for this CBU around the Mt Irvine hinterland and the whole of the Bon Accord Lagoonal area hinterland.	Low to Medium. According to the Halcrow Coastal Vulnerability Index (2014), whilst flood risk likely to increase in the future to the Bon Accord lagoon areas and hinterland the risk to communities and business is ranked as low to medium, so long as inappropriate future development does not occur in flood risk areas. A number of Adaptation Response option are likely to be needed to address manage the stakeholder vulnerability.
What is the structure and function of the ecosystems, and are means in place to manage and monitor them?	Mt Irvine Bay has a fringing reef offshore in western end of bay. Buccoo Bay has a low lying backshore, with dense vegetation, mangrove low limestone cliffs at the eastern and western ends of the bay. Sheerbirds Point is a sand spit located at eastern end with coral reef/seagrass offshore. Bon Accord mangrove forest along the east), south and west side towards Pigeon Point. Beach monitoring takes place (IMA).	
What are the important economic issues that will affect the ecosystem and its inhabitants?	Mt Irvine has residential properties, Golf Course, Hotel, Beach Facilities, Fishing Facility south of beach facility and the Coastal Road. Buccoo Bay has Buccoo Integrated Facility, Jetty for reef tour boats and Guest Houses, restaurants and shops. Road access from south is a key economic feature to the south of Bon Accord Lagoon. Road runs along coastline very near the beach along Mt Irvine Bay and this could be affected by coastal erosion and flood risk. The road infrastructure in Bon Accord Lagoon is positioned away from flood risk areas on the whole.	
What are the likely impacts of the ecosystem on adjacent ecosystems?	The health and integrity of the wetland system in this CBU comprising the Sheerbird's Point seagrass, Buccoo Reef and the Bon Accord mangrove forest are linked to human habitation, development and water quality (in addition to tourist pressure and overfishing issues). The likely impact is unknown until more targeted information is captured through the future ICZM Strategy Plan process for T&T. Halcrow VA (2014) needs to be updated to assess social and ecological vulnerability.	
What are the long-term goals, and have flexible ways of reaching them, been determined?	Long term goals for the CBU have not been set. These are most likely to be created as part of the future ICZM Strategy Plan process for T&T. Stakeholder engagement processes, in tandem with support from GoTT and THA will be pivotal in defining these long term goals. These, as a result, cannot be set within this table.	

Source: Juman and Hasanali (2015). [18]

Table 6.5: Adaptation Response Option — Rocky Point to Pigeon Point

Coastal Behaviour Unit B — Rocky Point to Pigeon Point		
Adaptation Response Title	**Years 0–5 (2019)**	**Years 5–20 (2034)**
Adaptation Response A: Maintain/restore wetlands and mangrove ecosystems;	wetland health and integrity within Buccoo Bay is critical	longer term wetland health and integrity within Buccoo Bay is critical
Adaptation Response B: Maintain sediment transport;	sediment supply within Mt Irvine Bay is critical	longer term need to maintain sediment supply within Mt Irvine Bay is critical
Adaptation Response C: Preserve coastal land/ development (including infrastructure);	part of a future ICZM Plan that identifies clear setbacks, policies etc	longer term land acquisition programs.
Adaptation Response D: Maintain shorelines utilizing "soft" measures;	Short-term "pilot" projects required to learn successes	implementation of short term "pilot" projects into the longer term within the CBU
Adaptation Response E: Maintain shorelines utilizing "hard" measures;	Short-term asset protection at Mt Irvine Bay only	X long-term asset relocation at Mt Irvine Bay
Adaptation Response F: Preserve Habitat for Vulnerable Species;	Reef and mangrove conservation programmes for marine species protection	longer term reef and mangrove conservation programmes for marine species protection
Adaptation Response G: Maintain water quality	Important for tourism sector and for the integrity of the wider marine ecosystem	Important for tourism sector and for the integrity of the wider marine ecosystem
	Existing Coastal Defences	vulnerability (people)
Current status	Failed rock and concrete seaward sloping concrete wall at Grange Bay	St Patrick Parish = 14,733 (2011Census). No detailed break down exists for communities/villages within this CBU.
Preferred Adaptation Responses (see Table 1 for possible "Courses of Action").	A, B, C, D, F, G. E (short term—Mt Irvine only);	

Source: Juman and Hasanali (2015).[19]

The outcome of the process is that EbA principles have been used to demonstrate which climate change adaptation responses are the most appropriate to employ and implement. A simple approach towards linking EbA principles with objectives in the draft ICZM Policy Framework is needed. This can be achieved by recommending a screening process that asks the 5 EbA questions. It is intended that the EbA principles are used not only to shape climate change adaptation options, but also the delivery of ICZM policy.

Conclusion

Mainstreaming climate change into ICZM should help improve sustainable development of coastal resources. A major issue is ensuring that changes to national plans and impacts from new sectoral priorities start to reach people on the ground. This will require continued coordination across the range of different activities going on at the national, subnational and local levels. Going beyond government-led mainstreaming issues such as 'green jobs', social enterprises, and wealth accounting are among other initiatives which are increasingly being seen as ways to address the integration of true social and environmental costs for a better quality of sustainable development. Climate risk analysis should become an integral strategy for policy development. When the climate risk is appropriately addressed at the national level within strategic plans and policies, this creates an enabling environment for government agencies to engage with climate risk reduction and risk management, and for the private sector and local communities to take their own steps to reduce their risks and manage residual risks.

Notes
1. McGranahan, Gordon, Deborah Balk and Bridget Anderson. 2007. 'The Rising Tide: Assessing the Risks of Climate Change and Human Settlements in Low Elevation Coastal Zones.' *Environment and Urbanization* 19 (1): 17-37. **See also:** Bueno, R., C. Herzfeld, E. Stanton and F. Ackerman. 2008. 'The Caribbean and Climate Change: The Cost of Inaction'. Stockholm Environment Institute-US Center Global Development and Environment Institute, Tufts University.
2. Rasmussen, Tobias N. 2004. 'Macroeconomic Implications of Natural Disasters in the Caribbean.' Working Paper 04/224, The International Monetary Fund, Washington, USA.
3. The Intergovernmental Panel on Climate Change (IPCC) estimated that the Caribbean region experienced an increase in temperature between 0.0 and 0.5 degrees over the last two decades IPCC 2007. **ALSO:**The IPCC 2007

estimated that sea levels rose, on average, 1 mm yr during the 20th century. A sea-level rise of 0.35 meters on average may lead to an 8% loss of land, impacting critical infrastructure and habitats (mangroves, turtle nesting sites, etc.) Toba 2007.

4. Nurse, L.A., R.F. McLean, J. Agard, L.P. Briguglio, V. Duvat-Magnan, N. Pelesikoti, E. Tompkins and A. Webb. 2014. 'Small islands'. In: *Climate Change 2014: Impacts, Adaptation, and Vulnerability. Part B: Regional Aspects*. Contribution of Working Group II to the Fifth Assessment Report of the Intergovernmental Panel on Climate Change [Barros, V.R., C.B. Field, D.J. Dokken, M.D. Mastrandrea, K.J. Mach, T.E. Bilir, M. Chatterjee, K.L. Ebi, Y.O. Estrada, R.C. Genova, B. Girma, E.S. Kissel, A.N. Levy, S. MacCracken, P.R. Mastrandrea, and L.L. White (eds.)]. Cambridge University Press, Cambridge, United Kingdom and New York, NY, USA.

5. Bueno, R., C. Herzfeld, E. Stanton and F. Ackerman. 2008. *op. cit.*

6. Bueno, R., C. Herzfeld, E. Stanton, F. Ackerman. 2008. *ibid.*

7. Bueno, R., C. Herzfeld, E. Stanton and F. Ackerman. 2008. *Ibid.*

8. Zhang, Y., M.K.Lindell and C.S. Prater. 2009. 'Vulnerability of community business to environmental disasters.' *Disasters* 33(1): 38-57. **See Also :**Acs, Z.J. and K. Kallas. 2008. 'State of Literature on Small- to Medium-Sized Enterprises and Entrepreneurship in Low-Income Communities', in G. J. R. Yago, G, Barth, J.R. and Zeidman, B. (Eds), *Entrepreneurship in Emerging Domestic Countries, Barriers and Innovation*, Milken Institute, Santa Monica, 21-45. **And:** Agbeibor Jr, W. 2006. 'Pro-poor economic growth: Role of small and medium sized enterprises.' *Journal of Asian Economics* 17(1):35-40.

9. Francis David.C, Meza Jorge Luis and Yang Judy 2014. 'Mapping Enterprises in Latin America and the Caribbean. World Bank Group

10. Mohammed, Asad and Perry Polar. 2015. 'Small and Medium Enterprises as indicators of resilience to climate change in the Caribbean'. Paper presented at the Forum on the Future of the Caribbean, Port of Spain, Trinidad.

11. Halcrow Group. 2015.'Vulnerability and Risk Assessment for Piloting the integration of coastal zone management and climate change adaptation in Southwest Tobago'. Document Prepared for Institute of Marine Affairs, Trinidad and Tobago.

12. IPCC. 2014. 'Climate Change 2014: Impacts, Adaptation, and Vulnerability. Part A: Global and Sectoral Aspects'. Contribution of Working Group II to the Fifth Assessment Report of the Intergovernmental Panel on Climate Change [Field, C.B., V.R. Barros, D.J. Dokken, K.J. Mach, M.D. Mastrandrea, T.E. Bilir, M. Chatterjee, K.L. Ebi, Y.O. Estrada, R.C. Genova, B. Girma, E.S. Kissel, A.N. Levy, S. MacCracken, P.R. Mastrandrea, and L.L. White (eds.)]. Cambridge University Press, Cambridge, United Kingdom and New York, NY, USA.

13. Sustainable Seas Ltd. 2014a. 'Design and Implementation of a Coastal Ecosystem based Climate Change Adaptation Plan and Guidelines for incorporating an Ecosystem Based Approach (EbA) to Adaptation into a National Integrated Coastal Zone Management Policy'. Document prepared for the Institute of Marine Affairs, Trinidad and Tobago.

14. Sustainable Seas Ltd. 2014b. *op. cit.*
15. Halcrow Group. 2015. *Op. cit.*
16. Ibid.
17. Ibid.
18. Juman, Rahanna, and Kahlil Hassanali. 2015. 'Integrating Climate Change Adaptation into Coastal Zone Management'. Paper presented at the Forum on the Future of the Caribbean, Port of Spain, Trinidad.
19. Ibid.

CHAPTER 7
Achieving Sustainable Development

Preeya Mohan

One issue with implications for Caribbean development is the absence or unavailability of relevant data at the national and regional levels, which consequently hinders the creation of appropriate development indicators and empirical studies. Reliable and robust data are critical for devising appropriate policies, monitoring, decision-making, carrying out empirical research and informing the public. Also, development indicators simplify complex information, highlight problems, identify trends and help set priorities for policy formulation and evaluation. Despite considerable advancements in strengthening national statistical offices along with international coordination, reliable and timely statistics remain inadequate in the Caribbean. Data gaps, data quality, compliance with methodological standards and non-availability of disaggregated data are among the major challenges in data collection and availability that the Caribbean faces. Better, faster, more accessible and more disaggregated data along with improved development measurements and empirical studies are needed to develop strategies to achieve sustainable development.[1]

Two critical areas of data collection and analysis, namely poverty and inequality and vulnerability and resilience, were highlighted by presenters and participants at the forum as two areas in particular that demanded appropriate data in the context of development planning. In the paper 'An Empirical Analysis of Poverty and its Determinants in Trinidad and Tobago', Raynata Wiggins noted the scarcity of empirically grounded work on poverty. Her research, using 2006 primary data, indicates that a household's education and residency are important factors that help identify the poor; therefore, these factors may also be used for better targeting of poverty reduction programmes. Lessons on data collection in Martha Morena's presentation 'Data Transparency: Multidimensional Poverty Measurement in Mexico', which outlined the experience of data collection in Mexico for the purpose of targeting the poor, can be drawn for the Caribbean. Additionally, presentations by George Gray Molina, Philomen Harrison, Clement Sankat, Joaquin Guzman Aleman and James Hospedales touched upon the varied factors that impact poverty, such as education, gender, age and health for which there is hardly any data available. The audience also clamoured about the correlation between tertiary education and poverty where some participants noted that the current structure of the tertiary education system did not always produce graduates with necessary skills. Hence the need for apprenticeship programs as well as an overhaul of the current on-the-job-training programmes.

Valerie Angeon presented a paper entitled 'Are Small Islands Developing States More Vulnerable than Others? Evidence from the Net Vulnerability-Resilience Index. Focus on the Caribbean'. She highlighted the weaknesses of existing vulnerability indicators and alternatively proposed a vulnerability-resilience composite index from a sustainable development perspective, the Net Vulnerability-Resilience Index. The analysis showed that countries in the region are not more prone to vulnerability than other countries, but there is no determinism dictating that a country will remain either vulnerable or resilient despite its intrinsic and structural features. Alison DeGraff presented the paper 'Participatory Mapping: Caribbean Small Island Developing States' which argued that participatory mapping is a powerful tool for the collection and use of geospatially oriented traditional and local ecological knowledge across a variety of disciplines. Notably, the paper outlined several examples of participatory mapping in the region. The growth of this initiative in small island developing states has been widely applied to strengthen public awareness and capacity, particularly for environmental conservation, cultural preservation, and climate change adaptation. Participatory mapping strives to build community resilience and has proven to be a valuable technique in taking positive steps towards sustainable development, especially in vulnerable communities.

This chapter expands these issues in four sections. Section 2 summarises the work on poverty and its determinants in Trinidad and Tobago. Section 3 outlines the issue of multi-dimensional poverty and inequality. Section 4 presents the paper on the vulnerability resilience indicator. Section 5 outlines participatory mapping.

AN EMPIRICAL ANALYSIS OF POVERTY AND ITS DETERMINANTS IN TRINIDAD AND TOBAGO

There is empirical evidence of high poverty levels in Trinidad and Tobago. For instance, a report from Kairi Consultants Ltd estimated that 16.7% of the population lived below the poverty line,[2] while another study by Kedir and Sookram estimated this figure to be closer to 22%.[3] Currently, there is no articulated framework for strategically addressing poverty reduction in Trinidad and Tobago, and in other Caribbean islands, which impedes efforts to effectively address poverty. The paper applies econometric techniques, specifically a probit model to micro-data from the 2008–2009 Trinidad and Tobago Household Budgetary Survey from the CSO, to empirically investigate the economic, demographic and social determinants of poverty which can inform policy making. Although the paper was written in 2015, 2008–2009 is the latest available household survey executed in Trinidad and Tobago. This reflects the severe shortfall in data availability in the region. Moreover, the government has set a target of reducing the incidence of poverty in the country by 2% annually. However, it is difficult to achieve this outcome and track progress without the appropriate data.

Trinidad and Tobago 2008–2009 Household Budget Survey

Data collection is a resource-intensive process. Caribbean countries have limited resources, and as such this may account for the paucity of data in the region. The following outlines the process by which I carried out the Household Budgetary Survey in Trinidad and Tobago. The Trinidad and Tobago 2008–2009 Household Budget Survey is a nationally representative survey of private households conducted by the CSO, and it provides detailed information on the expenditure patterns of private households and individuals. The 2008–2009 survey was conducted over a 12-month period: May 2008–April 2009. It comprised 12 monthly-representative sub-samples that were further divided into 24 fortnights/ periods of enumeration. To account for the effects of seasonality on expenditure patterns, new households were interviewed each fortnight. Data collection methods used in this survey were interviewer-administered questionnaires and self-administered diaries.

There were five questionnaires used in the survey to collect information not included in the Household Questionnaire, namely the Household Questionnaire, the Individual Questionnaire, the Diary (self-administered, covering a two week period), the Main Food Purchases Form and a Supplementary Form on Social Programmes. Retrospective moving-reference periods were employed to record the expenditures in the household and individual questionnaires, with reference periods of up to twelve months being used in most sections. Expenditures on food and non-alcoholic beverages, alcoholic beverages, tobacco and relevant purchases in restaurants and hotels were collected over a fourteen-day diary period.

The initial sample of this survey consisted of 7,680 households, which was determined as the sample size necessary so that the estimates of expenditure derived from the sample would have a 3% margin of error after accounting for an expected 15% non-response rate. However, the realized sample was 7,090 due to non-response, with an overall non-response rate of 7.7%. In an attempt to compensate for non-response, substitution for non-cooperative households was allowed. The survey covered all cities, boroughs and regions. The sample design employed was a stratified, two-stage cluster sample of households divided into 12 equal sub-samples which were nationally represented by region and income area.

The survey collected expenditure information on approximately 1,563 consumption items. This category comprised 12 main divisions: (1) food and non-alcoholic beverages; (2) alcoholic beverages, tobacco and narcotics; (3) clothing and footwear; (4) housing, water, electricity, gas and other fuels; (5) furnishings, household equipment and routine household maintenance; (6) health; (7) transport; (8) communication; (9) recreation and culture; (10) education; (11) restaurants and hotels and (12) miscellaneous goods and services. The CSO used the acquisition-cost approach to measure consumption expenditure on goods and services with the exception of owner-occupied tenancy. Owner-occupied tenancy consumption expenditures were measured using the flow of services or consumption cost approach.

Consumption expenditure was used as a proxy for income. Although income has been traditionally used as a proxy for well-being, consumption has the advantage of being a smoother measure that is less inclined to short-term fluctuations and thus tends to give a more accurate depiction of a household's living standards. Also, people are more inclined to lie about income but cannot, or usually do not, lie about consumption because of the detailed nature of the questions. Any seasonal fluctuations in consumption patterns are typically less amplified than income. Additionally, consumption expenditure provides information on a household's actual intake and use of resources as well as detailing the type of resources consumed. Also, in economies with a sizeable informal economy such as Caribbean economies, consumption-based expenditure acts as a better measure of lifetime income.[4] This measure serves as a more accurate gauge of living standards than income, which informs on a household's earning capacity or stated maximum potential to acquire a particular standard of living. The welfare measure for each household is calculated using the consumption-expenditure aggregates.[5] These aggregates comprise food and non-alcoholic drinks, alcoholic drinks, clothing, housing (calculated using a consumption cost approach), furnishings, health, transport, communications, recreation, education, hotel meals, miscellaneous goods, home-grown foods and gifts.

The Determinants of Poverty in Trinidad and Tobago

Given the dichotomous nature of the dependant variable poverty, the determinants of poverty are estimated using a probit model, that is, poor or not poor. Also, the probit model allows for the assessment of how each independent variable affects the probability of being poor. It does this by determining the probability of being poor or not based on the characteristics of the household. The independent variables include socioeconomic and demographic characteristics of households such as household size, number of children, marital status, main employment status, area of dwelling and other relevant characteristics.

The results indicated that household size and number of children are good predictors of household poverty—that is, poor households tend to be larger with more children than non-poor households. Empirical studies have found that household composition plays a key role in the link between household size and poverty.[6] This points to a potentially vulnerable group—households with a high percentage of children—that can benefit from targeted public programmes of poverty alleviation. The study also found that single-parent–headed households are more likely to live below the poverty line than are their counterparts. This is not surprising given the absent income from the missing parent that the household would have to survive without. This result is compatible with the earlier findings regarding larger households and households with a larger number of children, where both groups were more likely to be poor. All three results clearly indicate the correlation between household size and poverty in Trinidad and Tobago, which should be given key consideration in the formulation of poverty reduction policy.

An examination of the marital status showed that single persons and legally separated couples are significantly less likely to be poor. This is attributed to housewives entering the labour force to support their new status during the uncertain transitional period of a separation, which can result in either divorce or marriage.[7] Education was shown to be correlated to poverty—less educated people are more likely to be poor than more educated people. A head of household whose highest educational attainment was at the pre-school level, the primary school level, the secondary level or other were significantly more likely to live below the poverty line than those with a university level education. Although the government of Trinidad and Tobago invests heavily in education, offering free education from the pre-school to the tertiary level, these results suggest that more emphasis needs to be placed on the tertiary level as a mechanism for poverty alleviation. Currently the government offers free tertiary education through the Government Assistance for Tuition Expenses Program; however, this is a universal programme in which the poor are under-represented.[8] It is suggested that policy be formulated to address this issue that would target individuals from households with low welfare levels to facilitate a university education. However, as it was noted during the Forum, to reach university people, we must first climb the regular education ladder, which reminded participants of the relevance of education for the well-being of the population.

The results revealed that the employment level of the head of household is correlated to poverty. Compared to those with permanent employment, temporary workers were more likely to fall below the poverty line. This result highlights the importance of social safety nets, and in particular of automatic stabilizers, that provide unemployment benefits during economic contractions. An investigation into the tenancy of household variable revealed that households that were renting, whether furnished or unfurnished spaces or if they occupied the tenancy rent free, were significantly more likely to be poor than those who owned their home. This is even extended to those households that were living in rent free tenancies who might be staying with friends and family because they could not afford a place of their own, which further supports the finding on household size and poverty.

Finally, the results indicated that the area of residence is highly correlated to poverty. In comparison to those in Port of Spain, households residing in the San Juan/Laventille, Tunapuna/Piarco, Couva/Tabaquite/Talparo, Princes Town and Tobago are less likely to be poor based on consumption patterns. These results are surprising given that the above mentioned areas are traditionally low income areas. However, this finding can be attributed to the high cost of living in Port of Spain (the capital). This must be taken into consideration when drafting regional poverty reduction initiatives.

Given the government's goal of poverty reduction, the paper indicates that greater attention should be placed on poverty correlates such as household size and composition when formulating and designing poverty reduction policy. Further, the results suggest that investing in tertiary level education that directly targets low income families, addressing social protection coverage as it relates to workers that are periodically unemployed and affordable rent, particularly for low income households, should be made priority policy areas.

DATA AND MULTIDIMENSIONAL POVERTY AND INEQUALITY

While the region suffers from severe data limitations, there is some income data available; therefore, income thresholds are commonly used to measure poverty. This measure however overlooks the multi-dimensional complexities of poverty and human deprivations and masks stark inequalities within countries. While an increase in income tends to be correlated with improvements in well-being such as education and health, the strength of these correlations can vary considerably. In this regard, poverty and inequality, in addition to the other 'constraints and challenges associated with development must not be treated as related in a linear fashion to countries' per capita income levels'.[9] Given the myriad ways in which poverty manifests itself and its effects on the vulnerable members of society, using a narrow definition of poverty by measuring income—for example, defining as poor those persons living on less than US$ 1.25 per day is unlikely to meaningfully identify who is poor and who is not.[10] This is evident in the fact that many people who have escaped poverty as defined by the MDG goals are either still poor or experience its associated deprivations. In addition, there are persons who no longer live in poverty but remain vulnerable to risks at various stages of their life-cycle, and in different situations they can move in and out of poverty. Poverty is therefore not simply about income, nor is it static. Furthermore, the use of global aggregate indicators like the MDG's poverty line is unable to capture the efforts of individual countries, obscures important differences and fails to reflect unequal gains in reducing poverty within and across countries, communities and demographic groups.

Inequality must similarly be examined from a multidimensional perspective as it involves an analysis of differences in opportunities and outcomes. It reflects persistent differences in opportunity between defined groups. The level of inequality can also change over time, shifting across individuals. Thus, inequality of opportunities and resource redistribution are equally legitimate policy considerations. High levels of inequality, like poverty, can impede economic growth and sustainable development. Also, inequality weakens the linkage between economic growth and poverty reduction since a relatively small reduction in inequality can have a significant positive effect on the poverty headcount. Thus, it is important to increase economic growth which results in higher income with reduced poverty and improved well-being along with measures to equalise opportunity.

The fundamental weakness in data availability and indicators used in measuring poverty and inequality which influences the targets chosen and policies adopted must be addressed in all its dimensions. It is therefore important to look at a broader range of people than just those falling below a defined income threshold as well as non-income dimensions of poverty. To focus solely on income without taking into account the multi-faceted nature of how people experience poverty and inequality can lead to short-term unsustainable policies and strategies. This is why economic growth alone is not sufficient to end poverty and inequality or to benefit everyone and tackling vulnerability and promoting resilience among individuals is paramount. A multidimensional approach to poverty and inequality is required, which highlights the effects of the compounded vulnerabilities on the lives of individuals for the most strategic and impactful response and allocation of resources. The promotion of inclusive and sustainable development policies that enhance well-being and enable everyone to participate in and benefit from growth is critical. Multi-dimensional measures of poverty should however also account for national and subnational realities, employing appropriate strategies to build resilience and integrate environmental objectives. To ensure success in the utilisation of multi-dimensional measures of poverty, data collection needs to be improved and indicators of the many dimensions well-defined.

The Caribbean Context

There have been noticeable improvements in the overall quality of life in the Caribbean, but poverty and inequality continue to challenge development in the region. A number of reasons have been proposed including labour market imperfections, class, status, power, education, income and even a 'culture of poverty' created by the colonial history of the region which set the initial conditions of a highly concentrated distribution of income and an equally concentrated and cheap labour supply influenced by a 'dependency syndrome'.[11] Despite this, there has been insufficient attention to understanding the nature and dynamics of poverty and reluctance by some countries to undertake surveys and improve data quantity and quality as a prerequisite for designing effective poverty reduction programs. It is therefore imperative to launch a comprehensive review of poverty reduction programs to improve targeting, ascertain results, redesign for effectiveness and, most importantly, to ensure sustainability.[12]

Since 1995 the Caribbean Development Bank (CDB), with support from the Canadian International Development Agency (CIDA), the Department for International Development (DFID) and the United Nations Development Program (UNDP), has been assisting Caribbean countries in conducting Country Poverty Assessments (CPAs). CPAs provide the most current information on living conditions in the region and creates a conduit through which citizens, institutions and agencies can contribute their own perspectives on and solutions to poverty and inequality. The objective of CPAs is to determine the characteristics, geographic concentration, severity and causes of poverty and inequality, as well as propose possible solutions. They seek to identify and analyse possible relationships between employment statistics in both the formal and informal sectors and estimates of poverty, rural and urban poverty and macroeconomic policies and consequent structural changes in the society which continue to create and/or maintain conditions of poverty and inequality. They combine quantitative and qualitative methods to measure income and non-income poverty and estimates the level of inequality in income distribution using the Gini coefficient.

The UNDP has also been carrying out work using the Multidimensional Poverty Index (MPI) in the Eastern Caribbean. 'The global Multidimensional Poverty Index (MPI) reflects the combined simultaneous disadvantages poor people experience across different areas of their lives, including education, health and living standards. If people are deprived in at least one-third of ten weighted indicators, they are identified as multi-dimensionally poor'.[13] The MPI is currently used in more than 100 countries.

Improving approaches to measuring poverty in the Caribbean context and addressing inequality and vulnerability would involve the following:

Improving Measures of Poverty and Inequality

Proposals on measures that sufficiently capture the multi-dimensional nature of poverty and inequality and go beyond global, national and sub-national aggregates to reflect each country's situation and poverty characteristics with a view to informing targeted policies that could address the multiple deprivations experienced by vulnerable groups. Approaches for measuring well-being across or within countries based on indicators identified as essential for material living conditions and quality of life. A well-being approach may elucidate the implications of excessive inequality and encourage policies for more inclusive and sustainable economic growth in both developed and developing countries. Measures should focus on the political and sociocultural domains of life with the aim of strengthening social cohesion.[14]

Improving Data Quantity, Quality and Availability and Strengthen Statistical Capacities

The importance of strengthening statistical capacity in the region, particularly the implications of the introduction of new measures based on a broader definition of poverty, deprivation, well-being, opportunity and empowerment and the need for greater disaggregation at all levels. The opportunities presented by new technologies and new sources for data collection, possibly involving new types of partnerships among national statistical offices, universities, donor agencies, the civil society, private sector, and so forth.

Linking poverty and inequality with social cohesion

Poverty reduction strategies that go beyond economic growth and promote inclusive growth to improve well-being, empowerment, participation and resilience are critical for sustainable development.

Integrating Poverty and Inequality Reduction with Environmental Sustainability and Natural Resource Preservation

Integrating an environmental dimension in the fight against poverty and inequality is important. Climate change, natural disasters and unsustainable consumption and production patterns put added stress on the natural resource base which the world's population depends on for its survival. Increased environmental pressures and competition for limited natural resources will make the poorest country even more vulnerable. Poverty and inequality reduction policies and solutions should recognise the intricate link between poverty, growth strategies, environmental sustainability and natural resource preservation.

Improving Partnerships and Financing for Poverty and Inequality Reduction

The importance of strategic partnerships and increased cooperation and collaboration among stakeholders such as government officials, policy makers, multilateral and regional institutions, civil society and the private sector are critical in the fight against poverty. The importance of this is further increased given the reduced access of Caribbean countries to concessional funding, the need to engage donor organizations in a new discourse around different modalities of assistance to High and Upper Middle Income Countries seeking to reduce poverty and inequality.

Data Transparency: Multidimensional Poverty Measurement in Mexico

Only if something can be measured can it then be improved. For example, in Mexico the Social Development Law mandates recurrent data collection efforts to assess the impact of social programs on poverty reduction by focusing on eight poverty dimensions: income, educational gap, access to health services, access to social security, quality of dwelling, access to housing basic services, access to food and social cohesion. The measurements are periodic and must be done consistently, for the whole country and for states every two years and at the municipality level every five years. The information source used at the state level is the socioeconomic conditions module. At the municipality level the census is utilized. Two spaces are investigated, the 'Social rights space' which is measured through deprivation and the 'Well-being space', measured by income. A person is considered to be poor if he or she has at least one social deprivation and an income below the economic well-being line. This has led to a calculation of 45.5% of the population being poor, 9.8%

being extremely poor, 35.7% being moderately poor (2012 estimates). Social deprivations are also calculated. In 2012, social deprivation for the education gap was 19.2%, access to healthcare 21.5%, access to social security 61.2%, quality of dwelling 13.6%, access to housing and basic services 21.2% and access to food 23.3%. Poverty estimates are also calculated spatially at the state and municipal level in Mexico. From the poverty indicators, Mexico was able to implement a mix of targeted and universal poverty policies.

ARE SMALL ISLANDS DEVELOPING STATES MORE VULNERABLE THAN OTHERS? EVIDENCE FROM THE NET VULNERABILITY-RESILIENCE INDEX

There is a debate in the literature that small islands developing states (SIDS) present structural characteristics which impede their development. As such, several empirical tests have been implemented to measure their vulnerability using a range of methodologies. The numerous vulnerability indices can, however, be criticized on three main points: (i) most of these indices stress the economic dimension of vulnerability only; (ii) although some of these indices can be interpreted from a sustainable development perspective, they do not simultaneously cover all dimensions of sustainability; (iii) the multiplicity of variables and computation methods used to create these indices raise the question of whether there is a set of variables that consistently describes the state of vulnerability and resilience.

In the literature, vulnerability is defined as the degree of exposure of a country to external shocks, and it arises from intrinsic permanent or quasi-permanent features and exogenous factors. These factors impede long-term sustainable development. On the contrary, resilience depends on internal determining factors that are policy-responsive to external shocks and determines the capacity of a country to recover from a shock and to withstand its impact. Resilience is therefore the ability of a country to cope with its inherent vulnerability and reinforces long-term sustainable development.

This paper proposes a vulnerability-resilience composite index, the Net Vulnerability-Resilience Index (NVRI) from a sustainable development perspective. The index takes into account five equally weighted dimensions of resilience and vulnerability: economic, social, environment, peripherality and governance and is not just limited to SIDS but is applied to a worldwide sample. The economic and the political are the control dimensions of vulnerability resilience and the environmental; the social and peripheral dimensions are the contingent dimensions of vulnerability resilience. The two control dimensions determine the remaining three dimensions which reflect the key dimensions for policy management of vulnerability resilience.

The aim of the paper is to assess the relative position of SIDS, in comparison to non-SIDS, by considering these five dimensions. The index is tested on a worldwide sample in order to classify the different countries depending on their degree of resilience. For the robustness of the results, only countries whose missing data are less than 10% are selected. This led to 97 countries' being included with only seven SIDS (Bahamas, Bahrain, Dominican Republic, Jamaica, Maldives, Mauritius, and Singapore).

NVRI Results

The worldwide ranking of the NVRI showed that developed countries are ranked higher than other countries, meaning that they are relatively less vulnerable. The results also show that SIDS are more vulnerable than developed countries. Developed countries generally have a positive NVRI of 33.29 % mainly due to the contingent variables (36.08%) rather than the control ones (29.09%), compared to non-SIDS (Iceland, United Kingdom, New Zealand, Japan, Ireland, Cyprus, Malta, Indonesia, Philippines, Sri Lanka, Madagascar) and SIDS (Singapore, Bahrain, the Bahamas, Mauritius, Jamaica, Maldives, the Dominican Republic), are more prone to vulnerability. The Dominican Republic is the most vulnerable in terms of control dimension (-5.38%). Nevertheless, although SIDS are more tending to vulnerability, some of them show net resilience (positive value of NVRI) as in the case of Bahrain and the Bahamas. Moreover, Singapore (24th, NVRI = 20.84%) is close to the group of developed countries in terms of net vulnerability resilience. It is located between Italy (23rd, NVRI = 21.15%) and Portugal (27th, NVRI=16.94%). This result confirms the 'paradox of Singapore', that is, the very good performance of Singapore despite its smallness and insularity.

The different configurations of vulnerability and resilience allow for four situations. **Situation 1** defines vulnerability in terms of control dimensions only. A net vulnerability in the control dimensions is a sufficient condition for a net vulnerability in the contingent dimensions. This vulnerability is uncontrolled since there is no correcting power of the net vulnerability in terms of contingent and control dimensions. There is no possible limitation against the strength of features of vulnerability from the economic and the political dimension, which have fallacies. One can say that this vulnerability is resolutely built in and that there is no correcting power from the control dimensions. Nevertheless, resilience in the control dimensions is not a prerequisite for having a positive NVRI. Hence, when the control dimensions are sources of vulnerability, the consequence is an absolute vulnerable country, when the control dimensions are sources of resilience, the results in terms of the net vulnerability resilience for a country depends on the state of contingency dimensions. By leading to this conclusion, the paper justifies the argument, according to which, vulnerability resilience is resolutely built or maybe external. Nevertheless, in an absolute way, neither social, environmental nor insular (associated with the peripheral dimension) determinism can immutably and per se fix the state of vulnerability resilience even though they are dependent factors that strengthen or mitigate the net vulnerability resilience obtained from the control dimensions.

Situation 2 is characterised by a negative NVRI because the capacity to be resilient from the control dimensions is overthrown by the vulnerable features of the contingency dimensions. Nevertheless, since there is still a capacity to absorb shocks, the level of exposure to adverse (exogenous) shocks is widely mitigated. This is why situation 2 shows a limited vulnerability contrary to the unrestricted (absolute) vulnerability in situation 1. In this situation, the vulnerability is external rather than built in. It means that these countries have the potential to absorb an eventual adverse shock but that the capacity is too limited and there is a low correcting power of the control dimensions.

Situation 3 is characterized by a net resilience due to resolutely resilient features in terms of control that exceed the vulnerable features from the other dimensions. Hence, as the capacity to achieve a maximized resilience is impeded by vulnerable factors from the social, the environmental or the peripheral dimensions, countries in this group are headed for the top of the ranking, but some effort remains to be made. Consequently, their resilience is limited or unstable. The correcting power of the control dimensions is thus revealed in this situation, but it is not maximal like in situation 4. **Situation 4** is ideal since these countries have less probability of struggling against any context of vulnerability, but when it is the case, they have more potential in terms of economic power and governance to tackle this issue. In such a case, the resilience is absolute or stable, and the correcting power of the control dimensions in such countries is high.

Singapore displays an absolute and stable resilience due to mainly economic features and its quality of governance. However, Singapore suffers from environmental deficiencies. Consequently, the margins for Singapore to anchor itself to the group of the best countries (mainly the developed ones) come first from the correction of its environmental deficiencies and second from the fact that its governance can still be improved. Caribbean states suffer from other dimensions: their periphericity and in lesser extent their governance. They have in that sense strictly opposite features to Singapore. Nevertheless, as a SIDS whose resilience is partially based on a capacity to stay connected to opportunities offered by international trade, Singapore demonstrates that there is no determinism to suffer from isolation. Besides, as the Bahamas shows a better political capacity and a more resilient economic dimension among the Caribbean states, it registers a higher ranking of the NVRI. This allows the Bahamas to have a limited resilience instead of remaining vulnerable.

These examples evidence another advantage of the way that paper can measure the state of vulnerability resilience. It is possible to clearly identify where the deficiencies of any state are and what has to be adjusted to promote resilience thereby leading to sustainable development. To go further in the analysis of vulnerability resilience, a natural scenario of evolution can be defined from situation 1 to situation 4. In a dynamic perspective, one can imagine that a country can go through one situation to another. However, an unstable situation of resilience (situation 2) can shift into a worst situation if a negative external event occurs. But an unstable resilience can also tend to be a better situation if the country has actively implemented effective resilience measures before any adverse shock. So, the country can achieve a stable resilience. Countries in situation 1 can hardly reverse their vulnerability. This situation of built-in vulnerability due to the lack of resilient control variables can persist if no radical (economic or political) changes occur. Nevertheless if drastic actions are taken, the worst situation can progressively move to a state of undergone vulnerability before leading possibly to a state of resilience.

These results indicate that that SIDS are not specifically more prone to vulnerability than other countries. Moreover, there is no determinism that dictates that a country will remain either vulnerable or resilient despite its intrinsic and structural features. The index also showed the importance of determining factors (economic and governance) in the result of the net position of vulnerability resilience. These dimensions can strengthen or impede resilience or vulnerability that results from social, environmental, and insular/peripheral aspects (contingency dimensions). Hence, two main conclusions can be made: (i) there is no determinism in terms of vulnerability and (ii) vulnerability can be built. If we assume that resilience is more nurtured and can be built than structural and external, SIDS are not intrinsically vulnerable compared to other countries.

The NVRI is beneficial on two fronts. Firstly, for any country, the NVRI indicates its sources of deficiencies. Therefore, policy orientation should focus on the problematic dimensions that strengthen vulnerability in order to promote resilience. As the five recognised dimensions have the same weight, the suggested index leads to consider vulnerability as a whole in a holistic and systemic view. Secondly, by implementing prospective scenarios on the five dimensions, an idea of societal and institutional change that should occur to reverse vulnerability or to improve resilience is given. This could be considered a significant warning to seriously take into account in a political agenda in order to reinforce sustainable development programs. The profile of each country reveals the dimensions to be targeted in order to improve resilience and lessen vulnerability. SIDS can belong to any category of vulnerability resilience. However, it seems to be more crucial for any country to increase its probability to be more resilient by getting a net positive value of the NVRI in terms of control dimensions (economic and political), even though the contingent dimensions may hamper this target. The control dimensions can provide or stop resilience processes and thus can increase (or decrease their vulnerability).

PARTICIPATORY MAPPING: CARIBBEAN SMALL ISLAND DEVELOPING STATES

Participatory mapping is the solicitation of local stakeholder knowledge in geospatial data collection, and the incorporation of this data in a cartographic format appropriate for a broad audience—in the context of geographic information systems (GIS). This process provides a wide decision-making information base that takes into consideration both collaborative collection and validation of data. Through the solicitation and incorporation of local knowledge in data collection, participatory mapping can strengthen public participation in governance and social change. By leaving the control of access to the data and spatial information in the hands of the community, this practice is ideal for protecting traditional ecological knowledge that stakeholders are hesitant to record due to a history of exploitation.[15]

In a participatory mapping project, it is essential to have proper facilitation and respectful interaction with stakeholders, as well as respect for the value of local or traditional knowledge, regardless of what organisation, institution or government facilitates or funds the process. All information about the process, as well as the data collected, should be shared regularly, transparently, and fairly with stakeholders; and stakeholders should be consulted and given frequent opportunities to validate and provide feedback. Participatory mapping processes depend on a level of trust and mutual understanding by communities. There are many levels of participation, from simply informing a community of initiatives to assuring that the final decision-making remains in their control. The term 'participation' can take on three forms under the umbrella of participatory mapping: 'participation for legitimation', mostly top-down consultation projects seeking to justify claims; 'participation for publication', short-term projects initiated for research initiatives; and 'popular participation', genuine projects providing local stakeholders with a say in decision-making.[16] Figure 7.1 summarises the levels of public participation that can be readily applied to participatory mapping processes.

Figure 7.1: Levels of Public Participation

Co-option	Compliance	Consultation	Cooperation	Co-learning	Collective Action
Token community participation; no real community power or input.	Research agenda decided by outsiders, communities are assigned tasks.	Local opinion is sought, but outsiders analyse situation and decide actions.	Local people work with researchers to determine priorities, but the process is directed by outsiders.	Local people and outsiders share knowledge and work together to form action plans.	Local people set their own agenda and carry it out in an absence of external initiators.

Source: De Graff and Ramlal 2015.[17]

The more collaborative a process is, the more valuable the outcome will be for both the community and the project. Facilitators must tread carefully so as not to accidently co-opt local agendas and always strive for 'bottom-up' approaches and decisions that are instigated by stakeholders themselves.

In order to appropriately utilise mapping initiatives, facilitators must have a working knowledge of GIS and cartography, community facilitation and participatory development. Effective applications place as much value on the participatory process as the development of mapping or Geographic Information systems (GIS). Nevertheless, it is also important to choose appropriate mapping tools. GIS software varies drastically in pricing and capabilities. The software and hardware for the project should be chosen based on the analytical needs of the project, the costs for the technology, the costs of training facilitators and/or stakeholders and the institutional capacity. It is impractical to choose expensive software that is overly complicated, when less complex software would suffice, especially given the technical capacity of involved stakeholders.

Depending on the map audience, cartographic outputs can be in the form of GIS data, photographs, static maps, and/or interactive maps. Additionally, web mapping allows for the interactive display of a variety of different vector and raster data. Regardless of methodology or technology, community members should be encouraged to follow a common cartographic construct that will allow for any non-ephemeral maps to be both easily understood and utilised in the future, additionally all outputs and vocabulary should be understood and agreed upon by stakeholders. The audience of final map products should be determined at the onset of the project as well so that they can be appropriately designed for communities, in contrast to governments or international audiences.[18]

Upon deciding to use GIS technologies in participatory mapping, there comes an added responsibility to ensure that a local organisation, or a variety of local stakeholders, are sufficiently trained in that geospatial technology in order assist in analyses and in order to access and work with the data after any external facilitators or GIS specialists have left the location. Alternatively, if the use of GIS is necessary and local capacity insufficient, data should be provided in as many convenient forms as possible. Genuine custodianship of the final product should be ensured through community nominations of representatives to maintain the data. Information can also be stored on a website or online database for community download.

Participatory Mapping in the Caribbean

Participatory mapping remains fairly new to the Caribbean despite dating back to the 1980s–1990s in other parts of the world. Participatory mapping in most developing countries around the world has been primarily externally driven. This raises concerns of ownership of the process and the resulting data, as well as what happens to the project once the foreign facilitators/funders leave.[19] However, since the early 2000s when participatory mapping projects in the Caribbean began, foreign organisations and funders have partnered with local and regional organisations to implement these projects, combining facilitation efforts and providing a venue to maintain data and research within the local community.[20] It should be additionally noted that it is just as important for local and regional organisations to provide prompt feedback and maintain open contact with local stakeholders as it is for foreign facilitators and organisations. There have been a variety of participatory mapping projects in the Caribbean. Figure 7.2 provides a brief timeline of when projects happened, what methods were used, and where they took place.

Figure 7.2: Participatory Mapping Case Studies in the Caribbean Timeline

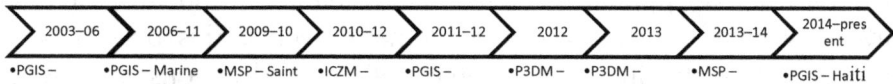

2003–06	2006–11	2009–10	2010–12	2011–12	2012	2013	2013–14	2014–present
•PGIS –	•PGIS – Marine	•MSP – Saint	•ICZM –	•PGIS –	•P3DM –	•P3DM –	•MSP –	•PGIS – Haiti

Source: De Graff and Ramlal 2015.[21]

Participatory 3D Modelling (P3DM) integrates local knowledge of a community or island with elevation or bathymetric data to create a scaled and geo-referenced relief model. It can be a very effective tool to assist with applications from vulnerability assessments to protected area planning. However, it requires engaged stakeholders with sufficient spare time to commit to the project and adequate funding for the facilitation and materials.[22]

The first P3DM in the Caribbean took place in Tobago as an initiative of the Caribbean Natural Resources Institute (CANARI), the Technical Centre for Agricultural and Rural Cooperation (CTA), the University of the West Indies (UWI), St. Augustine, and the Tobago House of Assembly in 2012. It was further financially supported by the United Nations Development Programme Global Environment Facility Small Grants Programme (UNDP GEF SGP) and The Nature Conservancy (TNC). Designed to utilise LEK in climate change adaptation, this P3DM project additionally served as a pilot to train facilitators and build capacity for the use of P3DM in other Caribbean countries (representatives were trained from Grenada, Saint Vincent and the Grenadines, Barbados, Saint Lucia, Jamaica, Haiti, and the Dominican Republic).[23] Lessons learned included the importance of trained facilitators, the use of multiple strategies to engage stakeholders, a central location for P3DM creation, and the inclusion of sessions to improve stakeholder understanding of climate change and its impacts.[24] Further P3DMs have since been completed in Roxborough, Tobago and Laventille, Trinidad.

The Sustainable Grenadines Inc. (SusGren), a nongovernmental organisation (NGO) with support from TNC, CTA and the Grenada Fund for Conservation (GFC) facilitated a P3DM on Union Island, St. Vincent and the Grenadines in 2013. The project sought to gain further spatial local knowledge that could be applied to TNC's At the Water's Edge (AWE) project which has been working with communities in St. Vincent and the Grenadines and Grenada to find ecosystem-based adaptations to climate change. The P3DM project, through the collection of local ecological knowledge and community participation, gathered relevant information on infrastructure, populated areas, natural habitats, and locations that have experienced changes due to climatic events. This data is being utilised in the identification of what policies and actions need to be taken to address climate change on a tiny island within in a small island developing state. The resulting model for Union Island is on display at the Revenue Office in downtown Clifton, and the Nature Conservancy has data on their website in the form of a coastal resilience interactive map portal. Lessons learned included the use of other community initiatives to get stakeholders involved, ensuring local ownership of the model, the importance of allowing for critical analysis throughout the process, the value of local knowledge and how the model can be further used as a planning tool across disaster management sectors.[25] After completion of the Union Island P3DM, another initiative spearheaded by the Grenada Fund for Conservation and partnered with TNC, CTA, and SusGren completed a P3DM from Telescope to Marquis in Grenville, Grenada.[26]

Participatory mapping and Participatory Geographic Information System (PGIS) initiatives allow for the collection and use of highly accurate data through GPS data collection, and for a greater flexibility in combined processes through diverse stakeholder interviews, field work, community meetings, community workshops.[27] CANARI assisted by the UWI Coastal Management Research Network and funded by the United Kingdom Department for International Development, conducted a three-year study in Laborie, St. Lucia. They looked at the relationship between marine resource users' livelihoods and their involvement in resource management and coral reef health. Given the lack of recent or accurate geospatial data for this area, participatory mapping field surveys with community members were facilitated to collect data on local toponyms, locations of decreased water quality and important marine information. Mapping this local ecological knowledge provided up-to-date, accurate geospatial information that could be used in application towards participatory management processes. Lessons learned included that stakeholders found aerial imagery easier to interpret than vector maps and that, especially in a case when disseminating data could be damaging to the community, it is important for the stakeholders to have a say in what data and in what form should be left in the hands of whom.[28]

Participatory mapping initiatives in the transboundary Grenadines (St. Vincent and the Grenadines and Grenada) began with the doctoral research (2006–2011) of Kimberly Baldwin at the UWI – Cave Hill in Barbados entitled 'A Participatory Marine Resource and Space-use Information System (MarSIS) for the Grenadine Islands: An ecosystem approach to collaborative planning and management of trans-boundary marine resources'. Research was conducted in coordination with UWI's Sustainable Grenadines Project (which transitioned into the Sustainable Grenadines, Inc. NGO in 2010) whose objective was to engage stakeholders through the support of activities that allow for meaningful collective action. Baldwin collaboratively developed the Grenadines MarSIS with local stakeholders, both countries' governments and local and international NGOs to include geospatial information on marine habitats, marine resource users, space-use patterns, biologically important sites, conservation areas and areas of threat. All of the marine conservation data were collected in coordination with, ground-truth and validated by the local community and is now a publically accessible database available in the form of ArcGIS shapefiles, Google Earth (.kml) files and static maps on the Grenadines MarSIS website.[29] Lessons learned included the importance of the investment of time by facilitators in the community, the significance of a custom project that combined PGIS with conventional scientific mapping methods and the value of transparency throughout the entire process via a regularly updated website, listserv and social media.[30]

As an addition to Baldwin's marine PGIS research in the transboundary Grenadines, the Compton Foundation funded supplementary terrestrial research in the transboundary Grenadines from 2011–2012. DeGraff worked with UWI–Cave Hill and the Sustainable Grenadines Inc. to create a comprehensive local knowledge geospatial database of important historical, cultural, and ecological terrestrial heritage sites to fill data gaps in the Grenadines MarSIS. Through the facilitation of interviews, field visits, community meetings and workshops with local stakeholders, the resulting database of surviving heritage sites provides an important resource for preservation. Together, this marine and terrestrial geospatial data served to strengthen St. Vincent and the Grenadines and Grenada's current joint application as a mixed (natural and cultural) marine transboundary UNESCO World Heritage Site. Data are publically accessible online in the form of ArcGIS shapefiles, Google Earth (.kml) files, interactive maps and static maps. Additionally poster-size, laminated copies are displayed in a community-recommended public building on each island, and static maps were distributed across the islands following the completion of the data collection and validation. Lessons learned included the importance of flexibility in cartographic mediums as chosen by each stakeholder (that is, aerial imagery, basic maps, field visits and verbal descriptions) and providing meeting locations that made community members feel comfortable and heard (that is, informal settings).[31]

OpenStreetMap (OSM) and the Humanitarian OpenStreetMap Team (HOT) have been widely used across the globe for disaster risk management and disaster response. They began work in Haiti following the earthquake in 2010 to assist in rescue efforts and response planning, as very little detailed geospatial data existed, particularly in rural areas. HOT continued work in Haiti to ensure that crowd-sourced OSM data was validated and improved upon by the local community through the support of the International Organization of Migration and the Comunite OpenStreetMap de Haiti (COSMHA).[32] An additional partnership with CartONG has deployed volunteers to Haiti to assist in the use of unmanned aerial vehicles (UAV) to improve the imagery available for participatory mapping in the country. CartONG is working to train stakeholders in UAV data collection and use for participatory mapping for disaster response and risk prevention so that communities can lead their own projects. An ongoing project, lessons learnt include choosing a mini-server for processing UAV images without consistent electricity and internet and training communities in UAV flights and image processing in ArcGIS and QGIS.[33]

Intensive coastal development in the Caribbean has resulted in conflicting demands on the coastal zone and near-coastal waters, particularly threatening the marine habitats that provide ecosystem services such as coastal protection, tourism destinations and food security. Governments and communities are increasingly realizing the importance of mitigating and adapting to the impacts of climate change. However, stakeholders and decision-makers alike often do not understand the costs and benefits of adapting to these changes or to increasing development, limiting their ability to prepare for future challenges. There are few cases thus far in the Caribbean; however, comprehensive marine zoning could be used as a strong approach to address effects of climate change on the coastal and marine environment.[34]

In 1998, the government of Belize established a Coastal Zone Management Authority and Institute (CZMAI); however, it was not until 2010 that they began the work on a plan to balance sustainable development and ecosystem protection. Partnering with the World Wildlife Fund and the Natural Capital Project, CZMAI chose to use Integrated Valuation of Environmental Services and Trade-offs (InVEST) software to develop a plan for managing the coastal zone. This software assists in environmental economic valuation, which seeks to put a monetary value on ecosystems to value their anticipated benefits. This part of an integrated coastal zone management process is particularly effective with stakeholder engagement practices as community members, policymakers and scientists come together to validate and add local knowledge data and analyse scenarios that highlight conservation versus development, as well as 'middle-ground' informed management scenarios. Stakeholder input was incorporated into the entire process through coastal advisory committees and public consultations. Furthermore, the Natural Capital Project experimented with their online mapping tool, InVEST Scenario Modeler (InSEAM), to allow community members to virtually collaborate and add data to a base map; however, facilitators found other methods to be more effective for the stakeholders involved.

The marine spatial planning process on St. Kitts and Nevis was facilitated by the Nature Conservancy and USAID in coordination with the government. This pilot project developed a draft marine space-use zoning plan while adhering to a guiding principle to continuously engage community members across government departments, NGOs, and individual stakeholders. Technology and accurate geospatial data are necessary to implement an MSP, yet transparency and community engagement in the planning process are also important. Interactive decision support systems (DSS) enable scenario analysis in order to attempt to resolve user conflicts and reveal trade-offs in management scenarios; in this case, the chosen software was the freely available Marxan with Zones. Accurate, current and relevant spatial databases are essential for marine zoning, but they are rare in SIDS without the financial resources to consistently create and update data. TNC/USAID carried out detailed ecosystem health field surveys and supplemented that with participatory mapping with local stakeholders. Community members continued to be engaged through the entirety of the MSP process, as zoning plans show a much higher rate of success when supported and appreciated by user groups. To allow for public access to the data, TNC made it available in the form of a geospatial database, georeferenced portable document formats (PDF) and a web-based map viewer. Lessons learned included the importance of integrating ecological and socioeconomic data into conservation planning tools, assuring transparency and stakeholder understanding with DSS, and strong in-country partnerships.[35]

The Blue Halo Initiative—a collaboration with the Barbuda Council and the citizens of Barbuda, funded by the Waitt Institute, initiated a community-driven ocean zoning project in 2013 using a DSS called SeaSketch. SeaSketch allowed for the visualization of how stakeholder-generated zones could combine with scientific data and policy to maximise ecosystem protection and minimise negative economic impacts on fishermen.[36] The three primary steps for the project were to '1) establish scientific guidelines, 2) identify stakeholder priorities and 3) balance stakeholder preferences while meeting scientific guidelines'.[37] Through the collection of habitat and fisheries data, ocean use surveys, and documentation of stakeholder priorities, baseline information to use a DSS was established. Through the use of a local cellular service-based Internet connection, facilitators held stakeholder interviews and public meetings to take community members through the web-based SeaSketch maps. The project settled on six no-take marine sanctuaries, three net-banned zones on coral reef/sensitive habitats, and four mooring areas, restricting anchorage to everywhere else. In 2014, the Barbuda government passed new ocean regulations that protect this 33 per cent of the coastal zone.

SIDS could greatly benefit from an increase in publically accessible, accurate geospatial data, especially local knowledge that relates to the conservation of ecosystems, preservation of cultural heritage and adaptation to the effects of climate change. Conservation and planning strategies show a higher rate of success when local stakeholders support a project through informed decision-making, and the use of participatory mapping initiatives and decision support systems are powerful tools for public awareness and capacity strengthening (Agostini et al., 2010).

NOTES

1. United Nations. 2014. *The Millennium Development Goals Report 2014*. http://www.un.org/m,illenniumgoals/2014%20MDG%20report/MDG%20 2014%20English%20web.pdf.
2. Kairi Consultants Ltd. 2007. 2005 Analysis of the Trinidad and Tobago survey of living conditions.
3. Kedir, Abbi, and Sandra Sookram, 2011. 'Poverty and Welfare of the Poor in a High-Income Country: Evidence from Trinidad and Tobago.' *Journal of International Development* 25(4):520–535 Doi: 10.1002/jid.1824.
4. Kedir, Abbi, and Sandra Sookram. 2011. *Ibid*.
5. Deaton, Angus, and Salman Zaidi. 2002. 'Guidelines for Constructing consumption Aggregates For Welfare Analysis'. Paper 192, Woodrow Wilson School – Development Studies. New Jersey: Princeton University.
6. Kedir, Abbi, and Sandra Sookram. 2011. *Op.cit.* See Also: Downes, Andrew S. 2010. 'Poverty and its Reduction in the Small Developing Countries of the Caribbean'. Paper presented at the conference on 'Ten Years of "War Against Poverty,'" Chronic Poverty Research Centre, University of Manchester, UK. **Also:** Lanjouw, Peter, and Martin Ravallion. 1994. 'Poverty and Household Size'. Policy Research Workng Paper 1332, Policy Research Department. Washington DC: The World Bank. And: Lipton, Michael, and Martin Ravallion. 1993. 'Poverty and Policy'. Policy Research Working Paper 1130, Policy Research Department. Washington DC: The World Bank.
7. Kedir, Abbi, and Sandra Sookram. 2011. *Op.cit.*
8. Wiggins, Raynata and Sandra Sookram. 2014. 'The Participation of the Poor in Universal Social Assistance in Trinidad and Tobago'. Paper presented at the 15th annual conference on "Caribbean Development: Standing Still or Standing Tall? Theoretical, Empirical and Policy Challenges", SALISES, University of the West Indies, Trinidad.
9. ECLAC Secretariat. 2012. "Middle-Income Countries: As structural- gap approach". Thirty-fourth session of ECLAC. San Salvador: United Nations Economic Commission for Latin America and the Caribbean.
10. Alkire, S., and A. Sumner 2013. "Multidimensional Poverty and the Post-2015 MDGs", OPHI Policy Briefing, Oxford Poverty and Human Development Initiative, Oxford.

11. Thomas, McDonald, and Eleanor Wint. 2002. 'Inequality and Poverty in the Eastern Caribbean'. Prepared for ECCB Seventh Annual Development Conference 21-22 November 2002, Basseterre, St Kitts.

12. Bobb, Euric. 2013. 'The Reduction of Poverty and Inequality' Opening Address to UWI's Conference on the Economy 2013.

13. Oxford Poverty and Human Development Initiative. 2015. 'The world's poorest people don't always live where you'd expect'. Oxford Poverty and Human Development Initiative, Oxford.

14. Organization for Economic Cooperation and Development (OECD). 2012a. 'Perspectives on Global Development 2012: Social Cohesion in a Shifting World', OECD, Paris.

15. Rambaldi, G., R. Chambers, M. McCall, and J. Fox. 2006. 'Practical ethics for PGIS practitioners, facilitators, technology intermediaries and researchers.' *Participatory Learning and Action* 54(1): 106–113. See also: Rambaldi, G., M. McCall, P. Kyem, and D. Weiner. 2006. 'Participatory Spatial Information Management and Communication in Developing Countries.' *The Electronic Journal on Information Systems in Developing Countries* 25(1): 1–9.

16. Rambaldi, G., and D. Weiner. 2004. Summary proceedings of the 'Track on International PPGIS Perspectives.' Paper presented at the Third International Conference on Public Participation GIS (PPGIS), Madison, Wisconsin.

17. DeGraff, Alison, and Bheshem Ramlal. 2015. 'Participatory Mapping in Caribbean Small Island Developing States.' Paper presented at the Forum on the Future of the Caribbean, Port of Spain, Trinidad.

18. DiGessa, S. 2008. 'Participatory Mapping as a tool for empowerment: Experiences and lessons learned from the ILC network': International Land Coalition. See also: Rambaldi, G., R. Chambers, M. McCall, and J. Fox. 2006. 'Practical ethics for PGIS practitioners, facilitators'*op.cit.* 106–113.

19. Rambaldi, G., and D. Weiner. 2004. Summary proceedings of the 'Track on International PPGIS Perspectives.' *Op.cit.*

20. Agostini, V., S. Margles, S. Schill, J. Knowles, and R. Blyther. 2010. 'Marine Zoning in Saint Kitts and Nevis: A Path Towards Sustainable Management of Marine Resources.' The Nature Conservancy. See also: CANARI. 2012. 'Report on the Participatory three-dimensional (P3DM) modelling exercise in Tobago.' Laventille, Trinidad: Caribbean Natural Resources Institute. Also: CartONG. 2014. 'First feedback on UAV & OpenStreetMap mission in Haiti.' Retrieved October 26, 2014, from http://www.cartong.org/news/mission-uav-openstreetmap-en-ha%C3%AFti-premier-bilan.   And: Sustainable Grenadines. 2013. 'Participatory Three Dimensional Modeling (P3DM) Workshop (Working with Nature and Communities to Reduce Climate Change Impacts):' Sustainable Grenadines, Inc.

21. DeGraff, Alison, and Bheshem Ramlal. 2015. *Op.cit.*

22. Bobb-Prescott, N. 2014. 'Case study on the use of participatory three-dimensional modelling to facilitate effective contribution of civil society in the Caribbean islands in planning for action on climate change. Laventille, Trinidad:' CANARI Technical Report.

23. CANARI. 2012. *Op.cit.*

24. Bobb-Prescott, N. 2014. *Op.cit.*

25. Sustainable Grenadines. 2013. 'Participatory Three Dimensional Modeling" (P3DM) Workshop (Working with Nature and Communities to Reduce Climate Change Impacts): Sustainable Grenadines, Inc.

26. Grenada Fund for Conservation. 2013. 'Report on the P3DM Activity in Grenville. Grenada, West Indies'. Grenada Fund for Conservation.

27. DeGraff, A., and K. Baldwin. 2013. 'Participatory Mapping of Heritage Sites in the Grenadine Islands. Cave Hill, Barbados'. Centre for Resource Management and Environmental Studies, University of the West Indies.

28. Smith, A. H. 2006. 'Using GIS Tools for Participatory Management of Coastal Resources in Laborie Bay, Saint Lucia.' Paper presented at the Gulf and Caribbean Fisheries Institute.

29. Baldwin, K. 2012. 'A Participatory Marine Resource and Space-Use Information System for the Grenadine Islands: An Ecosystem Approach to Collaborative Planning for Management of Transboundary Marine Resources.' (Doctor of Philosophy in Environmental Management), Centre for Resource Management and Environmental Studies, University of the West Indies, Cave Hill, Barbados.

30. Baldwin, K., and H.A. Oxenford 2014. 'A Participatory Approach to Marine Habitat Mapping in the Grenadine Islands.' *Coastal Management* 42(1) 36–58.

31. DeGraff, A., and K. Baldwin. 2013. *Op.cit.*

32. Humanitarian OpenStreetMap Team. 2011. 'Introducing COSMHA.' Retrieved October 26, 2014, from http://hot.openstreetmap.org/updates/2011-01-14_introducing_cosmha.

33. CartONG. 2014. *op. cit.*

34. Agostini, V., S. Margles, S. Schill, J. Knowles, and R. Blyther. 2010. *Op.cit.* Natural Capital Project. 2013. Marine InVEST: A Decision-Making Tool for Mapping and Valuing Ecosystem Services Provided by Coasts and Oceans: Natural Capital Project.

35. Agostini, V., S. Margles, S. Schill, J. Knowles, and R. Blyther. 2010. *Op.cit*

36. SeaSketch. 2014. 'Barbuda Blue Halo: Planning Marine Sanctuaries in the Caribbean with the Waitt Institute.' Retrieved October 27, 2014, from http://www.seasketch.org/case-studies/2013/10/01/ barbuda.html.

37. Johnson, A., and W. McClintock. 2013. '3 Steps to Community-Driven Ocean Zoning.' Retrieved October 27, 2014, from http://voices.nationalgeographic.com/2013/12/16/3-steps-to-ocean-zoning/.

H.E. Irwin LaRocque

PART THREE
RETHINKING THE CARIBBEAN FUTURE

The Honourable Ralph Gonzalves with the
Honourable Winston Dookeran

CHAPTER 8
New Thinking for New Times: Caribbean Leaders Share Their Views

David Anyanwu

INTRODUCTION

Leaders of the region along with other Forum participants called for the development of new models of Caribbean cooperation and integration. They recognised that for most purposes CARICOM is ineffective and plagued with institutional rigidities. Winston Dookeran notes that the search for a Caribbean economic space must be based on new models of cooperation and integration which can position CARICOM countries and, by extension, countries of the entire Caribbean to capture the opportunities that the world provides.[1] This does not entail supplanting existing integration processes, nor does it deny the benefits of a narrow integration process. In fact, as the leaders themselves present in this section, the process requires deepening relations within CARICOM, and extending those relations from CARICOM to the broader Caribbean.

However, the region cannot be serious about confronting today's challenges with models of integration from the 1970s and 1980s. The world has moved on dramatically and as such, convergence must be based on the widening of the region to include countries in the broader Caribbean, such as Cuba and the Dominican Republic. Antonio Romero Gomez of the University of Havana also supports this view. He noted the need to think beyond CARICOM and to seek deeper economic cooperation with Cuba. Despite political obstacles, the same can be said about the Dominican Republic which is already part of CARIFORUM. With Cuba and the United States normalizing diplomatic relations in July 2015[2], ongoing efforts including the successful negotiation of bilateral trade and partial scope trade agreements with several countries in the hemisphere have to be built on towards socioeconomic convergence. Convergence has been articulated by Dookeran as a process in motion.[3] Anyanwu further defines convergence as a natural response to global requirements for efficiency in this new economy and which demand

CARICOM countries to explore newer platforms for economic, political and diplomatic cooperation, to avoid being left behind.[4]

The improvement in relations between the two countries has been viewed by CARICOM countries not only as an overdue political development but also as an economic challenge for the sub-region. American and Caribbean companies are going to be exploring opportunities in key sectors such as telecommunications, tourism, transport, health and others. Within this context, CARICOM can develop strategic terms of engagement with Cuba so as to benefit from the gains of investment and interest that will emerge when the US Congress lifts the embargo and travel bans on Cuba. A Caribbean Sea convergence that includes Cuba presents an opportunity for the development of a regional destination tourism strategy which will not only sell the diverse offerings from the region, but also ensure that tourism in one country can have a positive effect on the rest of the region.

These new models of cooperation and integration which Dookeran posits provide the context for capturing the possibilities of a Caribbean Sea economy that is not limited by geographical borders. According to Dookeran, Caribbean Sea economic convergence will 'allow us in the English-speaking CARICOM region and of course the new entrance to Haiti to move from a gross domestic product something like $70 billion to operating in a wider Caribbean Sea with a gross domestic product of $350 billion'.[5] It will also provide a new growth path for the expanding business activity and realign regional institutions to encourage freer movement of goods, services, capital, ICTs and people. Ambassador Munera adds that a convergence of countries washed by the Caribbean Sea will open up the space for permanent cooperation with 25 countries with total population of about 285 million people and will create a market bigger than that of Brazil, Japan and Russia with 202 million, 126 million and 142 million inhabitants, respectively.[6]

For example, the Pacific Alliance as presented by Arriazola Peta Rueda of Mexico, represents an accumulated GDP of $3 trillion, which is equivalent to 43 % of the GDP of the entire Latin America and the Caribbean region. It also represents 2 % of intra-regional trade among the members, 19 % of trade with the rest of Latin America and the Caribbean region and 62 % of trade with the European Union. A primary merit of the Pacific Alliance is its representation in international organizations which gives it an important perspective and reach through membership in the

G-20 (via Mexico), Organization for Economic Cooperation (via Chile), Asia-Pacific Economic Cooperation (Chile and Mexico), Association of American States, CELAC, UNASUR, and the Andean Community. The experiences of the Pacific Alliance show gains that can be accrued from joint action. In 2014 alone, tourism alone brought $1.3 billion to the member states of the Pacific Alliance. Mexico in particular saw an increase of 200,000 visitors from member states of the Pacific Alliance following its removal of visa requirements for nationals of Peru and Colombia.

With convergence, there can be a deepening of relations to create the kinds of incisive institutions which can deal with today's challenges. A country as small as Grenada might be constrained to effectively engage in negotiations with multilateral finance institutions such as the International Monetary Fund (IMF). Navigating issues around conditionality and structural reform can be tasking on small countries. Broome argued that 'small states are likely to struggle to level the playing field in their attempts to negotiate the constraints and opportunities provided by engagement with the IMF during international crises, when they face higher stakes compared with larger economies'.[7] However, it would be incorrect to state that this capacity cannot be found in small states given that countries like Greece, Ireland, Iceland and Guyana have successfully negotiated debt relief with these institutions. Arguably, a collective approach by a region of 17 million negotiating on behalf of its countries might produce more positive outcomes for small economies. The proverbial strength in numbers has never been more relevant than in this context. Collective action can help small economies increase their bargaining power, as a group, in negotiations with financial institutions.

Indeed, the justification for the repurposing and modernization of Caribbean institutions is also predicated on the fact that convergence requires institutions that provide the enabling environment and facilitation for the expansion of business activity in the region. These kinds of institutions are trade enhancing, have a regional focus and are also aligned with the global and political forces. Unfortunately, institutional redundancies have become one of the region's greatest challenges because, as Dookeran surmised, there is an unrealistic expectation that the institutions of yesterday which continue to exist, and indeed the personalities and leadership models which influence them, can effectively respond to the global and political forces of today.

TRANSFORMATIONAL LEADERSHIP FOR A NEW FUTURE

Governments and, by extension, leaders are often constrained by the environment within which they operate, hence the belief that their behaviour is shaped by the environment. For example, fiscal indiscipline that exists in many CARICOM countries can be linked to the political environment in which their governments and leaders operate. In the Caribbean, political survival has historically been dependent on quick-fix solutions to satisfy the electorate with little or no lasting impact for the sustainable development of the region. It therefore requires significant political courage and purpose for a Caribbean leader to overcome this challenge and shape the environment in positive way. If leaders can have an effect on their environment, Blondel suggests that such an effect depends on the personal origins of the actions they take and the instruments by which these actions are implemented. While he notes that political leadership at the international level depends on the leadership of the most important states[8], the same could be said about leadership at the regional level. Thus, the call for Caribbean leaders to deliver the kind of leadership which can transform the region or for Trinidad and Tobago to play a leadership role in the region cannot be seen as unfounded.

Robert Rotberg, on the other hand, has argued that individual leaders and the choices they make impact the development of political cultures and institutions especially in former colonies. According to him, 'leadership actions greatly determine the kinds of political cultures that arise in newly emergent or post conflict nation-states. Additionally, leaders beget good governance, and the practice of good governance nurtures and enables robust institutions and strengthens the rule of law. The latter do not emerge in a vacuum but only as a result of early and careful leadership attention to core values'.[9] Transformational leaders according to Rotberg, embody a range of leadership qualities which he referred to as critical competencies and which give such leaders the ability to lead appropriately and with legitimacy. Arguing that such styles are most effective in still developing or postcolonial countries, he used illustrative case studies of leaders such as Nelson Mandela in South Africa, Seretse Khama in Botswana, Lee Kuan Yew in Singapore, and Kemal Ataturk in Turkey to show how they transformed their respective developing countries.

Indeed, there is evidence in the Caribbean that small states can experience dramatic changes in growth thanks to transformational leadership. The qualities exhibited by both Eric Williams and Norman Manley during their political careers are exemplary in this context, particularly, Williams' conviction that a successful future for the entire Caribbean is contingent on its constituent states being part of an economic and political unit greater than their own. As a transformational leader, he paved the way for Trinidad and Tobago to become more than just an exporter of oil, but into an industrial power – using the country's endowment in energy as a tool to develop the industry. Similarly, the dramatic rise of Singapore under the transformational leadership (under authoritarianism) of Lee Kuan Yew who over a period of 31 years as President of Singapore propelled that country's economic growth and development, raising the former British colony from a Third World backwater, to the front ranks of the First World. The government and public sector in Singapore are regarded as being among the most efficient in the world, and its infrastructure facilities can be compared against the best in developed countries. All these factors combined, contribute to Singapore's being ranked amongst the top in the world competitiveness league[10] What is perhaps most admirable of Williams' leadership compared to Lee Kuan Yew's is that Williams' achievements were attained in the context of a functional democratic system.

In this context, the overwhelming message from the Forum was a call to action for regional leaders. The Forum, a first of its kind, sought to catalyse change through provision of a space for debate and a rethinking of solutions to rectify what has been seen as a development problematique. There was a unanimous view by Forum participants of the need for action and a focus on execution. Interestingly, the message has also been communicated directly to regional leaders who patiently engaged participants over the three days of the Forum. Prime Ministers, Ministers of Government, Heads of Sub-Regional, and Regional and International Organizations engaged participants as well as presented some bold ideas for refocusing Caribbean development in this new economy.

How does the Caribbean optimally position itself to benefit from a rapidly progressing global convergence agenda? That was the question Winston Dookeran sought to answer in his opening remarks and introduction at the Forum. He focused on the political logic and on the quest of unlocking the politics of the region so as to realign it with the geopolitical, economic and financial realities of the time – particularly in the context of the challenges the region is faced with and the need to put aside the limitations of politics for a broader development agenda. In doing this, he acknowledged the many great strides of the region in the past five decades and noted the foundation which those achievements must now serve for 'the creation of the potential for the future'. Positioning the Caribbean to benefit from this changing global landscape, he argued, would require an evaluation of the pillars of the current architecture, particularly in terms of how they might be altered and redesigned to fit the purpose in the new economy. The political logic must align with the economic imperative in order to equip the region with the mandate and leadership required to accelerate Caribbean convergence. The region's socioeconomic realities demand bold and farsighted leadership and not the mediocrity that is fast becoming commonplace in Caribbean politics.

Referencing two former Prime Ministers of Jamaica, P.J. Patterson and Norman Manley, Dookeran expounded on the challenge of leadership which is at the heart of the Caribbean development problematique, noting that politics must not be seen as a deterrent for the advancement of the Caribbean region and that today's politics must be equal and responsive to the needs of the region. This is consistent with the position of Acemoglu and Robinson in their publication on *Why Nations Fail*, in which they argued that 'it is man-made political and economic institutions that underlie economic successes or the lack of it'.[11] Caribbean regional economic space and the institutions that promote it must reflect the alignment of global and political forces towards new models of convergence within a new convergence of the Caribbean region. Global trends suggest that countries are converging more than they are diverging and that these movements are in response to the demands of the changing global economic architecture.

REIGNITING THE CARIBBEAN AGENDA

Caribbean leaders are committed to energising the integration and cooperation process in the region and beyond. CARICOM's leadership was represented at the highest level, as well as leaders representing all corners of the Caribbean including the Spanish, Dutch and French speaking islands. Importantly, the Forum counted on the participation of young people who comprise some 60% of the Caribbean population. CARICOM, as the primary regional body, recognizes the timeliness and relevance of the Forum given the enormous regional and international challenges with which its member states are currently faced. In his speech to the Forum, Secretary General, Ambassador LaRocque noted, 'There is no doubt that serious fore-sighting and visioning need to be undertaken about the future of the Region. In so doing, we must be prepared to open our minds to new ideas, and to thinking differently. Allowing ourselves to be shaken out of our conventional thinking modes and approaches is an essential prerequisite in our quest for the future development of the Region'.

In making the case for the rekindling a Caribbean revolution, Sir Hilary Beckles reminded Caribbean people that self-reliance must never be alienated from their thinking.[12] He noted that he felt a strong perception within the Caribbean region that many of its development failures and limitations can be accounted for in terms of the stalling of the revolutionary momentum.[13] In this context, he argued that contrary to historical models of development in the region in which the production of goods and services and wealth accumulation were primarily for the benefits of societies external to the Caribbean, the idea that the production and equitable distribution of wealth can be for the benefit and advancement of its people is revolutionary.

Noting that the path to the 'Caribbean potential' lay in its history, Prof Beckles argued that the 'notion that the Caribbean is at a crossroad is not a complete truth because it *is* and has always been a crossroad'. It may be argued that the realization of this truth would be in many ways the first step in shaking the region out of its conventional thinking modes and position it on a path to development. Reflecting on an important historical impediment to this 'Caribbean potential', Beckles, argued that the perpetrators of historical crimes against humanity in the Caribbean must be held accountable. He further argued that 'economic models rooted in the colonial dispensation cannot be legitimized as sustainable and as such reparatory justice must be a part of the healing and development process and a critical aspect of the definition and defence of citizenship'.

Reflecting further on this revolutionary change in thinking, he argued that the region has gone adrift because its compass is no longer fixed on that which matters most, 'the liberation of the potential of the Caribbean people'. In his view, the region's economic dependency on the West and its social backwardness was predicated on the challenge that even though times have changed, the Caribbean remained fixed to inhibiting structures while the world is rapidly changing and moving on. Nevertheless, he was optimistic that the Caribbean development agenda had not failed, at least not yet, but rather its progress has stalled. Reignition of growth and development is therefore dependent on the region's ability to free itself of this dependency syndrome and see itself not as appendices and extensions of other power systems, but rather new alliances formed in a new convergence to propel this agenda.

SHARED FUTURE IN NEW CARIBBEAN ECONOMY

In making the case for deepened regional engagement, Prime Minister Kamla Persad-Bissessar of Trinidad and Tobago noted that 'where we want to be will be created by us sharing our resources, pooling our wealth and expertise, and structuring our medium and long-term policy frameworks based on a vision' – perhaps in a new convergence. Certainly, the region's exposure to global economic issues reveals the strength in standing together in the face of challenges. Contemporary security issues such as food, agriculture, energy crisis, economic and financial crises, and the pandemics of Ebola, Chikungunya, HIV/AIDs as well as transnational organized crimes pose serious challenges for global governance and multilateral institutions including the United Nations. More than exposing the vulnerabilities of CARICOM states, they have also reinstated the need for greater cooperation increasingly within the construct of a wider Caribbean. Therefore, despite the disparities across the region which can limit regional collaboration, there are great benefits which must be pursued. Disparities in access to tertiary, technical and vocational training; employment and job creation; economic diversification and new industries; access and availability of ICTS; and competitiveness of industries can be overcome with greater political fortitude.

Indeed, the Prime Minister, like other regional leaders in attendance, was cognizant of the Caribbean people's expectations for such transformational leadership and the need to realign the politics of the region with the economic realities of today as well as with the strong Caribbean identity among majority of Caribbean people. Reflecting on the expectations for regional leaders to formalize this aspiration, she noted that 'the challenges can at times be harsh, but when our people look to us for leadership, they expect to see it; and with collaboration, we share the burdens as a unified force, and meet the challenges with greater strength'.

It is also clear that in addition to political leadership, Caribbean institutions must also be modernised towards the development of frameworks that prioritize action over process so that important and necessary decisions to accelerate the integration process can be promoted. Questions yet remain about the kinds of institutional arrangements needed to take the region forward. There is consensus that the current regional integration model that resulted in the creation of CARICOM is unsuitable for today's challenges and is incapable of responding to the requirements for growth and development in this new economy.

For example, what impact would widening the regional space have on the region's ambitions of achieving a single economy and on foreign policy coordination? Would the benefits of Caribbean economic convergence be significant enough to forsake an ambition which CARICOM leaders themselves agreed to put on hold in favour of consolidating the supposed gains in the single market component?[14] Nevertheless, convergence is not about supplanting CARICOM; rather, as a process in motion, it 'represents a new way of thinking about integration in the region and injecting the process with new life and energy'.[15] It is about accelerating the pace of this process so as to exploit its potential benefits.

Owen Arthur, who carried lead responsibility for the CARICOM Single Market and Economy, underpinned regional cooperation as a critical element in the region's confrontation of the global economic crisis. But he observed that if economic integration is to become a strong force to drive Caribbean development, and if it is to be the means by which the regional economy is inserted into the global economy, 'that process must involve the building of strong and competitive enterprises by allowing them to have access to the skills of the people of the Caribbean, wherever they are available'. He argued that the Caribbean has never realized its developmental potential, in large measure because it has never succeeded in putting the creative imagination of its people fully to work on the region's behalf, and according to him 'that creative imagination must be liberated for the Caribbean to progress.'

ON REGIONAL ENERGY

Reflecting on Trinidad and Tobago's long active and strong participation in the global energy industry, Prime Minister Persad-Bissessar of Trinidad and Tobago referenced the evolution of Trinidad and Tobago's industrial policies from one that focused on its leading position as a top producer and exporter of petrochemicals including ammonia, methanol, urea, urea-ammonium nitrate (UAN) and melamine, to one that prioritises diversification and inserting smaller businesses in the energy value chain. Indeed, Trinidad and Tobago's petroleum industry's profile has changed significantly in the past four decades, from one centred on crude oil production in the 1970s to a focus on natural gas which became increasingly lucrative for the country in the late 1970s and 1980s with the decline in crude oil reserves. The manufacture and export of petrochemicals has significantly diversified the range of exports in the energy sector.

Significant downstream investments were predicated on the importance attached to downstream value chains as vital for the redirection and value and benefits to the local economy, and this was facilitated by regulations and incentives that enabled all levels of the local private sector to participate in the industry either through share-ownership, in the form of mergers and acquisitions, or manufacturing. Even though recent global events such as the 2008 economic crisis and the Middle East crisis have increased production of shale gas in the United States, caused a general softening in the global demand for energy commodities and contributed to the reduction of energy commodity crisis, the country's long history of successful participation in the global industry has offered it significant financial room for manoeuvre and solidified its positioning in the region as a financial services capital. To sustain the energy industry, Trinidad and Tobago is engaging new projects and cross-border activities with key actors such as Venezuela on the Loran/Manatee and Mannequin/ Coquina gas fields. These activities will, in essence, support the use of non-renewable resources to develop renewable and alternative sources of energy power generation for sustainable development. Similarly, the multi-donor US$1 billion Caribbean Energy Fund for which a memorandum of understanding was signed with the Inter-American Development Bank (IDB) will finance projects to convert power generation from oil to natural gas and the execution of renewable energy projects.[16]

In using the energy sector as a springboard for the rest of the economy, Prime Minister Persad-Bissessar argued that energy collaboration can provide the basis for reducing the costs of manufacturing and also increase competitiveness in attracting foreign investments. The role of foreign private capital, especially in the development of the local petrochemical industry is well noted in this regard. As a deliberate government strategy to meet the need for capital injection and access to international markets, this entailed a number of joint venture arrangements with varying levels of state participation. Similarly, foreign investments will provide the capital needed to enhance the productive capacity of local enterprises so as to create more market and business opportunities.

ON REGIONAL FINANCING

As an important issue for the region, 'the inward gaze and the economic difficulties of the developed "countries" in the face of recent economic crises, have further diminished an already shrinking pool of development finance'. The events in Europe, with countries such as Greece becoming the first developed country to default on an IMF loan, further support the argument that the priorities of donors are no longer fixated on former colonies. Outcomes of the Third International Conference for Financing for Development in July and the UN Summit on the Post-2015 Development Agenda in September will, in great measures, impact the future directions of the international development agenda and related priorities of countries and regions. These changes in the global financial architecture, as well as those anticipated based on current trends, will impact development in the region, thereby necessitating proactive action by regional governments and regions.

By virtue of their graduation from low to middle income countries, several CARICOM states find themselves in a conflicting situation in which much needed development finance is no longer attainable at below market terms from multilateral and bilateral sources of funding. Even as countries must now look to domestic and international sources of development financing, challenges in capital mobility in the region have meant that fast-growing economies such as Suriname's is starved of the capital needed to fuel development. In this regard, aligning capital markets for the purpose of full integration will facilitate the systemic creation of financial markets balance excess reserves with excess demand for credit.

ON REGIONAL ICTS

Having identified disparities in the access and availability of ICTs as a challenge for regional collaboration, Prime Minister Persad-Bissessar described the emergence of a national broadband strategy as an outcome of one of the structural reforms that Trinidad and Tobago prioritized for the purpose of energizing growth, diversifying the national economy (away from the energy sector in which commodities make up over 85 %

of Trinidad and Tobago's exports) and building national competitiveness. Indeed, connectivity has been identified as another critical factor for competitiveness.

The region certainly cannot imagine a future void of the transformative role of innovation and technological change. We live in a knowledge economy, and according to Ambassador LaRocque, 'In all spheres of life, ICT is making a profound difference ... and its influence stretches through all sectors and must be a key factor in driving the development of our human resources and in increasing our competitiveness'.[17] Similarly, Sir Hilary Beckles noted that creative innovation remains the key to the region's potential. Compared to price and quality, he argued that this is one area, throughout the region's economic history, in which they have not been able to compete. Given the importance attached to innovation in this new economy, the region must find ways to release itself from this entrapment.

In fact, the role of ICTs in the history of international cooperation and organization is well noted. It was, after all, the technological changes in communication (via telegraph) and transportation (via railroad and steamship) brought about by the industrial revolution in the nineteenth century that enhanced interdependence among states and gave basis for more stable forms of cooperation. Prime Minister Persad-Bissessar shares similar views on the importance of ICTs and connectivity. In noting the importance of connectivity in facilitating a convergence, she argued that 'if our economies are to talk with each other and establish common ground, connectivity is perhaps the most important factor'. Thus, she expressed the view that the region must work together towards the potential use of broadband for integrating connectivity and competitiveness objectives.

ON REGIONAL KNOWLEDGE DEVELOPMENT

There is now a prevailing appreciation of the importance of knowledge and information, including their production, distribution and application as prerequisites for competitiveness in this new economy. Also as pillars of growth and sustainability for the future. Bhattacharya notes the convergence in views by researchers of the inadequacy of the prevalent one-size-fits-all model of school information, to meet the challenging demands of this fast, innovation-driven economy.[18] Knowledge paves the way for innovation to address the country's ability to adapt to changing dynamics and enhancing competitiveness.[19] In a global economy in which knowledge is growing exponentially, Prime Minister Persad-Bissessar argued that 'an innovation thrust can become the trigger for a regeneration of entrepreneurship, in an environment that is linked to the global economy in a robust way'. A nation's competitive advantage is therefore increasingly dependent, among many things, on its ability to effectively manage knowledge, increase innovation and build an entrepreneurial society with a creative mindset, the capacity for transformative thinking and the flexibility to respond to high uncertainties.

Similarly, 'creative innovation', which Sir Hilary Beckles mentioned, is dependent upon education, research and the commercialization of collective ideas. According to Beckles, despite the challenge of mistrust and rivalry between industry and academia, this kind of innovation requires respect for research and the application of resources to value creation.[20] He referenced Asia as an example of a region that demonstrates the outcome of a successful partnership between academia and industry. Our development objectives and plans have, for the most part, been limited by the disconnect between private capital and education. Prime Minister Persad-Bissessar opined that it is through effective links among CARICOM nations and beyond in a vital knowledge system that the path for knowledge and information collaboration can be created. A convergence of Caribbean economies can lead to deepened levels of engagement in trade and other strategic areas including ICTs, energy, transport and so forth. This will not only boost economic growth and development in the Caribbean, it will also strengthen the region's stake in the global economy and increase its share of hemispheric and global trade. This is the essence of convergence—making the region resilient and globally competitive. Even CARICOM has noted the opportunity advancements in innovation, creativity, digital literacy, entrepreneurial attitudes and skills as platforms for growth and development in this new economy present for the region in its Strategic Plan.[22]

Creating a vital knowledge system to reignite Caribbean growth and development, which Sir Hilary Beckles argued is stalled, will require changes and investment in the education system, particularly in training and skills development. As Prime Minister Persad-Bissessar noted, the success of industries and economic sectors that are supported by knowledge and innovation depend on harnessing the energy of young people through skills and training to prepare them for a new era of prosperity. Participants at the Forum would have expressed frustration that the current structure of the tertiary education system did not always produce graduates with the kinds of skills needed to drive the regional development agenda. Collaboration and knowledge sharing will be difficult if disparities among countries in the region are not addressed. As Bhattacharya notes, the education system has to focus on developing skills built on creativity and prepare human labour with entrepreneurial ability capable of troubleshooting and experimenting with vague ideas.[22]

Sir Hilary Beckles further made the case for more investment in education in youths given that the Caribbean has the lowest enrolments of youth (age cohort 18 to 30 years) at the tertiary level among countries in the hemisphere. When further disaggregated, the differences among countries in the Caribbean do not bode well for a competitive future given the dependence of economic development and social transformation on the quality and skill-base of a society's people. While the global economic downturn has severely impacted Barbados' investment in higher education leading to a 30% collapse of nationals enrolled in university education during the period of 2012–2014, participation in tertiary education has increased to 65.23% as of December 31, 2013, in Trinidad and Tobago.[23]

Contrary to what politicians might want the Caribbean people to believe, it is not completely clear if the increase in higher education in Trinidad and Tobago is due to an expansion of the Government Assistance for Tuition Expenses (GATE) which approximately 67,000 students currently access.[24] This is because the facility is not accessed based on need – it is there for the rich and the poor, again bringing into question the efficiency and sustainability of the program. Perhaps the program would be more efficient if it were based on a combination of need and merit; that way the government could ensure that finances are not an obstacle to higher education and that the right people are trained. Trinidad and Tobago is probably the only country in the region that can afford this luxury in this economic climate.

Nonetheless, this a problem that requires a regional solution given the impact on growth and development. If the approach to education, particularly at the tertiary level is fragmented, then the region will collectively suffer. The demands of this new economy require a collective regional approach to ensure the provision of skills to the region's youth so that they can be able to access the training and education needed to become the innovators of tomorrow. How can manufacturing be taken to the next level if the region is not producing technologically driven innovators and entrepreneurs? The challenge for the region according to Sir Hilary Beckles is not the absence of capital to fuel development projects, but rather a chronic and acute shortage of relevant skills in critical areas. According to him, "We have a human resource crisis, not a capital crisis …investments follow skills and consciousness…the Caribbean needs to be sharpened up and made aggressively investment ready'. As seen in the Singaporean case, the engine of development for the Caribbean in this new economy largely defined by access and application of knowledge and technology will be driven by a well-educated and technically savvy citizenry.

LANGUAGE AND COMMUNICATION – KEYS TO CONVERGENCE

The region would benefit from improving communication links between higher education and skills training. Sir Hilary Beckles noted that the Caribbean has maintained an educational system which does not mandate every child to speak Spanish and English. This is an interesting point, not just for the Caribbean agenda, because it has implications for the region's engagement with the rest of the world. Globally, we see a consistent change in the status of English as the common language of business. The emergence of an 'internationally mobile, highly skilled labour force offering a number of languages'[25] has coincided with the emergence of new economic and financial actors in the aftermath of the 2008 financial crisis.

The Chinese and Indians have excelled in this area in that most of their college degree holders can speak at least English. Yet despite a strong Spanish and French influence in the region, most people only speak and understand their mother tongue—English. Bilingualism and increasingly multilingualism, will assist in increasing regional awareness and also a regional and global mindset—all prerequisites for a successful convergence. National competitiveness and indeed regional competitiveness will be shaped by the linguistic abilities of the labour force of any country or region, their ability to converse in the language of investors and other trading partners. Interestingly, Ambassador Munera recognized linguistic barrier as one of the invisible barriers to Caribbean convergence.

Reflecting on the path towards Caribbean convergence, Ambassador Munera drew a reference to what he termed 'invisible barriers' such as culture, language and old ideologies of confrontation which keep the countries of the Caribbean apart. Yet, as he noted, attempts have been made to bridge these gaps in the past, particularly with the establishment of the Association of Caribbean States (ACS) which was founded twenty years ago with the purpose of creating an organization that could overcome the rigidities instituted by colonial structures to facilitate a space for dialogue for the cooperation of Caribbean territories. Like many participants in the Forum who shared a deep sense of optimism in the Caribbean project, Ambassador Munera noted that Caribbean countries have been able to work together in many functional areas such as disaster prevention, sustainable tourism, trade facilitation and transport. He further noted the successes of the government of Colombia during his tenure as Ambassador to Jamaica, in building exchanges across the region. Of importance in this context is the ten-year long exchange of knowledge and the training of students in English and Spanish, a part of the long-term vision of the Government of Colombia to advance a wider Caribbean agenda.

ON POLITICAL WILL

However as Ambassador LaRocque cautioned, 'all ideas presented at the Forum had to take account of the baseline realities of the region, if they were to result in plans and policies'. In all fairness, much has been achieved in the long history of the Caribbean integration project. Truly, the region has made significant strides in the area of functional cooperation, particularly in education, health, security, trade and economic integration, movement of persons though still problematic; the coordination of public policy in the areas of renewable for energy, agriculture and tourism, air transport, financial services, and foreign affairs, and disputes-settlement through the Caribbean Court of Justice (CCJ).[26] CARICOM was the first among other regions to present to the 2001 United Nations' General Assembly Special Session an actionable response on HIV/AIDS, and the subsequent declaration which provided the framework for the establishment of the Global Fund for HIV/AIDs, tuberculosis and malaria.[27]

Indeed, the successes of CARICOM have often been overshadowed by its shortcomings and that might have historical links to the Caribbean people's perception of and confidence in their institutions. Ambassador LaRoque noted that Caribbean people have not always given deserved credit to the framers of the Revised Treaty, and referred to the CCJ as an example both in terms of its role in interpreting the Revised Treaty as well as the appellate jurisdiction for member states of CARICOM success. The CCJ as he noted, has in the past couple of years delivered two landmark judgements on the case of the Trinidad Cement Limited vs. CARICOM and also the Shanique Myrie vs the Government of Barbados, both of which alongside the Revised Treaty constitute a body of community law insofar as they confer the rights and create obligations on member states, industry and citizenry of the community.

Yet much remains unaccomplished, and it is this sense of unfulfilment that has fuelled much critique by the people of the region. It is, however, the individual responsibility of each member of government to put in place the right institutional arrangements in its national executive and administrative apparatuses to ensure that CARICOM's decisions are implemented in a timely and effective manner. Over the years CARICOM has identified priorities for action, but announcing them as done deals raised expectations of change and reform, but seldom were those promises fulfilled. Research by Paul Clement showed that the path to convergence can be slowed, as have other regional processes that required action at the domestic level. Hence his argument that in the absence of a supranational structure, the regional process is stuck in motion due to government's inability to comply with CARICOM directives.[28]

As a result, CARICOM has been criticized, albeit unfairly at times, for making 'overpromising the norm', and not the exception to the rule. It has also been accused in this context of presenting as imminent, complex and difficult sets of promises that reflect the goodwill of leaders but ignore the difficulties of implementation. As Prime Minister Persad-Bissessar noted in her speech, nothing moves without political will. Yet she recognizes the urgency of the times in which we live: an era in which inaction is severely punished by relegation to the bottom of the chain. 'Business as usual' can no longer be attainable in this current economic landscape shaped by different events, emerging powers, technology and innovation, new networks, alliances and collaboration. It is anti-development and cannot be the norm if CARICOM economies must respond to the global demands for efficiency in a highly competitive and knowledge driven economy.

Instead, it is through transformative leadership and with political action that Caribbean convergence will be accelerated to reignite Caribbean economic growth particularly in the smaller economies of the region and create value chain opportunities for small businesses across the region. Thus, the only way economies of the region can 'stop swimming against the tide' is through 'finding common ground for collaboration, partnership, political will and confidence" in ability to commandeer its destiny'.[29]

CONCLUSION

Sir Hilary Beckles opined that CARICOM cannot be blamed for inaction that has dogged the region's integration history, wherein individual states would rather see themselves as nations that desire to be larger than the whole. Countries in the region have tended to see themselves as discrete nations when in fact they are just communities within the Caribbean Nation. As Prime Minister Persad-Bissessar surmised in her speech, this time in the region's history calls for collective action—one that will see the application of the joint human and technical resources of the Caribbean people to secure a sustainable future. She stressed that the discussions and outcomes of the Forum must translate to quick and deliberate action given the urgency of the demands of the global economy as well as negative consequences of political inaction. This requires bold action and transformative leadership to recognize that the trajectory of the region's progress may be destined to go in a new direction.

Even in a new convergence, leaders must apply the necessary political action to commit to the path for the greater good. Sir Hilary concludes that 'the state must pass laws and create legal infrastructure that empower entrepreneurship, particularly in balancing public and private capital in order to create public goods and accumulate private property. The state is the custodian of the wealth for the development of the many', and as such cannot retreat to the margins of economic thinking and action, thereby rendering its citizens vulnerable.

As Dookeran noted, the search for a Caribbean economic space must be based on new models of intervention which can position CARICOM countries to compete and reignite the growth and developed which has stalled for too long. The political logic must be realigned to meet the geopolitical, economic and financial demands of today and tomorrow. Putting aside the limitations of politics for a broader growth and development agenda will require bold and courageous leadership and, more than anything, putting words to action.

Common problems and challenges exist throughout the Caribbean region. While the solutions are not easy, they are more daunting for individual countries to tackle on their own. The general sentiment of the Caribbean people at the Forum was a strong call for action and not talk from their leaders. The collective destinies of the Caribbean reside in their own hands and in the creative and disciplined use by leaders of the mandate they have been given by the Caribbean people. The types of leaders that can make bold and transformative decisions towards accelerating Caribbean convergence have never been more important than now. Convergence must be embraced as an inevitable response to the demands of global efficiency, and countries must start implementing feasible and high value-added regional initiatives to tackle the range of common challenges that the region is faced with. We summarise some of these short-term proposals in section III, chapter 3.

NOTES

1. Dookeran, Winston. 2015. 'Emerging Caribbean space in the global setting of our times: will the Caribbean miss this opportunity?' Opening speech by Winston Dookeran, Minister of Foreign Affairs of Trinidad and Tobago at Forum on the Future of the Caribbean. Hyatt Regency Hotel, Port of Spain, Trinidad. May 6, 2015.
2. The United States officially reopened its embassy in Havana on August 14, 2015. Some 55 years after it was closed.
3. Dookeran, Winston 2012. Caribbean convergence: revisiting Caribbean integration. Caribbean Development Bank Roundtable. May 2012.
4. Anyanwu, David. 2015. 'Caribbean convergence: an essay.' Paper commissioned by ILO for the Forum on the Future of the Caribbean. May 2015.
5. Dookeran, Winston. 2015. *Op.cit.*
6. Cadavia, Alfonso Munera. Speech by Secretary General of the Association of Caribbean States at Forum on the Future of the Caribbean. Hyatt Regency Hotel, Port of Spain, Trinidad. May 6, 2015.
7. Broome, Andre. 2011. 'Negotiating the crisis: the IMF and Disaster Capitalism in Small States.' *The Round Table* Vol. 100, No. 413, 155–167, April 2011.
8. Blondel, Jean. 1987. *Political Leadership: Towards a General Analysis.* London: SAGE Publications
9. Rotberg, Robert. 2012. *Transformative Political Leadership: Making a Difference in the Developing World.* Chicago and London: University of Chicago Press.
10. Transformational leadership http://www.adityabirla.com/Media/ Transformational-leadership.
11. Acemoglu, Daron and James A. Robinson. 2013. *Why nations fail; the origins of power, prosperity and poverty.* New York: Crown Business.

12. Beckles, Hilary 2015. Expanded version of the opening statement delivered by Sir. Hilary Beckles on the Day 2 of the Forum on the Future of the Caribbean, May 5-7, 2015, Port of Spain, Trinidad and Tobago.

13. Beckles, Hilary *ibid*

14. In May 2011, CARICOM leaders agreed to stall further implementation of the CARICOM Single Market and Economy, saying the region was better off consolidating the gains made under the single market component before taking further action on elements such as the creation of a single currency.

15. Dookeran, Winston. 2013. 'A new frontier for Caribbean convergence.' *Caribbean Journal of International. Relations & Diplomacy*. Vol. 1, No. 2, June 2013: pp. 5-20.

16. Persad-Bissessar, Kamla, 2015. Opening remarks by Kamla Persad-Bissessar, Prime Minister of the Republic of Trinidad and Tobago at the Forum on the Future of the Caribbean. Hyatt Regency Hotel, Port of Spain, May 6, 2015.

17. LaRocque, Irwin. 2015. Speech by Ambassador Irwin LaRocque, Secretary-General, Caribbean Community (CARICOM) at the Forum on the Future of the Caribbean, University of the West Indies, St. Augustine Campus, 6 May, 2015.

18. Bhattacharya, Abhijit, 2015. The innovation-driven economy and education system moving in different directions.' *Daily O O* http://www.dailyo.in/politics/india-schools-education-crisis-bihar-board-exam-cheating-hrd-ted-talks/story/1/3439.html accessed June 15, 2015.

19. Persad-Bissessar, Kamla, 2015. *op.cit.*

20. Beckles, Hilary, 2015. *op.cit.*

21. LaRocque, Irwin 2015. *op.cit.*

22. Bhattacharya, Abhijit, 2015. *op.cit.*

23. Beckles, Hilary 2015 *op cit.*

24. Karim, Fazal 2014. Speech by the Minister of Tertiary Education and Skills Training (MTEST) at a symposium on The Future of Learning through Technology at the Hilton Trinidad and Conference Centre on September 15, 2014. http://www.ttonline.org/minister-karim-increase-in-tertiary-education-enrollment/#accessed on June 25, 2015

25. Murray, Janet, 2015.'Learning languages is key to UK's success in the global economy.' *The Guardian* http://www.theguardian.com/education/0014/jun/19/learning-language-key-to-economic-success accessed June 24, 2015

26. KNEWS. 2014. Gonsalves notes CARICOM's progress at 25th Intersessional. *Kaieteur News*. March 11, 2014. http://www.kaieteurnewsonline.com/2014/03/11/gonsalves-notes-caricoms-progress-at-25th-intersessional/

27. Admin.2011 Incoming CARICOM chairman hails achievements in health sector. Guyana Times Internationalhttp://www.guyanatimesinternational.com/?p=8031. Accessed June 19, 2015

28. Clement, Paul. 2015. 'Implementation deficit: why member states do not comply with CARICOM directives.' Paper presented on day 1 at the Forum on the Caribbean, May 5, 2015.

29. Persad-Bissessar, Kamla, 2015. *op.cit.*

CHAPTER 9
The Private Sector

Miguel Carrillo, Sylvia Dohnert, Kayla Grant, and Carlos Elias

COMMON ISSUES

'Caribbean Convergence...represents a new way of thinking about integration in the region, and a potential strategy for injecting the process with new life and energy.... The convergence argument is that trade and markets should be buttressed by production, distribution and competitiveness'.[1]

The quest for expanding economic activity in the Caribbean requires opening space for private sector firms to grow. Growth, in this context, requires that firms strengthen their production processes and find efficient new practices, by investing in coordinating actions with other firms but also in new technologies that would allow them to be more productive. As productivity increases, firms would be able to compete across the region and move beyond the Caribbean to enter into new markets. This chapter argues that in some cases this process would need to be facilitated by public–private partnerships.

The process of Caribbean integration continues to evolve, and participants of the Forum on the Future of the Caribbean, voiced widespread demand for it to take on new meanings and a more proactive stance. Recognizing that the economic incentive framework for growth and development in the twenty-first century has significantly changed, Caribbean leaders are coordinating efforts for the definition of a new framework for cooperation. These efforts have been summarized under the broad umbrella of 'Caribbean convergence', which recognizes the imperative for integration going beyond trade to include production, distribution and competitiveness, increasing the choices and options for economies in the region to grow and develop. Private-sector initiatives play the central role in the convergence process, with the participation of the public sector as a partner.

URGENCY TO ACT NOW AND PRIORITIES

From a strategic perspective, this chapter notes the imperative to act now to expand the political and economic space for all firms: large, medium and small. As recent research indicates, the Caribbean is diverging from its global small economy peers with respect to competitiveness and long-run growth-related indicators, such as total factor productivity growth.[2] Given firms' central role in organizing production, a convergence model that provides the framework conditions for firms to become competitive and expand is more urgent than ever. In the current Caribbean context of stagnant growth and fiscal retrenchment, expanding the capacity of firms in the region to become competitive is the most expedient and sustainable path to resume growth.

This chapter describes the landscape of private-sector development in the Caribbean, the challenges and opportunities that it confronts, and a series of policy recommendations that could address these challenges and could be incorporated under a new Caribbean convergence model. This chapter also notes that the priorities that emerged from the Forum can be summarised as follows: (i) the need to open up to international markets as businesses in the region are not linked to global value chains; (ii) the need to address the limits related to smallness as it limits the evolution of economies of scale and economies of scope, with large regional corporations focusing on control rather than evolution; and (iii) the need to focus on value creation through innovation.

THE CHALLENGES FACING PRIVATE SECTOR DEVELOPMENT IN THE CARIBBEAN

The Caribbean has a sizeable private sector which accounts for about two-thirds of employment, four-fifths of consumption, four-fifths of total credit, and a potential to contribute to approximately two-thirds of investment. Given its size and contribution to tax revenue, employment, and the production of goods and services, this sector has the ability to drive economic growth. However, it faces a number of challenges.

First challenge: Size of the players

Not surprisingly, given the region's relatively small population and GDP sizes, Caribbean private sector firms are predominantly small. Some authors have even coined the term 'nano-firms' to describe the Caribbean situation of firm size relative to international players. Even large, multi-country firms in the region are medium-sized firms by international standards. Moreover, and despite the small market sizes, 82.5 % of firms are concentrated in selling to domestic markets, and the region has few global players.

Figure 9.1: Number of Firms by Employee Size (2014 firm level surveys)

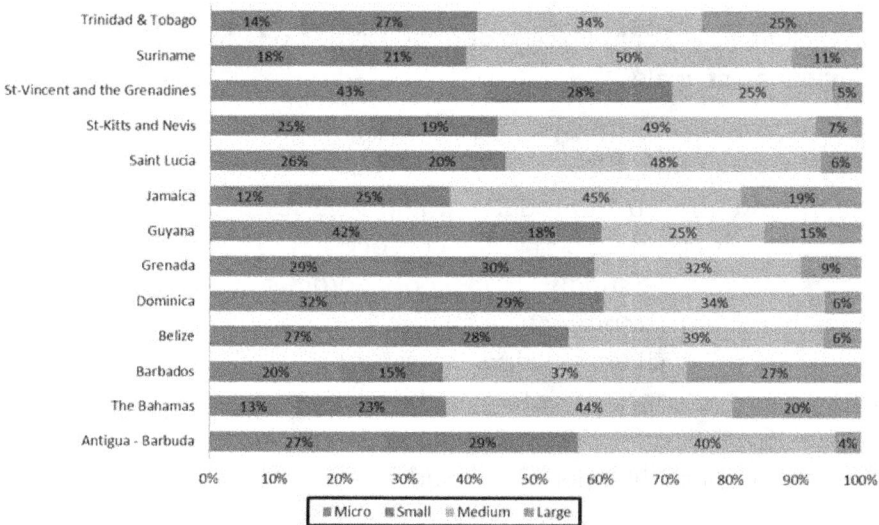

Source: 2014 Compete Caribbean funded firm level surveys.
Definitions for size: Micro (<10 employees), Small (10-19), Medium (20-99), Large (100+)

From a demographics-centered perspective, the problem of size is a 'chicken-and-egg' one. Relatively small markets give the region's firms insufficient fuel to grow from a demand-side perspective. In response to these demand-side conditions, large regional firms perceive diversification strategies as superior to specialization strategies, contrary to the global trend of successful firms and economies that focus on specializing. Moreover, perhaps influenced by their very small markets operations-base, Caribbean large firms' management is extremely risk averse compared to management in non-Caribbean countries. Profits are driven by market dominance strategies as a by-product of tariff and non-tariff barriers and a reduced number of relevant competitors, and firms have little sense of urgency in the quest for growth. These last two points in particular illustrate the difficult balance between stimulating economies of scale versus increasing competition that regulators in the region may be confronting.

The problems for small- and medium-sized companies in the region are also acute. Most of these companies have succeeded in establishing a foothold on a segment of domestic economies. However, their playing field is small, as their future expansion depends mostly on their capacity to export and/or their capacity to compete against larger firms or imported goods and services, in what are already small markets.

Second challenge: Scant linkages on the supply side to overcome diseconomies of scale

Once a Caribbean firm has penetrated foreign markets—thus overcoming the challenge of small domestic market size—it faces constraints on the supply-side linked to production and logistics. Difficult and costly transportation is compounded to the cost of coordinating small domestic suppliers all along the supply chain. Poor coordination and collaborative efforts among firms represent an obstacle to achieving economies of scale and scope, weakening value chains and increasing operating costs. Notably, there is a lack of synergies due to firms operating in different and unrelated industries. Most large firms, especially conglomerates, are SME aggregates usually operating independently and in silos missing the opportunity of synergies and strategic coordination. The resulting lack of competitiveness effects is particularly observed amongst the large established companies in the region, who have a limited appetite for venturing beyond the Caribbean, self-imposing constraints on penetrating larger markets in Central and South America.

Third challenge: Framework of conditions that increase production costs

Some large regional conglomerates and interlinked SMEs are either exporting or already replacing imports, which indicates that the region has private sector driven growth and export potential. However, to do so, they have to overcome a framework of conditions that makes their production costs higher than those of their competitors abroad, such as limited access to finance, lack of skills in the market, registration and regulatory issues, and in general, higher costs of doing business.

Research funded by Compete Caribbean[1] is particularly illuminative of the difficult business environment that firms in the region navigate. The table below summarizes the top four common challenges that firms face, as identified in Compete Caribbean funded firm level surveys.[2] In order of importance to the region, these were found to be: 1) an inadequately educated workforce, 2) the cost of finance, 3) access to finance, and 4) macroeconomic conditions. The relative importance of each constraint per individual country is summarized in the following figure:

Figure 9.2: Relative Constraints to Production

	Tax rates	Tax administration	Customs and Trade regulations	Labor regulations	Inadequately educated workforce	Business licensing and permits	Access to Finance (e.g. collateral)	Cost of Finance (e.g. interest rates)	Political environment	Macroeconomic environment (inflation, exchange rate, interest rate)	Corruption	Crime, theft and disorder	Practices of competitors
Region					1		3	2		4			
Barbados					2		1	3					
Belize					1						3	2	
Antigua and Barbuda	1				3				2				
Dominica							1	3		2			
Grenada			2					3				1	
Guyana	2							3			1	3	
Jamaica	1											3	2
St. Lucia				2	1			3		3			
St. Kitts & Nevis								2	3	1		3	
St. Vincent & the Grenadines								2	3	1			
Suriname					1			3			2		
The Bahamas		3			1		2						2
Trinidad and Tobago				3				2		1			

In addition, a Compete Caribbean collection of 2014 Private Sector Assessment Reports revealed that firms in different countries faced common difficulties in the areas of energy costs, logistics, and a weak inclination towards entrepreneurship and innovation. The four constraints highlighted by the survey as well as the common challenges identified by the PSARs will be explored further below

Inadequately skilled labour force: Firms across the region report difficulty in hiring workers with the skills demanded of their sector. Although countries in the region have an overall good reputation for education/training programmes to deliver professionals into the labour markets, investors surveyed in a 2011 CAIPA study on the region's investment climate have expressed dissatisfaction with recent graduates who are found to be trained in outdated technologies (particularly ICT) and have had to be re-trained on the job. Investors further complained about the number of technically skilled workers that can work in a high-tech environment (i.e., engineers, geologists, architects) vis-à-vis the number of professionals in occupations such as teaching, law or the health-related professions. Lastly, firms complain about a lack of workers with supervisory/management skills in all countries.[3]

In addition to these deficiencies, the Caribbean experiences a high 'brain drain' of its skilled labour force. The table below shows the high levels of the tertiary educated that has migrated to OECD countries and the estimated education expenditure as a percentage of GDP. A key finding is that education expenditure for these migrants is higher than the incoming remittances level as a percentage of GDP.[4] Given that a high level of both general and specialized skills are crucial to supporting productivity and competitiveness, policy makers in the Caribbean face the tough decision of how much to invest in education given the numbers of tertiary educated labourers who migrate abroad.

Figure 9.3: Migration, Estimated Education Expenditure, and Estimated Remittances as a % of GDP

	% of labour force that has migrated to OECD member country by education level		Emigration loss plus estimated education expenditure (% of GDP)	Remittances (% of GDP, average 1980-2012)
	Secondary	Tertiary		
The Bahamas	10	61	4.4	
Barbados	28	63	18.5	2.3
Guyana	43	89	9.5	1.9
Jamaica	35	85	20.4	7.4
Suriname	74	48	7.8	0.5
Trinidad and Tobago	22	79	16.8	0.3
OECS	50	75	10	7
C6	35	71	13	2
Average	43	73	11	4

Access to finance: In Caribbean policy discussions about private sector development, access to finance is often cited as a top constraint that firms face in the region. The data seem to back this assertion. From 2,000 firms surveyed in the region in 2014, 26 % cite that obtaining finance is a major or severe obstacle while 30% indicate it is a moderate obstacle. Moreover, firms' complaints about access to finance as an obstacle tend to be much higher in the Caribbean than those reported by firms surveyed in other small economies.[5] Further evidence of the difficulty of obtaining finance is provided by the fact that only 16.5 % of firms use banks as a source of investment funds. Moreover, Caribbean firms surveyed report collateral requirements as high as 180 % of the total loan value/line of credit in order to accede to funding (see figure). It is no wonder that many Caribbean firms surveyed reported financing their own investment through family members or friends who may often be located in the diaspora.

Figure 9.4: Approximate Value of Collateral Required (2014 firm level surveys)

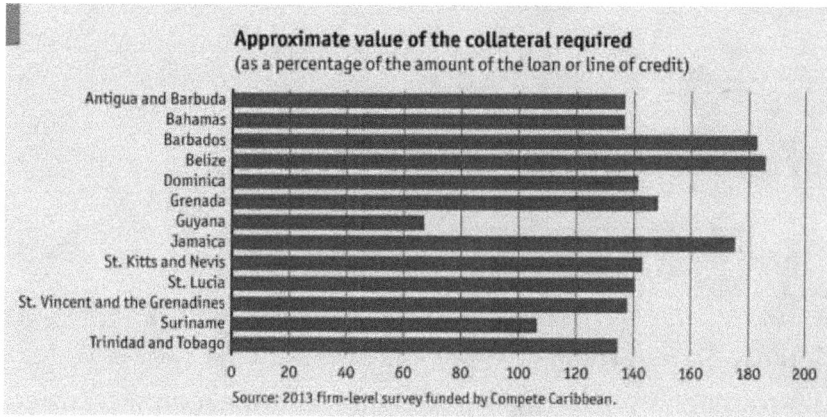

Approximate value of the collateral required
(as a percentage of the amount of the loan or line of credit)

Source: 2013 firm-level survey funded by Compete Caribbean.

Cost of finance: Intertwined with the issue of access to finance is the cost of finance as reflected by the interest rate. Although the terms and conditions attached to these rates differ by country, thus limiting their comparability,[6] average lending rates in the region are significantly higher than the US. Interest rate spreads, on average, are slightly lower than comparative small states but still higher than world averages.

Figure 9.5: Lending Interest Rate

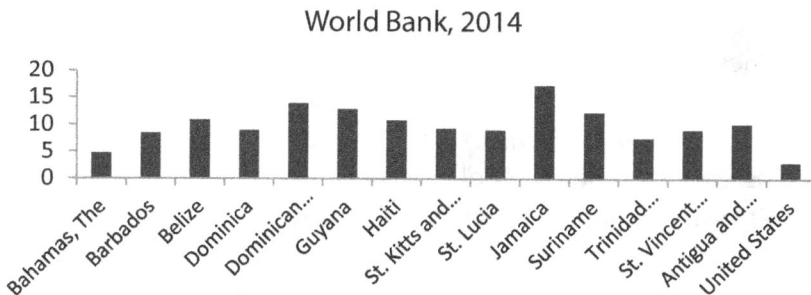

World Bank, 2014

Figure 9.6: Average Interest Rate Spreads

(In percent)

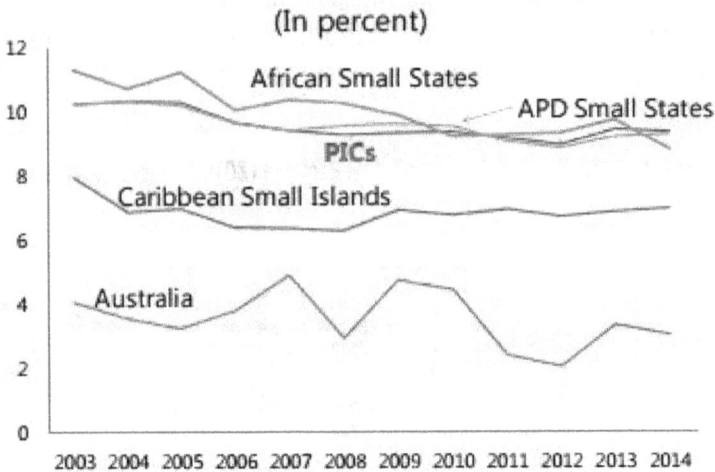

Source: IMF 2015

The interest rate essentially captures (i) the perceived risk of lending to a borrower and (ii) the costs of administering the loan. To tackle high interest rates then, financial policy reform needs to address improving lending institutions' understanding of SME consumers and introducing opportunities for reducing administrative costs. In the Caribbean, particularly as noted in a study on the OECS, high administrative/operating costs for services has been identified as an area requiring improvement.[7] Small market size, the concentration of banking institutions, macroeconomic uncertainty, and institutional quality (such as contract enforcement, collateral systems, and credit history) may also be contributing factors.[8] Investments in digital technology can reduce administrative cost and can assist in expanding market size through the introduction of new online products and services tailored to meet consumer needs. Addressing lending agencies' understanding of perceived risk amongst SME consumers can be accomplished through generic training sessions aimed at sensitizing banks to these types of consumers. Introducing countrywide data collection systems (such as credit history) can aid banks in developing more sophisticated data analytics techniques for assessing risk and for increasing their understanding of start-ups and SMEs.

Macroeconomic conditions: For the past three decades, the Caribbean region's GDP growth has slowly declined from an average of 3.9% per annum in the 1980s to 1.7 % per annum in the first six years of the twenty-first century.[9] The recent global economic and financial crisis magnified this phenomenon, with growth averaging –0.84 per cent between 2009 and 2013 in nine of the Caribbean tourism dependent economies plus Trinidad[10]. Public debt also increased following the global crisis, and by 2012, nine Caribbean countries had debt-to-GDP ratios above 60%.[11]

Figure 9.7: Public Debt, 2014

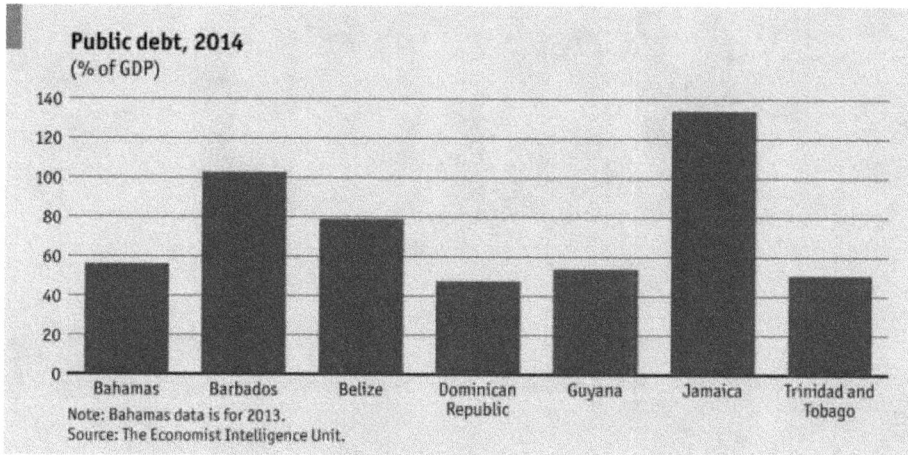

Public debt, 2014
(% of GDP)

Note: Bahamas data is for 2013.
Source: The Economist Intelligence Unit.

In Barbados, public debt as a proportion of GDP has continued to increase since 2012, from 84% in that year to 103% in 2014. In Jamaica this measure has remained above 130% since 2009. Guyana's ratio has dropped from a recent high of 65% in 2010 to 54% in 2014.[12] Constrained by this debt overhang and competitiveness in attracting FDI, the region's average level of investment as a percentage of GDP has been in decline since 2012 compared to increases in average performance by the rest of the world.[13] The resulting context of fiscal retrenchment underscores the importance of export-oriented private sector development as an engine of growth for the region.

Energy costs: High energy costs constitute major challenges to private-sector operations in the Caribbean[14]. Retail electricity prices in the Caribbean (as seen in the next figure) averaged 33 US cents/kWh in 2012 compared to 12 US cents/kWh in the US (late 2014 figure)[15]—nearly triple! Another, less well-known aspect of energy that affects firms in the region is the reliability of electricity supply. With the exception of Trinidad and Tobago, demand for electricity in the region exceeds supply, and 'black outs' are common.[16] Data from the 2014 Compete Caribbean firm level survey found that in Guyana, for example, nearly 35% of power is sourced from generators and in Barbados, that figure is around 30%.

Figure 9.8: Average Residential, Commercial and Industrial Tariffs per Utility (US$ per kWh)

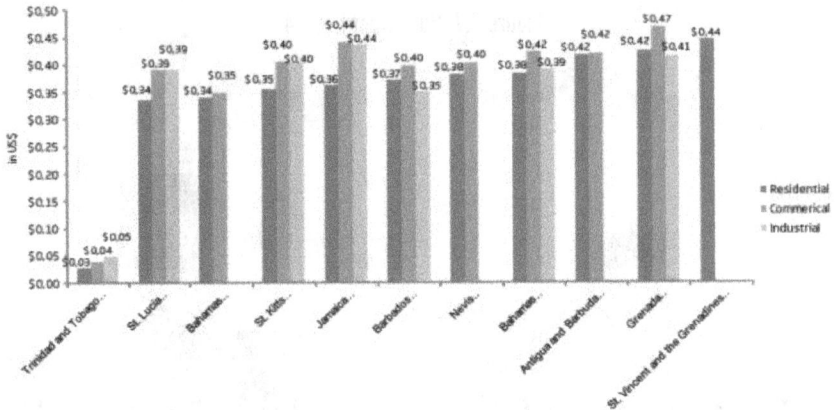

Source   Average tariffs were calculated by taking the average monthly bills calculated for the different customer types and dividing by the average month usage in the Caribbean by customer type for each utility

Fourth challenge: A nascent support system for the creation and growth of innovative firms. There is growing targeted support to create better skilled entrepreneurs who are able to develop productive, competitive businesses. The actors that typically provide this support include state-led organizations and universities who design entrepreneurial support programs that provide technical assistance (training in product development, market analysis, financial management, export strategies, etc.), financial assistance (i.e. seed capital/grants, loans, investment from investors), workforce development, knowledge transfer (i.e. mentorship programs), and promoting cultural acceptance and social safety nets towards those who take on entrepreneurial roles. The creation, variety and performance of such programs differ according to each country and further diverge in performance relative to the business and innovation ecosystems the firms operate in.

Lack of entrepreneurial framework conditions: The business environment is harsh on entrepreneurship ventures and institutions to support entrepreneurship, and SMEs are weak[1.7] Throughout the region, for example, the financial system penalizes business failure through harsh bankruptcy laws. The 2014 Global Entrepreneurship Monitor's (GEM) national executive survey (NES) specifically monitors the entrepreneurial framework conditions by surveying a minimum of thirty-six experts in each country. The NES revealed that the Caribbean (in this case, Barbados, Belize, Jamaica, Suriname and Trinidad and Tobago) on average, performs below total averages for all countries surveyed by GEM in the areas depicted in the below table. The extent to which it is perceived that public policies support entrepreneurship through government support and policies is lowest for Trinidad and Tobago (1.81). The presence and quality of government programmes that directly assist SMEs is similar across the Caribbean countries surveyed but falls below the total global average of 2.66. Basic school for entrepreneurial education and training, another key framework condition, is very low across the Caribbean countries surveyed. Assessing both the NES and GEM data reveals the types of entrepreneurial support needed to create a more dynamic entrepreneurial environment. The region has been responding through a focus on creating a more business friendly environment (i.e. through policy reforms) and through SME support centres, financial assistance, and entrepreneurship competitions but more can be done.

Figure 9.9: GEM 2014 National Executive Survey

Economy	The extent to which public policies support entrepreneurship - entrepreneurship as a relevant economic issue	The extent to which public policies support entrepreneurship - taxes or regulations are either size-neutral or encourage new and SMEs	The presence and quality of programs directly assisting SMEs at all levels of government (national, regional, municipal)	The extent to which training in creating or managing SMEs is incorporated within the education and training system at primary and secondary levels
	Governmental support and policies	Taxes and bureaucracy	Governmental programs	Basic-school Entrepreneurial Education and training
BARBADOS	2.42	1.87	2.3	1.71
BELIZE	2.55	2.2	2.45	2.05
JAMAICA	2.2	1.99	2.34	2.07
SURINAME	2.69	2.36	2.42	2.11
TRINIDAD&T	1.81	2.38	2.34	1.83
Caribbean Average	2.33	2.16	2.37	1.95
Total AVERAGE:	2.61	2.45	2.66	2.08

*On a scale of 1–5, with 5 being the most positive as rated by surveyed persons.

Weak support structure for innovative firms: The region is known for its comparative advantage in the production of creative content that holds the potential to fuel a culture of innovation. Despite the prior, the region has failed to link its creative ingenuity to sustainable, profitable business ventures. In part, a risk-averse culture affects the level of innovation but also the innovation system in the region is weak. Innovation systems should encourage commercial linkages between knowledge generators/ research and development institutions (such as universities) and firms or funding agents. Encouraging this type of innovation can take place through state investment in innovation which can include establishing innovation funds, accelerators, aid for innovation, and technological extension programs. The bar chart below depicts the level of innovation undertaken by firms surveyed.

Figure 9.10: Innovative Firms (2014 firm level surveys)

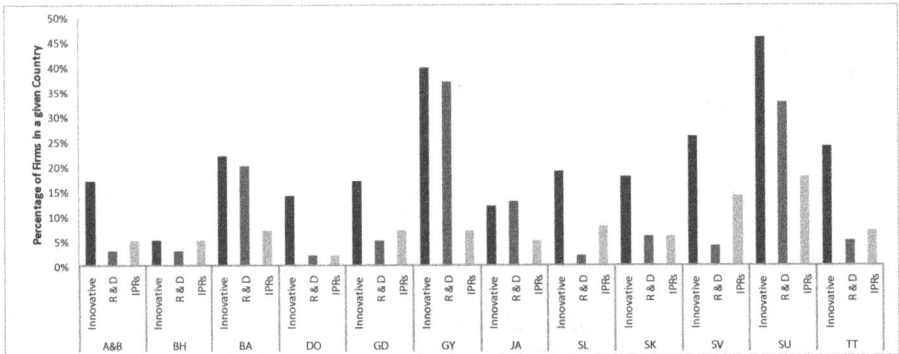

EMERGING SECTORS/OPPORTUNITIES FOR GROWTH

Despite these factors affecting competitiveness, a recently completed collection of private sector assessment reports (PSARs) for the CARICOM economies shows that there are certain industries throughout the region that are emerging and/or that offer new possibilities for growth. Most island states are seeking to increase the competitiveness of their product offering. Moreover, all of them are seeking to diversify into other high-growth sectors that can offset some of their economic vulnerability. This section highlights examples of sectors with potential for growth in these economies as determined by analyses in the private sector assessment reports.

Food processing and agri-business

Many of the once plantation-based economies have shifted to higher value-added agricultural products by focusing on food processing and agri-business. The main export markets have been to locations where Caribbean diaspora presence is strong and demand for homemade products is high. Several diasporic entrepreneurs are in fact involved in agri-business/food processing concentrated in Caribbean food (i.e.

Jamaica patties) or spices.[18] Dominica, St. Vincent and the Grenadines have defined a unique niche in the agro-processing of organic products. The organic industry is a fast-growing market. One estimate by the *Organic Monitor* puts the 2013 global market for organics at US$72 billion. The consumer demand for organic products in the United States, for example, has grown by 11.5% and is the world's largest organic market followed by Germany and then France.[19] Market access is a major challenge for many producers who have to invest heavily to ensure their facilities and products meet the quality and standards determined by the market they wish to enter. It is here that business support organizations often provide assistance to firms in understanding the intellectual property and certification processes including basic marketing and bookkeeping training. Furthermore, government and political support is necessary to ensure environmental standards for the organic market.

Ecotourism

The industry definition for ecotourism varies and with it, the estimated size and demand of the industry.[20] The UNWTO in 2004 estimated demand was growing at three times that of the tourism industry. The Tourism Network put the annual growth rate at 5% in 2005. Nevertheless, countries such as Grenada, St. Kitts and Nevis, Guyana and Dominica have been promoting ecotourism and are encouraged to focus on upgrading to higher value added services in the value chain. With ICT, there are greater marketing opportunities to reach emerging markets (i.e. in Asia), product development to grow current key markets, and multi-destination travel amongst CARIFORUM countries. Natural challenges to growth are airlift capacity, logistical infrastructure, and limited financial access for SMEs in the industry.

Cultural/creative and sports industries

The creative industries have received high levels of attention in many countries such as Jamaica, St. Lucia, and Trinidad and Tobago. The region can capture a larger share of the world's $18.7 trillion dollar cultural products market of which CARICOM, in 2014, was estimated to export only $25.4 million – a slight decrease from 2013 export levels.[21] Items high on the regional export list were perfumes, soaps, jewellery and printed material. The market for exports of cultural services is hard to determine but also holds vast potential. The region is exploring film and animation, music, sports and fashion industries as areas to support creative content producers in accessing new markets.

Business services such as business process outsourcing and financial services

These two areas continue to present opportunities for further growth and increased employment opportunities, especially for youth, in the countries that have focused in these areas. Countries such as Trinidad and Tobago, Jamaica and Belize have been taking advantage of providing BPO services mainly to the United States as the main target market. The United States is the largest player in a global BPO market projected to reach US$220 billion by 2020.[22] Though technological advances such as cloud computing and mobile applications have reversed a trend of insourcing, costs continue to be a competitive factor in offshoring destination choice.[23]

Barbados and the Bahamas have strongly focused on financial services. The offshore financial sector in the Bahamas is very large, with total offshore bank assets equivalent to 75 times GDP (at end of 2011).[24] To stimulate growth, countries can introduce new products and consider double taxation agreements with attractive markets. In Barbados, the financial services sector is the main contributor to corporate tax and foreign exchange.

Mining

Mining continues to be a main economic resource for Trinidad and Tobago, Suriname, Guyana and to a certain extent Jamaica but may also pose potential growth opportunities for the Bahamas (mining of aragonite and salt which was the fastest growing sector between 2000 – 2011).[25] A main challenge for the industry is incentivizing the use of clean technology to replace environmentally unfriendly and obsolete technology.

Opportunity for Growth – ICT-based and other Technology

ICT-based technology is a growing sector that is applicable to improving the functioning of a wide array of sectors such as film and broadcasting, provision of educational and other social services and tourism marketing. Key to ensuring its growth is broadband connectivity. New, disruptive technologies built and patented in the Caribbean also provide one unforeseen but very large potential for growth in the region. Creating the right environment and programmes that support horizontal and innovative technological solutions, could lead to stimulating the right conditions for the Caribbean to produce disruptive technologies that lead the region to discovering and exploiting a new export avenue.

HOW THEN TO BRIDGE THE CHALLENGES IN ORDER TO FULFIL THE OPPORTUNITIES OF THE EMERGING GROWTH SECTORS?

Recommendations

Forum participants provided the following recommendations to facilitate the expansion of private sector activities in the region. The implementation of these recommendations falls within the responsibility of institutions that represent the private sector, government and, more generally, stakeholders. However, given its potential for enhancing overall economic growth, this chapter recommends the formation of a committee that would develop each recommendation and adapt it to the special circumstances of each country. Such a committee would have to be represented by regional leaders, and the Arthur Lok Jack Graduate School of Business will take the lead in the creation of such a committee and in developing the reform agenda according to the following recommendations.

Establishing a regional public–private partnership (PPP) policy framework

The gap between the needs for infrastructure investment in the Caribbean and the capacity of governments to invest is wide. Many countries in Latin America find themselves in the same situation, and many have found that filling in infrastructure gaps may be facilitated by the inclusion of private companies as partners. Roads, transportation, airports, ports, energy, water, sewage treatment and irrigation are among many sectors in which a healthy partnership between private sector firms and governments have resulted in win-win solutions to the problem of funding infrastructure. The Caribbean can benefit from public–private partnerships if the 'rules of the game' are properly defined. Because of the size of the economies in the region, such rules of the game would be more powerful if they apply to the Caribbean and not just individual countries. The Bahamas, Barbados and, to a less extent, Trinidad and Tobago have been active in generating PPPs. The experiences of these countries, added to the experiences in other Latin American countries, would be used to design a regional Caribbean PPP policy framework which would facilitate regional investments designed to close infrastructure gaps that currently limit growth and development.

Building trust/transparency between the public and private sectors and inserting small and medium enterprises (SMEs) into PPP.

The development of PPPs in the region is just beginning, and participants in the Forum noted that in part because of the relative youth of these deals but also resulting from friction in the deals between the public and private sectors, there is a perception of mistrust and lack of transparency. The outcome of the current situation is that the marketplace for investors and projects, the place where demand and supply meet, is underdeveloped. The market for these investment opportunities would be enhanced if a regional inventory of projects is identified, noting that this initiative should be complemented by the previous proposal to establish a regional PPP policy framework. Importantly, the inclusion of SMEs into the larger PPP deals would promote transparency and enhance these deals. CARICOM in partnership with UWI's three business schools and multilateral partners may play a role in setting up this market.

Promoting Foreign Direct Diaspora Investments (FDDI)

The large number of Caribbean nationals living outside the Region offers a unique opportunity for the promotion of investments in the region. The previous two initiatives, to establish a regional PPP policy framework and to build trust and transparency, are consistent with building mechanisms that would allow Caribbean nationals living abroad to invest in projects in the region. This is an effort that has been frequently discussed, but few concrete actions have been taken to materialize it. The creation of a Foreign Direct Diasporic Investment (FDDI) council empowered to coordinate efforts from the ACS, CARICOM and Ministries of Trade and Chambers of Commerce in the region would be the first step to the definition of an incentive framework that would provide confidence to investors to bring their resources to the Caribbean.

Creation of a Regional Youth Entrepreneurship Programme

Such as in other parts of the world, most noticeably in Europe, the Caribbean unfortunately shows high levels of youth unemployment. In some cases, this fact leads to high levels of crime and brain drain. This initiative will be designed to channel the energy and creativity of Caribbean youth into productive activities. The private sector's corporate social responsibility funds could be directed towards specific activities that can result in the creation of job or business opportunities for the youth. In addition, Forum participants suggested a Regional Forum for Youth Development driven by the Prime Ministers of the region. Such an effort should be designed to identify concrete regional proposals to be implemented in the near term.

Creation of a regional policy that facilitates the expansion of firms in the Caribbean and beyond

Poor harmonisation of tax regimes, labour regulations, fiscal incentives among more become barriers for the expansion of Caribbean firms into new markets. For this reason, many firms find it difficult to continue growing beyond their domestic markets, limiting growth potential and wealth generation. Forum participants suggested the creation of a task force including government and private sector representatives to design a regional policy to facilitate the expansion of firms into new markets—in the Caribbean and abroad.

Promoting privatisation of public enterprises

Governments in the region own too many firms that could be privatised. In most cases, these companies were created at a time when markets did not offer opportunities for private sector investments, or the private sector was too small to take on needed investments. Over time conditions have changed, and governments now have the opportunity to improve economic efficiency by selling some of these companies to the private sector. These opportunities for divestment can have significant impact: they may increase fiscal resources to be directed to needed projects; they may offer investment opportunities to the general public through public offerings; and finally they may also offer diversification opportunities to established economic groups in the region. This initiative, as noted in the Forum, is fully consistent with the recommendation for PPP opportunities in the region. During the Forum, participants recommended the creation of a task force including private and public sector representatives to establish the rules for the selection of prime candidates for privatisation, and the modality of these efforts, noting the importance to include labour representatives.

Producing a regional cluster development strategy

This initiative is consistent with the concept of Caribbean convergence as presented in this publication, and it recognises the weak value chain links in sectors in the region. In particular, Forum participants noted the need to focus on at least two sectors—agriculture and energy—and on improving logistics throughout the economic space. The realisation of this effort requires the definition of a strategy that would guide private and public sector representatives in facilitating policies designed to strengthen regional clusters.

Using PPPs to develop niche markets and promote entrepreneurship

This initiative was presented by Forum participants in the context of using PPPs as a tool to promote entrepreneurship and also to develop niche markets. This is not easy to do, but the opportunity for the public and private sectors in sharing risk was, according to Forum participants, worth taking. Such an effort requires clear rules of engagement so that agent principal problems do not arise. Forum participants suggested the preparation of such an initiative led by the Arthur Lok Jack Graduate School of Business.

Creating a more sophisticated demand/market driven market for innovation

The last recommendation presented by Forum participants included an effort to promote innovation in the region. This is a critical factor to reignite growth in the region, especially in those economies that are lagging. The Forum participants suggested that the Competitiveness Councils in the region take the lead on this effort.

APPENDIX

Appendix 1 – Key Challenges of the Private Sector

The key challenges were derived from country specific PSARs which utilized information gathered from (i) interviews conducted by the consultants who authored the PSARs, (ii) results from Caribbean Growth Forums and (iii) 2010 enterprise surveys.

Country	Key Challenges Identified
Antigua and Barbuda	Lack of effective representation of the private sector; access to finance; corporate taxation; general political and governance issues; customs and trade regulations; infrastructure: high electricity costs and limited intraregional transport options; technology and innovation; labour skills; gender and the environment
Barbados	Access to finance; business environment; research and development and innovation; labour regulation; infrastructure, communications and energy; gender and the environment
Bahamas	Labour force skills; access to finance; infrastructure and energy; customs and tariff rates; innovation and information and communications technology; Environment and gender
Belize	Access to finance; corporate taxation; technology and innovation; trade policies; infrastructure; education and training; competitiveness; Gaps in Information
Dominica	Governance/lack of strategy for private-sector development; access to finance; cost of electricity; transportation and trade; corporate taxation; labour market and gender; environment
Grenada	General political and governance issues; access to finance; cost of doing business; labour market; trade tariff levels; gender and the environment
Guyana	Structure of business supporting institutions; property rights; access to finance; corporate taxation; technology and innovation; cost, reliability and ease of access to electricity; educated labour force; gender and the environment
Haiti	Private-sector development coordination; basic services provision that enables the private sector to grow; access to markets; access to finance; property rights
Jamaica	Access to finance, corporate taxation, crime and corruption, key inputs such as electricity and infrastructure, and lack of innovation

St. Kitts and Nevis	General political and governance issues; access to finance; cost of electricity; labour market issues; trade issues; gender and the environment
St. Lucia	General political and governance issues; access to finance; taxes; adequately trained workforce; cost of electricity; transport; technology; gender and the environment
St. Vincent & the Grenadines	Access to finance; corporate taxation; key inputs and infrastructure; foreign direct investment; technology and innovation; labour regulations; gender and the environment
Suriname	Structure of institutions supportive to business; access to finance; business environment; technology and innovation; trade and FDI policies; labour regulation; gender and the environment
Trinidad & Tobago	Registering property; crime, theft and disorder; access to finance; an inadequately trained workforce; labour regulation; and poor physical infrastructure

Source: Private Sector Assessment Reports, Compete Caribbean 2015.

Appendix 2: Snapshot of the Caribbean Private Sector

The consortium of indicators in the annex captures the size and general characteristics of the region's private sector. Labour force surveys (and in some cases census surveys) reveal that the private sector employs the majority of the work force with the remaining 30% of employment being government employees (inclusive of state-owned enterprises) and those classified as other. Some studies[i] cite that SMEs in developing countries are responsible for roughly 90% of employment.

Indicator Size of the Private Sector	Caribbean Average
Employment by Private Sector	70.0%
% of Total Credit to Private Sector	83.3%
% of Total Consumption by Private Sector	82.2%
Private Sector Participation in Infrastructure Investment from 2006-2013 ($ millions)	$390.182
Characteristics of the Private Sector	
GDP Composition by Agriculture (%)	8.08%
GDP Composition by Industry (%)	20.15%
GDP Composition by Services (%)	71.78%
Age of Establishments (years)*	19.2
Average Proportion of Investments Financed by Banks (%)*	22.6%

Sources: 2010 Enterprise Surveys (World Bank and Compete Caribbean); 2 Number of countries with data: 11. Source: World Bank 2015.

i.   ECLAC. 2009. 'SME Competitiveness in the Caribbean: Challenges and Opportunities'.

Appendix 3: Summarized Recommendations from the Forum

Action	Proposed By	Rationale and Context	Suggested Action Champions
To establish a legal and policy framework for PPP development	Albert Ramdin	There is not a regional approach to establish productive/ investment linkages between private and public sector.	Bahamas and Barbados have been very active in generating effective PPP. We suggest these countries to take the lead.
Built Trust/ Transparency between the public and private sector while inserting SME into PPP	Albert Ramdin and Ian Chinapoo	There is not a marketplace for investors and projects in the context of PPPs.	CARICOM in partnership with the UWI 3 business Schools, CAF and IADB.
Promote Foreign Direct Diaspora Investment (FDDI)	Didicus Jules	There has been a sharp decline in FDI in the region.	Create a council of FDDI coordinated by either ACS, CARICOM, and representatives of Ministries of Trade, and Chambers of Commerce.
Youth Entrepreneurship Program	Didicus Jules	Channel the youth energy into productive activities rather than criminal activity.	Combine private sector CSR initiatives with World Bank and IADB with the International Youth Foundation and the UN inter-agency network of youth development.
Alignment of businesses international trajectories with policies and fiscal incentives	David Dulal-Whiteway	Private sector leads the way in identifying the need for understanding and harmonizing policies to support the internationalization of firms.	Create a task force of officials in Ministries of Finance and Trade along with CEOs of large regional Caribbean corporations.

Promote Privatization and Semi-Privatization Initiatives	Albert Ramdin	A critical PPP must include a privatization and semi-privatization strategies.	Create a task force of officials in Ministries of Finance and Trade along with CEOs of large regional Caribbean corporations. It is critical to include in this task force the union movement.
Regional Cluster Development Strategy	Richard Lewis	It is critical to align efforts at a regional level and jointly develop 3 clusters: Agriculture, Energy and Logistics.	Energy Cluster: TT Energy Chamber.
Logistics Cluster: Port authorities, airport authorities, Ministers of Planning and Major distribution firms.			
Use PPP to develop niche markets and promote entrepreneurship	Didicus Jules	This is a critical measure to promote inclusive development.	Combine private sector CSR initiatives with World Bank and IADB with the International Youth Foundation and the UN inter-agency network of youth development. Link all these potential donor with local public sector institutions.
Develop a regional comprehensive youth development agenda	All	This action was demanded by participants and proposed by 3 panellists.	This shall be driven al the Prime Minister Level. We propose a regional forum for Youth Development driven by CARICOM PMs.
Create a more sophisticated demand/user-driven market for innovation	Richard Lewis	Demand/Market driven innovation is a critical factor to re-ignite growth in the region.	Competitiveness Councils in the Region.

NOTES

1. Dookeran, Winston. 'A new frontier for Caribbean convergence'. *Caribbean Journal of International Relations & Diplomacy.* Vol. 1, No. 2, June 2013: pp. 5–20.
2. Ruprah,Inder; Melgarejo Karl Alexander and Sierra Ricardo ,2014. 'Is there a Caribbean sclerosis?Stagnating growth in the Caribbean'. IDB. The authors find that since the 1990s, the Caribbean economies' relative total factor productivity growth has diminished with respect to similar small country peers. Total factor productivity includes the growth-enhancing effects of technological innovations, externalities, and the adoption of lower cost production techniques. Much of the cross-country literature on economic growth suggests that the bulk of long-run economic growth is driven by productivity (i.e. Easterly & Levine 2001).
3. Based on author's calculations using most recent data available.
4. Lack of data makes estimations of the Caribbean private sector's capital investment difficult. A rough estimate based on available investment data finds that approximately two-thirds of total investment is from the private sector.
5. SMEs in the Caribbean employ 4 to 50 employees with assets ranging from US$40,000 to $800,000 and sales not exceeding US$1.6 million. ECLAC (2009) presentation on SME Competitiveness in the Caribbean: Challenges and Opportunities. Countries include Trinidad and Tobago, Suriname, St. Lucia and Jamaica.
6. Bernal, Richard. 'Nano-Firms, Regional Integration, and International Competitiveness: The Experience and Dilemma of the CSME. In Benn, Denis and Hall,Kenneth eds. *Production Integration in CARICOM: From Theory to Action.* Kingston: Ian Randle Publishers, 2006.
7. Ruprah, Melgarejo and Sierra (2014). op. cit. See also : Misra, Prachi 2006.'Emigration and brain drain: evidence from the Caribbean'. IMF Working Paper WP/06/25.
8. See 2014 Private Sector Assessment Reports for CARICOM countries and PROTEQin firm-level survey on www.competecaribbean.org, and World Bank 2011 Enterprise Surveys.
9. The 2014 PROTEQin firm level surveys commissioned by Compete Caribbean utilize the World Bank's Enterprise Survey methodology, and covered a representative sample of 2000 firms in 13 countries.
10. Ticon Holdings Inc. & Ideas to Business Limited (2011), Investment Climate Study prepared for CAIPA and CEDA
11. This does not factor other contributions the diaspora make to the local economy.
12. Ruprah, Melgarejo and Sierra (2014) op. cit. compare access to finance difficulties for Caribbean firms and Rest of Small Economies firms in 2010, using consistent Enterprise Surveys for both sets of countries.
13. World Bank. 'Defining Lending Interest Rate'.
14. Randall, Ruby. 'Interest Rate Spreads in the Eastern Caribbean.' IMF. 1998.

15. See IMF working paper on 'What drives interest rate spreads in Pacific Island Countries?' by Fazurin Jamaludin, Vladimir Klyuev, and Anuk Serechetapongse (2015)

16. UNICEF. 2005. 'A Time to Choose: Caribbean Development in the 21st Century.' In this study, the included countries are The Bahamas, Belize, Barbados, Dominican Republic, Guyana, Haiti, Jamaica, Suriname, Trinidad and Tobago, and the OECS group--Antigua and Barbuda, Dominica, Grenada, St. Kitts and Nevis, St. Lucia,and St. Vincent and the Grenadines.

17. The average GDP growth for the CARIFORUM region as a whole between those years was 0.57%, but this was strongly influenced by the growth of the commodity exporters (BL, GY, SU), plus DR and Haiti (average 3.38% GDP/year growth for these 5 countries between 2009 and 2013).

18. Estimates for the Caribbean indicate that when the debt-to-GDP ratio is above 56 percent, there is a negative marginal and average effect of debt on growth. Ruprah and Sierra (2014). op.cit.

19. EIU. 2015. PSAR Overview Report.

20. IMF. 2015. Investment as a % of GDP: 1980 – 2020.

21. EIU. 2015. PSAR Overview Report.

22. Ibid.

23. Ticon Holdings Inc. & Ideas to Business Limited (2011), Investment Climate Study prepared for CAIPA and CEDA

24. Tennant, David. Jamaica PSAR. 2014.

25. Nurse, K., and Claremont. 2014. Caribbean Diasporic Entrepreneurship. Compete Caribbean

CHAPTER 10
Building the Resilience of Small States: A Strategic Vision for the Caribbean 2050

COMSEC

Editor's note: This chapter presents the unedited synthesis of the forthcoming COMSEC publication 'Building the Resilience of Small States: A Strategic Vision for the Caribbean 2050'. During the Forum COMSEC presented preliminary results and received comments and suggestions. COMSEC agreed to allow the publication of the synthesis, which is presented in its entirety in this chapter.

THE COMMONWEALTH[1]

Overview

The Caribbean region faces numerous economic, social and environmental challenges. The economies have been caught in a low-growth trajectory and falling total factor productivity, accompanied by high-debt ratios. Since 2000, while real per capita growth rates in developing countries averaged around 4% per annum, the comparable figure for the Caribbean Common Market and Community (CARICOM) was just around 2%. While the small size of the private sector, the lumpiness of government investment and unfavourable external circumstances have contributed significantly to the poor performance of regional economies, weather-related shocks have also served to derail their development efforts. With the anticipated intensification of adverse weather events resulting from climate change and Caribbean countries' limited resources and capacity to respond, the road ahead for the region is expected to be even more challenging.

The region will also continue to face economic shocks arising from their dependence on fuel and food imports. Building resilience will help to buffer the region against over-dependence on imported foods and fuel. Oil price shocks (high prices) have historically derailed economic growth prospects and provide an incentive for alternative energy. Indeed another strong incentive for developing alternative energy sources is the pending threat of climate change, and the growing imperative to mitigate its impact by reducing CO_2 emissions. The development of clean alternative energy is paramount. Climate Change also poses an existential threat to the small island economies of the Caribbean. Their geographical location and natural beauty that make it attractive to tourists also present challenges related to hurricanes and storms.

Climate Change is projected to bring an intensity of climatic and environmental occurrences. In recent times, the world has experienced an intensification of extreme weather patterns—namely extreme droughts and severe flooding, tsunamis, earthquakes and cyclones—which have led to the loss of lives, property, crops and environmental resources. Moreover, it is also recognised that Caribbean countries individually lack the capacity and financial resources needed for contingency planning and dealing with the challenges of climate change. Resources are needed to build capacities to adapt and capitalise on emerging technologies aimed around clean energy. The threat here is significant with the countries that have contributed the least may be required to bear disproportionate share of the burden of climate change.

These countries are also confronted with socio-economic issues in the form of high unemployment and underemployment, especially among the youth. Youth unemployment and underemployment result from a complex set of circumstances, such as the absence of economic opportunities, a mismatch between skills and available employment openings and inadequate educational exposure. Regardless of the reason, the impact is evident-inadequate human and social capital development and high rising crime (World Bank and UNODC 2007; UNDP 2012; Clarke and Popo 2014) constitutes one of the more intractable issues confronting the region. It threatens citizen security and imposes heavy costs on the economies and society. Another social trend, aging population structure, is predicted to escalate through to 2050, resulting in high dependency ratios that are likely to threaten the solvency of pension schemes and other forms of social security.

The region must also come to grips with a number of global trends, some of which may offer economic opportunities, while others may test resilience. Technological advances will accelerate the cross-border flow of goods and services that are increasingly knowledge intensive.

Communication technologies are expected to facilitate the 'on demand' economy, app-based and cloud-based solutions link the supply of and demand for services with the touch of a button.

While we cannot say with certainty what new technologies will be operational in 2050, we are fairly certain that the future will be one that is integrally linked with technology. Caribbean economies must, out of necessity, be strategically positioned to participate in and benefit from the opportunities. Strategic positioning calls for honing the skills and competencies required for meaningful participation in the knowledge economy. A number of studies have identified these requirements as intra-personal, inter-personal and technological or ICT, in addition to the core of educational subjects. Critical thinking, problem solving, creativity and entrepreneurial skills, together with an ability to work in teams, are identified as requirements for all cadres—middle management, professional and senior management.

MOTIVATIONS

A review of regional issues and global trends, along with the expressed aspirations of national and regional stakeholders, reveals a long list of critical issues. These include, but are not limited to:

- development of human resources for optimal engagement with the knowledge economy;
- considering the aging population and its implications from social and economic perspectives;
- fuller integration of youth into productive and rewarding pursuits;
- engineering a shift in the economies to encourage greater participation by the private sector;
- mainstreaming the environment, particularly mitigation and adaptation in the development process;
- dealing with oil price volatility and energy security; and
- addressing the issue of high and rising crime and citizen security.

Failure to address these issues will undoubtedly hamper the ability of the region to capitalise on the wave of opportunities emerging globally and achieve its growth and development goals. Indeed, on the current policy path, it is expected that the region is likely to regress to lower levels of development. Motivated by the need to urgently arrest these developments and safeguard the future of this region and transform it, the Commonwealth Secretariat has undertaken this research.

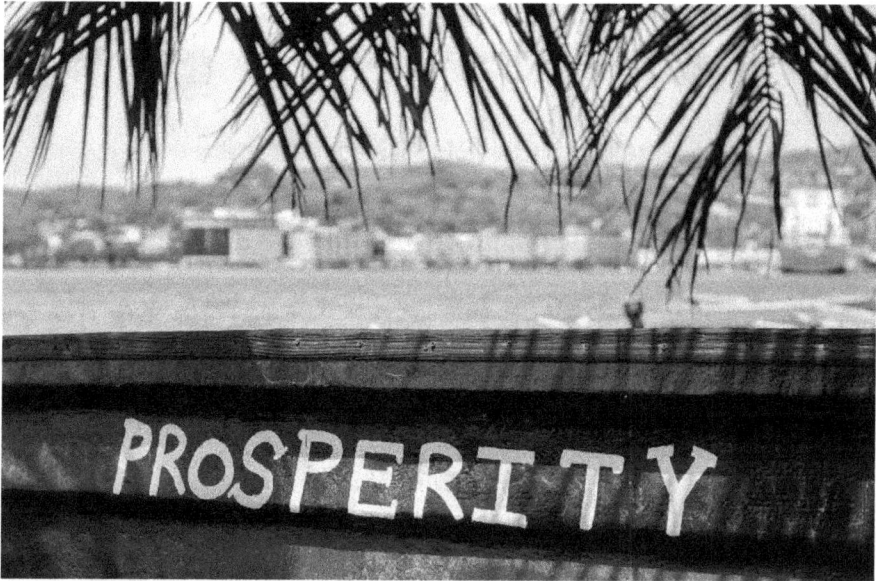

The analysis begins with an investigation of where the current policy path will lead, using a model to simulate the potential future impacts of emerging trends, likely shocks and current policy initiatives over the medium-term (35 years, 2050). The modelling framework is a tool for examining the impact of the social, economic and environmental problems facing the Caribbean and exploring alternative development pathways for the region.

Using a sample of Caribbean countries, it was found that the current development path would lead to higher and even more unsustainable debt burdens. Five out of the six countries under study would have a debt-to-gross domestic product (GDP) ratio above 100 %, while for two countries this could exceed 200% (see figure 10.1).

These projections suggest that interest expenditure on the debt will likely become a major drain on public finances in the future, reducing the funds available for development. When combined with the slowdown in growth expected over the medium term due to declining competitiveness, it is likely that most Caribbean countries would face worsening socioeconomic conditions.

Under this 'business as usual' scenario, crime and disorder is forecast to rise in the region. Figure 10.2 shows that in Jamaica, as well as Trinidad and Tobago, the rate of homicides per 100,000 is projected to rise to alarming levels. This trend, however, is not limited to these countries.

By 2050, the smaller states of the Eastern Caribbean are also projected to have rates of homicide similar to those currently being reported in Jamaica.

Figure 10.1: Projected debt-to-GDP ratio under baseline

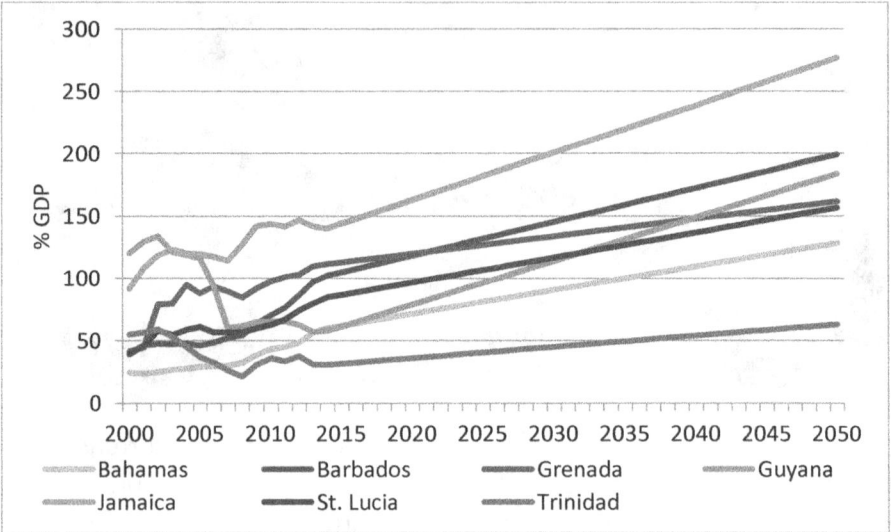

Source: *Authors' projections*

Figure 10.2: Homicide rate per 100,000 under the baseline

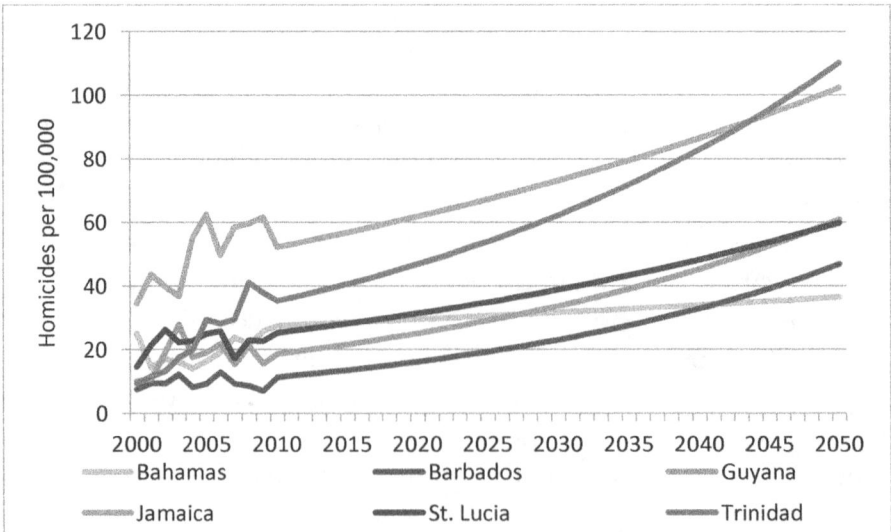

Source: *Authors' projections*

Not surprisingly, as shown in Figure 10.3, based on the socioeconomic projections highlighted above, the resilience of most Caribbean countries is likely to fall over the period under analysis. Figure 10.3 provides the baseline projections for the resilience index put forward by Briguglio et al. (2008) and is based on the indices of macroeconomic stability, microeconomic efficiency, governance and social development.

Figure 10.3: Resilience index under baseline

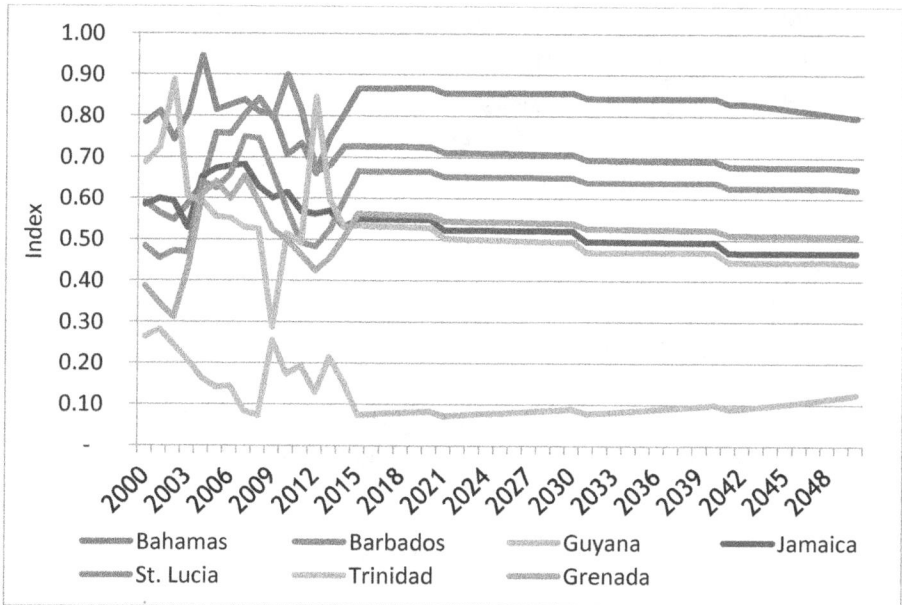

Source: *Authors' projections*

Most countries in the region are expected to experience a reduction in the resilience index, particularly Jamaica, due to rising debt, deteriorating socioeconomic conditions with the added implication of increasing their susceptibility to external shocks, lengthening their recovery period.

THE CARIBBEAN WE WANT

Clearly this is not the Caribbean we want, but what if anything can be done to arrest these developments and safeguard the future of the region? How can the region be truly transformed? The important question is transformed to what? What is the Caribbean we want? In our assessment both of the current situation and emerging trends, the Caribbean we want could include and be characterised by:

- creative and enterprising economies in which innovation is the driver of productivity;
- youth fully integrated into national development;
- a stable society where people are safe, secure and prosperous;
- environmental sustainability mainstreamed into the development process; and
- countries built on clean, resilient energy systems that make use of plentiful, local renewable resources, and are capable of providing stable supplies of energy to all sectors of their society.

Building on these possible visions for the region, this study articulates a strategy to circumvent the projected low levels of growth, high debt and low resilience in the region. The model considers a number of policy interventions aimed at building resilience including: increased productivity, export growth, increasing youth employment and fiscal reform. In the model, an assumed 2% per year increase in productivity has the greatest impact on resilience among the Caribbean countries considered. While these are clearly not new policy prescriptions, the value added in distilling the imperative for change, which we hope will catalyse a move from visioning and strategizing to implementation of a set of concrete actions.

Figure 10.4: Impact of policy to increase productivity by 2%

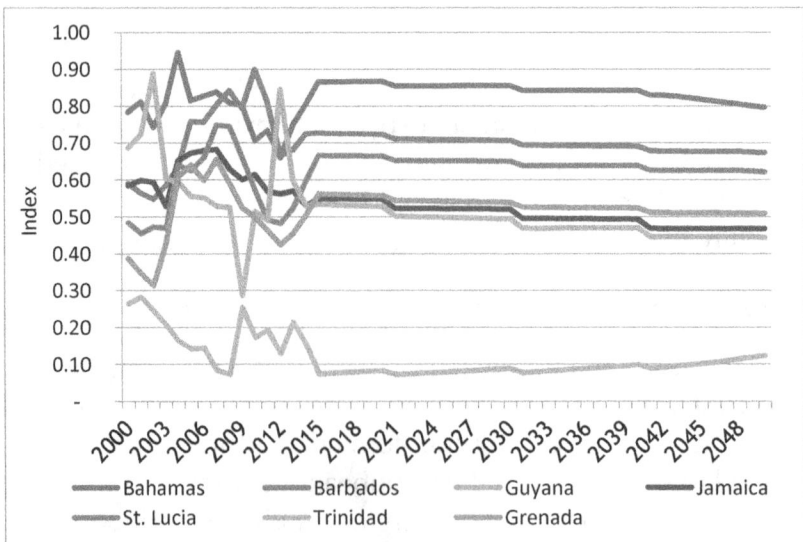

Source: *Authors' projections*

The transformative impact of implementing many already acknowledged actions-clearly outlined in pre-existing development strategies - is again illustrated using the modelling tool. It shows the Caribbean region with significantly improved development outcomes arising from longer term planning and focus on implementation. The key is not just the actions/policy prescriptions but the also the approach to development planning.

The growth in productivity would also have a positive impact on resilience in the region. By 2050, most of the countries in the sample would be on their way to building resilience (see figure 10.5). Most countries would exceed their peak resilience index score. The results are vastly different from a 'business as usual' scenario.

Figure 10.5: Resilience Index: Projected impact of policy to increase productivity by 2%

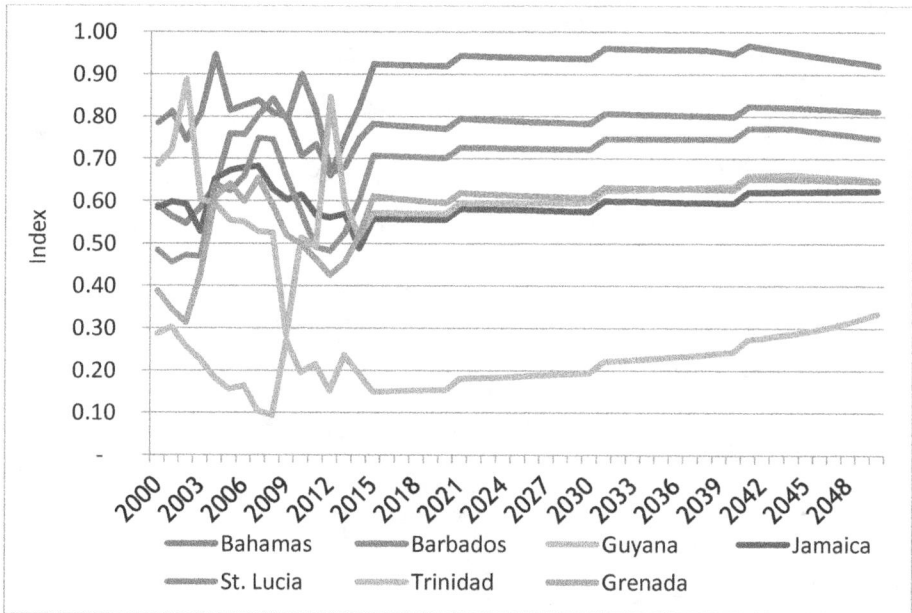

Source: *Authors' projections*

If such a focus on regional productivity is combined with policies aimed at stimulating export growth in the Caribbean, it is likely that the growth and debt targets set by the regional governments would be within reach.

Interventions aimed at enhancing productivity and exports are also expected to improve public and external current account balances in all countries. Only three countries (Barbados, Guyana and Jamaica) exceeded the debt-to-GDP ratio of 100 % by 2050, and only Grenada and Jamaica are unable to attain external current account surpluses by 2050.

Given the trends highlighted for crime in the baseline scenario, the study also considered a policy scenario aimed at enhancing the skills of the youth in the region and providing job opportunities among others. Such policy interventions resulted in a reduction in crime to modest levels in most countries.

Figure 10.6: Projected impacts of enhancing skills of youth and providing job opportunities on crime

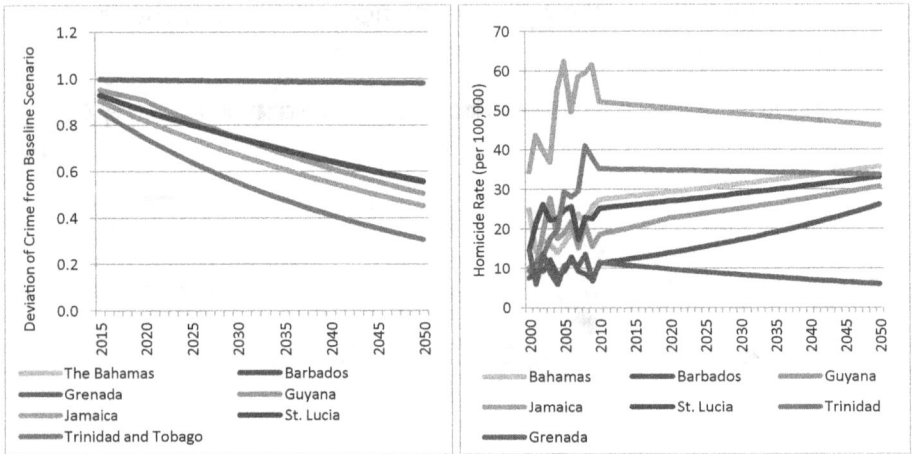

Source: *Authors' projections*

Figure 10.7: Projected impact of fiscal reform on debt-to-GDP ratio

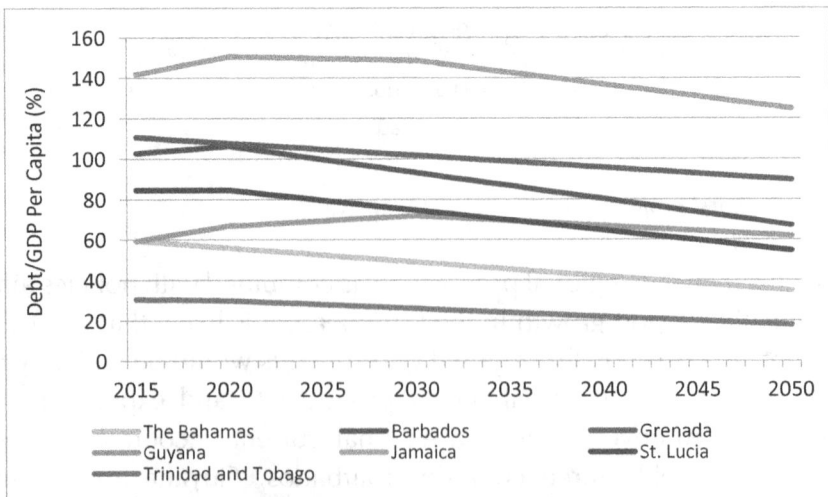

Source: *Authors' projections*

Fiscal reform in the future is expected to be targeted around reduced government expenditure, given the challenges faced in relation to raising revenue.

A fiscal goal of reducing expenditure by 30% is projected to significantly reduce the debt levels in all countries, with only Jamaica having a debt-to-GDP ratio above 100% by 2050. Such reform would also have benefits in relation to the external current account.

This improved outlook however hinges on a shift from short term problem solving to long term strategic planning. As is evident from the analysis, should regional economies continue on their current policy paths, they will regress economically—with serious social and environmental ramifications. The challenges posed by their size and the complexity of the environment within which these countries operate have been compounded by development strategies that focus on short-term problem solving to the detriment of long-term strategic planning. Indeed, patchy approaches to reforms and inconsistencies in addressing key challenges have contributed to volatile and, often times, mixed development results. A myriad of problems and their complexity have overwhelmed regional policy-makers and development partners alike. In this context, we believe that the best approach for moving forward is to ask ourselves the seemingly simple questions, what is the Caribbean we want and how do we begin to a map a way to get there?

This project, entitled *Building the Resilience of Small States: Caribbean Vision 2050,* seeks to address these questions and provide key recommendations on how Caribbean member states can build their resilience and improve their development prospects. Answering these questions must be done over a long enough period to effect meaningful change and achieve the desired results: hence the choice of the year 2050.

This study offers strategies that will seek to: balance the concerns of survivability today and sustainability tomorrow, with a focus on a long enough period to affect necessary changes; recapture the potential of young people across the Caribbean; renew and re-energise the focus on the need to secure the energy requirements of the region; and address the need for a truly transformational system of governance across the region, while strengthening systems that safeguard against corruption and ineffectiveness. The study contains an assessment of the main challenges and opportunities for the region, scenario modelling of where the region could be by 2050. The vision itself contains sector-specific goals for achieving the vision, which are further elucidated in the sector-specific strategy chapters.

The detailed reports are contained in a forthcoming book to be published by the Commonwealth Secretariat. The publication is divided into two sections. The overall findings of the study are presented in section one of the book, while section two contains the detailed sector studies. Section one, chapter 2 outlines the context within which Caribbean countries are operating and includes a discussion of emerging global trends to frame the understanding of what the world is likely to look like in 2050. Chapter 3 considers a range of possible paths for the region, depending on the policy choices made and the context within which countries are operating. Chapter 4 presents our view of the Caribbean we want and how to get there, entitled 'The Road to 2050: The Caribbean We Want'. Section two provides detailed studies on the energy sector (chapter 5), private-sector development and innovation (chapter 6), youth development (chapter 7), and finally citizen security (chapter 8).

The Commonwealth is committed to supporting the region in planning for, and realising the Vision for, the Caribbean we want by 2050, built on resilience. We believe this publication, with its in-depth analysis and action-oriented recommendations, is a critical step in the right direction and will be of interest to policy-makers, stakeholders, key development partners, academics and those with an interest in the Caribbean. The publication will be available from the Commonwealth Bookshop which can be accessed via this link: https://books.thecommonwealth.org/small-states-0 for those who are interested in obtaining the complete publication.

NOTES

1. This synthesis report was prepared by the Commonwealth team: Mr Deodat Maharaj, Deputy Secretary-General for Economic and Social Development at the Commonwealth Secretariat. He is a national of Trinidad and Tobago with over 20 years' experience working on development at the national, regional and international levels; Dr Denny Lewis-Bynoe, Head of Climate Finance and Small States, Economic Policy Division at the Commonwealth Secretariat and Ms Alicia Matheson, Research Officer in the Climate Finance and Small States Section. Contributions to this report came from the following consultants: Dr Sylvia Charles, Dr Christine Clarke, Professor Anthony Clayton, Dr Marsha Atherley-Ikechi, Dr Winston Moore, Professor Ryan Peterson and Dr Tom Rogers.
2. See Appendix 2 for more information on the Project Approach.

REFERENCES

Briguglio, L, G Cordina, N Farrugia and S Vella (2008), *Economic Vulnerability and Resilience*, United Nations University, Helsinki, Finland.

Clarke, K, and D Popo (2014), *Social Development and Protection in the OECS Member States*, Organization of Eastern Caribbean States (OECS) Commission, Castries, Saint Lucia.

The Economist (2015), 'The Future of Work: There is an app for that. New York and San Francisco', *The Economist*, available at: www.economist.com/news/briefing/21637355-freelance-workers-available-moments-notice-will-reshape-nature-companies-and (accessed 16 June 2015).

UN Development Programme (UNDP) (2012), *Caribbean Human Development Report 2012: Human Development and the Shift to Better Citizen Security*, UNDP, New York.

World Bank and UN Office on Drugs and Crime (UNODC) (2007), *Crime, Violence and Development: Trends, Costs and Policy Options in the Caribbean*, UNODC, Washington, DC, available at: www.unodc.org/pdf/research/Cr_and_Vio_Car_E.pdf (accessed 16 June 2015).

PHOTO CREDITS:

P15: iStock

APPENDICES

Appendix 1: All Contributors

Dr. Marsha Atherley-Ikechi has more than sixteen years of environmental engineering and utility regulation experience. Marsha has worked within the civil service and statutory organisations, holding both senior management and technical staff positions. Marsha has guided a number of projects across a broad spectrum of environmental and energy issues. She maintains comprehensive industry knowledge relevant to the sustainable development of small island developing states in areas such as climate change mitigation strategies, integrated water resources management, wastewater treatment and disposal, solid waste management, energy economics, energy efficiency, renewable energy adoption, water/energy nexus, and utility regulation. One of Marsha's most recent works investigated Barbadians' perceptions about renewable energy and estimated consumers' willingness-to-pay for the local water utility's use of renewable energy.

Dr. Sylvia Charles is a consultant, with significant experience in economic development issues, both in government and academic environments. Her appointments include employment with the Government of Dominica over a ten-year period as Economist, Development Economist and Chief Technical Officer, Trade, Industry and Tourism; a two year assignment with the Government of Grenada as CFTC Macroeconomist/Planner, where she co-ordinated the development of the National Strategic Development Plan process (2005–2007) and was reassigned to undertake the plan's update (2011). She also conducted middle management training in strategic planning and project appraisal and senior management orientation in strategic management. Sylvia Charles was engaged by the Organization of East Caribbean States (OECS) to review policies and plans of member states in order to identify gaps and synergies and to recommend interventions. She has consulted in the Caribbean, South Africa, Mozambique, Botswana and Nigeria in sector studies, surveys and cost-benefit analyses.

Dr. Christine Clarke is a lecturer and researcher at the University of the West Indies in the Department of Economics. She has served as Director of Economic Planning and Research at the Planning Institute of Jamaica, and previously Economic Adviser to the Director General of the PIOJ and Project Development Specialist for Vision 2030 Jamaica. She holds a PhD from Rice University, with a specialisation in public finance. Her economic research covered a wide range of topics including the drug/murder nexus in Jamaica, the demand for M1 in Jamaica and old age assistance in the United States. She co-authored the Minott Report 2005. More recently, her work has related to issues such as the economic impacts of climate change and fiscal sustainability issues in the Caribbean. She has served as a co-opted member on the Board of Directors of Graduate Studies and Research Entrepreneurship at the University of Technology (UTECH) and the Statistical Institute of Jamaica (STATIN).

Professor Anthony Clayton is the Professor of Caribbean Sustainable Development at the University of the West Indies. He is also a Visiting Professor at the University of Surrey, the University of Edinburgh and the University of Technology. He is a Fellow of the Caribbean Academy of Sciences and the World Academy of Sciences. He has more than thirty years' international experience in policy development for national security and policing, energy and environmental security, and governance and planning. In 2010, Professor Clayton was lead author on the intelligence-led policing strategy for Jamaica. Between 2012 and 2013, he served as lead author on Jamaica's National Security Policy. In 2014, he conducted a review of the Jamaica Constabulary Force, and in 2015 he undertook a review of the Department of Correctional Services.

Ms. Crystal Drakes is a currently a research associate at the University of the West Indies, Cave Hill Campus. Crystal holds an MPhil in Economics and a BSc in Economics and Management from the University of the West Indies. Her research interests include economic development in small island states, future foresight analysis, and the nexus between climate change and socioeconomic development.

Ms. Stacia Howard is the Managing Director of Antilles Economics, where she leads business development, drives the development of the forecasting models, and develops and contributes to articles of the company. Ms. Howard holds a MA in International Business and Languages from Heriot-Watt University and received economics training at the Central Bank of Barbados, the Economic Commission for Latin America and the Caribbean, and the International Monetary Fund.

Dr. Denny Lewis-Bynoe is the Head/Economic Adviser for Climate Finance and Small States, Economic Policy Division (EPD) at the Commonwealth Secretariat. An economist of more than 20 years' experience, her research interests are in the area of development economics broadly and, more specifically, trade, labour markets, finance, growth and tourism in small states. A former Director of Economics at the Caribbean Development Bank, Dr. Lewis-Bynoe has held several other posts during her career, including the Assistant Director of Research at the Central Bank of Barbados, Lecturer and Research Fellow at the University of the West Indies and Adviser to the Executive Director for Canada, Ireland and the Caribbean at the International Monetary Fund. She has researched and published numerous papers, including studies of the potential for south–south trade, determinants of growth for small states, labour market flexibility in the Caribbean and growth strategies for small developing countries.

Dr. Winston Moore is presently a Senior Lecturer in Economics at the University of the West Indies, Cave Hill Campus. Prior to this, he held the position of Senior Economist at the Central Bank of Barbados. His recent research has examined the issues surrounding the green economy, private-sector development, as well as the economic impact of climate change on tourism. Dr. Moore has published more than 70 peer-reviewed articles and his research has appeared in the *Journal of Forecasting, Journal of Policy Modelling*, annals of tourism research, applied economics and contemporary economic policy. He holds a PhD in Economics from the University of Surrey; a MSc in Economics from the University of Warwick; and, a BSc in Economics from the University of West Indies, Cave Hill.

Professor Ryan R. Peterson, PhD, is full academic Professor of Innovation Economics at the University of Aruba. He holds the university research chair on institutional capabilities for sustainable islands. Professor Peterson's scientific and business endeavours span over two decades, across three continents, on the innovation capability, sustainability and resiliency of (small) enterprises, (island) economies and (creative) communities.

Dr. Tom Rogers, a mechanical engineer by training, is a lecturer at the University of the West Indies Cave Hill Campus in Barbados, where he teaches at the undergraduate and postgraduate level on the subject of clean energy systems for small island states. He has been involved with a number of Caribbean-focussed energy projects, including the UN Environment Programme (UNEP) and Government of Barbados-led 'Green Economy Scoping Study for Barbados', the European Union and African, Caribbean and Pacific states (EU–ACP) Edulink-funded 'DIREKT' project, the DAAD-funded 'INEES' project, the Inter-American Development Bank (IADB)-funded 'BRIDGE' project and the EU–ACP Edulink II-funded 'CAP4INNO' project. He has also been instrumental in the development of the English-speaking Caribbean's first renewable energy-focussed MSc programmes, and is currently working with local and international collaborators on the concept of realising 100 per cent renewable energy systems for small island states.

Appendix 2: Project approach

To gain insight into potential areas of focus within the remit of the project, an Advisory Group—comprising regional 'thought leaders', including senior policy-makers within the Caribbean, and chaired by the Commonwealth Secretariat Deputy Secretary-General—was convened. Given the multifaceted nature of development, the Commonwealth adopted a multidisciplinary approach in the selection of experts for the group covering economic, social and environmental disciplines. The members of the group were Hon. Winston Dookeran (Minister of Foreign Affairs in Trinidad and Tobago); Mr. Rod Pennycook (Chair of the Board of the Royal Bank of Canada); Dr. David Smith (Coordinator of the University Consortium of Small Island States); Dr. Wendy Grenade (lecturer at the University of the West Indies [UWI]); Ms. Farmala Jacobs (Caribbean Youth Network representative); the Deputy Secretary-General of Economic and Social Development, Mr. Deodat Maharaj; and Dr. Denny Lewis-Bynoe, Head of Climate Finance and Small States in the Economic Policy Division of the Commonwealth. They met in Trinidad and Tobago and deliberated on the concept and approach for building the resilience of Caribbean economies and developing a vision for the Caribbean that embodies the aspirations of its people. In their choice of topics for consideration, the Advisory Group drew on their considerable knowledge of the region, identified those issues that are likely to be most transformative for the development of the region, and decided those that were to be the project's areas of focus.

The study commissioned by the Commonwealth includes research by a team of consultants, who contributed their expertise in the areas of economic modelling, the private sector and innovation, citizen security, development strategies and visioning to the report. In addition, the Commonwealth drew on internal expertise for the sections on youth and financing for development.

The project also involved broad stakeholder consultation, including with Caribbean youth networks, and social media interventions. In addition, initial findings were presented and shared at two high-level fora in the region—the Commonwealth Youth Ministers Meeting and the UN Development Programme (UNDP), UWI and Government of Trinidad-sponsored Caribbean Future Forum.

This vision was developed from a wide range of sources, including through a range of consultations from across the Caribbean region (outlined in Box A.2). The process is illustrated in Figure A.2.

Box A2: Development of the Caribbean Vision 2050

The vision for the Caribbean was developed using a widely consultative process, which included reviews of national strategic and development plans, in order to identify the elements that were common to all countries in the region and the CARICOM Strategic Plan for 2015–2019. The plans vary from short to long term and they all present a situational assessment for each country that is then addressed through a strategic framework with a vision, goals, objectives and strategies. The commonalities that were identified were then interpreted as the key areas of focus—both in terms of assessment and strategies—across the region. Together with those from the CARICOM Strategy, the common themes emerging from the country plans were synthesised in order to develop the elements of Vision 2050 (see appendix 4.1 for a synthesis of the review of national strategic and development plans).

The second element in the process of developing Vision 2050 involved eliciting the perspectives of a cross-section of Caribbean stakeholders on: his/her vision for the Caribbean to 2050; the greatest challenges/threats to achieving this vision in his/her sector during the timeframe and how these can be surmounted; the extent to which any of the strategies for surmounting the identified challenges are already being implemented; and his/her views as to the potential benefits to regional co-operation in relation to addressing the challenges previously identified. Consultations were undertaken through various means:

1.   A survey of the public and private sectors, as well as civil society and youth representatives in four Caribbean countries, in order to determine their views on some of the critical issues facing the region.

2. A meeting of Caribbean 'thought leaders': the Commonwealth selected a Caribbean Advisory Group to guide the development of the analytical and strategic work. The group, which covered economic, social and environmental disciplines, deliberated for a full day on the concept and approach for building the resilience of Caribbean economies, offered their vision for the Caribbean

3. A Facebook page to solicit contributions to the strategies and vision.

4. A presentation of the initial findings of the study at the Caribbean Region Commonwealth Youth Ministers Meeting in Antigua on 29 April 2015.

5. Finally, the vision—as well as key elements of the strategic framework stemming from the imperative for change—was presented at a three-day future forum of approximately 300 regional and international stakeholders in Trinidad and Tobago in early May 2015. The session was highly interactive and provided substantive interactions and feedback, which enabled the further refinement of the framework.

Figure A2: Methodology used to develop Vision 2050

Global
National
Regional

Critical Issues

Goals
Objectives
Strategies
Activities

Vision

Environmental Scan & Consultations

Road Map

Destination

Left to Right: Richard Blewitt, Winston Dookeran, Clement Sankat, Antonio Prado and Alfonso Munera

PART FOUR
TRANSLATING WORDS
INTO ACTION

CHAPTER 11
Measuring Success

Philomen Harrison and Carlos Elias[1]

INTRODUCTION

This chapter is intended to highlight the need for systematic data collection, compilation, dissemination and analysis, and its use for decision-making. The experience of users seems to suggest that there is little or no data available on countries of the Caribbean Community. Perceptions abound about social and demographic issues, for example, about poverty, crime, youth unemployment, disease, economic growth and life expectancy among others. The truth is that when decision makers and stakeholders talk about these issues in the region, they do it with their hearts, not with their minds. Speaking from the heart isn't bad, as our personal experiences informed by anecdotal information build up to what is, at the personal level, a value judgement of reality. Speaking from the heart, however, is bad for policy formulation and evaluation because personal preferences, well intended as they may be, do not necessarily reflect reality.

There are critical gaps in the data required for policy formulation and decision-making, uneven availability of some key data sets across countries, coverage issues in data that are available and a general lack of timeliness in the dissemination of data sets and in conforming to international standards. In spite of this, Caribbean countries do have some data, and it is often the case that users do not know what data are available or statistical offices while having the data are unable to respond in a timely manner to requests for information by users. Challenges with access to and dissemination of data serve to exacerbate the unmet demands for data and to reinforce, in some cases, the perception that there is none. In summary, while countries have data even in some of the areas highlighted above, a lot remains to be done based on increasing demands for data in new areas of statistics; more detailed data in existing areas and more timely delivery of data to users—these are some critical unmet needs.

This problem has been a long standing one and is not confined to the Caribbean. Recently the United Nations post-2015 report by the High Level Panel of Eminent Persons identified the need for a 'Data Revolution' in statistics production.[2] The Data Revolution was also an underlying theme at the Second High Level Advocacy Forum on Statistics (HLF) in CARICOM held in May 2014 in Grenada, inspired in part by the PARIS21[3] mandate to improve statistics in developing countries.[4] Over time, many high-level meetings both in the region and elsewhere have noted the problems of scarcity of data, and the need for a systematic effort to collect and analyse relevant information.[5]

This chapter covers a topic that is perceived as low priority but is included in this publication to highlight the urgent need to measure more of what matters to citizens of the Caribbean. The chapter first highlights the early focus on statistics in the community followed by an assessment of some of the critical data gaps across countries of the region that pose limits to the information needs of users. It then identifies some key challenges that contribute to the existing data gaps while highlighting some of the data that are produced across countries. An exploration of the national and regional statistical information architecture, including some key interventions made at the regional level, follows.

After showing how little everyone really knows about what matters the most, this chapter calls for a regional solution to this problem. It focuses on increasing transparency by ensuring that information is treated as a public good, that is, it should be freely and easily available to all. The chapter concludes with specific recommendations on data collection to measure CARICOM's performance, and to measure relevant information in general and in particular in the four key issues identified during the Forum: in transport, energy, finance and food security.[6]

EARLY FOCUS ON STATISTICS IN CARICOM

The CARICOM Secretariat, in recognition of the data needs of users across the region, established at its inception, a Regional Statistics Programme (RSP), which is completely dedicated to the compilation and dissemination of data for and from the CARICOM Member States and Associate Members. Without such data, countries and the Region cannot plan policy and forecast the future whether in the economic, social, environmental or financial sectors. Statistics as a science which is grounded in mathematics is a basic cross-cutting factor in all levels of policy-making.

The staff structure and size of the RSP is currently under review, but given the increasing demands for statistics in new areas or for new characteristics and details of existing data, there is need for the staff structure to be patterned after Eurostat—the Statistical Office of the European Community—to enable the execution of key activities such as harmonising statistics; compiling and disseminating regional databases on member states; supporting the strengthening of statistical capacity in countries and acting as a repository and dissemination platform for the archiving, storage and release of high-quality information about the Region.

In addition to the RSP, the then Common Market Council of Ministers in 1974 established the Standing Committee of Caribbean Statisticians (SCCS) to facilitate the following:

> To foster increased recognition of the importance of adequate statistical services to the countries of the Region; to widen the scope and coverage of statistical data collection; and to improve the quality and harmonization, of statistics produced. (Resolution No. 54/74/4 of the Fourth Meeting of the Common Market Council of Ministers).

The SCCS was to be subject to the general supervision of the Common Market Council which reflected the high status given to statistics in the Community. The SCCS which still exists today, comprises Directors of Statistics/Chief Statisticians, representatives of national, regional and international organisations and members of academia. What is missing is private sector membership.

The early focus on statistics in the Community has been in two key areas: Trade Statistics and the Population and Housing Census. The backdrop to trade data was the establishment of the Caribbean Free Trade Area (CARIFTA) in 1968. The first digest of trade statistics of member states of CARICOM, which was produced in 1976, represented efforts by the Secretariat spanning several years, to produce 'estimates of the flow and pattern of intra-CARICOM' trade. The time period for this first digest was 1960 to 1974. The information published in the first digest of trade statistics was intended to correct *misunderstandings* about intra-CARICOM trade performance. The sources of data were the trade publications as well as unpublished data provided by the National Statistical Offices (NSOs) of member states.

In the case of the Census, the Ninth Meeting of the Commonwealth Caribbean Government Statisticians in September, 1976, recommended that the CARICOM Secretariat and the Council of Ministers establish a Regional Census Coordinating Committee (RCCC). This decision marked another turning point with the Regional Statistics Programme (RSP) of the CARICOM Secretariat being charged with the responsibility of facilitating regional coordination and assistance supported by the RCCC in CARICOM from the 1980 Census Round to the present time.

AN ASSESSMENT OF THE DATA GAPS AND KEY CHALLENGES – HIGHLIGHTS OF MAJOR DATA GAPS

Caribbean information is often characterised as outdated, incomplete and inharmonious. Is this view of statistics anecdotal? Timeliness affects many areas of statistics except for the Retail Price Indices, which are in general produced and disseminated in a timely manner; and Trade Statistics. Regional trade data may experience challenges due to missing information from a key country, but for many countries this data set is timely, harmonised and up-to-date. Some key challenges that impact the data produced and its reliability include the failure to conform to international statistical standards, poor source data based on low response rates by the public to surveys and the absence of data sharing from administrative data sources within the National Statistical System (NSS).

The following are some of the main data sets that are produced across the region:

Population and Housing Census data: All member states and Associate members of CARICOM have been able to conduct the Population and Housing Census in the 2010 Census Round, the most recent internationally. Tables are generated to provide information on the population of a country and its demographic and social characteristics and on the housing stock. Census-taking in the Caribbean has followed a regional approach dating back to colonial times to ensure greater uniformity both in the questions asked and in the conceptual framework. It also ensured support for countries needing it in the conduct of the census exercise. In the 2010 census round, there was funding of a Common Census Framework project activity by international development partners comprising the Inter-American Development Bank(IDB); United Nations Population Fund (UNFPA); Department for International Development (DFID) and the European Union (EU) which served to formalise the efforts at harmonising the census questionnaire, methodologies and framework for dissemination. The census is the largest statistical activity that a country can conduct and so the coordinated approach to census-taking in the Caribbean strikes a critical rebuttal to the view of inharmonious statistics since efforts at a common census approach including the methodological guidelines have been addressed. However, delays in the processing and disseminating of the census results by countries contribute to these data sets' not being made available to users in a timely manner. The use of the census as a benchmark for data that is collected across the entire national statistical system, render it a valuable data set to the country, provided it does not take ten years to be made available.

National Accounts data is also produced by countries, mainly Gross Domestic Product (GDP) by Industry—Current and Constant Prices—and GDP by Expenditure—Current Prices—and of course the GDP growth rate. Countries are required to follow the international standards of the System of National Accounts (SNA), the latest being the 2008 SNA. To the extent that countries are unable to achieve compliance with this standard, the data will be less harmonised. In addition, many countries rely on financial statements of firms to produce these accounts which are often collected with a one-year lag, and it may also take an additional year to publish actual data. Interestingly a few countries are moving to produce quarterly GDP, and many countries produce preliminary revised and actual figures over a three-year period. Key National Accounts are tables that are recommended at the international level; the minimum required data sets are not produced by all countries in the region. There is therefore, uneven performance with respect to the issues of incomplete, inharmonious and outdated data relative to this data set.

Retail Price Index is the source from which the rate of inflation is derived. The frequency of this data set is monthly, which makes it the timeliest data for most countries. In a couple of cases, there may be incompleteness relative to the coverage of the index within countries.

Labour Force Statistics (including the employed, unemployed, the unemployment rate and youth unemployment rate) are produced by some countries on an annual or quarterly basis with the exception of most of the countries of the Eastern Caribbean and Guyana that rely on Census data. Work is in progress in this area in the countries of the Eastern Caribbean relative to the conduct of Labour Force surveys.

Merchandise Trade Statistics are data on imports, exports, and total trade which is often subject to volatility in its timeliness due mainly due to challenges in the administrative source of this data set. The provisions for confidentiality under the Statistics Act may at the very worst imply that the trade data on exports may be too aggregated to be meaningfully incorporated in the regional trade data bases (many products lumped in a 'not elsewhere stated' category). Quantity data on trade is also poorly recorded at the source, the focus being on the value and the duty to be collected.

Balance of Payments Statistics include current account (deficit/ surplus) and foreign direct investment and can be described as complete and a bit outdated for a few countries, partly due to the transitioning to the most recent international standard, but this area is by no means inharmonious.

External Debt Statistics is the data set produced by the NSOs and is subject to release by the relevant government ministry. It is therefore sometimes outdated (due to non-release), but is also effectively harmonised.

Government Statistics – Central Government Revenue and Expenditure: Formats may differ across countries despite the availability of an international manual to guide the production of this data set. This data set is also produced in the relevant ministries.

International Trade in Services Statistics data do exist, but, relative to demands for users for more characteristics such as by trading partners and possible coverage issues, this data can be described as incomplete. An International Manual exists to facilitate harmonisation. In some cases, this data come from the Central Banks.

Other Social/Demographic Statistics: education, migration, health, crime, poverty and decision-making statistics are produced unevenly across countries. Belize, for example, produces the best set of health statistics and Grenada education statistics but whether these data sets are accessed by users is debatable.

Tourism Statistics/ Tourism Satellite Accounts (TSAs) are produced by very few countries.

Environment statistics and Information Communication Technologies (ICT) statistics represent fairly new areas of data gathering. Inroads have been made in this area by some countries as well as by the RSP. The major data gaps are in areas for which agencies from outside the region are responsible for collecting data from countries.

In sum, data on crime/violence and HIV/AIDS are key areas with data gaps as well as Labour Force Statistics, particularly for the OECS countries. Challenges in the production of sex-disaggregated data, which are necessary but not sufficient for the production of gender statistics, contribute to the data gaps.

SOME KEY CHALLENGES THAT IMPACT THE DATA GAPS

NSOs in CARICOM are being asked to produce more with less. The following are some of the key challenges:

a. Small size: Small Island developing states (SIDS): underscoring the small size of some of the statistical offices/agencies and in general the lack of absorption capacity to training/technical assistance to produce a wide range of statistics.

b. Financial/budgetary issues: inadequate budget which does not increase with increasing workload (to compare in absolute and relevant terms).

c. Human resources staffing: inadequacy and shortage of trained statistical staff.

d. Increased demand for statistics in an environment of declining resources, resulting in critical data gaps.

e. Non-response by businesses and households to surveys carried out by the NSOs.

f. Outdated legislative frameworks.

g. Need to stay relevant (by providing timely and user-friendly data) in a changing environment.

h. Uncoordinated national statistical systems (NSS) reflected in an absence of data sharing among agencies (data from administrative sources for statistical purposes only).

i. Inadequate information technology (IT) resources.

j. Need for a focus on strategic planning (NSDS framework) to produce high-quality statistics to support regional and national policy objectives.

k. Weak satellite units – line ministries often have inadequate statistical and IT capacity.

Some of these challenges are explored more fully in section 6 relative to possible solutions that can enhance the availability of data to users.

THE NATIONAL AND REGIONAL STATISTICAL SYSTEMS

The National Statistical System (NSS)

A National Statistical System (NSS) can be said to consist of all statistical authorities in a country that collects, compiles and disseminates official statistics. Invariably, the central authority is normally a statistical office or institute. The other data-producing agencies are usually statistical units in Ministries Departments and Agencies (MDAs). The statistical units in the MDAs largely produce data for administrative purposes such as the tax authorities. However, this data is often required by the NSO to bridge the gaps in the compilation of data such as in National Accounts. It is often the case that the NSS in many countries including those of the CARICOM Region are uncoordinated. This can lead to a number of problems such as the absence of data sharing and the production of poor quality information. It is necessary therefore that attention be paid to the strengthening of the NSS.

A critical issue in the strengthening of the NSS is having an appropriate legal framework that would be the basis for providing solutions to the systemic challenges of data sharing and production and the independence of the statistics produced and its dissemination while ensuring desirable data quality. In this context, an IDB-funded project executed by the CARICOM Secretariat produced a CARICOM Model Statistics Bill that addresses the establishment of an integrated NSS. This Model Bill has been made available for adoption by countries and is highlighted elsewhere in this chapter. Another fundamental mechanism that is being supported by PARIS21 relative to the strengthening of the NSS is the National Strategy for the Development of Statistics (NSDS). The NSDS provides a framework for strengthening statistical capacity of the entire NSS through a development and strategic management perspective that underscores the link between statistics and the national developmental policy framework of countries. Elements of the NSDS include an assessment phase of the status of the NSS; a design phase, including envisioning and preparing a roadmap with identified actions and resources; and an implementation phase.

The Role of the Regional Statistical Programme – Strengthening of Statistical Capacity and Compilation of Regional Databases

The RSP of the CARICOM Secretariat does not collect primary data in countries but relies on the data collected by the statistics-producing agencies, mainly the NSOs of member states. The data is submitted to the CARICOM Secretariat and are then validated and compiled to produce regional databases and/or publications that are disseminated on the website of the RSP, www.caricomstats.org. Occasionally, in the absence of the submission of data by member states, the RSP will search on their websites or in publications that are available for data to fill the data gaps.

A key factor that informs the compilation of regional statistics is the need for harmonisation to enable comparable data across countries. In this regard, a critical mechanism is the common Regional Statistical Work Programme (RSWP) which serves to ensure that there are common themes for data compilation across countries. The objectives of the Regional Statistical Work Programme are: to focus on the statistical needs to establish, monitor and evaluate the CARICOM Single Market and Economy (CSME); to make available statistical information for decision-making; and to keep pace with the changing socioeconomic and global environmental changes, as well as technological advances.

In addition, conformity with international and regional statistical standards is also encouraged, such as the Common External Tariff (based on the international trade classification system), the System of National Accounts; the International Labour Standards and the latest Framework for the Development of Environment Statistics of the United Nations Statistics Division (UNSD).

In this regard, the RSP with funding received from international development partners focuses on the strengthening of statistical capacity in countries including the production of a number of regional public goods. However, inadequate funding challenges the implementation of these frameworks by countries. The most important initiatives to date include:

- the Regional Statistical Work Programme (RSWP)
- the design of a CARICOM Model Statistics Bill that targets an integrated NSS
- the design of Data Management Frameworks—including Archiving and Dissemination
- a position on access to micro data

- CARICOM Minimum Data Set (MDS)
- Common Census Framework
- Regional Implementation Strategy for the System of National Accounts 2008
- Common Literacy Survey Framework
- Guidelines and manuals in a number of areas such as Merchandise Trade Data processing Manuals, Literacy Survey and the Development and Conduct of Statistical Business Registers
- The creation of the Professional Association of Statisticians, which is in its initial stages and which would require some support from IDPs/governments
- CARICOM Code of Good Statistical Practices.

There are varying degrees of implementation across countries of the above frameworks and solid and consistent support is required to enable an even, strategic and structured approach. This is where a CARICOM Regional Strategy for the Development of Statistics (RSDS) can lead the way ensuring a results-oriented approach in building upon these frameworks.

Box 1. Highlights of Selected Frameworks — the RSWP and the Model Statistics Bill

The CARICOM Regional Statistical Work Programme

The preparation of a Regional Statistical Work Programme (RSWP) is a vital contribution to a better understanding of the Region. Indeed, the driving force behind the RSWP included the following:

1. The recognition of the requirements for the production of statistics, given the deepening and widening of the integration process through the implementation of the CSME;

2. It is further driven by the recognition by the Standing Committee of Caribbean Statisticians (SCCS) of the pressures that would be placed on the poorly resourced national NSOs to produce any additional data sets to monitor the establishment and performance of the CSME;

3. The response to the Mandate of the Eighth Meeting of the Resumed Session of the Community Council of Ministers (Council) of 2001 that the CARICOM Secretariat, in collaboration with the SCCS, were to prepare a three-year statistical work programme to improve the range and quality of statistics in the Region;

> 4. A clear need for harmonisation which requires at least a minimum level of common programmes, compatible series and quality level in the production of statistics across the Member States.
>
> The CARICOM Model Statistics Bill:
>
> 1. Seeks to establish an Integrated National Statistical System;
> 2. Recognises the need to create a body corporate, with some degree of autonomy in the operations of the NS);
> 3. Enables the exchange of data from Ministries Departments and Agencies for Statistical purposes only;
> 4. Specifies that the Statistical Legislation will supersede other legislation relative to the exchange of data for statistical purposes only.

In addition, relative to the data gaps highlighted earlier, a number of interventions have been coordinated by the RSP in collaboration with IDPs (or vice-versa) over the past ten to fifteen years, without which these gaps would have been more severe. Interventions in two areas are highlighted as follows:

1999–2004 Social/Gender and Environment Statistics

This is a project executed by the RSP and the UNSD on 'Strengthening Capacity in Social/Gender and Environment Statistics for Conference Follow-up'. Key outputs from the project were a regional publication in each area of statistics; national compendia in the area of environment statistics by at least eight countries; general training and sensitisation and the coming together of policy-makers and statisticians to identify the major gender and environmental concerns and corresponding indicators. In 2002, prior to the end of the project, the RSP established a CARICOM Advisory Group comprising a sub-group of the Directors of Statistics and IDPs to promote permanent programmes in these two areas of statistics. Core data sets were refined, and routines for the submission of data to the RSP as well as time periods for the production of national publications in these areas were identified.

Outcome of Intervention in Social/Gender and Environment Statistics

Prior to this intervention, only two countries had started work on environment statistics with one producing a publication. Since the project and the establishment of the programme, six countries have produced two or more publications and in a couple of cases five publications each. The RSP itself has been able to produce two additional regional publications in environment statistics. In the area of social/gender statistics, programmes for collecting these data are now more structured with templates for data collection. A publication on 'Power and Decision-Making'; a publication on 'Population, Household and Families'; and one on 'Education, Health and Work' and the documentation of the metadata have been some of the highlights in social statistics. In addition, a number of training workshops have been held over the years in both areas as well as in specific areas such as civil registration and vital statistics, which brought together personnel from the Registrar General Departments/Health Ministries and Statisticians and a workshop on Harmonisation of Statistics focusing on Economic and Social Statistics. The Secretariat is also trying to collate information on Crime Statistics and Poverty from all available sources in countries for online dissemination.

Statistics on International Trade in Service

Three phases of intervention have been undertaken. This area of statistics, while being constrained by major discontinuities in the availability of funds, saw the execution of project activities including the conduct of a situational assessment, regional and national-level training and the production of a first regional publication in the first project. The second phase of work in this area was in-country technical assistance which included the review of the data collected at NSOs/Central Banks to facilitate the production of tables at the recommended international level as well as regional training. The third phase of work occurred under the Ninth European Development Fund and focused on in-country technical assistance, regional training and the production of common guidelines to facilitate harmonisation of these statistics. This area of statistics also sought to engage policy-makers and statisticians including central bank personnel and representatives from various ministries. There was some focus on Tourism Satellite Account by both the RSP and the Caribbean Tourism Organisation; efforts to support development work to measure the Creative Industries have also occurred.

Outcome of intervention on Statistics on International Trade in Services

The only data that was published prior to intervention in this area was the services component of the balance of payments. Since the interventions, at least twelve countries are extracting and compiling data at the recommended international level and submitting to the secretariat. Related to trade in services, data on foreign direct investment by source, industry and type are available for more countries than before. The RSP has produced three regional publications. The sensitisation provided in the area of tourism statistics has led to further work being carried out in a few countries.

Latin American efforts to collect and analyse data have been attempted for the past several years. Arguably the most successful is the Socio-Economic Database for Latin America and the Caribbean (SEDLAC). This project, funded mostly by the World Bank, has its roots in the MECOVI program, which focused on the execution of multi-purpose household surveys as the main tool to collect socioeconomic information.[7] The coverage of Caribbean countries in the SEDLAC database, however, is limited as it only includes The Bahamas, Belize, Guyana, Haiti, Jamaica and Suriname. For these countries most of the household surveys reported are old: The Bahamas in 2001; Belize in 1999; Guyana in 1993; Jamaica in 2002 and Suriname 1999. Therefore poverty estimates for these Caribbean countries are more than ten years old. This contrasts sharply compared to other household survey data available for other Latin American countries: Argentina in 2013; Bolivia in 2012; Brazil in 2012 among others.[8]Looking at 'before and after the interventions', it can be deduced that appreciable inroads have been made. In many instances, users are not aware of what activities have been conducted, what data exist, and that continuous investment in the National Statistical Systems of member states is a key requirement along with continuous training of staff in technical and managerial areas to build upon what already exists..

Recent efforts by the government of Trinidad and Tobago to strengthen the capacity of the Central Statistical Office for use in policy development in the areas of national accounts, trade (that experienced some challenges but is now on track); inflation and nemployment/employment (again with a little longer lag than is desired) are welcomed. However, most countries of the region lag behind in data collection and dissemination. As an example, in table 11.1 a main indicator of poverty is the Headcount Index: the proportion of population below the poverty line is shown for member states for two periods of data (one year in each period). Generally it can be concluded that data are available for at least two data points over time for most countries. Some of these countries benefitted from funding support from the Caribbean Development Bank that engaged consultants to work with the national agencies including the NSOs in conducting Country Poverty Assessments. Jamaica is a key exception in that this country conducts continuous Surveys of Living Conditions, and therefore this country has more up-to-date data. Table 1 clearly shows that data does exist but also highlights some of the challenges such as the generally low frequency of the surveys reflected in lack of up-to-date information except for Jamaica and The Bahamas. Evidently, the outdated data series point not to the lack of data but, by its outdatedness, to data that probably will not reflect the current reality of poverty in member states. Most of these countries are unable to have these surveys on a more regular basis and, therefore, regional solutions as discussed elsewhere in this chapter can be utilised to fill this gap. In sum, more data are often available in countries but are not collated and disseminated due to key challenges in the NSOs/NSS.

Table 11.1: Proportion of Population Living below the Poverty Line

Country	1998–2002		2005–2013		Sources
	Percent	Year of Data	Percent	Year of Data	
Member States					
Antigua and Barbuda	...	...	18.3	2005/6	Living Conditions in Antigua and Barbuda – 2005/6 Poverty in a Services Economy in Transition prepared Kairi Consultants Ltd. in collaboration with the National Assessment Team of Antigua and Barbuda, Volume 1, Main Report. August 2007
The Bahamas	9.3	2001	12.5	2013	Bahamas Living Conditions Survey 2001 printed in 2004; Bahamas in figures 2013 (website)
Barbados	13.9	1996/7	19.3	2010	Barbados Country Assessment of Living Conditions 2010, Volume 1, Human Development Challenges in the Global Crisis: Addressing Growth and Social Inclusion prepared by SALISES and the National Assessment Team of Barbados
Belize	34.1	2002	41.3	2009	Country Poverty Assessment, Final Report. Volume 1, Main Report August 2010. Halcrow Group Limited in association with Decision Economic and Penny Hope Ross working with The Belize National Assessment Team
Dominica	39.9	2003	28.8	2008/9	Country Poverty Assessment- Dominica: Reducing Poverty in the Face of Vulnerability Volume 1 Main Report 2008/9, prepared by Kairi Consultants Ltd. in collaboration with the National Assessment Team of Dominica
Grenada	32.1	1998	37.7	2007/8	Country Poverty Assessment – Grenada, Carriacou and Petit Martinique-2007/8, Volume 1, Main Report prepared by Kairi Consultants Ltd. in collaboration with the National Assessment Team of Grenada
Guyana	43.2	1993	36.1	2006	MDG Progress 2011, Government of Guyana and UNDP

Country					Source
Haiti	...	...	77	2011	World Bank Development Indicators
Jamaica	19.7	2002	19.9	2012	www.pioj.gov.jm Moderate Poverty Line (individuals) Survey of Living conditions, 2012. Prepared by The Planning Institute and the Statistical Institute of Jamaica, 2012
Montserrat	...	...	36.0	2008/9	Government of Montserrat and the CDB: Final Report- Montserrat Survey of Living Conditions 2009 Volume ,1 Main Report- July 2012 prepared by Halcrow Group Limited working with the National Assessment Team of Montserrat
St Kitts	30.5	2000/1	23.7		Country Poverty Assessment St Kitts and Nevis Report 2007/8, Living Conditions in a Caribbean Small Island Development State.
Nevis	32.0	2000/1	15.9	2007/8	Volume 1: Living Conditions in St Kitts and Nevis prepared by Kairi Consultants Ltd. in collaboration with the National Assessment Team of St Kitts and Nevis
Saint Lucia	25.1	1995/6	28.8	2005/6	Trade Adjustment and Poverty in Saint Lucia 2005/6, Volume 1, Main Report 2007. Prepared by Kairi Consultants Ltd in collaboration with the National Assessment Team of Saint Lucia
St Vincent and the Grenadines	37.5	1995/6	30.2	2007/8	St Vincent and the Grenadines Country Poverty Assessment 2007/2008 -Living Conditions in a Caribbean Small Island Developing State, Volume1, Living Conditions in St Vincent and the Grenadines. Prepared by Kairi Consultants Ltd.
Suriname	73.0	2000	7.5	2010	National Development Strategy Report on Poverty Eradication Plan for the Government of Suriname and UNDP by Vanus James, June 2001(estimate in report) 2010- Human Development Atlas 2013 prepared by the Government of Suriname and UNDP. Methodology for 2010 is based on multidimensional concept
Trinidad and Tobago	21.0	1992	17.0	2005	Human Development Atlas 2012, prepared by the Government of the Republic of Trinidad and Tobago and UNDP

WHY DO WE NEED REGIONAL SOLUTIONS TO THE INFORMATION PROBLEM IN THE CARIBBEAN?

Justification for a Regional Approach

A regional approach to improving the availability of information is supported by the fact that the economies of the region are small, and the cost of filling information gaps can be high for individual countries, but economies of scale can be realised if data is collected and analysed from a regional perspective. Also, harmonisation in methodologies and frequency of data collection and analysis are necessary given the similarities of issues across countries in the region. Finally, NSS would benefit from a strengthened regional approach to openly and freely sharing information. A regional approach to data collection and dissemination would guarantee that information in the Caribbean becomes a public good.

Data collection and analysis can be expensive. The main tool for data collection is through surveys. The cost of surveys is related to the design, testing, execution and analysis of results. Significant cost savings can be realised if household surveys, and other data collection efforts, are executed and/or led by a regional institution. These savings would be related to the design, execution and analysis of results. Sample sizes would not change because of the need to have results at the country-level of measures of the main socioeconomic characteristics of the population —therefore, sample design should consider representative samples at the national and sub-national levels, as is done now. However, a common design, management of survey execution and analysis would result in significant savings by avoiding the duplication that currently exists. For example, a single multi-purpose household survey design may be used for all countries. Such a survey would share the same modules for all countries as the issues of interest, such as poverty measures or education would be common to all and can be adapted where necessary to suit specific issues that are relevant in the respective countries. Minor adjustments would be required in some cases to take into consideration the fact that some names change across the Caribbean—for example, food and currency names. In this context, a specialised team of practitioners would design and vet the survey, including the sample design, to ensure that it is exactly what is needed to collect relevant information. This team would also modify at the margin the survey to make it country specific.

During survey execution, the team would monitor execution and provide quality control to all the surveys throughout the region. Finally, data cleaning, compilation, and quality control, would be consolidated at the regional level to ensure building a good database. Data analysis would also be consolidated, providing the opportunity to provide primary data to governments, academia, and other stakeholders.

This approach would guarantee significant cost savings, and a homogeneous set of information for the countries in the region. An important consequence of a common approach is that survey results would be comparable across countries in the region. Importantly, it would provide the evidence necessary to identify correlations between problems and interventions to solve those problems. For example, a highly effective poverty reduction programme based on automatic provision of unemployment benefits executed in one country may provide the evidence necessary for the expansion of such a programme to other countries in the region. The evidence of success would be presented by the results of surveys executed throughout the region, with the control group represented in those countries in which the poverty reduction programme is not implemented. Analysis of differences between countries would provide additional evidence that would feed the policy-making process. Because at the moment the information necessary for this approach is not available, governments are missing on the opportunity to learn from each other's failures and successes.

A final benefit of a regional approach is to ensure that information is treated as a public good in the Caribbean. The frequency, quality and availability of information varies greatly across the region. Information about macroeconomic indicators is easier to find at websites of national statistical offices or central banks, among other data providing services on the Internet. This information is useful for macroeconomic analysis, although some information gaps exist and others appear based on circumstances—for example, international reserves kept at the central bank during times of macroeconomic stress tend to be delayed. In some cases, electoral cycles also play a role in the availability of information, especially related to politically sensitive data on socioeconomic characteristics of the population. More persistent gaps appear in the collection and dissemination of socioeconomic characteristics of the population. In most cases, these gaps reflect the cost and difficulty to execute surveys in the region. As has been noted in this chapter, the budget allocation to national statistical offices is insufficient and has been falling over the past few years. Because of the relatively high cost of data collection, most countries in the region do not offer timely information, and therefore the contribution of hard data in the decision-making process is limited.

A key mechanism that is aimed at facilitating a regional approach while ensuring that the statistics produced across countries are comparable is the common Regional Statistical Workshop (RSWP) that was prepared by the CARICOM Secretariat and the Standing Committee of Caribbean Statisticians (SCCS) as mandated by the Community Council of Ministers.

Table 11.2: Budget of National Statistical Offices as a Percentage of Total Government Budget – Selected Member States and Associate Members, 2012–2014

COUNTRY	2012	2013	2014
MEMBER STATES			
1	0.15	0.12	0.13
2	0.18	0.19	0.19
3	0.20	0.19	0.16
4	0.22	0.23	0.26
5	0.13	0.11	0.10
6	0.16	0.25	0.14
7	0.24	0.19	0.20
8	0.44	0.26	0.34
9	0.12	0.14	0.13
10	0.23	0.23	0.22
ASSOCIATE MEMBERS			
11	0.23	0.24	0.27
12	0.31	0.41	0.41
13	0.35	0.31	0.30
14	0.26	0.24	0.25

Source: Information provided by responding NSOs from Member States and Associate Members

The major rationale for the RSWP is to focus on the statistical needs to establish, monitor and evaluate the CARICOM Single Market and Economy (CSME) and also to make available statistical information for decision-making, For these objectives to be achievable, it is necessary that the NSOs and other data-producing agencies in the national statistical system be effectively equipped to deliver the outputs of the RSWP in a timely manner to users. Relative to the budget allocation, table 2 provides information for selected member states on the percentage of the total budget of the respective countries allocated to statistics. It is clear that on average this budget approximates to 0 per cent when rounded. This is a major contributing factor relative to the unmet demands and lack of timeliness in the production and dissemination of data that NSOs face. In absolute terms, the budget allocation for member states ranges from approximately 0.19 Mn. USD to 6.6 Mn USD.

At the heart of a regional approach are efforts that are being made by the CARICOM Secretariat, such as the development of Centres of Excellence (COE) to enable knowledge sharing across member states which can be instituted through a 'permanent' attachment programme of cooperation. These mechanisms would ensure that the skills set that are required to fuel this regional approach is available in a number of countries across the various areas of statistics. For example, a COE in sampling design can be established in a few countries, national accounts, merchandise trade data processing and social and demographic statistics in others. The COE along with the attachment programme will be mechanisms for sustaining this regional approach, as well as enabling training of statisticians.

Is the information that is made available used or do decision makers prefer anecdotal information and gut feelings? It is very difficult to provide evidence of the use of information for decision-making, and even less for the impact of information of decisions made by governments in the region. The literature on this issue is sparse, and more needs to be done to research this important issue. Russell and Munoz is one of the first attempts to measure how to use information for decision-making purposes in Latin America.[9] These researchers propose three indicators to measure the use of information for the design of policy—contrasting supply and demand for statistics as they relate to policy formulation, an econometric analysis to identify correlations between supply and demand for statistics and the evaluations prepared by the IDB PRODEV programme. Using these three indicators, Russell and Munoz rank countries in Latin America based on how the relevance of statistics for policy formulation.[10] Table 3 shows the results of ranking countries by the IDB PRODEV evaluation methodology, arguably the indicator with the most accurate results. As the table shows, Caribbean countries do not perform well compared to other countries in Latin America as there are no Caribbean countries in the top two quintiles, and they are over-represented in the first two quintiles. Importantly, this ranking presents the relative position of countries compared to each other, which does not mean that the best ranked are models to follow in how they use statistics for decision-making. In other words, it may be that the best ranked countries also suffer from significant problems in terms of their use of statistics for policy formulation.

Table 11.3: Ranking of Countries on The Use of Statistics

Quintile	Countries
1 (lowest, worst)	Belize, Guatemala, Haiti, Jamaica, Suriname
2	Bolivia, El Salvador, Guyana, Paraguay, Dominican Republic
3	The Bahamas, Barbados, Trinidad and Tobago, Nicaragua, Honduras
4	Argentina, Ecuador, Panamá, Perú, Uruguay
5 (highest, best)	Brasil, Chile, Colombia, Costa Rica, México

Source: Russell and Munoz, 2014.

The efforts to populate information for the identification of public policy priorities remain a key issue for the Caribbean. The international community refers to this issue as evidence-based policy-making, that is, the need to identify issues, prioritise them, and then design public policy that is firmly rooted in good information.[11] A summary of the assessment prepared by the UK Statistics Authority on The Use Made of Official Statistics notes the 'need for more systematic engagement with those organisations and individuals whose decisions, or actions, are informed by official statistics' but it also notes that 'producers of official statistics need to do more to investigate and document...the use made of official statistics and the types of decision they inform and publish alongside official statistics information on the quality and reliability of statistics in relation to the range of potential uses.'[12] Therefore the solution to the problem of poorly informed policy-making requires a two-pronged approach. Decision makers need to acknowledge, and demand, the need for solid information; and statistical offices need to supply such information as needed and of good quality. Because of the special characteristics of the region, we suggest that this two-pronged approach would be best if implemented from a regional perspective.

REGIONAL SOLUTIONS FOR KEY ISSUES THAT IMPACT THE AVAILABILITY OF STATISTICS

Three key issues are presented as priorities to improve statistics production and dissemination. These issues include insufficient investment in human resources, poor strategic planning and insufficient use of modern ICT for the collection and dissemination of information.

First challenge: human resources. Inadequate human resources in statistical offices throughout the region are responsible for poor capacity to produce the most basic data in a timely manner, and preclude the expansion of supply of information to satisfy demand. There are a number of challenges that impact the statistical offices' capacity to provide information:

- Staff retention is limited because of inadequate compensation policies, which results in the incentives for rapid turnover of young professionals.
- In turn, rapid turnover of professional staff results in loss of institutional memory.
- Because staff turns over quickly, there is a permanent demand for training, but supply of training and specialization courses cannot keep pace with demand.
- In general, statistical offices in the region are small with small budgets, and cannot keep up with increasing demand for information.
- In general, anecdotal evidence indicates poor work ethic and leadership in most statistical offices.

How should we address human resource challenges?

- Governments in the Caribbean should invest more in NSS to provide for adequate staffing requirements; the budget should be adequate, be predictable and allows for investing in recurrent collection of primary data.
- Public funding should be complemented by an effort from statistical offices in the region to generate their own resources. Importantly, this should be done through the sale of specialized services to the private sector, but not through the sale of data that should be made available free to the general public.
- Statistical offices should be reorganised by reviewing the internal allocation of resources to identify inefficiencies. This effort should

also include the identification of priority information gaps, and a plan to fill them in the near term.

- Statistical offices throughout the region, with support from the RSP, should design training and skills development plans to reinforce the competencies obtained in the past and to acquire new knowledge and skill sets, bridging the gap between the existing competencies and the new ones that are required in a changing environment. In particular, there is a need for a new generation of data scientists. According to Hal Varian of Google, the 'sexy job over the next ten years will be statisticians...' ,which spoke to the need for a new breed of statisticians, namely, data scientists.[13]

- As previously noted, in an effort to retain trained staff, compensation should be related to the value of skills in the market. Compensation policies should be complemented with appropriate working conditions, including a good work environment

- Statistical offices throughout the region, with the RSP support, should promote mentoring and internships programmes.

- The RSP should be strengthened to facilitate coordination with universities in the region to reorient the education/training to the new breed of statisticians as data scientists; promote cooperation between statistical offices, including secondments and the development of Centres of Excellence and e-learning; and facilitate twinning and documentation/electronic Help Desk/Knowledge based creation (online at the regional statistics office).

Second challenge: strategic planning. Statistical offices throughout the region lack proper strategic planning processes, which leads to the following:

- There is uncoordinated NSS and lack of relevance and general unresponsiveness to user needs and to the speed with which information is required for policy making, monitoring and evaluation of results.

- Most statistical offices in the region lack adequate user consultations and are unaware of market demand for information, so there are critical gaps in the data.

- Lack of transparency is reflected in poor sharing of information by agencies, specifically administrative data.

- Fragmentation in the production of statistics leads to an absence of harmonization within and across countries.
- Administrative data that are not produced for statistical purposes may not reflect the required level of quality with implications for reliability and conceptual consistency.

How can we strengthen strategic planning for the production of usable and timely information?

- A strategic approach is required to steer the statistical programmes to satisfying the needs of users and enable NSS to respond in a precise, coordinated and sustainable manner.
- Such a framework has been developed by PARIS21[14] which is the National Strategy for the Development of Statistics (NSDS) and a regional aspect—a CARICOM Regional Strategy for the Development of Statistics (RSDS).
- NSDS helps countries build a reliable statistical system that produces the data necessary to design and implement national development policies and programmes, supporting results-based management and better governance and aid-effectiveness as well as empowering people in their daily lives and in holding governments accountable.
- A CARICOM RSDS is the master plan for regional statistical development in CARICOM and should be aligned to the national strategic plans to cater for country specific issues.
- We must ensure that there is public trust in the statistics. Including the integrity, credibility and independence of the statistics produced will be integral to the NSDS/RSDS.
- Conformity to international and regional standards such as the CARICOM Code of Good Statistical Practices, the IMF General Data Dissemination Statistical System, use of Advance release calendars and the UN Fundamental Principles of Official Statistics can lead to greater independence and impartiality in the statistics produced.

Third challenge: taking advantage of modern Information and Communications Technologies. The challenge in this area is twofold: inadequate IT Infrastructure in the production, dissemination and analysis of statistics; and absence of IT skills that specialize in statistics. Many statistical offices in the region do not have dedicated in-house IT staff, leading to the inability to leverage IT in statistics data processing and analysis. As a consequence, speed of production and dissemination of data is slow; access to data by users is poor; and the potential for using timely information for analysis is low.

The Prime Minister of Grenada emphasized the need to use modern ICT for statistics in the keynote address at the HLF as follows:[15] 'ICT had the potential of in helping countries to move forward quickly and effectively and should therefore be the engine of the data revolution in transforming the national and regional statistical systems to inform solutions to the majority of the data challenges that existed'.... 'The data revolution in CARICOM must be powered by ICT and therefore ICT and Statistics must not be isolated from each other'.

How can modern ICT be leveraged for the production and dissemination of relevant information in the Caribbean?

- significantly cutting costs and reducing the time taken to collect and produce data, thus enhancing efficiency;
- taking advantage of electronic data capture of IT such as a paperless surveys and maybe paperless censuses in the future;
- implementing data management systems;
- deepening data analysis and dissemination;
- using anonymization of data to be made available to researchers;
- making use of data scientists, and their role in data visualization, in creating opportunities for unlocking the power of data and translating statistics into knowledge and action;
- introducing Big Data in the NSS: part of the data revolution, BIG Data is collected by corporations, such as Banks and Credit Card companies, through online shopping and through the use of social networks.

RECOMMENDATIONS AND PRIORITIES FOR ACTION

First and foremost strengthening the availability and the quality and relevance of timely information requires increasing funding for the RSP and NSS in the Caribbean. Financing the NSOs/Systems is the greatest challenge because it has major implications for the execution of the current statistics programme, for expanding into new areas of statistics, and for the adoption of updated or new international standards and classifications.

The post-2015 development era as a successor to the MDGs will result in the increasing demand for statistics over the next fifteen years. The Community Strategic Plan and the Samoa Pathway also imply additional core funding for statistics. Funding would come from local sources, but also from International Development Partners (IDPs). To coordinate efforts and funding from all sources, CARICOM should develop a Regional Strategy for the Development of Statistics.

To address funding shortcomings, this chapter recommends the creation of a Caribbean Regional Fund for Statistics. This fund would be administered by the CARICOM Secretariat through its Regional Statistics Programme and would be used for strengthening data collection and analysis, transparency and harmonisation of information in the Caribbean. The fund would be designed under the following framework:

- It would be substantial—it is a suggested minimum recurrent budget of US$2.5 million per year.
- All information collected through this fund would be made available for free in the website of the Regional Statistics Programme which will be a repository and the major dissemination portal for the collation of the data collected by countries.
- Funds would be allocated via a competitive process and through the identification of priority information gaps by the Regional Statistics Programme. The competitive process would be open to national statistical offices, academia, government entities and private sector institutions.

In addition, this publication recommends focussing on four outstanding short-term issues identified during the Forum:

- air and sea transport to facilitate movement of people and goods throughout the region and from the region to countries in the broader Caribbean and beyond (i.e., why a person pays more to fly from Port of Spain to Paramaribo than from Miami to Port of Spain —the logistical convergence challenge);
- energy to reduce high costs and provide incentives for the development of regional energy networks, increasingly relying on the production of energy from renewable resources (i.e. why prices for kwh vary so much across the region—the energy convergence challenge);
- finance to facilitate a market making mechanism(s) that connects financial markets in the region, making feasible the creation of financial markets that meet excess reserves with excess demand for credit (i.e.,why entrepreneurs pay different prices for loans in the region – the financial convergence challenge);

- food security to facilitate trade within countries in the region, the broader Caribbean and beyond to ensure good quality supply, stable prices and long-term viability of agriculture (i.e., why food is expensive and scarce in Bridgetown yet plentiful and cheap in Georgetown—the food security and climate change convergence challenge).

Each one of these issues requires the collection of primary data that is not currently available. These issues are also new as compared to traditional data collection efforts. For each one, the necessary data will involve the identification of data needed, its frequency and the level of detail necessary. We recommend that this data collection effort become a regional priority, and that it follow the following general guidelines.[16]

Priority issue	Primary data needed, suggested methodology
Air and sea transport to facilitate movement of people and goods throughout the region and from the region to countries in the broader Caribbean and beyond.	Definition of supply and demand curves for air and sea markets in the region—for people and goods; by market segmentation; current and forecasts for the next 10 years; emphasizing the estimation of price elasticities of supply and demand by market. With this information, decision makers should be able to design a new regional policy for the supply of private and public air and sea transportation, including if necessary cross subsidies and its distribution.
Energy to reduce high costs and provide incentives for the development of regional energy networks increasingly relying on the production of energy from renewable resources.	Complete mapping of supply networks and demand for electricity in the region. Definition of supply and demand by market—current and forecasts for the next 10 years. Definition of energy costs by type of generation. With these information decision makers should be able to design a regional energy policy, including the expansion of transmission networks and the provision of incentives for power generation from renewable sources and cross subsidies if needed.

Priority issue	Primary data needed, suggested methodology
Finance to facilitate a market-making mechanism(s) that connects financial markets in the region, making feasible the creation of financial markets that meet excess reserves with excess demand for credit.	Definition of supply and demand for credit in markets in the region. This effort would require careful segmentation of markets for households, businesses, public institutions and governments. Because of the highly volatile characteristic of financial markets in terms of interest and exchange rates, which lead to frequent opportunities for arbitrage, the data collected would need to be updated frequently—an issue that should be easily accommodated by information provided by banks in the region. Compared to energy, the creation of regional financial markets is significantly easier to achieve but probably more difficult to maintain. However, decision makers should be able to design appropriate mechanisms for flows of funds in a regional financial context.
Food security to facilitate trade within countries in the region, the broader Caribbean and beyond to ensure good quality supply, stable prices, and long-term viability of agriculture.	This effort would require a significant data collection effort to estimate demand and supply for main products in the region, including segmented markets and seasonal characteristics of food supply and demand. With this information, decision makers should be able to design a regional food policy.

To complement these efforts, we also recommend the creation of a Virtual Statistical Office to be hosted by the CARICOM's Regional Statistics Programme. This Virtual Office will serve two key purposes. First, it will act as a knowledge base to enable the access to resources by NSOs and agencies relative to manuals, guidelines, tools, software and other forms of assistance to statistical agencies in member states to assist with the acquisition of methodological and technological skills for data production. Second, it will also incorporate a Data Repository/Library. This would include all data from Member States which will be lodged at the Secretariat with the more recent data being made available data in the website of the RSP along with additional news and relevant information, documents and research and any other information related to CARICOM's main programs and projects. As it related to data, the virtual library cum data repository will provide searchable data which may be presented and downloaded by users into several formats – such as MS Excel or Stata. A policy on the availability of archived data has been prepared under an IDB Regional Public Project, and this can be utilised for the purposes of archiving of historical series.

'These proposals cost money. This chapter recommends the creation of a Regional Fund for Statistics. This fund would be solely dedicated to fulfil the objective of filling the information gaps in the region.

Access to information is the cornerstone to good governance, meaningful participation, and increasing transparency, and is recognized as a fundamental human right.'

(Carter Centre)

NOTES

1. Dr. Philomen Harrison, Project Director, Regional Statistics, Caribbean Community (CARICOM) Secretariat. Dr. Carlos Elias, Radford University and DHC Consulting.
2. 'A New Global Partnership: Eradicate Poverty and Transform Economies through Sustainable Development' -The Report of the High-Level Panel of Eminent Persons on the Post-2015 Development Agenda, 2013.
3. PARIS21 stands for Partnership in Statistics for Development in the 21st Century.
4. 'A Roadmap for a Country-led Data Revolution', Paris21, 2015.
5. Reports from High Level Forum on Statistics 2009, 2014 MDG meetings.
6. In the rest of this chapter, the information is presented will be primarily for Caribbean Community member states: Antigua and Barbuda, Bahamas, Barbados, Belize, Dominica, Grenada, Guyana, Haiti, Jamaica, Montserrat, St. Kitts and Nevis, St. Lucia, St. Vincent and the Grenadines, Suriname, Trinidad and Tobago.
7. In 1996, the Measurement of Living Conditions in Latin America (MECOVI) was created as a programme jointly funded by the Inter-American Development Bank, the World Bank, that included support from the United Nations Economic Commission for Latin America and the Caribbean (ECLAC).
8. http://sedlac.econo.unlp.edu.ar/eng/statistics-detalle.php?idE=34
9. Russell, Mariko, and Jorge E. Munoz. 2014. *¿Cómo medir el uso de las estadísticas para el diseño de las políticas públicas?* Mimeo.
10. It is important to clarify that the results of this paper should be considered preliminary, and that there is no attempt to measure the impact of statistics on the 'quality' of public policy.
11. Scott, Christopher. (2005). 'Measuring up to the measurement problem. The role of statistics in evidence-based policy-making'. Mimeo for Paris21 Partnership in Statistics for Development in the 21st Century.

12. UK Statistics Authority. (2010). The Use Made of Official Statistics. Monitoring Brief 6/2010, 19 October 2010. http://www.statisticsauthority.gov.uk/assessment/monitoring/monitoring-reviews/index.html.

13. Harvard Business Review October, 2012- Data Scientist: The Sexiest Job of the 21st Century by Thomas H. Davenport and D.J. Patil).

14. Partnership in Statistics for Development in the 21st Century www. paris21. org.

15. Report on the CARICOM Second High Level Advocacy Forum on Statistics, May 2014, Grenada.

16. It is expected that each data collection effort would require the preparation of terms of reference, the definition of a budget. The Regional Statistical Programme is ideally situated to lead the process to collect these information.

CHAPTER 12
The Role of Diplomacy

David Anyanwu[1]

PART ONE

DIPLOMACY, GLOBAL GOVERNANCE AND MULTILATERALISM

Diplomacy plays a central role in achieving the foreign policy objectives of small countries such as those in the Caribbean. Over the years, the region has exceled at joining forces for concrete results in world stages. Some of the benefits of coordinated diplomacy in several processes include the hosting of the China-Caribbean Economic and Trade Cooperation forum.[2] Yet much remains to be done, especially given the comparative disadvantages of size and resources which present limitations for the region's quest to put their foreign issues and interests at centre stage. During the Forum, there was a strong sentiment of the need for greater joint-action by Caribbean states to achieve results for the benefit of the region.

Sovereignty has often inappropriately been blamed for the failures at integration, and it has been used as an excuse for inaction. The region has suffered from chronic bouts of mistrust, a lack of foresight, shared vision and bold and transformative decision-making. Its inherited political system has also confined politicians to short-term cycles of decision-making, sometimes limiting a pro-Caribbean and integrationist agenda. Collectively, these factors have accounted for the failures of CARICOM and cynicism about integration that have progressively worsened post-independence. Despite the similarities and common challenges shared by its members, CARICOM is now seen as consisting of a group of independent microstates with little tolerance for the idea of shifting sovereignty to any principal institutions.

The conundrum therefore is how to share and manipulate power at the regional level while still allowing for significant national authority in decision-making. In the absence of a supranational entity to commandeer a regional agenda, a shared approach to sovereignty at least in key areas and for certain foreign policy goals appears to be a most effective way of maintaining the independent sovereignty of states while at the same time strengthening foreign policy coordination in the region. Shared sovereignty arrangement with CARICOM in this instance will assist in achieving national foreign policy goals of states and can help in repositioning the region on the global map and enhancing its profile in the international system. It will also ensure that the region is pushing a clear, coherent and consistent message to the international community.

The presentations by Professor Andrew Cooper not only noted the relevance of small states diplomacy but also reinstated the value of regional coordination especially in the context of maximizing the region's numbers in multilateral processes and institutions. Similarly, in noting the comparative disadvantages of small states diplomacy, Dr. Obijiorfor Aginam pressed for more practical alternatives for the Caribbean focusing on areas of strength. In this context, he focused on the benefits of pursuing a regional health diplomacy as one facet of a broader multi-dimensional diplomacy in which CARICOM states must effectively engage. The need for a more strategic approach to Caribbean diplomacy was discussed by Professor Jochen Prantl. It is within this context that this chapter discusses requirements for twenty-first century diplomacy. The chapter focuses more on the process of improving capacities of CARICOM diplomacy than on creating new relations, so as to ensure that the region's interests are served in this hyper-globalized world.

Small states and multilateralism

In this current interdependent multiplex world,[3] geographical limitation is increasingly less deterministic of states' political and economic relations, and diplomacy is driven by the phenomenon of globalization. Countries are much more interdependent because of the trans-boundary and global nature of the challenges confronting them and the level of interconnectedness and cooperation required to find lasting solutions. The polarizing forces of multilateralism and regionalism are forcing countries, particularly small states, to engineer policies, strategies and institutions that are in sync with international regimes. As Dookeran observes, 'On the one hand, the world is moving towards multilateralism and global integration with a strong commitment to open markets and international institutions.... On the other hand, it is entering a new era of regionalism as nations seek to guarantee their markets'.[4] As such, Caribbean countries' foreign policies and diplomacy must be strategic yet coordinated enough to respond to global forces at work.

A Caribbean Sea convergence has been postulated as one such scenario for meeting the requirements of this current global economic landscape. Evolving transformations in this multiplex world[5], particularly in areas such as security, technology, economy and financing as well the involvement of non-traditional actors, necessitate changes in countries' approaches to diplomacy. Similarly, the complex questions that these major transformations present demand that small states upgrade their diplomacies or at least syncronize them with current political and economic realities.

Seen as a solution to the complex challenges of peace, stability and development with which the international system and its constituents are faced with, Ambassador Rudy Insanally, a former Permanent Representative of Guyana to the United Nations, notes that the effectiveness of multilateralism and multilateral cooperation is evident in the different treaties, conventions and agreements which reflect cooperation by states and other actors in the international system.[6] Small states and developing countries in general have the most to gain from the multilateral process, hence their loyalty to key multilateral institutions such as the United Nations. Multilateralism according to Ambassodor Insanally offers small states an enlarged political space and the room to develop effective working alliances to further those aims. As such, we have seen the importance of configurations such as the Non-Aligned Movement (NAM), the Group of 77 and the Association of Small Island and Low-Lying coastal States (AOSIS) in providing small developing states the platform to counter western powers from a position of relative strength. Multilateral diplomacy is therefore a primary safeguard against hegemonism and unilateralism for small states.

Just as multilateralism remains the most favourable context for small states to engage more powerful countries in the international system, diplomacy is a necessary tool for a small state to carry out its foreign policy and to be present as well as active in globalized international politics. Given the constraints of size and military might, diplomacy is the channel via which CARICOM states can influence the international community. The former Secretary General (Ag.) of CARICOM, Ambassodor Lotita Applewhite of Guyana, noted that diplomacy represents 'the force of ideas and creativity that are our strengths as we grapple with the issues and attempt to make a difference in the international arena. It is the use of these strengths that give our small states a voice on equal terms with the most powerful states to advance those issues which are of particular concern to us'.[7]

Diplomacy remains a most indispensable tool for small states as actors in the international system. Where these countries fall short in areas of hard power, they will have make up with soft power. As a region with several microstates, their strength does not lie in their military capabilities or in economic power. Yet, like all states, they have to navigate the international system to create opportunities to promote their national and foreign policy interests. To do this, they have to be policy flexible, they need strong leaders and an active and responsive diplomatic corps to advance those issues beyond national borders. Diplomacy however, has changed dramatically in both the way it operates and the substance it transfers. This is not unexpected because the international system is constantly evolving as seen with the proliferation of new actors and the gradual shifts in power from the west to the rest. As a bona fide instrument of global governance, there is an expectation that it must continuously evolve in order to remain relevant, effective and to meet the current geopolitical and economic requirements. Cooper and Shaw note that despite some challenges in the multilateral system, there are still 'select avenues of agency' which small states such as those in the Caribbean can exploit (often by unconventional means). They argue that 'small states must find innovative and often unorthodox forms of diplomatic engagement to ensure their interests are well served in a hyper-globalized world'.[8]

Changes, power shifts, new structures, actors and modern diplomacy

Whereas for most of the history of international relations, diplomacy has been understood variously as 'state centric,' 'the domain of the ministries of foreign affairs and departments of external relations,' 'communication between states and institutions using traditional forms of information exchange' as well as the 'control of domestic-international events', modern diplomacy has witnessed changes in the constitution of actors and parties. Foreign ministries and departments are increasingly delegating functions or being forced out of them by other units in government. It is no longer unusual for each ministry to have its own international affairs department such as exists in several ministries in Trinidad and Tobago namely National Security, Gender, Youth and Child Development, Labour and many more creating competition and rivalry around issues.

The attempt by other government ministries to streamline, shape or direct the terms of their engagement with international actors presents serious challenges to the role of foreign ministries and the traditional practice of diplomacy.

Advancements in information communication technologies have also changed the way information is shared and communicated between states, and therefore a new level of expertise is demanded from states in a broad range of negotiating areas as well as timeliness in response to international matters. It also presents new challenges in the exercise of foreign policy because diplomats now have to ensure that there is policy coherence and that the different ministries and agencies are in sync and understand what the country's foreign policy goals and objectives are. Diplomats must also ensure that they work well together so that commitments made in an international setting such as the WTO do not contradict the government's positions on other related or unrelated areas such as human rights, gender or regional security, and that they do not deter the attainment of other national and regional interests in future years.

Petrovsky also notes that the major political factor that has radically reshaped diplomacy is the decline of the role of national governments which has coincided with the rise of non-state actors including non-governmental organizations in modern diplomacy.[9] He calls this growing interest and participation of non-state actors and other non-executive branches of government in diplomacy the 'degovernmentalization' of foreign affairs. He also notes the pressure placed on traditional politics-oriented diplomacy by economic diplomacy necessitated by the sizeable expansion of global trade and competitiveness as well as the influence of the telecommunications revolution on modern diplomacy.[10]

Ambassador Insanally agrees that multilateral diplomacy has now become 'everybody's business'—so much so that negotiating tables are no longer the sole domain of government representatives but also representatives of private sector, labour, non-governmental organizations (NGOs) and wider civil society.[11] In fact, it is not unusual these days for non-state actors to constitute part of official government delegations to international multilateral forums including negotiations. Today, non-governmental organizations are not just demanding representation and participation in these multilateral forums, but they are seeking special considerations in the rules of procedure of inter-governmental proceedings which can guarantee their right to interventions and to participate in both formal and subsidiary meetings amongst other non-traditional privileges. Yet, the role of the state and its diplomacy in presenting its foreign policy remains central in international relations.

Petrovsky also notes that multilateral diplomacy is adapting to a new multilateralism characterized by more complex agendas of conferences and negotiations with larger numbers of issues and the growing involvement of experts, citizens groups and NGOs.[12] These are important changes the region must embrace because it is in the region's interest to take advantage of the resources which can boost the dual capacities in negotiating and advocacy. Governments need to accept the new role and contributions of NGOs, and NGOs have a responsibility that goes beyond lambasting the government when things are not going in their favour. In the Caribbean's case, the most active 'outsiders' have been civil society groups. Even though they are not diplomats in the traditional sense, they have been able to stay active because many maintain strong connections and linkages with powerful and well-resourced international NGOs. Many government officials and politicians in the region still do not consider civil society as active partners in key areas. The old mentality of viewing civil society as enemies seeking to embarrass governments and expose their shortcomings in international forums remains very much alive. This has to change and is a critical part of the modernisation process that needs to happen. NGOs and private sector can make valuable contributions which can help improve the effectiveness of the Caribbean diplomacy. This engagement must be advocated at all levels of governance.

The interest and participation of NGOs have grown dramatically in the past five decades, with strong advocacy and mobilization capabilities as well as specialized technical knowledge and expertise on global issues in areas such as environment, health and gender. NGOs are increasingly playing pivotal roles in multilateral processes which were previously seen to be the sole domain of governments and diplomats. For example, the International Campaign to Ban Landmines (ICBL), a coalition of NGOs, was instrumental in securing the 1997 Mine Ban Treaty.[13] Similarly, Control Arms[14] played a pivotal role in securing the landmark Arms Trade Treaty.[15] From a regional point of view, the Caribbean Coalition for Development and Reduction of Armed Violence (CDRAV)[16] has played a pivotal role in the mobilization and advocacy of Caribbean states to support, sign and ratify the Arms Trade Treaty since 2008.

Caribbean governments have not traditionally seen civil society and other non-state actors as significant partners in governance and the decision-making process, so it is not surprising that the role of NGOs in this modern diplomacy has not been warmly embraced by all. The relationship is still very much marked by mistrust as NGOs are seen as watchdogs for international groups or other entities with an agenda to shame regimes they do not support. NGOs on their part, have not done much to change this perception since some have also become political. Anyanwu notes that the lack of structure and absence of clear provisions in national constitutions (of CARICOM states) mandating government to involve civil society in their national governance processes have created this sense of hostility wherein government workers feel uncomfortable working directly with civil society representatives.[17] While these changes in modern diplomacy can present challenges for coordination, national and regional NGOs with resources including technical expertise in issues of national interest should be welcomed by governments and indeed form part of official delegations to multilateral meetings because, as Ambassador Insanally rightly observed, 'the traditional Caribbean diplomat is [often] ill-equipped to handle some of the arcane and esoteric issues on today's international agenda'.[18]

In the context of these changes as well as the asymmetries that exist in the conduct of modern diplomacy, a key message presented in this chapter is that CARICOM countries will need to realign their foreign policy objectives in order to maximize their diplomatic impact. There needs to be a pragmatic and progressive approach to policy coherence and coordination at the national and regional levels so that, from the outset, the right linkages can be established between key areas such as trade, health, security and foreign policy. In accelerating the process of convergence, they must also seek to strengthen strategic alliances beyond regional borders towards a regional approach to diplomacy as opposed to acting individually.

Strategic regional diplomacy

A key feature of this modernisation process is the development of strategic diplomacy to reposition CARICOM as an unavoidable player in issues of interest in the international system. In his presentation to the Forum, Jochen Prantl made the point that strategic diplomacy is essential to navigate the most urgent contemporary problems the Caribbean region is faced with. Similarly, Allen and Smith argued that strategic diplomacy focuses on the pursuit of a vision and provides the principles and guidelines that facilitate the positioning of a region[19] in the international system in relation to its key strategic partners.[20] Foreign policy coordination as one of the four pillars upon which the CARICOM integration was designed and as enshrined in the Revised Treaty of Chaguaramas already provides the institutional base which is a prerequisite for such a diplomacy.

The development of Foreign Policy Coordination Strategy by CARICOM member states is a key achievement for the regional organization but, as previously mentioned, it has encountered some significant obstacles because the mechanisms of coordination have been fraught with instability. In CARICOM's 2015–2019 strategic plan, the heads of government identified the deepening of foreign policy coordination (to support strategic repositioning of CARICOM and desired outcomes) as one of its eleven (11) high-priority areas for focused implementation over the next five years.[21] The Committee of Ambassadors and Caribbean Diplomatic Corp can play significant roles in strengthening coordination and advancing a regional foreign policy agenda.

CARICOM is well positioned for a variety of reasons to advance a regional strategic diplomacy as a means of repositioning the Caribbean from a position of strength (not vulnerability or weakness in the international system) so the region can maintain strategic relevance in the resolution of key issues that they are interested in or that impact them. Having fourteen votes in the United Nations is a strength, and when applied effectively and in sync with likeminded states in the system, the Caribbean can use this diplomatic leverage to foster new directions and perspectives on regional and global issues. There is no doubt that strategic regional diplomacy will require not just a coordination of non-national positions on international issues, but will also the creative coordination and mobilization of the resources of the different CARICOM states. This will enable the region to take advantage of skills and expertise within and outside national foreign ministries and departments as part of the process of developing the strategic narrative needed to drive this diplomacy.

As a consequence, strategic thinking becomes pivotal. It entails prioritizing because as small states, there is a limit to what can be achieved over a specific period of time, given that they are part of a global system shaped and influenced by a multitude of factors. Therefore, the region must be able to analyse the existing situation properly, giving due thought and attention to what is attainable within any period of time and noting if any, the mitigating circumstances, and then apply the right mechanisms to achieve set objectives. It entails prioritizing because a small region should judge the objectives of its strategic partners—considering their motives, strategies, goals and limitations—and then prioritize the best option for mutual cooperation and gains by parties. Most importantly, there is the need to think regionally and globally to make Caribbean diplomacy more effective and productive.

THE VALUE BASE OF REGIONAL DIPLOMACY
Whither CARICOM foreign policy coordination?

Recent economic and financial trends reassert the regional and global nature of the challenges that Caribbean small states face and the requirement for a similar regional and global approach to effectively challenge them. Noting the institutional redundancies that have become commonplace in small states of which the Caribbean is not excluded, and the need for the modernization of these institutions to facilitate a new form of diplomacy to match contemporary global economic and geopolitical realities, Dookeran observed that CARICOM's voice has become dimmer in the international community and current structures of integration do not appear capable of reigniting it. Effective diplomacy in contemporary international relations requires the balancing of the domestic and international linkage with the understanding that the latter is often the product of the former.

The role of diplomacy as an important tool underscoring one of the four pillars upon which CARICOM is conceptualized is well noted. The region's approach to foreign policy coordination has earned it some respect in the international community for what has been described as 'independence of thought' in its 'adoption of sometimes controversial, yet courageous positions'.[22] Yet the foreign policy coordination responsibility of the CARICOM Secretariat remains filled with contradictions, mistrust and selfishness.[23] The increasing fragmentation of foreign policy coordination in the region is reflected in the inability of CARICOM member states or in the heads of government, to agree on the region's candidate for the head of the Commonwealth. The lack of consensus on this important issue damages the credibility and reputation of the region in the international community. In addition, the region might lose out completely on the opportunity to identify the head for this very important institution.

The state of implementation of the region's foreign policy strategy has also been strongly criticized by integrationists who continue to advocate for a more robust, stronger and interdependent CARICOM. As resource-challenged countries seeking to maintain some strategic relevance and ensure their interests are represented in the international community, there is simply no mystical path to reenergizing regional foreign policy coordination if CARICOM countries remain unwilling to sacrifice some sovereignty.

Similar concerns are expressed about the increasingly weakened diplomatic capacity of Caribbean states. Unlike developed countries and indeed larger developing economies that are able to rely on various instruments such as geopolitical strengths, economic and military might, and diplomacy in their engagement with other members of the international system, Caribbean states like many small states in the global South have little of those instruments in abundance. So when diplomacy—as the only instrument they have to advance their concerns in the international system—fails, they have little to rely on. From a critical mass perspective, regional diplomacy can be harnessed into an instrument of strength which can highlight the positive aspects of regional interdependence, while assisting the region in advancing their cause and defending their interests in the international community.

Does the region need a Caribbean Diplomatic Corp?

While Caribbean countries work and cooperate at least at the caucus level at the UN and other multilateral settings, much remains to be done to ensure maximum use of the collective capacity of the region's resources towards a more effective and successful Caribbean diplomacy. The region also needs to start thinking about how diplomacy can be used to accelerate the convergence process. There is no doubt that in modernising Caribbean institutions, the political logic must align with the socioeconomic and geopolitical realities of the times. The region's leaders cannot continue to use sovereignty as an excuse for inaction. The time for political mediocrity is long expired. It is important that key messages from the region are pushed with a common purpose and are not sidelined by self-serving national but ineffective priorities. The focus should be on how the Caribbean can become an unavoidable actor in hemispheric and even global affairs.

In his presentation, Cooper questioned why there isn't a collective or external action service equivalent in the Caribbean. Drawing on a reference from the United States – Antigua and Barbuda gambling dispute at the World Trade Organization (WTO) in which Antigua and Barbuda won the right to retaliate[24], he argued that the case exposed the vulnerability of a small country which has to rely on outsourcing commercial diplomacy because it neither had a resident WTO ambassador in Geneva nor had in-house the requisite technical knowledge and expertise in Geneva. This seems to support the logic for joint representation in those key universal institutions where technical representation and participation on behalf of the countries in the region are required on a daily basis. Similarly, a question that can be asked is why CARICOM as a region does not have a Geneva-based disarmament ambassador? For a region that is so adversely impacted by small arms and light weapons, and that is seeking to insert itself in the global governance of this industry through the Arms Trade Treaty process, one would imagine that this would be a priority.[25] Instead, they have to resign to commuting from Permanent Missions in New York, as well as from capital cities, to Geneva to attend meetings at often high costs and as a result can be left out of intersessional and extraordinary meetings that are more frequent and informal than actual conferences.

In this context, the region needs a new cadre of diplomats that think 'Caribbean' to be able to promote and pursue the region's interests abroad. The concept of a Caribbean Diplomatic Corp [focused squarely on Caribbean foreign policy] is not new and definitely not groundbreaking. Conceptually, the mere thought is confounded with many complex challenges, chief among them being the dual issues of supranationality and sovereignty. In this instance however, the success of this institution is not dependent on states' ceding sovereignty (shared-sovereignty might even be a stretch), but rather it is based on the realization that there could be several key multilateral issues and processes, and without such an institution, these small states would be unable to act or respond to developments in a timely and effectively manner. The Heads have actually taken a first step in this direction, in establishing a permanent committee of ambassadors to support the implementation of decisions of the regional body.

A Caribbean Diplomatic Corp will not only enhance coordination and support a Caribbean foreign policy agenda, it will also strengthen national capacities to achieve states' foreign policy objectives. The current global environment is creating a distinctive set of issues which for small states require an expanded approach to diplomacy to confront them. Climate change, space exploration, new vulnerabilities created by global trading rules, disarmament and nuclear technologies are increasingly complex and demand specialized and concerted efforts which are not readily available in small countries of the Caribbean. In a changing system of world diplomacy, this should be part of the medium-to-long term vision for the region. Also importantly, this reduces the cost of diplomacy for states. The fact is that no single country in the region is sufficiently positioned to confront the challenges and maximize the opportunities provided in the areas outlined above. By acting together and drawing upon the combined resources of all, the region will be better equipped to reposition itself as an important player in these areas.

As indicated in the trade and disarmament examples, the best use of this Caribbean Diplomatic Corp would be to represent the region at those highly technical institutions that require a certain level of expertise which may not be readily available to individual countries. In essence, it does not replace national diplomatic services, rather it will support the attainment of the region's foreign policy goals. As briefly discussed below, staff at national overseas missions are already stretched, given the workload and the limited number of diplomats a small state can afford in expensive cities such as New York, Geneva, Washington, DC, and Brussels. This is also compounded by rampant nepotism and political patronage which is fast becoming the norm in the selection of persons for posting to major cities. This regional Diplomatic Corp ensures that on those very critical issues, such as climate change, trade, nuclear disarmament, and space exploration, the region has some sort of permanent representation and that Caribbean leaders are continuously and periodically informed on the state of affairs in the relevant institutions. The Caribbean Diplomatic Academy based at the University of West Indies as a regional research institution (as discussed in subsequent sections of this chapter) is well placed to provide specialized training to this new cadre of diplomats —training them not as national diplomats but as regional diplomats tasked with promoting the collective interest of all who have agreed to participate.

This Caribbean Diplomatic Corp will be housed within the CARICOM Secretariat.[26] It will have its own legal identity but linked to CARICOM through COFCOR and the CARICOM Committee of Ambassadors. As a minimum, the Heads of Government would need to appoint a CARICOM High Representative from outside the Committee of Ambassadors whose role would be to oversee and manage the Diplomatic Corp. Given that ambassadors in the committee would be operating in their national capacities, the High Representative cannot come from that group. The High Representative will report to the CARICOM Secretary General and COFCOR but his/her mandate will be given by the Heads of Government. The High Representative will then oversee staff of the Diplomatic Corp including ambassadors that would be appointed to key international organizations.

This is basically the only way to ensure that as small countries, the region can carve out and maintain greater policy space in the major international issues. Depending on their accreditation and portfolios, each ambassador would be supported by a competent and specialized staff. While it is important that staff may be seconded from national diplomatic services, it might be most appropriate if they are sourced at the regional level. Given the very delicate issue of trust, recruitment has to happen at the CARICOM level and in accordance with CARICOM recruitment regulations with oversight from the Committee of Ambassadors. Instructions to, as well as reporting from, diplomats would have to be communicated via the High Representative to COFCOR and the Secretary General. It is important that both the appointment of ambassadors and recruitment of other staff is conducted in a transparent manner and on the basis of merit, expertise and a history of excellence given the gaps and the very technical nature of the areas they will cover.

While the institutionalization of this entity or implementation of the recommendation is fraught with other real challenges in a region, they are not insurmountable. Issues such as cost and maintenance, recruitment of staff, duration of tenure, lines of reporting and instructions as well as the actual rules of the receiving institutions of global governance will have to be finely addressed for this to work. On the issue of cost—the idea that one or two countries have to show leadership is well accepted and has been advocated given the success of that model in other regions such as in Europe; however, all interested Caribbean states would have to finance this institution on the basis of a formula agreed upon by COFCOR. Its objective is not to undermine the bilateral diplomatic activity of states —hence the reason that it will receive its mandate from the Heads of Government. As shown in figure 1, COFCOR and the Secretariat would also be responsible through instruction at the Heads level to set up the framework for the operationalization of this institution. Although this may not be necessary, nothing should prevent a country that has the resources for additional national presence.

Figure 12.1: Abbreviated Reporting and Instructing Structure Caribbean Diplomatic Corp

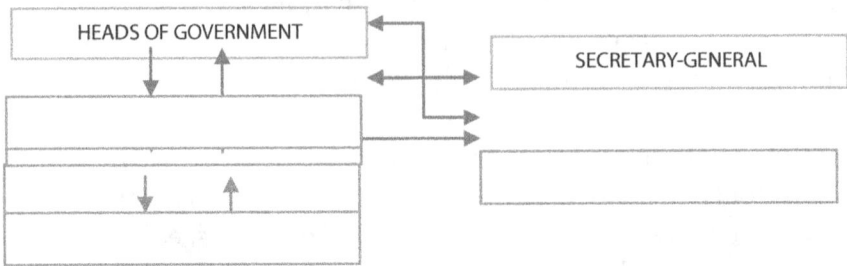

The same justification would apply to strategic locations around the world in which the region has no representation. This can only complement and not necessarily replace national diplomats. The issue is how CARICOM can transform its public image as a mere 'talk-shop' which only manufactures statements and communiques with little or no implementation record to back up its summits. If there is a Caribbean diplomacy and if the region is serious about building on the successes of the past, then the institution of a Caribbean Diplomatic Corp should form part of the modernising process. The message from the Forum was clear on the need to focus on action and Caribbean diplomacy will benefit immensely from a dedicated Caribbean Diplomatic Corp. Its dual role will therefore be to advance Caribbean interests in the international arena while anchoring the national pursuits of the individual member states. It will serve to accelerate the convergence process which is now clearly understood as a process in motion. This could be the way of implementing joint diplomatic overseas missions with which the region has struggled for too long.

Joint overseas representation

This was yet another issue that baffled many at the Forum including Professor Cooper given the challenge that small countries face in getting the right combination of missions in strategic locations and also the right persons to lead and work in them. In the past few years, Trinidad and Tobago has opened missions in China, India and Panama while Jamaica still maintains the most overseas missions of all CARICOM states. But as Cooper alluded to, specialized diplomacy including commercial diplomacy and diaspora diplomacy is not only done in capital cities but increasingly in major cities that are globally known as centres of excellence as in the case of San Francisco and technology, or culture in Los Angeles and indeed emerging cities such as Shanghai, Mumbai, Dubai and so on in which the region has no presence. The region needs some presence in these key cities of the world if the Caribbean brand is to be truly promoted.

As was reflected in the Forum, the inability of the CARICOM states to share missions overseas is still a concern for Caribbean people and scholars alike, especially given that a number of much bigger countries have shown that his process can work. As stated in the preceding section, this is not an issue of sovereignty but rather of finding common areas for cooperation to promote national interests. This can only accelerate the process of a Caribbean Sea convergence and also prop the region for greater presence on the global map. The experience of the Pacific Alliance (formed in 2012), which has established joint trade and diplomatic missions around the world in places such as Ghana, Azerbaijan and Vietnam shows that this can work and that it has yielded both results for countries in the alliance.[27] The Embassy of Colombia in Ghana provides the infrastructure for use by Chile and Mexico under the agreement signed by the countries in September 2012. Other joint missions in Algeria, Morocco, Vietnam, Singapore, Paris (at the OECD), and Azerbaijan show their appreciation of the value of cooperation and the need to maximize their resources and opportunities for representation in strategic locations where member countries do not have enough presence.[28] If countries with far more resources can find avenues for cooperation in the furtherance of their foreign policy objectives, then why are smaller countries with fewer resources but similar interests not able to do the same?

Granted, CARICOM may not have such a supranational entity in the likeness of the European Community, yet that does not preclude its member states from maximizing the opportunities provided in the framework of foreign policy coordination to set up these joint missions which at the least, can promote specific or niche dimensions of their foreign policies such as in culture, trade, energy and economy. As it stands, the Revised Treaty of Chaguaramas provides a workable framework for cooperation and should not be used as an excuse for inaction.

However, one can only imagine the effectiveness of a joint mission (in the context of the diplomatic asymmetries Aginam speaks about) that allows Caribbean states to work together, share resources (both financial, human and otherwise) while still advocating their national interests.

While the OECS states share some missions notably in Brussels, Geneva and Toronto, there are still many strategic locations in which these small states have absolutely no presence. Similarly, many important cities are not covered by consuls considering that Caribbean countries place a lot of service on consuls. Even some countries have shared their frustration about the apparent inability of Caribbean countries to establish presence. Such a view was expressed by a senior Austrian official who could not understand why, despite a generous offer presented to the region to set up a joint overseas mission in Vienna, it has not been able to do so. As Carolyn Rodrigues-Birkett, Guyana's former Minister of Foreign Affairs and former chair of CARICOM's COFCOR, noted in a speech to a meeting of CARICOM Foreign Ministers in 2014, *'If developed countries—with much more human and financial resources than we have—can pursue with each other shared space of diplomatic premises or, as in the case of the Pacific Alliance countries, establish measures in the area of consular assistance to benefit their nationals, then our small Community of nations must recognize the merit of adopting either these or similar options and of course we will be examining this in detail'.*[29]

The location of the mission is as important as who is being sent there and the commensurate skills and expertise they possess or require to be able to effectively negotiate and advocate the region's interests without being overstretched to a point of futility. Compared to their developed country counterpart who is generally specialized and assigned to specific issues, there is no denying that the average Caribbean diplomat or FSO is overstretched in terms of the number of issues he or she has to cover; and as a consequence is often unable to perform at their optimum level, which undoubtedly affects the quality of work they can produce especially with regard to the preparatory work needed ahead of major international meetings. This problem is especially pronounced at foreign missions for all CARICOM countries and less so in capitals, at least in the case of Trinidad and Tobago and Jamaica which have fairly sizeable foreign ministries. The smaller countries are not so fortunate.

Take for example the Permanent Mission of St. Lucia to the United Nations which has a staff of five (5) and according to its official website has to engage 'representatives of the other 192 United Nations member states, as well as observer missions, non-governmental organizations, and U.N. Secretariat in furtherance of Saint Lucia's multilateral interests ...collaborating with the CARICOM Caucus of Ambassadors, the Latin

American and Caribbean Group (GRULAC), the Group of 77 and China, the Non Aligned Movement (NAM), the Alliance of Small Island States (AOSIS), the Forum of small States and other relevant bodies'.[30] From an outsider's perspective, that seems to be an enormous amount of work for such a small number of staff. While some are more resourced than others, other CARICOM states' missions face similar challenges. Guyana's website lists only four staff members[31] while Jamaica with a bigger delegation lists eight.[32] How can they now be expected to effectively and consistently promote Caribbean interests against much larger and well-resourced countries seeking the same? Cooper noted that the region can enhance and project a positive, active image in the international landscape by having 'younger, culturally, technologically, sophisticated ambassadors that enhance soft power' within both a national and regional context.

Civil society is not an enemy

Cooper and Shaw acknowledge the role that civil society groups can play in advancing the regional agenda.[33] As major players in development and policy making, the interest of Caribbean civil society is not restricted to the promotion of good governance, participatory democracy and advocacy around human rights, but also on hard issues such as security and weaponization, environmental sustainability, market and trade facilitation, health, culture and much more. As active participants in the governance process, civil society can provide the advocacy and mobilization needed to ensure that issues most important to a nation or even a region win greater recognition. What CARICOM states need to do now, at both national and regional levels is to create the structures and spaces for engaging civil society. This includes the creation of opportunities to facilitate civil society participation in key governance and decision-making processes, as well as encourage exchange of information on issues of mutual interest.

As Richards noted, engagement of civil society in regional processes is not a gesture but an obligation which should be continuous, structured and well defined.[34] Anyanwu notes that despite its good intentions, the CARICOM Civil Society Charter, which had as its primary goal 'the creation of a truly participatory political environment within CARICOM which will be propitious to genuine consultation in the process of governance', was never completely implemented across the region.[35] CARICOM's 2015–2019 Strategic Plan once again references its intention to establish 'a permanent arrangement for engagement/consultation with the regional representatives of private sector and civil society NGOs, Labour, Youth, Media etc.) at the meetings of Councils' as part of its plan to enhance the participatory governance.[36] The bottom line is that small states such as those in the Caribbean need their diplomacies to work. Their diplomacies, especially from a regional perspective and approach need to be able to upgrade their engagement in the international system. A viable regional diplomacy for the twenty-first century cannot be realistically achieved without the inclusion of non-state actors. Gone are the days when diplomacy was simply confined to capitals and missions: the role of non-state actors, particularly in civil society, has never been more important.

Institutions for diplomacy

Much was said in the Forum about the need to modernize and reposition Caribbean institutions to respond to challenges of contemporary international relations and also to capture the opportunities therein. These calls have been made against the backdrop of the prominent role institutions play in the growth and development of any nation and also because of concerns that institutional redundancies are fast becoming primary challenges for the region's growth and development agenda.[37] Acemoglu and Robinson have argued that 'it is man-made political and economic institutions that underlie economic successes or the lack of it'.[38] Unfortunately, several Caribbean institutions are not seen to be providing the enabling environment needed to optimally advance the region's interest in the international system because the processes and modes of operation are outdated and out of sync with the global forces (economic, social, political, cultural etc.) at work; and as such, they are unable to advance a regional diplomacy that serves the collective interest of Caribbean states.

To facilitate regional diplomacy and ensure that the region maintains some strategic relevance in the international system, Caribbean institutions, chief among them CARICOM, must reflect the ability to consistently mobilize and advocate a strategic regional narrative on a range of key issues as part of a process of building and maintaining trustworthiness in the international system. A key aspect of that modernising process must be the Caribbean Diplomatic Corp. There have been calls for more long-term strategic planning at the regional level that prioritizes the attainment of inclusive and sustainable growth and development for all member states. In this context, regional institutions have to align the same strategic narratives to the global forces at work and ensure that in the constitution of the region's diplomacy, they can consistently advance those issues that are most important to the region.

PART B
TOWARDS A MULTI-DIMENSIONAL DIPLOMACY

The academic inquiry in the particular and unique features of small states' foreign policy has been insufficiently conceptualized and analysed. [39] This also goes for the application of the region's diplomacy. Small states' foreign policies are often not discussed in terms of how small states have made decisive and independent contributions to the international system but unfairly focus on 'core' and 'periphery' dependence-oriented relations. It is possible for small states such as those in the Caribbean to carve out a degree of relative autonomy by identifying those features of the external environment that are likely to work most effectively to their advantage. [40] There is more power in the Caribbean's 'smallness' if its engagement with the international community is strategic. As author of *The Color Purple*, Alice Walker rightly stated, 'The most common way people give up their power is by thinking they don't have any'.

Diplomacy according to Objiofor Aginam, is driven by phenomenal flows of ideas, finance, information communication technologies, and also affects countries in different ways. There is an increase in the understanding of the role of diplomacy in the context of key global arenas of diplomacy such as health, environment, disasters, humanitarianism, market multilateralism, conflict resolution and broadly human security. States therefore need multi-dimensional diplomacy to respond to the equally multi-dimensional nature of issues and security challenges which they are faced with in the international system. Sung-Joo notes that 'today's diplomacy deals with a country's culture, science, sports and other endeavours such as scholarship and arts'. [41]

Multi-dimensional diplomacy in this context emphasizes the multiple possibilities of power exercise and how they can be brought to bear on the instrumental capabilities of Caribbean small states towards ensuring that their interests receive support in the international system. Effective multi-dimensional regional diplomacy therefore requires greater policy coherence between national policies on key issues. The region needs multi-dimensional diplomacy to tackle poverty and equality, navigate progress on sustainable development, to strengthen their financial capabilities and build resilience in the wake of the changing global economic and financial landscape. Several facets of diplomacy including public diplomacy, economic diplomacy, environmental diplomacy, energy diplomacy, cultural diplomacy, gender diplomacy, health diplomacy, science diplomacy and much more can be strategically pursued to influence the behaviour of other actors in the international system as well as promote those issues of importance to Caribbean states.

Public diplomacy for example is an increasingly popular technique used by countries to achieve their objectives. Well-thought-out policies in this regard can assist Caribbean states to overcome opinion polarization, fluctuation and combativeness. It can lead to a deeper understanding of countries in the region and also beyond, particularly within the context of the deepened integration and convergence of countries of the greater Caribbean. This is especially important if a state is seeking solidarity in pursuit of a goal as in the case of Trinidad and Tobago which sought to host the secretariat of the Arms Trade Treaty. Trinidad and Tobago has invested resources to create an image that supported its capacity and suitability to host the secretariat. Given the interrelatedness of global issues, hardly any form of diplomacy is pursued alone. At any time, countries may be simultaneously engaged in multiple forms of diplomacy such as environment and health, economics and energy etc.

Similarly, governments engage in economic diplomacy by means of economic tools such as trade agreements to achieve state interests around economic growth and development. It may also entail some trade diplomacy which focuses on boosting a country's trade and financial sectors. It is international diplomatic efforts that set the foundation for increased economic relationships and increased investments. Consistent with the convergence model which has been advocated by Dookeran,[42] a regional economic policy must be focused on widening the economic space for the Caribbean and also on deepening the Caribbean integration process to a point of meaning. It should be focused on building the environment, the drivers and the conditions necessary to attract investments. The widening of the Caribbean is not a new proposal yet it is one that finds merit in the justification that investors will find a Caribbean market of nearly 30 million people attractive. [43]

Focusing on global health diplomacy in his presentation to the Forum, Obijiorfor Aginam noted that health diplomacy—the pursuit of matters of health through diplomatic negotiations—has undergone profound changes in the past few decades. Diseases and public health, both driven by other economic factors, increasingly feature as prominent challenges to contemporary foreign policy deliberations between actors in the international system. Labonte and Gagnon further note that the securitization of health is one of the permanent features of public health governance in the twenty-first century.[44, 45] As such, the processes that shape global health governance are no longer the sole domain of public health experts from health ministries, but increasingly that of trade officers, human rights officials and indeed many other major players at the national, regional and international levels including state and non-state actors.

Noting that global health is only possible though collective action, Sir George Alleyne, the United Nations' Secretary General's Special Envoy for HIV/AIDS in the Caribbean region, has argued that the health of all people and the reduction of health inequity cannot be achieved without health diplomacy.[46] The need for a regional approach has long been recognized and remains great today. We have seen the benefits of regional health diplomacy in the region's advocacy for a United Nation's High Level Conference on non-communicable diseases. The region therefore needs to remain sensitive to emerging global issues that may involve health diplomacy. The recently concluded Third International Conference on Financing for Development[47] was a missed opportunity to draw the international community's attention to health issues which are of great concern to the region. Yet, as Sir George Alleyne cautions, the region must ensure that health issues of interest to the region remain on the agenda ahead of the United Nations' summit for the adoption of the post-2015 human development agenda in September 2015 and what is now the 2030 Agenda for Sustainable Development.

In his presentation, Obijiorfor Aginam further noted the challenges of a hyper-globalized world wherein regional coordination is needed to confront health scares such as SARs, Asian flu and Ebola that have also become global security issues. He argued that in crafting a global health diplomacy, the Caribbean region would need to find the right mechanism to manage these trans-boundary health risks that have become extremely important for regional security. Yet, Drager and Fidler argue that although contemporary health issues are transnational in nature, 'countries remain core actors that must reorient their health and foreign policies in ways that align their national interests with the diplomatic, epidemiological and ethical realities of a globalized world'.[48]

CARICOM's regional health policy should focus on building global partners with a view to developing its 'epidemiological shield' against both transnational and trans-boundary communicable and non-communicable diseases which pose the greatest threats to its health security. Its strategic approach to global health should prioritize South–South cooperation, focusing on those hemispheric countries with similar interests such as Cuba and Brazil. Brazil's position on health as a human right has enabled it to mainstream health in all its policies, this position has also influenced its approach to South–South cooperation. Similarly, Cuba sees health as a human right although its approach to health diplomacy is more ideological and based on solidarity.

Another highlight of the roundtable on global diplomacy was the presentation by Dr. Camille Alleyne on space exploration as a tool for diplomacy and sustainability for small states. The key message is about harnessing the region's existing capabilities in science, innovation and technology towards a future in the space economy. Space exploration is not a common subject in the region and perhaps not one that CARICOM countries in their current economic conundrum will immediately embrace, yet it presents an untapped opportunity for the Caribbean region. These opportunities are in areas such as environment conservation, agriculture management, crop production, mineral exploration, health and disease mapping. As Alissa Trotz noted, space-based technologies can be adapted in innovative and exciting ways by locally trained and equipped homegrown users to solve local problems and reinvigorate regional economies.

The question therefore is how to build the capacity given the prevailing view that space exploration is no longer the domain of developed countries, but indeed smaller and developing countries are engaging in joint action and partnership activities. These partnerships cannot be restricted to developed countries but must be open to other emerging and developing countries which are willing to engage in such win-win partnerships. A Caribbean Sea convergence can provide the framework for these countries to start developing some space activity for mutual gains. There are possible economic gains through the commercialization of space products including earth imaging and also the potential for spin-off effects into other sectors such as a bio-technology, telecommunication, pharmaceuticals etc. A space diplomacy that focuses on meeting the capacity and human capital development requirements for tomorrow through convergence is needed in this context.

Technical basis for a multidimensional diplomacy

Small states have traditionally been seen as vulnerable with little economic and political influence, and their foreign policy has traditionally been discussed in terms either of relations of 'dependency' or relations between 'core' and 'periphery'.[49] Focus has largely been on maximizing relationships based on historical ties, and more lately on building relations with other countries of the South. Indeed, the international system in which Caribbean states operate is by and large shaped by the actions and inactions of larger and more powerful states. Yet as Al Bu Said suggests, there are a number of ways in which small states can make decisive contributions to international relations and in which they can exercise considerable freedom of action. The viability of Caribbean states' foreign policy power is dependent on its resilience to global pressures which in turn relies on their capacity to negotiate and advocate those issues that are most important to them. Caribbean states must find effective ways, preferably institutionalized, to promote their interests in the international community.

Negotiating capacity

Ambassador Insanally observed that Caribbean states 'find it difficult to hold their own in negotiations with their larger and more developed counterparts...not only do most of them suffer from the constraints of limited size and resources but they also lack the strategic clout to extract meaningful concessions from more powerful states'. Noting that since success in negotiations is the result of a mix of strategy and hard work, Caribbean states are not always persuasive enough in negotiations because they lack the bargaining power and leverage to influence the outcome of issues in the global agenda.[50] While the region has produced some renowned diplomats, there is the need to improve the related capacity of Caribbean diplomats in negotiation and advocacy, and also enhance the coordinating ability of regional institutions to accentuate the power of its diplomacy.

As opposed to building new relations for a new diplomacy, what is needed is to improve the negotiating capacities of Caribbean diplomats so that they can successfully and effectively present and defend the

Caribbean cause in the international community. It begs the question therefore: what kinds of additional skills are required in this new space? Alissa Trotz, in her presentation on gender diplomacy, agreed with the need to recalibrate Caribbean diplomacy and on the importance of strategic diplomacy, but she cautioned that it is also important that the region does not reinvent the wheel. Indeed twenty-first-century diplomacy requires a variety of skills including the art of negotiations and the ability to work in a rather diverse global environment. Although small states face other unique challenges such as the absence of bargaining leverage to extract sizeable concessions from more powerful countries, Ambassador Insanally argues that by means of soft power, a small state diplomat must be able to sway counterparts from more powerful countries that his proposition serves their common interests.[51]

To achieve these goals, CARICOM and by extension its member states must intensify the level of effort, training and prioritization it places on the development of skills, particularly the negotiating capacity of its Foreign Service Officers (FSO) and diplomats. Studies have shown negotiating skills as one of the most important requirements for a successful diplomatic career. Wood and Coates add that 'skilled negotiation requires solid communication skills, and is often enhanced by effective consensus-building".[52] The improvements in the negotiating capacity of Caribbean diplomats will be just one aspect of the region's commitment to advancing its diplomatic profile and capability.

Training

Institutions like the Diplomatic Academy based at the Institute of International Relations of the University of the West Indies (UWI), St. Augustine is playing a significant role in training FSOs and will be key in the development of a new cadre of diplomats for tomorrow, imparting in them the new tools and skills for a new diplomacy. The Institute of International Relations has worked with the Ministry of Foreign Affairs of Trinidad and Tobago and other regional and international institutions to develop training programmes which are delivered by local and international experts in a familiar environment and in a Caribbean context. This is a marked difference from trainings that happen abroad. Although focused on small states and developing countries in some cases, it cannot have the same impact as locally designed and delivered trainings. Perhaps the Diplomatic Academy will decide to tackle the elephant in the room, which is the linguistic inflexibility of many of the region's diplomats. This challenge was identified by Beckles and was reiterated by many others over the course of the Forum.

Yet, as Petrovsky argued, there is value in keeping links in time. Learning new methods does not suggest the erosion of past experiences of diplomacy as lessons by pioneers, and they remain very much relevant and critical to the success of any diplomat.[53] Rajiv Ramlal alluded to this in his discussion of the key points raised in the panel on global diplomacy. The premier and career diplomats from the region, with great insights and experience in the politics and intricacies of the multilateral institutions have a responsibility to pass on the knowledge to young diplomats through established structures such as the Diplomatic Academy. There is also much learning that happens from practical observation –learning by doing– so the new cadre of home-bred diplomats should be given the opportunities while still in school to participate in internships both in capital and missions so they can have a well-rounded training. With the right training, a diplomat can acquire a personal negotiator's toolbox which will assist them incrementally with consistent practice and experience to perform at the highest standards.

Intellectual preparation

Noting the difference between clever diplomacy and big/small diplomacy, Henrikson argues for the emphasis on intellectual preparation towards the development of a country's foreign policy positions and diplomatic engagement. He argues that this is a most important insight into the mind of one's interlocutor and into precision in the formulation of a country's interests.[54] An essential skill for any Caribbean diplomat is a thorough understanding of the Caribbean perspective or as a minimum national perspectives. It is impossible for a diplomat to 'get others to have his/her way' without a comprehensive understanding of the country or region he or she represents. Having already noted the strain which understaffed Caribbean missions and capitals face in dealing with the myriad of global issues that confront their countries, there is need to think more closely about how countries in the region can manage their resources more effectively through joint action to improve their capacity to be intellectually prepared ahead of major international meetings. Another essential requirement is to understand the interests of their counterparts – their unique needs, fears and intentions. This is not an easy feat and forms part of the intellectual preparation process.

The benefits of Regional Preparatory Meetings ahead of major conferences such as the Arms Trade Treaty Diplomatic Conference in 2012 are well noted. Those conferences allowed diplomats from across the region to sufficiently develop a CARICOM position ahead of the negotiations on the Arms Trade Treaty in New York. That process has also paved the way for more coordination of positions ahead of the First Conference of States Parties in Cancun in August 2015. Ahead of the Third International Conference on Small Island Developing States (SIDS) held in Samoa in September 2014, Trinidad and Tobago's Foreign Ministry worked with its officials at the UN office in Washington as well as in the different ministries in the country to prepare an agenda for the meeting. At the regional level, the Caribbean Regional Preparatory Meeting was held in July 2013 in Jamaica to discuss issues important to the region and agree on an outcome document which would have served as a basis for the regional position at the conference.

Beyond these preparatory meetings, there should be more joint research and data-sharing activities among foreign affairs ministries and departments in the region. This already happens, but more can be done to ensure the best intellectual preparation for Caribbean diplomats before major meetings. In a knowledge economy, research and data production for decision making is important if the region's diplomats are to effectively present and negotiate its interest in international forums. With advancements in technology, information can be transmitted so quickly via email, video conferencing, telephone and so forth that Caribbean diplomats cannot therefore restrict cooperation and exchange of information with each other to formal meetings. This will assist in their preparation for conferences and indeed their negotiating capacity. Given the limited resources in the region and the similarities of challenges and approach, there is no need for replication and duplication of efforts. This is where CARICOM, as the primary regional institution can play a key role in coordinating research pooling, data sharing and coordination. There is already a system in place but it has to work better. If functioning properly, countries, particularly the smallest and most resource-challenged will take advantage of these opportunities.

Advocacy skills

Strong advocacy skills are another essential component of successful diplomacy toolkit, and if Caribbean diplomats are to successfully influence international global policy, they must possess and systematically apply their advocacy skills. For small states relying solely on soft power to influence the international system, advocacy and networking skills are important if its representatives are to successfully articulate and elevate Caribbean issues at international forums. According to Professor Nigel Harris, regional diplomats have to 'keep [their] ears to the ground for opportunities to promote the region or for opportunities that may be advantageous to the region in various ways—trade, politics, culture, educational opportunities...while equipping 'themselves with soft skills such as socialising and networking' both requirements for success in the diplomatic arena'.[55]

Civil society organizations around the world have relied on their advocacy skills to bring issues of concern to them to the front in many international forums, and based on those skills, they have been able to mobilize support that led to landmark institutions such as the Arms Trade and Mine Ban Treaties. Advocacy skills are unnatural to FSOs and diplomats, and they are skills that are acquired through practical sessions. High-level diplomatic service requires the ability to persuade and advocate. Given the high importance of political neutrality and detachment for professionalism at the national level, some scholars go even further to distinguish advocacy skills, noting the ineffectiveness of 'passionate advocacy', especially in countries prone to regime changes, and where its FSOs and diplomats are nonetheless expected to continue an unbiased representation of policies even if those policies are set by regimes that they privately do not agree with.[56]

CONCLUSION

Diplomacy will continue to be an indispensable tool for Caribbean states in the multilateral system. A multi-dimensional regional diplomacy covering key areas such as energy, culture, trade, health and more is needed to advance the strategic interests of Caribbean states in the international area. More than building new relations, what is needed for a Caribbean regional diplomacy to thrive in this knowledge-driven economy are strong capabilities in negotiation and advocacy. In the context of lack of resources as the a significant constraint of the diplomacy of Caribbean states, more foreign policy coordination is needed to overcome these limitations, particularly in the areas of intellectual preparation and in possibilities of joint-diplomatic missions.

The idea of a Caribbean Diplomatic Corp is proposed in the context of strengthening foreign policy coordination—a foundational aspect of the regional integration movement. Although the region's institutions have yielded results for the region over the years, they are simply not adequate to take the region to the next level of global relevance. The fundamental question which leaders and decision makers must ask is by what yardstick is progress measured? If the goal is to attain the levels of economic development and strategic relevance that other small states such as Singapore have attained, then action is needed to accelerate the process of convergence. The possible role of a potential Caribbean Diplomatic Corp in this context is critical to advance the imperatives for the future.

NOTES

1. Consultant, Ministry of Foreign Affairs of Trinidad and Tobago.
2. The 3rd China/Caribbean Economic and Trade Cooperation Forum was held in Trinidad and Tobago on September 12–13, 2011. Jamaica hosted the first forum in 2005, while the second forum took place in Xiamen, China in 2007.
3. See Amitav Archarya's keynote address to the Forum.
4. Dookeran, Winston. 1996. 'Crosscurrents in Caribbean policy analysis'. In *Choices and Change: Reflection on the Caribbean,* Winston Dookeran (ed.). Washington D.C: Inter-American Development Bank.
5. Amitav Acharya, in his keynote presentation to the Forum, highlighted four characteristics of this multiplex world: multiple great powers and actors in the mix; complex global interdependence; multiple layers of governance; and a non-hegemonic de-centered world. For more, see *The End of American World Order,* 2014 Polity.
6. Insanally, Rudy. 'Multilateral diplomacy for small states: 'the art of letting others have your way" in *Caribbean Journal of International Relations & Diplomacy* Vol. 1, No. 2, June 2013: pp. 95-102.
7. CARICOM Secretariat. Diplomacy is small states' power says acting SG. Press Release 168/2011, May 4, 2011 http://www.caricom.org/jsp/pressreleases/press_releases_2011/pres168_11.jsp.
8. Cooper, Andrew and Timothy Shaw. 2009. 'The summitry of small states: towards the "Caribbean Summit". Policy Brief, The Centre for International Governance Innovation, No.15, April 2009.
9. Petrovsky, Vladimir. 1998. 'Diplomacy as an instrument of good governance' in *Modern Diplomacy* J. Kurbalija (ed.)http://www.diplomacy.edu/resources/general/diplomacy-instrument-good-governance, accessed July 16, 2015.
10. Ibid.
11. Insanally, Rudy. 'Multilateral diplomacy for small states: 'the art of letting others have your way" in *Caribbean Journal of International Relations & Diplomacy* Vol. 1, No. 2, June 2013: pp. 95-102.

12. Petrovsky, Vladimir. 1998. 'Diplomacy as an instrument of good governance' in *Modern Diplomacy* J. Kurbalija (ed.) http://www.diplomacy.edu/resources/general/diplomacy-instrument-good-governance, accessed July 16, 2015.

13. A legally binding international agreement that bans the use, production, stockpiling and transfer of antipersonnel mines and places obligations on countries to clear affected areas, assist victims and destroy stockpiles.

14. A coalition of non-governmental organizations from across the globe working on arms control

15. Another legally binding multilateral treaty to regulate the international trade and transfer of conventional weapons. The treaty entered into force on December 24, 2014.

16. CDRAV is a member of the Control Arms Coalition and has membership in fourteen (14) Caribbean states.

17. Anyanwu, David, 2013. 'Can Caribbean civil society effectively influence regional policy? Overcoming national and regional challenges in CARICOM,' in *Civil Society and World Regions: How Citizens are Reshaping Regional Governance in Times of Crisis*, Lorenzo Fioramonti (ed.) Plymouth, UK: Lexington Books.

18. Insanally, Rudy. 'Multilateral diplomacy for small states: 'the art of letting others have your way" in *Caribbean Journal of International Relations & Diplomacy* Vol. 1, No. 2, June 2013: pp. 95-102.

19. Their focus was on the EU.

20. Allen, David and Michael Smith, 2012. 'The EU, strategic diplomacy and the BRIC countries'. Policy Paper 11: February 2012. University of Loughborough.

21. CARICOM Secretariat. Strategic Plan for the Caribbean Community 2015-2019: Repositioning CARICOM. Vol.1 – The Executive Plan. Turkeyen, Guyana. July 3, 2014. http://caricom.org/jsp/secretariat/EXECUTIVE%20PLAN%20VOL%201%20-%20FINAL.pdf.

22. CARICOM Secretariat. 2011. Press Release: Diplomacy is small states' power says acting SG. May 4, 2011.

23. Francis, Ian. 2013. *Commentary: CARICOM faces increased foreign policy coordination challenges.* http://www.caribbeannewsnow.com/headline-Commentary:-CARICOM-faces-increased-foreign-policy-coordination-challenges-14034.html accessed July 21, 2015.

24. United States — Measures Affecting the Cross-Border Supply of Gambling and Betting Services. https://www.wto.org/english/tratop_e/dispu_e/cases_e/ds285_e.htm.

25. CARICOM countries led by Trinidad and Tobago and Jamaica have played leading roles in the Arms Trade Treaty process. Trinidad and Tobago campaigned vigorously to host the Secretariat in Port of Spain, but ultimately lost out to Geneva, Switzerland in a vote at the First Conference of States Parties in Cancun, Mexico in August 2015.

26. It is important that this entity does not suffer from the difficulties encountered by the Caribbean Regional Negotiating Machinery (CRNM), which was

established in April 1997 by CARICOM Heads of Government to develop, coordinate and execute an overall negotiating strategy for various external negotiations in which the Region was involved.

27. Schipani, Andres. 2014. 'Pacific Alliance: moving forward. Beyondbrics'. http://blogs.ft.com/beyond-brics/2014/02/11/pacific-alliance-moving-forward/. accessed July 23, 2015.

28. Lavut, Anna. The Pacific Alliance: the new star among integration groupings. Russian International Affairs Council. http://russiancouncil.ru/en/inner/?id_4=5238#top-content , accessed July 23, 2015.

29. *Stabroek News*. Joint diplomatic representation crucial – Rodrigues-Birkett tells CARICOM foreign minister. May 22, 2014.http://www.stabroeknews.com/2014/news/stories/05/22/joint-diplomatic-representation-crucial/.

30. Website of the Permanent Mission of St. Lucia to the United Nations, New York. http://saintluciamissionun.org/mission-role/.

31. https://www.un.int/guyana/staff .

32. https://www.un.int/jamaica/staff .

33. Cooper, Andrew and Timothy Shaw. 2009. Op.cit

34. Richards, Peter. 2008. 'Caribbean civil society groups want to have direct input at Americas Summit''.''.. Noticias Finacieras. November 5.

35. Anyanwu, David, 2013. 'Can Caribbean civil society effectively influence regional policy? Overcoming national and regional challenges in CARICOM,' in Civil Society and World Regions: How Citizens are Reshaping Regional Governance in Times of Crisis, Lorenzo Fioramonti (ed.). Plymouth, UK: Lexington Books

36. CARICOM Secretariat. Strategic Plan for the Caribbean Community 2015-2019: Repositioning CARICOM. Vol.1 – The Executive Plan. Turkeyen, Guyana. July 3, 2014. http://caricom.org/jsp/secretariat/EXECUTIVE%20PLAN%20VOL%201%20-%20FINAL.pdf.

37. Leadership and political inaction remain fundamental problems for accelerating Caribbean development.

38. Acemoglu, Daron and James A. Robinson. 2013. Why nations fail; the origins of power, prosperity and poverty. New York: Crown Business.

39. Chong, Alan and Matthias Maass, 2010. 'Introduction: the foreign policy power of small states'. *Cambridge Review of International Affairs* Vol 23, Issue 3, 2013.

40. Al Bu Said, Badr Bin Hamad, 2005. 'Small States' diplomacy in the age of globalization: an omani perspective' in Analyzing Middle East Foreign Policies and the Relationship with Europe Gerd Nonneman (ed.) Lecture delivered to Belgium's Royal Institute for International Affairs in September 2003.

41. Sung-Joo, Han. 2008. Strategic diplomacy in an age of globalization. Speech presented at the sixth symposium: Diplomatic Strategy in the Age of Globalization on May 9, 2008. The Tokyo Foundation.

42. See: Anyanwu, David. 2015. Caribbean convergence: an essay. Paper commissioned by ILO for the Forum on the Future of the Caribbean. May 2015 and Dookeran, Winston. 2013. 'A new frontier for Caribbean

convergence'. *Journal of International Relations & Diplomacy*. Vol.1, no, 2, pp. 5-20, June 2013.

43. The wider Caribbean in this instance would include Dominican Republic, French Guyana and other islands that are washed by the Caribbean Sea.

44. Labonte. Ronald and Michelle L Gagnon, 2010. 'Framing health and foreign policy: lessons for global health diplomacy,' in Globalization and Health, Ronald Labonte and Michelle Gagnon (ed.).

45. Health security is a feature of Human Security which was popularized in the early 1990s by the UNDP in the wake of the Cold War.

46. Alleyne, George, 2014. Health diplomacy; science diplomacy, can the twain meet? Distinguished lecturer at the Institute of International Relations of the University of the West Indies, St. Augustine Campus, March 18, 2014. https://sta.uwi.edu/uwitoday/pdfs/Sir%20George%20Alleyne%20on%20 Health%20diplomacy%20and%20%20Science%20diplomacy.pdf .

47. Held in Addis Ababa, Ethiopia on July 13–16, 2015.

48. Drager, Nick and David P. Filder, 2007. 'Foreign policy, trade and health: at the cutting edge of global health diplomacy.' Editorials, Bulletin of the World Health Organization, March 2007.

49. Al Bu Said, Badr Bin Hamad. 2003. 'Small States' Diplomacy in the Age of Globalization: An Omani Perspective". *The Review of International Affairs,* Volume 3, Issue 2, 2003.

50. Insanally, Rudy. 'Multilateral diplomacy for small states: 'the art of letting others have your way" in *Caribbean Journal of International Relations & Diplomacy* Vol. 1, No. 2, June 2013: pp. 95-102.

51. Insanally, Rudy. 'Multilateral diplomacy for small states: 'the art of letting others have your way" in *Caribbean Journal of International Relations & Diplomacy* Vol. 1, No. 2, June 2013: pp. 95-102.

52. Wood, George and Breena Coates2008. Strategic leadership course directive. Carlisle, PA, U.S. Army War College.

53. Petrovsky, Vladimir. 1998. 'Diplomacy as an instrument of good governance' in *Modern Diplomacy* J. Kurbalija (ed.) http://www.diplomacy.edu/ resources/general/diplomacy-instrument-good-governance, accessed July 16, 2015.

54. Henrikson, Alan. (Undated). 'Ten types of small state diplomacy.' The Fletcher School of Law and Diplomacy, Tufts University, Medford, Massachusetts. https://is.muni.cz/el/1423/podzim2008/MVZ157/um/TEN_TYPES_OF_ SMALL_STATE_DIPLOMACY.pdf

55. CARICOM Secretariat. "Advocacy and networking stressed as important skills for diplomats." Press release 160/2000. 18 May 2009 http://www. caricom.org/jsp/pressreleases/pres160_09.jsp .

56. Lenczowski, John, 2011. *Full spectrum diplomacy and grand strategy: reforming the structure and culture of U.S. foreign policy.* Plymouth, UK: Lexington Books.

CHAPTER 13
What do we do now? The Development Agenda For Action

Winston Dookeran, Iwan Sewberath-Misser and Carlos Elias[1]

During three days in May 2015, leaders of the Caribbean and stakeholders—including politicians and political activists, members of academia, representatives of international institutions and development practitioners, private sector representatives, students, and citizens from many countries of the region and beyond—gathered to share their knowledge and views, visions and priorities for action on how to enhance the future of the Caribbean. All these priorities merit careful consideration, and all the chapters in this publication are intended to summarise what transpired during the *Forum on the Future of the Caribbean*.

After presenting all the issues discussed during the Forum, this penultimate chapter serves to align all the proposals from the Forum in a format that facilitates the identification of priorities for action. We present here the development agenda for the Caribbean. As mentioned by the Principal of the University of the West Indies Professor Sankat in the preface and by the then Minister of Foreign Affairs Dookeran of Trinidad and Tobago in the first chapter, the Forum was a place to listen and encourage action, not just a place to listen for the sake of listening—and to act motivated by the potential benefits to be reaped by accelerating the current Caribbean convergence process.

This chapter presents a short list of initiatives that were proposed during the Forum and which are considered priorities because they resonated the most with participants; they were repeated often during the Forum; are concrete and doable, and the impact of their implementation is high and will be perceived as such by citizens in the near-term. However, it is with some reservations that this chapter only focuses on only a few, of many, initiatives put forward by the participants. For this reason, we include an annex to this chapter with a complete list of all initiatives put forward during the Forum, with a preliminary assessment of their technical and political difficulties, as well as the potential costs of implementation. This list will provide a wealth of information for the selection of additional initiatives in the future.

A CALL FOR ACTION WAS THE MAIN MESSAGE DELIVERED BY FORUM PARTICIPANTS

First and foremost, Forum participants clamoured for action now. They argued that the current regional integration model that resulted in the creation of the Caribbean Community (CARICOM) had served the region well for a number of years but was now obsolete. Participants also noted that CARICOM should not be considered a failure because of its many positive contributions to the development of the region, some of which will be presented later in this chapter. However, the elusive goal of a single market and economy remains the top, yet unfulfilled, priority.

CARICOM's problem is in its capacity to implement agreed upon actions, a recurrent comment brought forward by participants during the Forum. Over the years, CARICOM has identified priorities for action, announcing them as done deals, which raised expectations of change and reform, and seldom were those promises fulfilled. For CARICOM leadership, over promising is the norm, not the exception to the rule. CARICOM's implementation record is disappointing according to evidence presented by Professor Clement during the Forum.[2,3] He reported that every year CARICOM approves a significant number of directives, on average in excess of nine hundred per year, but that compliance is limited: on average about 38% of directives are executed by member countries. His analysis also shows that compliance varies significantly depending on the category: it is relatively good for legal and institutional infrastructure directives (compliance rates of over 75% per year) and single market directives (compliance rates of over 60% per year).However, it is disappointing for directives related to the single economy (compliance rates of less than 5% per year).[4] According to Professor Clement, the explanation of the large mismatch between directives compliance in general and by category is related to two complementary factors: first, the tendency of CARICOM to present as imminent a complex set of promises that reflect the good will of leaders but ignore the difficulties of implementation; second, the large impact of domestic politics on the implementation of directives that affect regional integration.

The evidence presented by Professor Clement points to significant difficulties in implementing single economy directives. The single economy directives are arguably those that 'bite' the most, as they open up opportunities for competition among private sector businesses throughout the region. Local businesses feel exposed to competition from abroad, and they consider that companies from large countries, such as Jamaica and Trinidad and Tobago, would have comparative advantages over companies in smaller countries, such as in the OECS. For example, the 'Investment Code' and 'Accreditation Directives' require a test of ownership and control. Companies that would qualify for benefits under the Investment Code would have to be controlled by a citizen of the region, and this test would disqualify firms in Barbados that are local yet have foreign ownership. Similar arguments may be made for the poor implementation outcomes of directives for facilitation of travel and right of establishment.

Interestingly, the research of Professor Clement identifies a positive correlation between election cycles and important CARICOM decisions. He notes for example that the Grand Anse Declaration in 1989 was made in the context of elections in nine out of twelve CSME member states. A similar scenario repeated itself when the revised Treaty of Chaguaramas was signed in 2001.[5] In this context, it would appear that large integration announcements, which are always welcomed by the people in the region because they reflect their deeply rooted sense of Caribbean citizenship, tend to coincide with electoral cycles and are used to improve incumbent chances of re-election.[6] As noted, the problem is that, in many cases, these announcements were not followed up by a focused implementation effort.

In spite of the negative view of the pace of implementation presented in the previous paragraph, participants at the Forum fully recognised the achievements of CARICOM.[7, 8] The Caribbean Court of Justice, perhaps the most relevant achievement, is in place and building a Caribbean jurisprudence that over time will strengthen its capacity to play a central role in the region. The Caribbean Disaster

Emergency Management Agency (CDEMA) and the Caribbean Catastrophe Risk Insurance Facility (CCRIF) are in place and will play a role in prevention and reconstruction in the future. The Caribbean Community Climate Change Centre (CCCCC) is also in place and has been influential in the global response to climate change. As it relates to the pillars of CARICOM, the Single Market core regimes are in place, and regional policies are being considered in agriculture and food security, energy, industry, ICT and security. The Caribbean Public Health Agency (CARPHA) was created to prevent and monitor communicable and noncommunicable diseases. The Pan Caribbean Partnership against HIV and AIDS has been in place since 2001 working on prevention and treatment of that virus and disease. The Caribbean Examinations Council (CXC) provides examinations and curricula relevant to the region. The Caribbean Vocational Qualification (CVQ) provides vocational certificates recognised throughout the region. Importantly, diplomatic efforts by the CARICOM have been successful; for example, the International Civil Aviation Organisation adopted the community of interest principle, facilitating as much as possible the expansion of routes by Caribbean airlines throughout the region.

What comes first?

Action requires modernising institutions in CARICOM. To reach this goal, the region now needs a modern institutional framework that is consistent with the new socioeconomic reality of the twenty-first century. The new framework should provide incentives for more dynamic decision-making processes leading to real integration within CARICOM, the broader Caribbean and even countries in Central and South America.

For CARICOM to modernise, it needs new institutions—that is, new rules of the game and a new political and economic incentive framework that determines which initiatives are prioritised and how they are implemented. Modernising institutions imply identifying and addressing CARICOM's governance shortcomings. That CARICOM needs to be modernised is not new, and a modernisation proposal was commissioned by CARICOM in 2012, but it did not trigger the expected reforms.[9] Current Caribbean institutions focus on process and not on execution, an issue that is widely recognised by leaders in the region. As previously noted, the problem is CARICOM's decision-making process. For years, Caribbean leaders have been talking about the 'implementation deficit' of CARICOM.[10,11] In October of 2014, Secretary General LaRocque noted that, in the context of the heterogeneous nature of the countries in the region and the relative youth of its nations, it is 'no surprise therefore that regional integration has had a long history of gradualism, moving, some will argue, at the pace of the slowest. ... Further, the governing arrangements for the CSME have become bureaucratic, unwieldy and lethargic and we spend more time and resources discussing the same issues rather than making decisions we can effectively implement.'[12]

The new integration model should deliver effective and efficient policies and services serving the purpose of genuine integration based on the region's common history, culture and goals. Convergence processes in motion throughout the region and the world offer opportunities for the region.[13] Convergence, as defined in this publication, is a sociopolitical and economic process that results in networks of people, businesses and governments. It includes trade and integration, but it goes beyond these traditional concepts to also include genuine formation of multinational socioeconomic networks for which borders are irrelevant. This was often noted during the Forum when participants noted that the 'feeling of belonging' to the Caribbean was widespread and far more advanced than the formal integration of its governments. To summarise:

> 'Caribbean Convergence...represents a new way of thinking about integration in the region, and a potential strategy for injecting the process with new life and energy.... The convergence argument is that trade and markets should be buttressed by production, distribution and competitiveness.'[14] The Caribbean is fully embedded in this process, which will continue over time as these networks expand and strengthen.

A NEW FRAMEWORK FOR POLICY MAKING IN THE CARIBBEAN

In times of change, which are mostly forced upon the Caribbean from events outside the region, Caribbean leaders are reminded of the need for integration—such as in 1989 when the threat of diminishing preferences to countries in the region, as a result of the creation of the European Single Market, led to the meeting in Grand Anse, Grenada, and to the aspiration of a Caribbean Single Market and Economy, causing the region to encounter new challenges. These challenges, faced again more recently, come from outside the region, but are now related to the lingering effects of the world financial crisis that started in 2007 and continues to negatively impact countries in the world, including the Caribbean. New world trends, noted previously in this publication described as a 'multiplex' world, also impact and challenge the status quo. Threatened by these events, the region leaders need to recognise that now, such as in the past, the Caribbean needs to strengthen integration efforts as a strategy to become self-reliant.

As noted by Ambassador LaRocque the goals of integration as presented in the revised Treaty of 2001 remain relevant today: *'Improved standards of living and work; full employment of labour and other factors of production; accelerated, co-ordinated and sustained economic development and convergence enhanced co-ordination of Member States' foreign policies; and enhanced functional co-operation. That last objective recognised the need for more efficient operation of common services in areas such as health, education, transportation and telecommunications.'*[15] Moreover, the pillars upon which the integration arrangements were designed also remain relevant today: economic integration, human and social development, security cooperation and foreign policy coordination. The challenge is not with the definition of goals and targets, but with the capacity of CARICOM to execute. In other words, the challenge is to close the implementation gap of CARICOM.

The current institutional framework should evolve—recognizing the achievements of CARICOM and addressing the challenges of the future— to facilitate the convergence process in the region. Citing again Ambassador LaRocque *'as we move to address those challenges, we must reach to the realisation that our national growth and development is inextricably tied to regional growth and development. Regional policies and national policies must be so intertwined as to be almost indiscernible, that sense of being part of a Community.'*[16]

The framework should lead to recognisable goals established in CARICOM for many years now:[17]

- Free movement of skills, goods, services, and capital including the right of establishment

- Abolition of exchange controls, free convertibility of currencies
- Integrated capital markets
- Convergence of macroeconomic policies
- Harmonised company legislation, and more generally harmonisation of laws and administrative practices
- Focus on facilitating production convergence

To make these goals reachable, CARICOM now needs to focus on action. Action, in turn, should be guided by the establishment of an institutional framework guided by the following principles:

- Market and convergence based
- Problem identification and results oriented
- Institutions oriented, including the need for rationalising institutions when needed
- Partial integration approach is preferable to more comprehensive integration approaches[18]
- Prioritising tangible outcomes[19]—or in the words of a report commissioned to propose reforms to CARICOM: 'targeting the delivery of a narrow range of specific, practical and achievable benefits over a reasonably short time horizon'[20]
- Consider strengthening the Association of Caribbean Community Parliamentarians (ACCP)[21]
- Focus on functional cooperation: the common provision of goods and services[22]

Strengthen foreign policy coordination, especially by expanding CARICOM horizons to the broader Caribbean and countries in Central and South America[23]

CONCRETE STEPS TO MOVE THE PROCESS FORWARD

The modernisation agenda will benefit from the creation of a "Blue Ribbon Committee on the Modernisation of CARICOM" empowered to update the 2012 proposal for modernising CARICOM, mapping out the current institutional framework, and based on that analysis making a recommendation on the modernisation of CARICOM institutions through changes in governance.[24] To make the work of the Blue Ribbon Committee relevant, it will be created with a clear mandate to reform CARICOM and would include a commitment by CARICOM Member states to formally vote on the modernisation proposal that would be the main output of the Blue Ribbon Committee: approve it to implement the modernisation proposal or turn it down and signal the continuation of business as usual. This committee would prepare a road map for changing the governance structure to facilitate decision making within CARICOM.

Caribbean citizens have heard proposals, such as the previous one, before. Caribbean leaders do not shy away from criticising CARICOM's slow pace of reform towards genuine integration. The previous proposal may sound uninspiring to many and may seem a poor result from the Forum. The modernisation process requires modernising CARICOM, but the implementation of this requirement will take time, and it may lead to lengthy discussions with no apparent real results.

For this reason, the Caribbean convergence process needs to be energised by solving concrete regional problems that affect most citizens. These problems were identified by participants during the Forum. Therefore while the Blue Ribbon Committee on the Modernisation of CARICOM delivers results, there is a need to focus on solving short-term regional problems. This chapter, therefore, suggests that the following four regional problems are resolved in the near-term:

- Air and sea transport to facilitate movement of people and goods throughout the region and from the region to countries in the broader Caribbean and beyond (Why a person pays more to fly from Port of Spain to Paramaribo than from Miami to Port of Spain; the logistical convergence challenge).

- Energy to reduce high costs and provide incentives for the development of regional energy networks, increasingly relying on the production of energy from renewable resources (Why prices for kwh vary so much across the region; the energy convergence challenge).

- Finance to facilitate a market-making mechanism(s) that connects financial markets in the region, making feasible the creation of financial markets that meet excess reserves with excess demand for credit (Why entrepreneurs pay different prices for loans in the region? the financial convergence challenge).

- Food security to facilitate trade within countries in the region, the broader Caribbean and beyond to ensure good quality supply, stable prices and long-term viability of agriculture (Why food is expensive and scarce in Bridgetown but plentiful and cheap in Georgetown; the food security and climate change convergence challenge).

Annex: Inventory of proposals put forward during the Forum

Near-Term Priority Proposals. The criteria used for the selection of these priority proposals include: general agreement and support by participants and presenters during the forum; they were properly articulated and developed; they may be executed in the near-term; they highly affect most of the Caribbean. The proposals are presented in the following tables in order of priority and are further divided between those that apply to the public sector and the private sector. The table includes an assessment of how difficult it is to execute the proposal from a technical, funding and coordination perspective (in all cases High, Medium or Low).

Table 13.1: Near-term public sector proposals

Proposal	Technical difficulty	Funding level	Coordination challenges
Regional air transportation policy (to ensure high quality, low cost air transportation across the Caribbean).	Low	High	High
Regional financial capital flows facility (to ensure that excess supply of funds meet excess demand for funds across the region).	Medium	High	High
Regional energy policy to reduce high costs and develop the capacity to produce energy from renewable resources.	Medium	High	High
Regional food security policy to ensure supply of quality products, and to lower price volatility.	Medium	High	High
Regional disaster prevention, emergency support and reconstruction facility (including direct support to citizens affected by high inflation and income loss because of the disaster) (including an insurance facility).	High	High	High
Regional program to reduce poverty and eradicate extreme poverty (the program would address the problem of poverty from a regional perspective, and it would set the stage for facilitating the implementation of free movement of labour in the region) (the region exhibits unacceptable levels of poverty and extreme poverty that are inconsistent with its income level) (the program would have a two-pronged approach: in the near-term it would strengthen safety nets and create automatic stabilizers; in the medium term it would focus on education and human capital to reduce dependency of the structural poor from the state).	Medium	Medium	High
Regional programme to address social impact of youth unemployment and gender issues (develop and implement a Caribbean youth entrepreneurship/National Service Programme in conjunction with tertiary institutions, private and public sectors with a focus on green, blue and social entrepreneurship) (promote an inclusive approach that reduces marginalization based on gender and sexual identity).			
Develop and implement a sustainable solution to protect and enforce the rights of domestic workers (CARICOM Free Movement of Labour issue).	Low	Low	High

Proposal	Technical difficulty	Funding level	Coordination challenges
Regional Public Partnership Policy Framework (definition of a common regional approach to PPP).	Low	Low	High
Regional broad band initiative (to expand quality connectivity across all the countries in the region; a regional approach ensures quality and lowers cost).	Low	Medium	High
Regional approach to reduce exposure and to be insured against sea transport accidents in national and international Caribbean Sea (oil spills, nuclear waste transport or other).	High	Low	High
Program to reduce the transaction costs linked to remittances.	Low	Low	High
Trinidad and Tobago becoming a transport hub for Caribbean-South America trade and building a bridge between Trinidad and Venezuela.	Medium	High	Low
Revise and implement the Caribbean Civil Society Charter which has been agreed since 1997 so as to provide a consolidated process for civil society to influence regional policy.	Low	Low	Low
Advocacy by ECLAC for IFIs to apply a broader set of criteria based on vulnerability rather than gross national income, in assessing Caribbean SIDS' access to concessional finance including.	Low	Low	Low
Research and institutional collaboration on new sources of domestic and regional financing for the Caribbean.	Low	Low	Low
Sharing of overseas missions by Caribbean countries in underrepresented regions.	Low	Medium	High
Develop a space science and technology education curriculum at tertiary, primary and secondary and also technical courses.	Medium	Medium	Medium

Table 13.2: Near-term private sector proposals

Proposal	Technical difficulty	Funding level	Coordination challenges
Develop a private sector strategy. The first step is to reconvene the Caribbean Business Forum.	Low	Medium	Medium
Strengthening the regional financial sector (onshore and offshore, call for a regional meeting of financial sector institutions to accelerate the interconnection/merge or convergence of financial sectors in the region).	High	Medium	High
Invest in strengthening businesses (cluster development) in energy, logistics and agriculture.	Medium	High	Medium

Long-Term Priority Proposals. These proposals have long gestation periods and they would not have an impact in the near-term.

Table 13.3: Long-term public sector proposals

Proposal	Technical difficulty	Funding level	Coordination challenges
Modernizing CARICOM—revise Chaguaramas Treaty to create the single market and economy and for policy coordination, including some proposals made by participants to the Forum, such as introducing sanctions to provide incentives for compliance; complete removal of trade barriers; creating a Union of Caribbean States; designing and executing Public Investment Programs independent of political cycles.	Medium	Low	High
DATA: Fill in information gaps (the region does not have accurate data to design, execute and evaluate interventions). This requires a regional approach, initially focused on measuring poverty and extreme poverty in the region.	Low	Medium	High
Use of renewable sources of energy – solar, wind, tides, and other (the PM of Trinidad and Tobago mentioned the creation of an Energy Fund: US$1 billion to fund the transformation of energy generation from oil to gas).	Medium	High	High

	Technical difficulty	Funding level	Coordination challenges
Program to mandate learning Spanish and English throughout the region (include student exchange programs).	Low	Medium	High
UWI becomes, such as before, a regional public university (this would require rationalizing/merging new universities throughout the region).	Low	High	High
Dedicating 1% of GDP to research and development and dedicating X% of GDP for tertiary education (this would require legislation). Making the link to productivity, and also facilitating the link between industry and research.	Low	High	High
Long-term solution to highly indebted countries in the region.	Medium	High	High
Tertiary and technical/vocational education. Matching supply and demand for skills and knowledge.	Medium	Medium	High
Regional approach to integrated coastal zone management.	High	Medium	High
Public sector reform (privatization of public enterprises, rationalisation and strengthening the public service, compensation).	Medium	Medium	High
Exploit opportunities in space economy through the development of a Caribbean Space Agency that will conduct research on space science and technology, satellite technology development and their applications.	High	High	High

Table 13.4: Long-term private sector proposals

Proposal	Technical difficulty	Funding level	Coordination challenges
Accelerating regional convergence (facilitating the strengthening and development of Caribbean value chains).	Medium	High	High
Developing high value added, mechanized, industrial agriculture (cocoa and others, export oriented initiative) (opportunity for investments in countries in the region that have land).	Low	High	High

NOTES

1. Dr Winston Dookeran, Minister of Foreign Affairs of Trinidad and Tobago. Mr Iwan Sewberath-Misser, Representative of the Banco de Desarrollo de America Latina. Dr Carlos Elias, Radford University and DHC Consulting.
2. Clement, Paul C. 2015. 'Implementation deficit: why member states do not comply with CARICOM directives.' Mimeo presented at the Caribbean Future Forum in Port of Spain, May 5–7, 2015.
3. The data presented by Professor Clement is dated because there is no publicly available detailed data for any year after 2007. A relevant issue for transparency and accountability of CARICOM is data availability, which unfortunately remains a problem.
4. The legal and institutional infrastructure directives include: treaty revision; national administration; enforcement of regulations; Caribbean Court of Justice; CROSQ (Standards and quality); and national competiveness. The single market directives include: free movement of goods; free movement of services; free movement of persons; free movement of skills; contingent rights; facilitation of travel; accreditation and equivalency; transfer of social security benefits; free movement of capital; removal of restrictions; capital market integration; double taxation agreement; and right of establishment. The single economy directives include: common external policy; harmonization laws; sector program and enabling environment; common support measures; and public education.
5. Paul C. Clement, 'Implementation deficit: why member states do not comply with CARICOM directives.' Mimeo presented at the Caribbean Future Forum in Port of Spain, May 5–7, 2015.
6. The intuition presented is well described in the economics literature by the Public Choice School. Led by the seminal work of Economics Nobel Laureate James Buchanan, public choice was best described as 'politics without romance' because it used economic tools to map out the behavior of politicians and the policies they design and execute. For additional information see the Center for Study of Public Choice at George Mason University (www.gmu.edu) or James Buchanan 'The Calculus of Consent' written with Gordon Tullock in 1962.
7. Ambassador Irwin LaRocque, Secretary General Caribbean Community. Distinguished Lecture delivered at University of the West Indies Port of Spain, Trinidad and Tobago, October 3, 2014.
8. Grenade, Wendy C. and Kai-Ann Skeete. 'Regionalism among small states-challenges and prospects: the case of the Caribbean Community (CARICOM). Published in Small States Digest Issue 1 2015, Commonwealth Secretariat.
9. In 2012 Richard Stoneman, Justice Duke Pollard and Hugho Inniss, 'Turning around CARICOM: proposals to restructure the Secretariat.' Consultancy to conduct an organizational restructuring of the Caribbean Community Secretariat. Report prepared by Landell Mills Ltd. This report was mandated by CARICOM Heads of Government and was contracted by the CARICOM

Secretariat with the financial support of the European Union and the Member States of CARICOM.

10. Wendy C. Grenade and Kai-Ann Skeete, 'Regionalism among small states-challenges and prospects: the case of the Caribbean Community (CARICOM). Published in Small States Digest Issue 1 2015, Commonwealth Secretariat.

11. Richard Stoneman, Justice Duke Pollard and Hugo Inniss, 'Turning around CARICOM: proposals to restructure the Secretariat' (2012). Consultancy to conduct an organizational restructuring of the Caribbean Community Secretariat. Report prepared by Landell Mills Ltd. This report was mandated by CARICOM Heads of Government and was contracted by the CARICOM Secretariat with the financial support of the European Union and the Member States of CARICOM.

12. Ambassador Irwin LaRocque, Secretary General Caribbean Community. Distinguished Lecture delivered at University of the West Indies Port of Spain, Trinidad and Tobago, October 3, 2014.

13. Winston Dookeran. 'A new frontier for Caribbean convergence.' *Caribbean Journal of International Relations & Diplomacy*. Vol. 1, No. 2, June 2013: pp. 5–20.

14. Ibid.

15. Ambassador Irwin LaRocque, Secretary General Caribbean Community. Distinguished Lecture delivered at University of the West Indies Port of Spain, Trinidad and Tobago, October 3, 2014.

16. Ibid.

17. Ambassador Irwin LaRocque, Secretary General Caribbean Community. Distinguished Lecture delivered at University of the West Indies Port of Spain, Trinidad and Tobago, October 3, 2014.

18. Paul C. Clement, 'Implementation deficit: why member states do not comply with CARICOM directives.' Mimeo presented at the Caribbean Future Forum in Port of Spain, May 5–7, 2015.

19. Ibid. Also the main recommendation that emerged from the Forum on the Future of the Caribbean held in Port of Spain, May 5–7 2015.

20. Richard Stoneman, Justice Duke Pollard and Hugho Inniss, 'Turning around CARICOM: proposals to restructure the Secretariat,' 2012. Consultancy to conduct an organizational restructuring of the Caribbean Community Secretariat. Report prepared by Landell Mills Ltd. This report was mandated by CARICOM Heads of Government and was contracted by the CARICOM Secretariat with the financial support of the European Unio and the Member States of CARICOM.

21. Ibid.

22. Wendy C. Grenade and Kai-Ann Skeete. 'Regionalism among small states-challenges and prospects: the case of the Caribbean Community (CARICOM). Published in Small States Digest Issue 1, 2015, Commonwealth Secretariat.

23. Ibid.

24. Ibid.

APPENDICES

APPENDIX 1 – SPEECHES

SPEECH BY PRIME MINISTER KAMLA PERSAD BISSESAR, FORUM ON THE FUTURE OF THE CARIBBEAN, MAY 2015

INTRODUCTION

I am delighted to join fellow leaders for this afternoon's high level panel **on the Future of The Caribbean**. I welcome you all to Trinidad & Tobago. We all share a kinship, and a mission of sustainable progress for our countries and our peoples. I note that the discussions yesterday and this morning were insightful and thought-provoking; perhaps even 'disruptive'. That is good! Because if we are to create *'New Thinking for New Times'* we must also be resolute in our responsibility to ensure that we use these forums to move forward.

CURRENT STATUS AS A REGION

With that in mind, a good place to start is to acknowledge our present status as a region. Our similar approach to governance has historically been on the basis of making things happen, whether they be the ordinary or the impossible. Our history of good relations is strong, and we have all benefitted at different moments over time from each other's support, shared resources and collaboration. Our populations combine to create a global resource of tremendous potential in the context of knowledge sharing and competitiveness. And we all now fully appreciate the exposure we have to world economic issues, and the strength we can build when we face challenges by standing together.

This is where we are as a region right now. Where we want to be will be created by us sharing our resources, pooling our wealth and expertise, and structuring our medium and long term policy frameworks based on vision. The most valuable link we all share and must keep, is that our vision for the future is based on people having the lives they want, and are willing to work for.

POOLING WEALTH FOR GREATER VALUE

Collaboration brings great benefits, but also brings great challenges. Those challenges arise in great part because of disparities which our short to medium term policies must seek to correct, including:

- Access to tertiary, technical and vocational training;
- Employment and job creation;
- Economic diversification and new industries;
- ICT access and availability, and
- The competitiveness of our industries.

Addressing these disparities may not necessarily mean that we must adjust our vision or policies; it may mean that greater fortitude is required. It may mean a deeper political must not only see where we, as a region must go, but also pursue the path resolutely. The challenges can at times be harsh, but when our people look to us for leadership, they expect to see it; and with collaboration, we share the burdens as a unified force, and meet the challenges with greater strength. We must not discount the value our partners can add to our economies and the lives of our people.

I use the example of Trinidad & Tobago as an active and strong participant in the global oil sector for over a century. We are now a gas-based energy economy and have been for almost two decades; pursuing strategies at different stages of implementation for economic diversification. Our industrial policies have evolved from focusing on our leadership as a petrochemical producer and exporter, to one which asserts itself more aggressively on the downstream value-chain. The downstream value chain is vital if we are to re-direct more value and benefit to ourselves and our economy by ensuring that all levels of business enterprises can participate in energy, whether by share-ownership or manufacturing.

Even amidst our progress with a rebirth of energy, economic diversification has picked up the pace on three fronts:

- By reforms and incentives for the business environment that will support new economic sectors;
- By new training programmes for our young people to build the skills-base to support these sectors, and
- By reforming the energy environment to promote new investments in exploration and production.

Concurrently with these developments, our role in the region as a Financial Services capital is also growing. So Trinidad & Tobago, as a partner to other nations, brings a great deal to the table, and we do so with a commitment to fairness and equity.

COLLABORATION – ENERGY

Standing together gives us greater opportunity to improve ourselves and strengthen our region—so how do we approach collaborative partnerships with energy?At a meeting with US Vice President Joe Biden last January, Trinidad and Tobago proposed a thematic Caribbean Energy Fund in partnership with the IDB.By 27th February we signed an MOU with the IDB for the development of this Caribbean Energy Fund.This fund, estimated to require US$1B will be a multi donor fund and discussions are going on as we speak with potential donor countries and institutions – the feedback is positive.The fund will finance projects to convert power generation from oil to natural gas, and the execution of renewable energy projects.

Alongside this fund, it was announced recently in Jamaica that the US will establish an energy task force to identify ways to advance energy sector reform, regional integration and clean energy development.Across in Venezuela, we are now advancing cross-border collaboration on the Loran/Manatee gas field as well as the Mannequin/Coquina gas field.This means that can sustain industry, engage new projects and also collaborate on how we can share resources for a mutually beneficial purpose.What better way is there than to pursue alternative energy and renewable energy power generation, by policies that put non-renewable resources to work to foot the bill!

COLLABORATION – BROADBAND

A critical factor in competitiveness, extending the value of our resources and building our knowledge platforms is **connectivity**.In Trinidad & Tobago we have prioritized a number of structural reforms to drive economic growth and promote diversification and competitiveness. Part of those reforms has seen the emergence of a **National Broadband Strategy**.This strategy will enable us to connect Trinidad & Tobago and its citizens to the Government and to the rest of the world in an efficient and value-creating manner.And if our economies are to 'talk' with each other and establish common ground, connectivity is perhaps the most important factor.As a region, we must discuss and collaborate on how we can unify our connectivity and competitiveness objectives on account of

Broadband .More than that, with a unified Broadband strategy, we can then pursue policies to make our economies, industries and public and private sectors fully connected.In this way, we can benefit not only from building a new era of communication, but also from direct engagement that links us to the world economy as a unified, influential force.

COLLABORATION-KNOWLEDGE

Knowledge and information is another area of abundant potential for collaboration.The production, distribution and use of knowledge and information as pillars of growth, sustainability and competitiveness are critical to stability as we proceed into the 21st century, beyond 2020.

Knowledge as a valuable commodity paves the way for innovation. Innovation is the thread of our ability to adapt to changing dynamics, and continuously enhance our competitiveness.An innovation thrust can become the trigger for a regeneration of entrepreneurship, in an environment that is linked to the global economy in a robust way.And key to knowledge, innovation and entrepreneurship, is **connectivity**.

So having put forward the argument for greater collaboration in broadband strategies, and the need to advance discussions quickly, we now see how it will pave the way for knowledge and information collaboration.This means effective links among us as well as between CARICOM nations and the vital knowledge system and networks around the world.And in crossing these hurdles, we can pioneer together into new and higher levels of engagement in trade and other areas which will strengthen our stakes in the global economy and reduce our costs for energy and power-generation.

This is why earlier, I underscored the importance of eliminating disparities that exist in our combined policies for growth and development.Without reforms and investments in training and skills development, achieving the gateway to collaboration and knowledge sharing will prove a very stubborn challenge.And now we begin to see the value of not only collaboration, but by strategic interventions and policies, creating a smooth sequencing for us to build upon strengths.To drive new industry and economic sectors that are supported by knowledge and hungry for innovation, we must act to harness the energy of our young people through skills and training to prepare them a new era of prosperity.Energy collaboration can provide the basis for reducing costs and increasing competitiveness in attracting foreign investments.

Increasing foreign investments provide the capital needed for local businesses to enhance their position, their markets and their productive capacity.

Increasing economic activity knocks on to create increased demand for existing and new skills.Better access to training and skills development will help to meet these new demands.And the best education and training systems, as well as the most progressive and competitive business environments are born out of highly efficient connectivity.So you see the potential for what can be a value-capturing economic loop. This loop creates a change-sensitive and self-adjusting cycle of all of these areas combined.What emerges is a robust platform for knowledge and information, fortifying the wheels of competitiveness, sustainable development and expansion by keeping it turning at a vigorous pace.

POLITICAL WILL (FORCE)

The creation of this change-sensitive and self-adjusting cycle will not be achieved easily if we each stand on our own.But the benefits to be gained from breaking the mould of *'the natural evolution of things'*and replacing it with *'disruptive'* new ideas for a new kind of engagement are clear.And nothing moves without political will.

At one time, *business as usual* would have been the safest generalisation for how we pursue development.*Business as usual* is part of the reason why we have remained vulnerable to global economic glitches, and why our economies have remained at the mercy of factors over which we have no control. But that generalisation has little substance in a modern environment that demands that we innovate, think strategically and find, or make ways to advance.That generalisation may very well be found at the heartbeat of the implementation deficits and a sort of resignation to vulnerabilities and risks.

The very basis of innovation, entrepreneurship and change comes alive by deciding that we will adapt vulnerability to influence…and risk to opportunity.Therefore the plateau that some of us has arrived at where:

- Productivity has become sluggish;
- Fiscal deficits are increasing;
- Economic growth remains at the lower end of the scale, and
- The poor and vulnerable are increasingly exposed

…is not a condition that we must choose to live with.

Stagnation and ceilings must never be the way our story as a region ends, or is told in the future.

We must break down barriers and initiate breakthrough actions to a desirable future place in the world for our people.So while we acknowledge that mere mention of progress, sustainability and strength on the global economy will not create action…we also see that:

- Finding common ground for collaboration begins with partnership;
- Partnership empowers political will;
- Political will motivates action, and
- Confidence enlivens political will.

This is how we, as a region, can stop swimming against the tide, and aim for an achievable objective of becoming the ones who influence the tide.This is the only way for us to re-shape our resilience as Small Island Developing States - to collaborate as a matter of urgency, and not simply choice.Because for every nation you can identify as having influence in the world economy, you will find broad collaboration, inter-connectivity, knowledge and competitiveness as part of their policy infrastructure.

A VISION FOR THE FUTURE

So I now return to where I began, to make a central point which must be the pivot for what we discuss, and what we intend for the outcomes of this conference to be.**New Thinking for New Times** means we must be resolute in our responsibility to find opportunities to move forward. The three areas I focused on – energy, connectivity and knowledge - are not the sum-total of how we must rethink, reform and reaffirm to collaboration.But they are among the most important sustainability issues we must face.The time has come however, for us to pool our collective human and technical resources and harness our formidable talents among our people.And our every endeavour must also be with tomorrow people in mind.

The region in 2015 sees countries that are grappling with increasing debt to GDP ratios that threaten hard-fought development gains that have lifted thousands out of poverty.The *Preliminary Overview of the Economies of Latin America and the Caribbean 2014*, published by ECLAC, cited the region's growth rate as continuing a decline which started in 2011, to an average regional growth rate of 1.1 % in 2014. In turn, this has been exacerbated by reduced Official Development

Assistance with the graduation of many of the region's countries into the Higher Middle Income Country (HMIC) category.

So there is an irony about the current status of our region.Our work to date has helped to create the conditions where our fundamentals are judged by higher standards and more stringent measures.But having achieved this enhanced status, we now have less access to sustained support for critical initiatives.In simple terms, this means that we must make our own way, on our own strength, based on the future we seek to deliver for our people.To me, this means that the things we discuss today simply must translate to action quickly and deliberately.As leaders, we do not have the luxury of time as our predecessors did, and our responsibility is much greater than before. We must be **bold** in considering that the trajectory of our progress may well be better off in another direction.If we so decided, we must have the political will to choose that direction, and the perseverance to hold to our path.

CONCLUSION

Trinidad & Tobago maintains support for the vision of our region by CARICOM Member States in 2014, which is set out in the Strategic Framework Plan for the 2015–2019 period.This vision, you will recall, is based on the implementation of eight (8) integrated strategic priorities over a five-year period including:

- Building Economic, Social, Technological and Environmental Resilience;
- Strengthening Community Governance, and
- Pursuing Coordinated Foreign Policy, Research and Development and Innovation.

The Community's call for a people-centred development paradigm is one that I firmly support.As Heads of Government, when we asked our citizens to elect us to office, the responsibilities we took on included a commitment to keep our promises.Some of those promises are ones we made categorically, but some of those promises were also inferred—that we will secure the present, build the future, and leave no one behind. Today, here, right now…is the moment we demonstrate how we will do that.We must stand up to that responsibility.

I thank you.

EMERGING CARIBBEAN SPACE IN THE GLOBAL SETTING OF OUR TIMES
Will the Caribbean miss this Opportunity?

By Winston Dookeran
Minister of Foreign Affairs, Trinidad and Tobago
Forum on the Future of the Caribbean
  Hyatt Regency Hotel
  May 6, 2015

SALUTATIONS

We have had a wonderful setting for what I hope will be a most intriguing day and a rather disruptive day.

I want to start to deal with an issue that is at the heart of the challenge of leadership in the Caribbean region. That issue was put together in a few words by the former Prime Minister of Jamaica, P.J. Patterson when he said and I quote,

> "It is high time that the perception of politics as an obstacle to the advancement of the Caribbean can be removed. To become the catalyst for meaningful change, politics must be visionary but, yet, pursued through positive activism and principled purpose.

> As we completed the first decade of the 21st Millennium, this is indeed the moment to espouse bold concepts which extend the frontiers of our knowledge, that also reflect a full appreciation of what is essential to fashion new political models, engender change and deepen the democratic process"

These words were somewhat echoed by his predecessor Norman Manley when he said,

> "old ways in politics are no longer equal to the new needs."

I thought from what I heard here this morning that these would come during the course of this session and tomorrows. We will focus on how we unlock the politics of our region in order to create the potential for that future of the Caribbean's civilization. To do so we recognize that what we have achieved over the last 50 years has indeed been an enormous achievement. But the time has come for a new process to begin, and it is in that context therefore that we recognize, all of us in the region, as we move out into a different phase of our development, what is really promoting that.

Globalisation has been with us for some time and in the case of the Caribbean for all time. It is not something new. Our experience in the Caribbean region has shown how we can adopt, mitigate and reduce the uncertainties that the external world imposes upon small developing countries, here in the Caribbean and elsewhere. Kishore Mahbubani, a noted diplomat and scholar said in an introduction to his book called **The Great Convergence**, and I *quote, "deep in our guts we all know that our world has changed significantly. Indeed the world has experienced greater change in the past 30 years than it did in the previous three hundred. What we are struggling to find is one big idea that explains what we feel."* That I believe is the concept of what he coined the great convergence.

Our challenge therefore, to insert our region into the new world must find a new architecture, and that is why we need to look deep into what are the pillars of the current architecture, and how they must be altered and redesigned. **Why Nations Fail** was the title of another provocative book recently, and it concluded *"it is man-made political and economic institutions that underline economic success or the lack of it."* That was a historical piece looking at the origins of power, prosperity and poverty in the world setting. This is why I have always been wedded to the idea that the greatest challenge we face is to wield together the synthesis between political logic and economic logic.

They are not separate and apart. Much of our teachings and much of our syllabus have been predicated on that. Political and economic logic must now go hand in hand, that is what must lead us to make some major departures that have gotten us no favours, and it was mentioned here earlier.

The economic shocks are not a temporary phenomenon for the Caribbean region. Indeed, we have always been negotiating how we respond in our entire economic history to economic shocks, but yet the international financial institutions of today have predicated their windows of support on the basis that economic shocks are a temporary phenomenon and can be dealt with by cash flow injections. It has not worked and therefore the time has come for us to redefine those windows of support on the basis of the new premises and the new realisation about our economic challenges. The issue of searching for economic space as one of the bases upon which we can ensure that we have the wherewithal in order to capture the opportunities that the world offers.

The time has come for the region and I sense in the submissions here this morning an acceptance of the fact that we must move out. The Caribbean region's economic space must be captured by new models of intervention, not in any way denying the benefits of a narrow integration process but capturing the possibilities that a new Convergence of the Caribbean Region, beyond borders can take place. It is that, that will allow us in the English- speaking CARICOM region and of course the new entrance to Haiti to move from a gross domestic product something like $70 billion to operating in a wider Caribbean Sea with a gross domestic product of $350 billion. The platform for expansion of business activity will have a new growth path and in that sense institutions that allow us to integrate beyond borders must be put into place to encourage the movement of capital; the movement of technology; the movement of people; and indeed the movement of goods and services. Our institutional framework now limits the orbit of our operations, and that we believe must also be addressed.

The third area within this framework of a new convergence process can be easily described as a currency of institutional redundancies in the region. All of us engaged in different institutions, sometimes we recycle each other's work. All of us engaged in development sometimes take the credit for somebody else's institution. We have reached a stage of institutional inertia, particularly with respect to development institutions in the region, whether they are in a world of finance, or in other areas of economic activity. There is need now to accept the fact that institutional redundancies is one of our great challenges. It is not only a challenge here in the Caribbean, but it is also a challenge also in the world at large with which we operate and in which diplomacy takes place.Many of the institutions of yesterday during another era of cold war continued to exist when in truth we now have a different alignment of global and political forces. These are all deep issues that must be addressed.

So today, I take this opportunity to raise these issues as we embark on what I hope will be a new exercise to reduce the gap between the expectations of the citizens of the Caribbean, the civilization in which we belong and indeed the entire Caribbean region and its expectations from the global arena. We can together, work out not solutions that can be implemented tomorrow, but thinking that would lead to such institutions for the next generation.

Thank you.

SPEECH DELIVERED AT THE FORUM ON THE FUTURE OF THE CARIBBEAN BY MINISTER OF PLANNING AND SUSTAINABLE DEVELOPMENT BHOENDRADATT TEWARIE, MAY 2015

"A New Approach to Sustainable Development Governance: Is it Happening?" This is the topic that I have been asked to speak on and if the question that I need to answer is – is it happening in Trinidad and Tobago?, then I think that the answer is – 'yes.' How can I say that? I can say that because we have been taking sustainable development seriously, striving for a balance between economic progress, environmental conservation and socio-cultural harmony and we have crafted governance institutions and mechanisms to achieve sustainable outcomes.

Let me say that sustainable development is a disruptive idea which our government has embraced since 2010. The sustainable development idea has gained currency because there is a worldwide rebellion against privilege, because there is a strong movement rethinking corporate behaviour and a new framework for a multi-stakeholder benefits approach to capitalism and because green thinking to save our plant has gained significant momentum.

Our *Manifesto* of 2010 established a Sustainable Development Framework and was adopted as government policy. The Medium Term Policy Framework 2011–2014 derived from this and has guided budgetary allocation for the 2011–12/ 2012–13/ 2013–14 and 2014–15 budgets on five (5) priorities;

- Crime, Law and Order
- Agriculture and Food Security
- Health Care Services and Hospitals
- Economic Growth, Job Creation, Diversification, Competitiveness and Innovation
- Poverty Reduction and Human Capital Development

Our *Manifesto* made a commitment to 'Prosperity for All' and our Medium Term Policy Framework envisioned that 'through creativity, innovation and collaboration, we shall prosper together.'

A SUSTAINABLE DEVELOPMENT REPORT WORKING FOR SUSTAINABLE

Development in Trinidad and Tobago, aligned to the Medium Term Policy Framework was developed to guide Trinidad and Tobago's participation at the Rio +20 Conference on Sustainable Development in 2012. Three pillars of sustainable development

– Economic Sustainability, Social Sustainability and Environmental Sustainability are highlighted in this document and 12 challenges to confront through action are identified.

Over the last five years, therefore, we have been guided by lofty ideas, we have budgeted for identified priorities, implemented through ministries and other state institutions and collaborated with the private business sector and the NGO sector to achieve objectives and to deliver results.

Plans and projects are meaningful only if implemented and implementation or execution is what makes development happen. To strengthen the disposition to implementation, actions need to be measured and evaluated.

We have, therefore, established a Monitoring and Evaluation Unit to do this, a Performance Framework to guide us (one of only a handful of countries in the world to do so) and a Performance Report to record actual performance on 48 indicators linked to the five priorities financed by the budget every year. These Annual Reports on Performance are duly laid in Parliament.

Over the last five years and especially over the last four there has been good alignment between philosophy, strategy policy, plan, execution and monitoring and evaluation.

This has been made possible because of the focus and orientation of the Ministry of Planning and Sustainable Development, the support of the Prime Minister and Cabinet, key structures within the same ministry which have been strengthened and new structures and/or institutions created to support ministerial action.

How does this work? First of all there is a division in the ministry responsible for socioeconomic planning which leads the socio economic development planning process through the formulation, coordination and continuous review of medium and long-term strategies and policies for national development in consultation with other government agencies and stakeholders. At the present time they are preparing an action agenda 2015–2025.

This Division, in collaboration with the Ministry of Foreign Affairs also handles government's relationship with the United Nations (UN) and Trinidad and Tobago's participation in the post-2015 process.

Complementing the SEPPD is the **Project Planning and Reconstruction Division (PPRD)**. They prepare the Public Sector Investment Programme (PSIP) which is the capital expenditure component of the national budget consisting generally of an amalgamation of individual projects and programmes that are linked to the five priorities and which strives for geographical spread.

The PSIP is the instrument available to the government to translate its plans, objectives and strategies into tangible projects and programmes with a view to accelerating growth and development within the country and therefore the transformation agenda of the government. This PSIP programme has, since 2012 been operating on a three year rolling plan basis.

While both the SEPPD and PPRD deal with socio-economic development issues, spatial planning, an ingredient for overall national development, is handled by the Town and Country Planning Division (TCPD).

TCPD is charged with the responsibility for administering the Town and Country Planning Act, Ch. 35:01 of the Laws of Trinidad and Tobago, on behalf of the minister responsible for town and country planning. The functions of the division are to secure consistency and continuity in the framing and execution of a comprehensive policy with respect to the use and development of all land in Trinidad and Tobago. The Town and Country Planning Division has been dramatically transformed to provide customer service, to be more responsive and helpful to the citizen, and a collaborative framework via special committee has been established to address larger projects.

Under my watch the Town and Country Planning Division outdid itself by working with the National Planning Task Force (made up of volunteering professionals) to complete the National Spatial Development Strategy (NSDS) and to support the passage of the Planning and Facilitation Bill which actually abolishes the Town and Country Planning Division and establishes in its place a National Planning Authority and decentralizes the processing of simple applications to Local Government Authorities and the THA. I thank the employees of Town and Country Planning and the PSA for their cooperation and collaboration and their trust in me and in this government.

The National Transformation Unit (NTU) is the newest addition and its mandate includes building assessment and evaluation capability for Trinidad and Tobago, which includes building public sector capacity in monitoring and evaluation.

Additionally, the NTU is also required to monitor and evaluate the implementation of National Policies and Plans on the basis of identified indicators. The NTU also monitors performance on the basis of commitments made in the Manifesto in nine areas of policy shifts. The nine policy shifts emphasize the fact that the management of policy over the last five years has involved continuity as well as change.

Advisory Bodies

The Economic Development Board (EDB) and the Council for Competitiveness and Innovation (CCI) were both established in 2011 to develop and implement comprehensive strategies to accelerate sustainable economic growth and prosperity for the nation and its citizens.

Both bodies work under the direction of the Minister of Planning and Sustainable Development. The role of the EDB is to 'reshape our strategies for economic development by facilitating diversification and achieving a diversified economy within the framework of sustainable development', whereas the role of the CCI is to 'take action to make our firms more competitive, expand exports and improve our competitiveness ranking in the world'.

The roles of the Economic Development Board and Council for Competitiveness and Innovation will naturally have some areas of commonality given the nature of their mandates. While the EDB is tasked with issues regarding the overall objective of economic development and the CCI with issues of business competitiveness, there will not only be the necessity for collaboration between the two bodies, but they will have instances of mutually reinforcing roles and activities. In practice both Boards work closely together.

Arising out of a 2012 national diversification conference, a National Committee of Stakeholders was created and its primary role, as agreed to by Cabinet, is to discuss and agree on a plan of action for stimulating investment expansion in the country. This is a collaboration between business, labour, ministerial and public service to enhance the diversification performance in seven areas.

In effect, the committee will provide a forum through which the government could constructively and regularly engage leaders of industry and commerce, trade unions and other key stakeholders involved in the economic diversification of the country, with a view to creating a more conducive environment for businesses to prosper and for the country to achieve sustainable economic growth.

The Economic Development Board also drives the development of five growth poles geographically spread and works with Town and Country Planning and other institutions to identify local strategies for development as well as identifies new growth poles.

Implementation is always a challenge. However, we have achieved significant success. In my view we have been successful because of leadership, clarity of purpose, organizational capacity structured to achieve results, a climate of collaboration, partnership and creativity and the setting of deadlines and targets. On policy issues, a swift turnaround is valued; the PSIP has timelines which need to be met during the course of any year, NTU has to operate within a budgetary cycle and collaborate with others to meet deadlines. Town and Country Planning was given targets as part of a process of reform.In addition, the spirit of collaboration and teamwork has been infused in traditionally rigid bureaucratic structure and in addition, we have encouraged collaboration between public and private sector.

Buttressing all of this has been the statistical basis for evidence-based decision making. We inherited a lot of problems in the Central Statistical Office in 2010, and problems continue but the CSO has also played a vital role in policy-making. A Human Development Atlas was completed in 2012 which identified human development challenges in 14 regions in Trinidad and Tobago. This made is possible to identify gaps.The National Census was completed in early 2012. This made it possible to work with contemporary data. The CSO has also serviced the country by the provision of GDP statistics every year for decades.

Trade statistics were a problem after issues emerged with the installation of the ASYCUDA system in Customs but are now current. In 2011, labour statistics were four quarters or one year behind. CSO has now caught up but is still two quarters behind. The normal expectation is one quarter and CSO will be on par with other similar agencies worldwide with up to date statistics on the labour market by June.

The inflation data has been provided on time every month for the last 18 months.We have worked collaboratively with the IMF to make this possible.

We have also now completed a Population Policy, an Innovation Policy and are working on a Manpower policy to support our ten year plan going forward which will strengthen and continue to develop the five priorities but will also, focus on (i) intensifying the diversification process, (ii) infrastructure development, including expanding the road network and building a post Panamax Port at one of the existing sites but also rolling our Broadband (iii) an internationalization of Trinidad and Tobago's energy platform focused on down streaming natural gas, exporting knowledge, experience and services, and on renewable energy and energy efficiency solutions and (iv) strengthening governance and building institutions.

This articulation of policy for action over the period 2011-2014 has brought development planning into focus and guided investment over the period. As the timeframe of the MTPF 2011-2014 is at an end, a successor development policy and plan, theNational Development Plan (NDP) 2015-2025, is being prepared to refine strategic interventions and focus future investments aimed at closing the development gap, beating the middle income trap and fostering economic inclusion and a better spread of equity.

The Government of Trinidad and Tobago strategic policy considerations for the next ten years, 2015–2025, will build on the Medium Term Policy Framework (MTPF) 2011–2014 and lay the foundation required for catapulting the country on a path of sustained economic and social progress. The proposed new National Development Plan 2015-2025 will be premised on:

- Principle of sustainable development i.e. maintaining a healthy environment to sustain the desired socioeconomic transformation for citizens to enjoy a high quality of life and for communities to flourish and prosper
- National Spatial Development Strategy (NSDS) 2013–2033 which aims to protect and enhance environmental assets, and where appropriate make economic use of them, and to prudently use natural resources to guide the nature and location of development and improvements at municipal and local levels
- Close alignment with the post-2015 global development agenda and the Sustainable Development Goals
- Pursuit of high per capita income and sustained economic growth based on innovative strategies to diversify the economy, disperse

economic activity throughout the country based on clustering of industries, leverage and build on the competitive advantages of the country, increase exports and investment, develop strategic partnerships regionally and globally to build the critical mass needed for economies of scale, markets, skills and innovation capacity, and facilitate enterprise development

- Socio-economic inclusion of the most vulnerable in society by providing opportunities for persons to access sustainable employment, education, health care, housing, food, utilities, etc.

Some of the priority areas of investment will centre on: national and personal security; health and wellbeing; youth and ageing; food security; diversification, growth and employment; human capital development; applied research for enterprise development; infrastructural development; climate change and environmental preservation (including alternative and renewable energy, disaster risk reduction and water management); and governance and institutional reform.

The next National Development Plan will therefore attempt to continue the process of ensuring that there is alignment with global sustainable development agenda and seek to integrate the new set of sustainable development goals within the strategic priorities for the period 2015-2025. To this end, the social development goals and targets will form the backbone of the planning horizon and would facilitate the ease of reporting to the international agencies under the UN system as to the progress in the implementation of the post-2015 development agenda. At the same time it will sharpen the focus for action at home.

Already we have been able to rationalize our relationships with the multi-lateral institutions, the European Union, the UN System. This has been systematically done over the last three years or so.

In some cases we have an understanding of how we engage each other, in the case of the UN, we have actually signed an agreement to bring programmes and executing agencies under one umbrella for implementation.

In consultation to prepare Trinidad and Tobago's post-2015 miscellaneous goals we engaged a large number of collaborators from civil society who signed off on what we sent to the UN as our country report.

We have also begun an active process of promoting and nurturing an entrepreneurial and innovation driven culture. Actions include the creation of the Centre for Enterprise Development which functions as a nurturing ground and hatchery for new business start-ups. The idea to innovation which has supported 200 innovations with grants up to 200,000 TT dollars to each recipient; Lumination which does the same for social innovators; an Apps Centre for software design; a partnership with Microsoft to create an Innovation Centre; a partnership with the World Bank to identify solution entrepreneurs for climate change problems.

What I have described to you so far are, in our context in the Caribbean, bold initiatives—bold for the public service, bold for accountability in government, bold in terms of Trinidad and Tobago's experience and bold in terms of policy action.

But this was a governance framework that we had to build to register our serious commitment to the alignment of philosophy, strategy, plan, institutional capacity, execution, monitoring and evaluation, account to parliament and the people. These bold but necessary actions disrupted the status quo of laissez-faire and allowed us to achieve practical outcomes which could be measured.

But we are entering a difficult world now, not so much of disruptive thinking but where, instead, disruptive changes are taking place and the meaning of these thing have yet to be fully absorbed and so perhaps our thinking on what is taking place around us is not so clear. The world as we know it is under challenge.

What are some of these disruptive changes transforming the world we live in?

1. The challenge of managing the global financial system.
2. The transformation of the global production system and the shifts in Ocean traffic and routes.
3. The restructuring of the energy matrix and market.
4. The opportunity that most growth will take place in emerging and developing countries.
5. Authoritarian, militaristic terrorist interventionists that disrupt peace and order, in a strategically arbitrary fashion.

Over the next decade the issues of how to manage, regulate and monitor a global financial system which was severely tested in 2008/2009 and which some believe to be fundamentally unsound will present a formidable challenge as the global economy continues to transform and restructuring of the production system intensifies.

The Schumpeterian changes now taking place in the global energy economy will have serious implications for competitiveness, trade and investment. Moreover, future growth in the world is predicted to occur overwhelmingly in emerging and developing countries. Least developed countries will therefore have an opportunity to move up and emerging and developing countries can seize the opportunities to triumph over the middle income country trap and achieve stronger success. The highly industrialized countries of the Commonwealth for instance with whom we are partners,will have new opportunities for investment, trade and partnerships.

A glorious future awaits the countries of the Caribbean, consisting of middle income and high human development countries in a transforming world economy. Moreover, the thrust for sustainable development is also likely to yield positive dividends for countries within the region as well as progressive partnerships between some developing and emerging countries and other global players. With this transformation and restructuring at the economic level, geopolitical shifts will also present new opportunities. The countries of the CARICOM are likely beneficiaries of a changing world order that has already been set in motion.

In the coming decade CARICOM will have a rare opportunity to shape its partnerships in institutions such as the Commonwealth and the UN, and to play a more meaningful role in the world's decision making—including decisions that will affect the multilateral system and development banking institutions.

What will be required will not be disruptive thinking as such, but strategic, critical and creative thinking that the disruptions already set in motion by forces in the world will demand.

How to take advantage of opportunities presented by these disruptions? How to protect oneself from the vulnerabilities that these disruptions may bring? The time for action on one's own is long gone; this is the age of collaboration, partnerships, and multiple alliances to achieve progress.

I could not close without proposing action solutions for the region to pursue- in the context of this forum, I would describe these as bold, disruptive actions:

i. Resolution of air and sea transport and security challenges in the Caribbean region.

ii. An action agenda for integration of the production system of the region for development integration within a sustainable development framework.

iii. Transformation of the energy matrix in the region to make the region competitive and these small states, many of them islands, greener.

iv. A broadband and internet based knowledge access and knowledge, creativity and innovation strategy for the region linked to productivity, entrepreneurship and applications for innovation.

v. Active facilitation of private sector growth and involvement and public/private partnerships across the region.

vi. Set objectives and targets for the five above and stick doggedly to the task of achieving them, supporting these institutions with infrastructure, talent, organizational capacity and political clout.

vii. Work with global and regional financial sector to actualize plans and achieve results by formulating programmes, projects and interventions that yield results.

The world is fast transforming and we must take the change in motion around us seriously and act in response as well as proactively. The world is not going to wait for the Caribbean region, so we must summon the will to act in our best interest seizing opportunities and building resilience for sustainability. Bold action is required in a world in which disruptive forces have already been set in motion by others.

OPENING REMARKS BY THE CAMPUS PRINCIPAL

Forum on the Future of the Caribbean

"DISRUPTIVE THINKING. BOLD ACTION. PRACTICAL OUTCOMES"

Teaching & Learning Complex, UWI St. Augustine Campus
Tuesday 5th May, 2015 | 8.30am

ENTERING A NEW CHAPTER IN CARIBBEAN DEVELOPMENT

Today marks a defining moment in the history of our Region as we initiate a new dialogue and begin a novel journey that challenges the status quo and philosophical paradigms of traditional Caribbean development.   Our aim is to create a fresh dispensation of ideas, thoughts and actions that will help our Region re-position itself as an important player on the international stage and secure sustainable development in an ever-evolving and competitive world system. Using this **Forum on the Future of the Caribbean** as a platform for discussion, debate and dialogue, we are therefore breaking new ground and entering an exciting new chapter of Caribbean Development in the second decade of the 21st century! We are re-charting our course to economic growth and social empowerment, with a bold spirit of radical thinking and resolve!

THE UWI – THE INTELLECTUAL CENTRE OF OUR REGION

Before I continue, I must tell you how thrilled I am that this transformative and mould-breaking forum is taking place right here on the grounds of our University! It brings to memory the vision of our founding fathers captured in the Irvine Commission Report of 1944. This report envisioned the regional UWI, and I quote, '...to be something more than the best possible institution for production of our graduates. It should be 'The Intellectual Centre of our Region'. It is precisely within this context that I say that there could have hardly been a better place for such a conversation to emanate, given the long and enduring involvement and prominent role of The University of the West Indies in Caribbean development. The hosting of this important Forum therefore bears witness that The UWI is indeed re-positioning itself at the centre of thought, being a catalyst and driver for the development trajectory of our Region! And let me thank the Ministry of Foreign Affairs and the UNDP in particular, and all the other supporting agencies for collaborating to host this Forum. And most importantly, let me thank all of you, our distinguished guests and stakeholders from various sectors for taking time out of your busy schedules to be present with us today

FORUM ON THE FUTURE OF THE CARIBBEAN – COMMITTED TO THE SUCCESS OF THE REGION

I would like to emphasize, that the significance of this Forum is much larger than any one of our co-hosting individual institutions. This Forum is really about our commitment to the success of the peoples of the wider Caribbean region, and by extension other developing nations and the global South; it is about working together to stimulate radical ideas, rethink the future of the Caribbean and taking bold actions with the aim of achieving sustainable development; it is about unlocking our potential as one Caribbean people; it is also about ensuring that people and human imagination are at the centre, with a focus on our youth! Our youths are the ones that will inherit this space we call the Caribbean Region, and therefore we need to hear the freshness of their thoughts so that they too can help shape their destiny!

NEW THINKING-NEW PARADIGMS-NEW SOLUTIONS – AN IMPERATIVE FOR THE REGION

Bearing this in mind, it is imperative that as a Region, we shift gears and look towards the future.   The time in which we live demands new thoughts and new paradigms which will result in new solutions. We need to create a new vision for our Region, our countries, our institutions and ourselves. As I reflected upon the future of the Caribbean myself, I could not help but think of some of the possibilities…this morning, I think aloud and share some of my thoughts with you….

> » *What if…*we removed every barrier to trade for manufactured and agricultural goods within the Caribbean region that have been certified by their States of origin?

> » *What if…*we ensured the free movement of people within the Caribbean region?… or what if we created a *Union of Caribbean States?*

> » *What if…* we brought together the resources of the Caribbean including capital,   technology,   labour,   energy, manufacturing, production and distribution knowledge, our land

and marine assets etc. to build a robust production capability within the region – a matter which the late Professor Norman Girvan passionately advocated for since the 1960s, but a matter that has never materialized up to today, much to our Region's loss?

» **What if...** Trinidad and Tobago utilized its geographic location and became a trans-shipment hub for goods going to South America? Would this not open up the Latin America market of over 350 million people to Caribbean and global exporters?

» **What if...** we build a bridge from Trinidad to Venezuela?

» **What if...** the regional UWI becomes the leading University not only for the English-speaking Caribbean, but also for the Spanish, French and Dutch speaking Caribbean, thereby serving great numbers of students from these countries;

» **What if...** the Regional UWI introduces a liberal fee regime that opens itself up to the wider world, including the sons and daughters of the Caribbean Diaspora and those from our ancestral origins?

» **What if...** all our state funded higher education institutions, universities, colleges and technical institutes are brought together to form one Regional Collegiate System anchored in quality, technology, mobility and efficiency?

» **What if...** all the countries of our region implemented legislation with structured funding for research at 1% of our GDP?

» Or **what if...** there was a Regional Research Funding Agency (funded also as a percentage of each country's GDP).....could we imagine how this may propel problem solving, creativity, innovation and knowledge generation for our societies?

» **What if...** University funding was guaranteed and enshrined in the constitutions of our countries in the Region and as a percentage of GDP, as it is in some Latin America countries... could we imagine how this will remove all publicly funded Universities from the financial challenges of the day?

» **What if...** the countries of our Region implemented long/medium-term visions, strategies, direction and major capital development projects which *CANNOT* be changed through the electoral cycle (apart from exceptional circumstances)?

I ask you distinguished ladies and gentlemen, to ponder upon some of these questions, and I hope that more of these will be generated today... *for although probing these questions may be seen in some quarters as 'radicalism' at work, I say that in the context of an ever evolving world system, bold solutions to our present challenges and building an exciting future for our peoples will not reside in past thinking! In moving forward, I am therefore of the firm belief that we must speak about fresh ideas, concepts and models; pursue new perspectives and paradigms; while discarding inappropriate old approaches! This is the spirit and philosophy behind this Forum on the Future of the Caribbean. Bold thinking must no longer be on the periphery, it must now be at the centre!* This is not to say that we must forget our past, our rich history and the significant strides we have made post- independence...but the time has come for us to begin to think outside the box, to be creative, innovative and industrious if our Region is to achieve sustainable development!   Hopefully, this forum will begin to interrogate some of these issues, remembering that The UWI must always remain a space for critical thought.

CONCLUDING REMARKS – A CALL TO ACTION/ EXECUTION

Let us not allow our new ideas and practical solutions to perish on the shelves of libraries across our Region. **Rather, our ideas must be brought to life! We must THINK today; STRATEGIZE tomorrow; and on Thursday – COMMIT TO ACTIONS that must be taken to get us to a desired destination! I have said on previous occasions that Vision without Execution is just mere words. Execution is tangible!   We must therefore entrench in our thinking that**

> **'shared vision' which does not translate into execution is a recipe for continued failure. Let us therefore focus on EXECUTION, as this has bedeviled us in the past!   In so doing, history will record this Forum on the Future of the Caribbean, as a turning point in the trajectory of Caribbean development. While the road ahead may be full of trials, I believe that it holds significant promise. As we summon the will to execute with commitment, diligence and not being distracted, we will deliver the change needed to unleash our Region's full potential which will redound to the benefit of our peoples.**

In closing, I thank my staff at The UWI St. Augustine Campus for managing today's event on campus as well as our partner organizations; I thank you the presenters and audience for participating; and I do look forward to a very productive, memorable and impacting Forum for positive change!

ADDRESS TO THE FORUM ON THE FUTURE OF THE CARIBBEAN

by Richard Blewitt
UN Resident Coordinator Trinidad and Tobago. Suriname, Aruba, Curaçao and Sint Maarten

I shall be very brief, a very good morning, here in the wonderful and sometimes complex T&T, the focus today is The Caribbean and it's journey:moving from survivability to sustainability.

The Caribbean is a victim of its own great successes. It's middle income status is well deserved but it still has much to do to tackle deep - rooted challenges including re-asserting its identity, tackling crime, persistent poverty, high corruption ratings which is linked to its debt levels, it's limited access to affordable energy and high level of non communicable diseases. Despite the region having some world breakers, it generally lacks world breaking institutions. The challenges of climate change impacts and disasters are very serious.

At the same time there is an abundant number of success stories, incremental development ini- tiatives that help in tackling these difficult challenges.The Caribbean leadership in the world is deeply impressive; take for example, the NCD UN General Assembly meeting four years ago when the Caribbean led for the world.

Here in Trinidad and Tobago for instance from the vantage point where I sit we have:

> » A very effective citizen security program, run by the government in partnership with NGOs funded by the IADB. The UN has peer-reviewed this to support its legitimacy and it's continued improvement though south-south collaborations and expertise sharing.

> » A national on–the-job training programme involving thousands of young persons, helping them get real work experience. We the UN have 30 such persons and Microsoft employs a similar number.

> » A world class oil and gas sector and a strong, albeit privileged manufacturing sector serving the Caribbean

> » There is a very powerful piece of procurement legislation that would profoundly reduce corruption and ensure efficiency and value for money.

» Civil society and corporate philanthropy are delivering on the ground strong projects and services. These need to be built on and scaled and supported for sustainability.

» A very skilled set of Tobagonians.working in many sectors and as part of global companies servicing the Caribbean and it's linkages to other regions.

» A carnival and fete season that is a cultural and commercial success, and the commercial and cul- tural value of pan, soca, chutney soca and calypso

» Now turning to Aruba where I also serve, there is world breaking innovation in the green economy, and a PM who says he want not just five star hotels, but five star hospitals and five star schools.

» UNDP is helping to develop a multi-stakeholder engagement in Curacao and Sint Maarten to ad- vance national development planning processes and strengthen nation building.

» In Suriname there are strong economic fundamentals, well managed from a central banker coming from the IMF

So what more needs to be done?

As an international development specialist of 25 years I remain convinced though my experience that it is tough running a country. I haven't done it myself of course but I have observed others.There are always many competing demands, ideas and needs, and it does not matter how small your country is, it is not easy.

Listening over the last two days to move from survivability to sustainability, it seems there are areas that have come up as priorities:

1. All of us supporting existing regional plans to get things done in action. Reinforcement for action.

2. Community empowerment, investing more in and expecting expecting more from your poor and unequal

3. Tackling corruption, nepotism and the lack of accountability and transparency

4. modernizing the education system to include much more critical thinking and problem solving

5. Greater levels of cross-party leadership towards good law and policy making

6. A continuous and deep process of civil service improvement and reform, delivering world class public services

7. Regionally and at the country level using and adjusting the UN frameworks, human rights, SGDs, health in all policies etc.

I commit the UN and the UN family in the Caribbean to do what we can do to partner in a practical way anything that supports this human development journey from survivability to sustainability

Thank you

ADDRESS BY ANTONIO PRADO, DEPUTY EXECUTIVE SECRETARY OF THE ECONOMIC COMMISSION FOR LATIN AMERICA AND THE CARIBBEAN ON THE OCCASION OF THE FORUM ON THE FUTURE OF THE CARIBBEAN

Port of Spain, Trinidad and Tobago
May 5, 2015

Excellences, academics, ladies and gentlemen,

I am very happy to be back in the Caribbean. This is my first trip to Trinidad and Tobago, and it is a pleasure to be in Port of Spain and especially to be here, at the celebrated University of the West Indies campus at Saint Augustine.

Allow me to pay tribute to the Honourable Winston Dookeran, Minister of Foreign Affairs of Trinidad and Tobago, for his vision and commitment to making this very important and timely event a reality. I congratulate him and the partner organizations led by UNDP for the effort in designing an agenda that promises to stimulate radical ideas that engender the disruptive thought required to tackle the persistent challenges facing this sub-region. ECLAC is very pleased to have been able to contribute to this effort.

Today, the Caribbean like Latin America is facing a future fraught with challenges and uncertainty. It is clear that the models and strategies that have delivered improved living standards in the past will be unable to continue doing so in the future. Across the region, leaders in government, business and other institutions have been tweaking these models to adjust to a hyper-competitive world whose economic and geopolitical epicentre is shifting by degrees from the North Atlantic and Europe to the East.

Among the other big tectonic shifts are the commitment of member states in the United Nations to the Sustainable Development Goals and the new architecture that will emerge on financing for development after the meeting in Addis Ababa alongside the new commitments to addressing climate change at the Paris meeting. In light of these considerations arguably, small adjustments that are meant not to 'rock the boat' too much will not be enough to address a challenging future. In the words of Luke Williams, in his book on disruptive thinking, the Caribbean needs a 'disruptive approach for a disruptive age'.

Disruptive thinking that leads to innovative models, products and technologies is often revolutionary rather than evolutionary. To succeed at this, the region needs an academy that is capable of reinventing itself- a revolutionary academy. How can the academy recast itself for the kind of functional disruptive thinking that is needed in the region? I would like to outline a few ways in which the academic community could act as this agent of change.

First, I think the academy needs to be more welcoming to ideas and interactions with the public at large. This could be facilitated by a regular 'open day' when faculty and staff share ideas with the public on various development challenges confronting the society. A strengthened culture of openness can provide the seeds for new ideas for basic and applied research that can lead to new products, services, methods and techniques to boost growth and development.

By way of example, the region urgently needs creative and innovative solutions in growing knowledge-driven competitive export businesses, boosting self-employment and tackling crime and dysfunction. A critical disruption is for the academy to realise that its best solutions would come from a robust collaboration with the wider community.

Second, the academy needs to revisit the attention it gives to theorising and micro-level research. More careful attention to theory will provide the basis for deeper and more nuanced understanding of the development challenges facing the region and how they could be addressed. Further, whether in the study of economics, sociology or technology, for instance, much of modern research in the academy today focuses on the macro level.

However, increased attention should be given to micro-level research that seeks to understand how individual agents and organisations function and succeed. The study of different categories of firms for instance could provide rich insight into their motivations and what makes them profitable and competitive. This would provide lessons that could inform the operations of new start-ups; thereby allowing them to leap-frog some of the hurdles faced by predecessor firms.

Third, it is critical that Caribbean universities strengthen their links with private businesses and business development agencies and bureaus of standards. The sharing of experiences with these institutions, both those that have failed and those that are successful, provide an ideal avenue for developing dynamic networks that can build the scaffolding for developing commercial products and services that can compete in international markets.

Indeed, this merging of theoretical and practical research provides probably the best opportunity to enable Caribbean products and services to capture niches in global value chains. Scaling up these arrangements also provide new revenue streams for universities which have been affected by the challenges faced by member states due to their high debt burdens and limited fiscal space.

I am aware that at the University of the West Indies and at other universities in the sub-region, you have been trying to tackle some of these challenges. For instance, the Cocoa Research Centre here in Trinidad and Tobago, has one of the largest gene banks for cocoa in the world and is doing exciting research, which could provide the foundation for a gourmet chocolate industry here. In addition, UWI Mona is collaborating with a US firm to advance its pioneering research in the medical use of marijuana.

Nevertheless, the Universities cannot do it alone. Development institutions and think tanks like ECLAC must complement the work of the academy. Over the decades, ECLAC has contributed to development thinking in the region. Indeed, Raul Prebisch and Sir Arthur Lewis were two of the leading disruptive thinkers of their era. In recent years, the global crisis has provided us with an opportunity to rethink our approach to development.

The countries of Latin America and the Caribbean are at a crossroads in terms of their future growth and distribution capacity. The so-called commodity price super-cycle is showing signs of weakening. Though prices remain high, demand is slowing and the prices of agricultural and mineral products are sliding. The region, which benefited from the commodity boom (albeit with considerable variation from one country to the next), is now suffering the impact of less favourable external conditions.

These conditions are threatening a growth phase that began in the mid-2000s in most countries, especially those with mining sectors, and has continued nearly unabated, with just a brief interruption in 2008 when the global financial crisis hit. For Caribbean countries whose economies are driven mostly by tourism services, the situation is much worse and this has been aggravated by high debt burdens.

Looking ahead, swift and sizeable productivity gains, as well as productive diversification beyond commodities and tourism services will be needed, and these developments will not occur without careful planning. Investment in basic and higher education, science and technology and technical capacity for production will be indispensable to usher in a new era of growth with greater equality in Latin America and the Caribbean.

The key pillars which must be addressed   are structural change and the   continuous upgrading of traditional sectors. This provides a platform for developing new competitive sectors that capture and sustain market share in global value chains. This however, is no easy task. It demands a clear industrial policy that integrates investments in education and skills training, productivity improvements in sectors such as tourism and light manufacturing, research and development in new products and a culture of readiness for technological change and innovation.

The reality is that the Caribbean urgently needs to raise growth to between 3.5% and 4% from the weak 1.9% that was achieved in the last decade, if we are to improve living standards in the region. To do this the region would need to raise the productivity of its weakest firms to that of its strongest at the domestic level and to push the productivity of export sectors much closer to international benchmarks.

In addition, the region would do well to reinforce the virtuous links between growth and equality. Improved equality should be facilitated by universal access to basic social protection; the use of more focused measures such as conditional cash transfers, incentives for self-employment to reduce the wage bill and more equitable access to capacity building instruments such as high quality education and training also health and infrastructure services, including ICT.

Improved equality as a result of such measures will also strengthen growth by boosting domestic demand. The region must also strive to improve the business environment and leverage the private sector for investment in areas such as infrastructure and improved regional interconnection. At the same time partnership with the private sector must take place within the context of transparency and accountability so that the public sector does not bear all the risks while the private sector reaps the profits.

To achieve equitable growth in an env ironmentally sustainable manner, the Caribbean will need to tackle some critical challenges. The first urgent challenge is high and unsustainable levels of public debt. Debt in the region averages some 64% of GDP and a number of countries have debt in excess of 80% of GDP. Debt service costs at 24.5% of revenue and 9% of exports of goods and services, combine to make the Caribbean one of the most debt-constrained regions in the world.

While it is true that some portion of this debt has been due to unanticipated shocks, a significant part has been due to lack of fiscal transparency, accountability and broad participation in public finance management. Thus while we may advocate for debt relief to create fiscal space, better fiscal management must also be addressed in any strategy aimed at institutional change.

High debt has been reinforced by weak export competitiveness, which has resulted in a failure to keep pace with technology. Indeed, the competitiveness challenge is the result of the failure of the Caribbean to invest sufficiently in research and development and technological innovation, especially in ICT and STEM training to develop new products and services that could enter global value chains.

This has been reinforced by an education system that is not geared towards problem solving and creativity but to echoing old approaches to new challenges. Comprehensive education reform aimed at entrepreneurship, must be the hallmark of new thinking to advance and excite the imagination of our youth.

Climate change and the risks posed by natural disasters are also important concerns for the region. The cost of adaptation and risk mitigation will be high. The region therefore needs to mainstream these costs in its development programmes. Further, there is need to invest in creating a 'green' economy since this is likely to be an important aspect of competitive advantage of economies in the future. Better partnerships with global climate financing and technical assistance institutions would help to accelerate this process.

The Caribbean also needs to better leverage ICT and statistics, including big data to advance its development. Focussed attention should be placed on both developing ICT based services and using ICT to improve the efficiency of service delivery in key sectors.

Strengthened data collection and management, including the collection of environmental statistics are also critical. However, beyond raw data the Caribbean also needs to focus on developing creative indicators to measure change in a number of important aspects of development.

Individual countries are not likely to succeed on their own. Regional integration and cooperation at the CARICOM and wider hemispheric level is critical to advance regional and global value chains which are the new vehicle for export expansion. In this respect, opportunities for greater interconnection and collaboration with countries in Latin America offer prospects for production integration.

To effect this we must remove all existing barriers to the movement of Caribbean people, the movement of capital and other resources and create a single space for creative engagement.

We must also create the institutional frame for the collaboration of our universities both within and outside of the region, including engagement with the diaspora, so that local scholarship can be continually combined with new ideas and perspectives. The time is ripe for the revitalisation of the CARICOM integration as a platform for intensifying links with Latin America in trade, technical and cultural cooperation. This could help the Caribbean scale up resources for its development.

The task of regional transformation is herculean, but within the creative space provided by this forum, I urge the presenters and other participants to dig deep and come up with workable solutions that could advance the region's development.

Ladies and gentlemen I challenge you this week to think outside your comfort zone, and disrupt the status quo.

Thank you.

The Commonwealth

BUILDING THE RESILIENCE OF SMALL STATES: A STRATEGIC VISION FOR THE CARIBBEAN

Deodat Maharaj, Deputy Secretary-General (Economic and Social Development), Commonwealth Secretariat

Port of Spain, Trinidad and Tobago, 5 to 7 May 2015

Honourable Prime Ministers, Honourable Ministers, Excellencies, Distinguished Ladies and Gentlemen and Members of the Media.

A pleasant good afternoon. It gives me great pleasure to be present at this forum today and to be able to have this conversation with you on this splendid Port of Spain afternoon.

I wish to thank and congratulate the Government of Trinidad and Tobago, the University of the West Indies and the United Nations family in Trinidad and Tobago and other partners for hosting this much needed Forum and we in the Commonwealth are happy to be involved as well. I am especially happy to be here in the land of steelband, calypso and chutney, the land of the hummingbird, Minshall and Naipaul.

This is the land of the great West Indian thinkers CLR James, Lloyd Best, Dr Eric Williams and the quintessential Caribbean man, William Demas. It is also my land and though I will not even dare contemplate being considered in the same category of these giants, I can certainly state that like so many of you, my love for this region of ours is no less.

I am grateful for the chance to share some thoughts on how we can possibly think a bit differently about the region and perhaps to suggest some ideas on the Caribbean we want by

2050. In terms of the session, I will speak for about 20 minutes followed by Dr. Moore and we will leave about one hour for what I hope will be a nice interactive dialogue.

Perhaps it will be useful to situate our discussions in an appropriate development context and it is best to start by noting that economic growth in the Caribbean has been slower than other regions. Since 2000, while the real per capita growth rates in developing countries averaged around 4.31 percent per annum, the comparable figure for CARICOM was just around 1.9 percent.

And as I stand before you today, seismic shifts are also taking place in the global development landscape. We are seeing the emergence of mega regional trading blocs such as the transatlantic and trans pacific trading partnerships. This will exclude 160 countries representing an estimated 80% of the world's population.

Our concern in the Commonwealth is that in this architecture, where is the place for the small islands and countries of the Caribbean- Barbados; Grenada; St Kitts and Nevis; St Vincent and the Grenadines; St Lucia; Dominica; and yes, Trinidad and Tobago? Quite simply, the answer is, there may not be a place.

Let us look at the trade data for a moment. For this region, trends in trade show that its share of global trade has decreased from approximately 0.24% or just one quarter of one percent in 1990 to 0.16% in 2013. If we look at the CARICOM region excluding the oil and gas producer Trinidad and Tobago, the mere fraction becomes even smaller if this is possible to imagine.

Without Trinidad and Tobago, the region accounted for 0.17% of World Trade in 1990, which has since decreased to 0.08% in 2013.

When you look at the debt data, the news quite frankly as presented yesterday is discouraging. The natural beauty of the region masks the fact that it is one of the most heavily indebted regions on the planet.

Nine of our member countries have gross debt to GDP ratios greater than 75% with 3 countries having public debt levels greater than 100%. This is unsustainable and development cannot take place with these crippling debt burdens with loan financing and lack of access to concessional terms only exacerbating this troublesome reality.

For good measure, I will add our susceptibility to natural disasters and economic shocks and we all know what happened with the tourism sector immediately after 9/11. We also know that Hurricane Ivan damaged 70% of the homes in Grenada, destroyed 30% of them; and the total damages stood at USD1 billion or equivalent to two years GDP!

So in essence we can move from high income to middle income to zero income in a few hours.

Just briefly moving to citizen security with a quick overview of the data. In terms of crime and violence we are not doing to well as a region with some of our countries having amongst the highest per capita homicides rate in the world. The Bahamas stands at 29.8 per 100,000 citizens and Jamaica, 39.3 per 100,000 nationals.

Just for your information, the homicide rate for the UK is 1 per 100,000. So the rate in Jamaica, for example, is about forty times higher than in the UK, while the rate in Barbados—a relatively low-crime society by Caribbean standards—is still over seven times higher than in the UK.

Based on current trends, the modelling exercise we commissioned has indicated that it is possible by 2050, that the smaller states of the Eastern Caribbean can have rates of homicide similar to those currently being reported and experienced in Jamaica. If we do not make progress in tackling crime, there will be countries in our region that could be amongst the most violent on this earth by 2050.

As Caribbean people, we always think about bequeathing a legacy to our children and the next generation, our treasured assets. That is just our way. My view is that with 60% of the population considered as young people, they are not the future, but the present.

Let us for the moment take an unscientific approach and I seek the forgiveness of Dr. Watson in this endeavour as we look at one variable to get a flavour of our legacy to the prized assets, the young people of the region.

Let us see how they are doing in terms of employment where youth are at a much higher risk of being out of work with teenagers having the highest unemployment rates. In Barbados, individuals aged 15 to 19 years old face an unemployment rate 5 times higher than adults with their unemployment rate at 47% compared to 14% for those aged 20-44 years old. In St. Lucia, 40% of the unemployed were younger than 25 years old in 2011.

If we only look at the initial data I presented and do not consider some advancements made, a reasonable person may conclude, that we in the Caribbean are in a race to the bottom...and we are winning.

However, there are some positive signs as well.

Having observed and been involved in the development of the region, I am pleased to note the advances that we have achieved. We need to build on the progress made to launch the next steps towards a strengthened vision for the region of the Caribbean we want by 2050.

Our experience has shown that we do indeed have a limited ability to withstand or bounce back from adverse shocks as we have done in the past be these external shocks or natural disasters. The Commonwealth's research on assessing vulnerability and building resilience highlights key gaps in economic, social and environmental management across the region. Governance has also been identified as an important component to resilience building strategies and for this reason the Commonwealth is focusing its current efforts on better understanding and supporting the development of enhanced governance systems across its small states members starting with the Caribbean.

We are also making progress in improving the efficiency of our economy. In the latest report by the World Bank's *"Doing Business 2015: Going beyond Efficiency"*, 50 percent of economies in the Caribbean implemented at least one reform making it easier for local entrepreneurs to do business—12 reforms in total, a historical high for the region. Though one can also note that in the same report the highest ranked country was Jamaica which stood at 58. Most of our countries trailed behind whereas Mauritius had a ranking of 28. They are getting something right.

The region is one with the youngest population in the Commonwealth sphere. I was in Antigua not too long ago addressing the region's Youth Ministers Meeting, recognising our young people as an asset to the region. The Caribbean region is already producing outstanding young people, one of whom I had the privilege of meeting at a recent Commonwealth Youth Ministers Meeting in Antigua and Barbuda. Due to her entrepreneurial achievement, Nolana Lynch from Trinidad and Tobago was awarded the Caribbean region winner of the 2015 Commonwealth Youth Awards.

Compared to other regions, we have relatively matured regional institutions, we generally think about ourselves as West Indians and Caribbean people and have a generally good track record on collaboration as a region with cricket being a good example of how we once collectively expressed ourselves as a people. It was also good to see the result of the just concluded Kensington contest where we prevailed and tied the test series. Sir Hillary and Professor Sankat, our University of the West Indies, my Alma mater is another example.

Notwithstanding these efforts, we still face many challenges as noted earlier, and we need to act to ensure that we have continued and sustained developmental progress. There is an imperative for change if the Caribbean is to fulfil its development aspirations or indeed survive as a viable entity.

Based on what we have heard since yesterday, I am convinced that the development model for the region cannot be based on a business as usual scenario if we are to deliver on our development goals. It is said that one definition of madness is doing the same thing over and over expecting a different result.

The challenges we face have serious ramifications for the future development and growth trajectories of the countries within the region and must be addressed.

Based on the modelling work we have done, the projections show that inaction or if left to business as usual, countries in the region will have debt to GDP ratios above 100 percent and in some cases, exceeding 200 percent. Interest expenditure is likely to become a major drain on public finances in the future, further reducing funds available for development. Therefore, we have to move away from decision-making based on expedience and convenience and where political imperatives trump everything else.

In pursuit of an inclusive and sustainable development for our Caribbean member states, I propose that we aspire towards a new Vision for the Caribbean by 2050, a strategic framework that recognises the Caribbean as peaceful, prosperous and inclusive, its people creative, enterprising and resilient, fully engaged in, and benefiting from, development within the framework of effective institutions that guarantee human rights and social justice.

Possible elements can include:

1. Goal 1 —A creative and enterprising economy in which innovation is the driver—aimed at supporting the region to effect a transition from low value added economic activities to ones that are driven by local creativity and enterprise, including the public sector. Business has to be the engine of growth and we must link ourselves to Global Value Chains.

2. Goal 2, youth fully integrated into national development— recognising our young people are valuable and creative assets, working with them as development partners towards Vision 2050 and with every household having a university graduate by 2050;

3. Goal 3, with a stable society where people are safe, secure and prosperous. A goal that is premised on the development of networks, institutional links, community based interventions and monitoring, and knowledge sharing. We need to re-energise our regional approach to the social challenges that are faced in the Caribbean;

4. Goal 4, environmental sustainability mainstreamed in the development process—an important element considering that the natural environment including The Blue Economy is a major element of the attractiveness of the Caribbean;

5. Goal 5 - A region built on clean, resilient energy systems that make use of plentiful, local renewable resources and are capable of providing stable supplies of energy to all sectors of society – aimed at promoting energy security and resilience, minimizing the region's carbon footprints. Indeed, we must be ambitious, a Caribbean that is powered by renewable energy by 2050.

I am sure there are others related to Governance and institutions both at the national and regional levels but we wanted to look at a few as a basis to initiate a conversation and to support a long-term vision for the Caribbean we want by the middle of the century.

When taken together, these elements could address some of the major challenges that are common to the region and that require regional efforts to solve. The framework offers strategies that will seek to: balance the concerns of survivability today and sustainability tomorrow; recapture the potential of the young people across the Caribbean; renew and re-energise the focus on the need to secure the energy requirements of the region; and, the need for a truly transformational system of governance across the region whilst strengthening systems that safeguard against corruption and ineffectiveness.

The consultancy team will have the chance to speak about their work so I will like to focus on just a few policy options starting with The Blue Economy.

I was in Samoa last September attending the SIDS Global Conference and we in the Commonwealth fully support the SAMOA Pathways and the call made for great recognition of the vulnerabilities of small states, and support for SIDS in building their resilience. However, after listening to all the presentations and thinking about the notion of SIDS, I thought it might be useful to look at some data that can help us think through this issue and perhaps turn the standard assumption on its head.

Let us walk through some data for a moment.

As we know, Barbados has a land area of 430 sq. kms but we may not know that it has an ocean space of 200,000 sq. kms; St Lucia has a land area of 616 sq. kms but a maritime zone of 15,260 sq. kms; Grenada's land area is 344 square kms and an ocean space of 27,500 square kms; When you look at Trinidad and Tobago, it has a land area of 5,198 sq. kms and an ocean space of 79,000 square kms.

In the case of the Bahamas, its land space is 13,900 square kms and an ocean space of 684,000 sq. kms. We are currently supporting Bahamas to extend their continental shelf which if successful will result in an additional 200,000 sq. km of ocean space giving it a total maritime zone covering approximately 884,000 sq. kms compared to its land space of 13,900 square kilometres.

To my mind, we need to get out of the prism that imprisons us into thinking that we are small island states and sometimes miss, what is most obvious. We could also think that we are medium or big ocean states as is the case of The Bahamas. It is in this context, we in the Commonwealth will like to propose an emphasis on The "Blue Economy"—embracing the concept of an ocean-based economy as a mechanism to realise sustainable growth. The premise being that the oceans can play a pivotal role in tackling the longer-term socio-economic and environmental challenges.

The Blue Economy is potentially of major value to all Caribbean countries—the opportunity to create more value out of existing and new resource streams cannot be overlooked. This must include both existing benefits and uses, such as fisheries and shipping. Among the opportunities identified as having potential in the Blue Economy are marine fish farming, renewable energy, seabed minerals and marine biotechnology.

The Commonwealth Secretariat has been working with a number of countries in the region in this regard and will continue to do so. National Ocean Policies have been prepared for several countries including St Kitts and Nevis, St Vincent and the Grenadines and The Bahamas.

A few countries have recognised the potential of the Blue Economy and are moving ahead at a fast pace. The recently elected Government in Mauritius has established a Ministry dedicated to the Oceans. Mauritius' neighbour, Seychelles just recently established a new Ministry, The Ministry of Finance, Trade and the Blue Economy. We need to act quickly before, yet another opportunity is lost.

Secondly, we will like to suggest a stronger focus on the diaspora from two standpoints, firstly that of the diasporic economy on which some studies have already been done and secondly from the perspective of remittances. On remittances, when we think about the issue, we do not ordinarily reflect on the cost of remittances. We have been advocating and Turkey as the President of the G20 on 14th April at the Commonwealth La Francophonie/G20 Development Dialogue made a renewed commitment to bring down the cost of remittances from 10% to 5%.

This may seem nominal or unimportant. However, in 2014 the region received an estimated $5 billion in remittances. Assuming the figure is constant for the next ten years, a reduction in the cost from 10% to 5% could result in an additional $2.5 billion injected into Caribbean economies. For this to happen, sustained advocacy is required in ensuring that this G20 commitment is met. This is another concrete and specific area where additional financing can be injected into economies of the region without resorting to a cap-in-hand policy.

Again on the issue of remittances and this is linked to the diasporic economy, when you look at the data for Bangladesh which received an estimated $15 billion in remittances in 2014, 40% of those resources went into investment and not consumption. We need to reflect on this and imagine, or reimagine how our remittances can be structured accordingly and more effectively leverage our diaspora as investors and networks. There are some good signs in this area with Antigua and Barbuda recently establishing a Diaspora village.

Again on the theme of innovative financing, we will like to table two specific initiatives on which we are working that can benefit the Caribbean. The first is a Small States Trade Financing Facility to help our entrepreneurs access trade financing through a system of guarantees. We are also aware that there is indeed funding for Climate Finance.

However, oftentimes our jurisdictions do not have the capacities to unlock the financing. Consequently, we are tabling a proposal to establish a Climate Finance Skills Hub which is intended to help countries unlock Climate Finance in the Caribbean, Pacific and Africa. Work is underway on these two initiatives and support will be required from member states to get both approved at our forthcoming Heads of Government meeting in Malta in November 2015. We also recognise the need for financing to deal with shocks.

On energy, less than five percent of energy generated is currently renewable, and less than 20 percent of the private sector is energy efficient in the region. This has to change and we need to have a towering vision to be 100% reliant on renewables by 2050. There is no other option.

For young people, entrepreneurship is a key driver of human capital, unleashing the economic potential of youth and promoting sustainable growth and development. 18 percent of new and emerging businesses are owned by young people in Latin America and the Caribbean—some distance behind Africa with 30 percent youth-owned businesses. The consultancy team will speak to this issue during the dialogue.

The evidence collated by the team indicate strong prospects for the region—with the appropriate policy intervention, and commitment, we can have a better trajectory. However, only with the right institutional arrangements and leadership. The time for the politics of expedience and convenience has come to an end. Too much is at stake.

To make this a reality, our efforts leading to 2050 must be underpinned by enhanced levels of support from the international community. For small states, international support is required in: accessing resources, on favourable terms to fund critical infrastructure projects; and filling capacity gaps that hamper their ability to cope with emerging economic, social and environmental issues.

This is where organisations like the Commonwealth can play a role in global advocacy. However, this should not take away from the fact that this is our region and we have to accept both responsibility and ownership in addressing the challenges and finding solutions.

I therefore hope that we will use this session to deliberate on these issues, and to identify concrete next steps towards implementing targeted solutions. As a Commonwealth, we are committed to supporting the region in the planning for, and realising a Vision for the Caribbean we want by 2050 built on resilience.

I thank you!!!

Allow me to welcome Dr Moore to make his presentation.

KEYNOTE ADDRESS BY AMINA MOHAMMED, UN SPECIAL ADVISOR ON POST-2015 DEVELOPMENT PLANNING

7 May 2015 (Trinidad & Tobago)

INTRODUCTION

- Ladies and gentlemen, I am delighted to be here today and glad to have the opportunity to discuss with you the essential role of the Caribbean in delivering on the post-2015 development agenda.
- The post-2015 agenda is a universal agenda that builds on the MDGs toward an integrated vision to ensure an inclusive, safe, resilient and sustainable future.
- The universal and transformative nature of the agenda must reach every corner of the Caribbean to address the specific risks and vulnerabilities that surround the Small Island Developing States.

PROMOTING A SUSTAINABLE ECONOMY TO ADDRESS CHALLENGES OF SIDS

- To address these challenges in the Caribbean, the Post-2015 agenda calls for a renewed Global Partnership for sustainable development.
- As you are aware, one of the most prominent challenges of SIDS is climate change, with its widespread adverse impacts to human health and the environment.
- The post-2015 agenda aims to tackle climate change in an integrated manner that maximizes the effectiveness and impact of the efforts of diverse stakeholders.
- Sustainability is critical for long-term economic growth. Utilizing a holistic approach emphasizes the close connection between economic development and environmental sustainability and incorporates the co-benefits that matter to different audiences, such as green job creation, utility costs savings, open public space or sustainable tourism.
- We must also address the issues of connectivity for the full integration of the Caribbean into the world economy by leveraging the power of information communication technologies (ICTs). The use of ICTs can improve the areas of health, education, agriculture, business,

government and disaster risk reduction, and lead to tre- mendous positive impacts on the lives of many.

- Therefore, governments in the Caribbean should align their national development plans and programs with the SDGs.
- This includes improving resource efficiency, facilitating investments in renewable energy and sustainability infrastructure, regulat- ing land use and other private behavior, and building resilience, including through climate adaption and mitigation.
- By tying in such measures into broader economic goals, we are investing in our future to ensure economic, environmental and social sustainability.
- The continued leadership and engagement of the Caribbean states in regional collaborations and in their individual capacities in this area will be essential to coordinating the global effort to fight climate change in the context of sustainable development.

ENSURING SOCIAL INCLUSION FOR ECONOMIC AND HUMAN DEVELOPMENT

- Ladies and Gentlemen, the core of the post-2015 agenda is poverty eradication. In achieving sustainable development and dignity for all, the agenda aims to address the essential needs of the most marginalized populations so that no one is left behind.
- To leave no one behind, the post-2015 agenda strives to reduce inequalities within and among countries, and promote the social, economic and political inclusion of all, including minorities and women. Good governance and the rule of law will be essential to reducing crime and violence and ensuring human security.
- Among the most vulnerable populations are women and children, who are disproportionately affected by conflict and climate impacts.
- Women's leadership and active participation are critical to promote peace, tackle climate change and ensure sustainable development.
- Due to their social roles, women are the nexus to food, water and energy. Therefore, they hold the keys to climate action – their knowledge contributes to adaption strategies and their participation is vital to implementing mitigation plans within communities.
- We must also unlock the potential of our youth, as they will be the torch-bearers of the post-2015 agenda and our future efforts to achieve sustainable development.

- The empowerment of women and youth will be key to driving economic growth and ensuring sustainable development. We must invest in our human capital to ensure stronger economies and peace- ful, inclusive societies.

MOBILIZING ALL MEANS OF IMPLEMENTATION TO FINANCE DEVELOPMENT

- The post-2015 development agenda will need to be supported by adequate Means of Implementation, through a renewed Global Partnership.
- Public financing will still be at the core, but it must be complemented with innovative forms of financing. We must mobilize all the resources available and unlock the trillions of resources that may be made available.
- Multi-stakeholder partnerships at all levels (global, regional, national and local) will be at the core of implementation.
- They have proven effective to galvanize broad-based joint action, define concrete objectives and clear timetables as well as serve as mutual accountability frameworks. They engage diverse stakeholders to deliver at multiple scales, from the bottom-up.
- Partnership is about the integration of visions, values, plans, re-sources and knowledge sharing. And at the core of renewed partner-ships is inclusiveness, transparency and mutual accountability.
- The private sector also has responsibilities and all must work in partnership, within and across sectors.
- Civil society's involvement in partnerships is one of the corner-stones of accountability within every partnership, be it local, na-tional, regional or global.

MAKING INSTITUTIONS FIT FOR PURPOSE FOR EFFECTIVE IMPLEMENTATION

- To truly deliver on a new development agenda, it is vital that we strengthen international, regional, national and local institutions through the coherence of policies and the implementation of all three pillars of sustainable development.
- National commitment is essential to provide the appropriate legal frameworks and institutional and financial capacity for local governments.

- Local and regional actors will be key players in public service delivery to ensure equal access to basic services such as primary education, health care, clean water supply, sanitation, solid waste and energy supply.
- The UN system must also be fit-for purpose, leading by example and supporting implementation at the country level.
- To eradicate poverty and build the path to a sustainable future, theinternational community must be equipped with equitable, long-term strategies toward economic development, social inclusion and environmental protection.

MAXIMIZING THIS TIME FOR GLOBAL ACTION

- This year offers a unique opportunity for global leaders and people to set the world on the path to a universal, transformative and integrated agenda that leaves no one behind. Never before has the world had the unique opportunity to address such a complex agenda in a single year.
- The three high-level international meetings in Addis Ababa, New York and Paris in the year ahead give us the opportunity to build on the MDGs and establish a paradigm shift in international development.
- During these next several months, we must keep the ambition high to ensure a truly transformative agenda. The active engagement and robust support of all relevant stakeholders in the intergovernmental negotiations is essential to set the landscape for the FFD Conference in July and adoption of post-2015 agenda in September.
- It is of vital importance that the special challenges in the Caribbean and the specific proposals to address them are reflected in discussions and included in the new agenda.
- Therefore, we look forward to your continued engagement in these processes.

I thank you for your attention.

FORUM ON THE
FUTURE OF THE
CARIBBEAN

MAY 5-7, 2015
The University of the West Indies
& the Hyatt Regency, Trinidad and Tobago

FORUM ON THE
FUTURE OF THE
CARIBBEAN

Disruptive Thinking. Bold Action. Practical Outcomes.

Day 1 - May 5, 2015, UWI St. Augustine Campus

Stimulating Radical Ideas

On the first day academics from across the world, and regional thought leaders and policy-makers will present radical ideas and outline deeply practical outcomes around our key themes, including Caribbean convergence, the resilience of Small Island Developing States (SIDS), the quality of data for decision making and pathways to a more sustainable future.

8:30 am	**Opening Remarks**
	PVC Professor Clement Sankat, Campus Principal, UWI, St. Augustine
	Opening Address
	Professor Patrick Watson, Director, The Sir Arthur Lewis Institute of Social and Economic Studies, St Augustine
	Welcome Remarks
	Dr Antonio Prado, Deputy Executive Secretary, Economic Commission for Latin American and the Caribbean (ECLAC)
9:15am	**Convergence of Ideas and Ideals**
	Moderator
	Dr David Anyanwu, academic consultant
	1. *Macroeconomic Instability in Small Island State*
	Dr Anthony Birchwood, Lecturer, Department of Economics, UWI, St. Augustine
	2. *Implementation Deficit: Why Member States Do Not Comply With CARICOM Directives*
	Professor Paul C. Clement, Chair, Department of Social Sciences, Fashion Institute of Technology, New York
	3. *Bank spreads in the Caribbean*
	Presented by Dr Dorian Noel, Lecturer, Department of Management Studies, UWI, St. Augustine
	Written with Professor Michael Brei, Assistant Professor, Econoix, Paris, Dr Antony Birchwood, Lecturer, Department of Economics, UWI, St. Augustine
	4. *Caribbean Offshore Financial Centres*
	Professor Rose-Marie Belle Antoine, Dean, Faculty of Law, The University of the West Indies, St Augustine Campus
10:30am	**Coffee break**

10:45am	**Building Resilience in Small Island Developing States (SIDS)** Moderator Ms Toni Thorne, World Economic Forum Global Shaper Bridgetown hub and CEO of Thorne Publishing Productions *1. Vulnerability in Small Island Economies* Presented by Dr Sebastian Auguste, Universidad Torcuato Di Tella, Buenos Aires, Argentina Written with Ms Magdalena Cornejo, Universidad Torcuato Di Tella, Buenos Aires, Argentina *2. Situating the Caribbean within the new Global Political Economy of Development* Dr Matthew Bishop, Lecturer, Institute of International Relations, UWI, St. Augustine *3. Case study for Building Resilience: A New Path to Sustainable Industry Development* Mrs Indera Sagewan-Alli, Executive Director, Caribbean Centre for Competitiveness
12:pm	**Lunch**
1:00pm	**Better Data = Better Measurement = Better Decision Making** Moderator Ms Jennifer Raffoul, World Economic Forum Global Shaper Port of Spain hub and Founder and CEO of Made in the Caribbean *1. Governance in the Caribbean SIDS – Evidence From Governance Global Indicators* Professor Lino Briguglio, Director, Islands and Small States Institute, University of Malta *2. Appropriate multidimensional indicators and measurements of poverty and vulnerability for the Caribbean* Presented by Dr Valérie Angeon, University of French West Indies, Guadeloupe Written with Dr Samuel Bates PSL Research University, Paris *3. An Empirical Analysis of Poverty and its Determinants in Trinidad and Tobago* Presented by Ms Raynata Wiggins, PhD candidate, The Sir Arthur Lewis Institute of Social and Economic Studies, St. Augustine Written with Dr Sandra Sookram, Research Fellow, The Sir Arthur Lewis Institute of Social and Economic Studies, St. Augustine

2:15pm	**From Resilience to Sustainability** Moderator Mr Kirk-Anthony Hamilton, World Economic Forum Global Shaper Kingston hub and Founder and CEO of The Infiniti Partnership 1. *Integrating Climate Change Adaptation into Coastal Zone Management* Presented by Dr Rahanna Juman, Institute of Marine Affairs, Hilltop Lane, Chaguaramas, Trinidad and Tobago Written with Mr Kahlil Hassanali, Institute of Marine Affairs, Hilltop Lane, Chaguaramas, Trinidad and Tobago 2. *The Inflationary Costs of the Extreme Weather: Evidence from the Caribbean* Presented by Professor Eric Strobl, Ecole Polytechnique, Paris Written with Dr Andreas Heinen, Universite Cergy-Pontoise, Paris, Dr Jeetendra Kadran, Inter-American Development Bank 3. *Micro, Small and Medium Enterprises as Indicators of Resilience to Climate Change in the Caribbean* Presented by Dr Perry Polar, Caribbean Network for Urban and Land Management, UWI, St. Augustine Written with Dr Asad Mohammed, Caribbean Network for Urban and Land Management, UWI, St. Augustine
3:30pm	**Coffee break**
3:45pm	**Metrics for Sustainability** Moderator Ms Kaierouann Imarah Radix (World Economic Forum Global Shaper Georgetown hub and Executive director S4 Foundation) 1. *Measuring the Effectiveness of Models of Cooperation:* Regional Integration and Cooperation as one of the Crucial Elements of Caribbean Development Mr Viktor Sukup, Member, Board of Directors, Club of Rome/Brussels Guest Professor, University of Buenos Aires. 2. *Participatory Mapping: Caribbean Small Island Developing States* Presented by Ms Alison K. DeGraff, Department of Geomatics Engineering and Land Management, UWI, St. Augustine Written with Dr Bheshem Ramlal, Department of Geomatics Engineering and Land Management, UWI, St. Augustine 3. *New Pathways to Sustainable Development in the Caribbean* Ms Shariann Henry, UWI, St. Augustine
5:00pm	**Reception hosted by PVC Professor Clement Sankat** **UWI Campus Principal, St. Augustine at the Office of the Campus Principal**

Day 2 - May 6, 2015, Port of Spain Hyatt Hotel

Rethinking the Caribbean Future

On day 2, we will begin to build a vision of how the Caribbean could transform itself by 2050. Comprising a series of keynote speeches by internationally renowned experts, followed by moderated roundtable discussions, delegates will discuss themes around global and regional convergence including CARICOM integration and opportunities for convergence from the private sector. We will address too the crucial role that the political economy and governance plays in delivering sustainable development.

8:00am	National Anthem of Trinidad and Tobago Introduction Ms. Frances Seignoret, Permanent Secretary Ministry of Foreign Affairs, Trinidad and Tobago Welcome Ambassador Irwin LaRocque, Secretary General, Caribbean Community (CARICOM) Ambassador Alfonso Múnera Cavadía, Secretary General, Association of Caribbean States Opening Statement Sir Hilary Beckles, Vice Chancellor , UWI
8:45am	**Session 1: Global Convergence: A Place for the Caribbean** **Ministry of Foreign Affairs, Trinidad and Tobago** To disrupt the current paradigm of Caribbean integration and place the region in the global convergence process. How does the Caribbean optimally position itself to benefit from a rapidly progressing global convergence agenda? What are the limits to Caribbean convergence: economics, politics or both? How can the Caribbean generate the political will to drive convergence? How can the region deepen integration with Latin America? How does the renewed US-Cuba relationship impact the Caribbean? What lessons can be learnt from highly successful integration models? Where does the Caribbean stand in the global convergence process? Opening Remarks and Introduction Moderator Mr Mark Wilson, Economist Intelligence Unit A Convergence of Caribbean Economies: Will the Opportunity be Missed Again?

8:45am	Introductory keynote The Honourable Mr. Winston Dookeran, Minister of Foreign Affairs, Trinidad and Tobago
	The Pacific Alliance: Lessons for Caribbean Integration
	Keynote Address
	Ambassador Armando Arriazola Peto Rueda, Special Advisor in the Division for Latin America and the Caribbean, Ministry of Foreign Affairs, Mexico
	Round Table: Convergence: The Caribbean and International partners
	Ambassador Henri-Paul Normandin, Director General of the Latin America and Caribbean Bureau of the Department of Foreign Affairs, Trade and Development, Canada
	Improving Cooperation among Caribbean States
	Ambassador Alfonso Múnera Cavadía, Secretary General, Association of Caribbean States
	CARICOM as an Integration Model
	Irwin LaRocque, Secretary General, Caribbean Community
	Perspectives on Caribbean Convergence
	Dr. Antonio F. Romero Gómez, Chair of Caribbean Studies, "Norman Girvan"- University of Havana
	Discussants
	Caribbean convergence, Dr Matthew Bishop, Lecturer, Institute of International Relations, UWI, St. Augustine
	US-Cuba relations, Dr Jacqueline Laguardia Martinez, Lecturer, Institute of International Relation, UWI, St Augustine
	Dominican Republic's role in Caribbean Convergence, Mr Iván E. Ogando Lora, Former Director General of CARIFORUM
	Questions and Answers
10:45am	**Coffee break**

11:00am	**Session 2: Location Strategies for the Caribbean: Convergence of Ideas and Ideals** **Arthur Lok Jack Graduate School of Business** To extract lessons for Caribbean convergence from disruptive action by the private sector. The private sector is a leading driver, beneficiary and blocker of regional integration. Caribbean convergence is moving a pace among private sector players. What incentives would encourage the private sector to play an active role in regional policy debates and push convergence? What are the best opportunities and examples of Caribbean convergence from the private sector including Small and Medium Enterprises? Presenter and Moderator: Professor Miguel Carrillo, Executive Director, Arthur Lok Jack Graduate School of Business Round Table Dr Didacus Jules, Director General Organization of Eastern Caribbean states (OECS) Mr Richard Lewis, Chairman, Council for Competiveness and Innovation, Ministry of Planning and Sustainable Development Mr Ian Chinapoo, Executive Director, The Unit Trust Corporation of Trinidad and Tobago Mr David Dual-Whiteway, Managing Director, Republic Bank Presenters Is There a Caribbean Sclerosis: A Critical Assessment of the Private Sector Dr Inder Ruprah, Regional Economic Advisor, Inter-American Development Bank Building Private Sector Partnerships beyond the Caribbean: Is this Real or Illusionary? H.E. Albert Ramdin, Assistant Secretary General, Organization of American States (OAS) Questions and Answers
1:00pm	**Lunch**

	Session 3: Building the Resilience of the Small States: A Strategic Vision for the Caribbean 2050
	The Commonwealth Secretariat
	To capture the burning aspirations of the Caribbean, outline concrete proposals for achieving them and to show the consequences of inaction.
	Concrete steps to improve Caribbean development require visioning techniques and a careful assessment of the current development challenges, in particular citizen security, youth development, energy, private sector development and innovation. What is the ideal Caribbean in 2050? Where would the current growth and development strategies in the Caribbean lead? How can the Caribbean improve development prospects and build resilience to external shocks and new vulnerabilities? What are the practical outcomes for achieving an ideal Caribbean in 2050?
	Moderator and Keynote Presenter
	Context and Motivations for Caribbean Vision 2050
2:00pm	Mr. Deodat Maharaj, Deputy Secretary-General for Economic and Social Development, Commonwealth Secretariat
	Presenters
	Summary of the Key Findings, Dr Sylvia Charles, Consultant and President of the Organization of Women of the Americas
	Dr Winston Moore, Senior lecturer, UWI, Cave Hill
	Roundtable
	Youth, Ms Eleanor Joseph, Caribbean Regional Youth Council Consultant
	Energy, Dr Marsha Atherley-Ikechi, Utility Analyst, Fair Trading Commission
	Citizen Security, Professor Anthony Clayton, Alcan Professor of Caribbean Sustainable Development, Institute for Sustainable Development, UWI Mona
	Private sector and innovation, Professor Ryan Peterson, Lecturer, University of Aruba
	Development Strategies, Dr Christine Clarke, Lecturer, UWI Mona
3:45pm	**Coffee break**

	Session 4: New Thinking for New Times
	To get the reaction of political leaders on adopting disruptive and innovative ideas and ways to avoiding implementation deficit.
	Political leaders play a crucial role in shaping the development path of nations. Top leaders with proper vision and decisive action are crucial for development. How can leaders in the region build the political will to take hard decisions?
	Opening Remarks
	The Honourable Kamla Persad-Bissessar, SC, Prime Minister of The Republic Trinidad and Tobago
	Moderator
	Sir Hillary Beckles, Vice Chancellor , The UWI
	Keynote Address
	International Economic and Trade issues
	H.E. Dr Mukhisa Kituyi, Secretary General, United Nations Conference on Trade and Development (UNCTAD)
4:00pm	Keynote Address
	Reinventing Caribbean Regionalism in an Emerging Multiplex World
	Professor Amitav Acharya, Professor, School of International Service, American University, Washington, DC
	High Level Round Table
	The Honourable Kamla Persad-Bissessar
	Prime Minister of The Republic Trinidad and Tobago, SC
	Represented by The Honourable Vasant Bharat Minister of Trade, Industry, Investment and Communication
	The Honourable Mr. Winston Dookeran, Minister of Foreign Affairs, Trinidad and Tobago
	Dr. The Honourable Ralph Gonsalves, Prime Minister of St. Vincent and the Grenadines
	The Honourable Freundel Stuart, Prime Minister of Barbados
	The Right Honourable Perry Christie, Prime Minister of The Bahamas
	To be represented by The Honourable Frederick Audley Mitchell Jr
	Minister of Foreign Affairs of The Bahamas
7:30pm	**Formal Reception hosted by The Honourable Kamla Persad-Bissessar**

Day 3 - May 7, 2015, Port of Spain Hyatt Hotel

Taking Action for Sustainable Outcomes

The focus of the final day of the Forum will be on creating the momentum and means to take bold action for the future. Prompted by thought-provoking keynote speeches and roundtable discussions, delegates will be invited to debate innovative, yet practical, ways of tackling poverty and inequality, reducing debt levels, delivering green and blue growth strategies and human capital development, and the role of Caribbean diplomacy in the global world of politics.

8:00am	**Welcome Message and Introduction**
	Mr. Richard Blewitt, United Nations Resident Coordinator
	Introductory Keynote Address
	A New Approach to Sustainable Development Governance in the Caribbean: Is it happening?
	Senator Dr The Honourable Dr Bhoendradatt Tewarie, Minister of Planning and Sustainable Development, Trinidad and Tobago
	Keynote Address
	The Caribbean in Post-2015 Development Planning
	Ms Amina Mohammed, Special Adviser to the UN Secretary-General
9:00am	**Session 5: Pillars for Sustainability**
	Moderator
	Dr Giovanni di Cola, Special Advisor of the Multilateral Cooperation, Department (Multilaterals), International Labour Organization (ILO), Geneva
	Education: The Anchor for Caribbean Sustainability
	Dr. Didacus Jules, Director General of the OECS
	Gender Deficit: The Challenge for Social Sustainability
	Professor Patricia Mohammed, Institute for Gender and Development Studies, University of the West Indies
	Potentials and Achievements in the ALBA-PETROCARIBE Area
	Luis Alejandro Sauce Navarro, PETROCARIBE Main Advisor
10:45am	**Coffee break**

	Session 6A: Poverty and Inequality: Could it End? United Nations Development Programme Finding innovative solutions and measurements of multidimensional poverty, well-being and inequality to improve resource allocation and decision making. In the fight against poverty innovative approaches to resource mobilization and decision making is critical. Moreover, poverty is multidimensional and should be measured beyond income to include wider human deprivations. What are appropriate multidimensional poverty and well-being indicators? How can they be used to improve resource allocation, decision making and monitor policy interventions? How to improve data dissemination, quantity and quality to better inform the public? What best practices can be adopted to improve data quantity and quality? What are innovative solutions to poverty and inequality reduction? Opening Remarks and Introduction Moderator Professor Patrick Watson, Director, The Sir Arthur Lewis Institute of Social and Economic Studies, St Augustine Presentations Are Measurement Indicators for Poverty and Inequality the Problem? Introductory keynote Dr George Gray Molina, Chief Economist, Regional Bureau for Latin America and the Caribbean, UNDP New York) Is Mexico's Experience on Data Transparency Transferrable to the Caribbean? Ms Martha Moreno Perez, The National Council for the Evaluation of Social Development Policy (Coneval) Are there Really Data solutions for the Caribbean? Dr Philomen Harrison, Project Director, Regional Statistics, CARICOM Discussants Education, PVC Professor Clement Sankat, Principal, UWI, St. Augustine Child poverty and gender, Mr Joaquín Guzmán Alemán, Regional Adviser, Social Policy, UNICEF Health, Dr James Hospedales, Executive Director, the Caribbean Public Health Agency Questions and Answers
11:00am	

	Session 6B: Bold Action and Outcomes: Governance Challenges
	United Nations Development Programme
	To advocate bold action and solutions to promote peaceful and inclusive societies for sustainable development
	What is the role of good governance in localizing the post-2015 sustainable development agenda? What is the role of political will and leadership required to overcome challenges to sustainable development challenges? How can the citizenry be adequately involved in the localization of the development agenda through inclusive and participatory decision-making and increase accountability and transparency? What are the new growth strategies for sustainable development? How can the rule of law be promoted at the national and regional level to foster a legal and political framework for sustainable development?
	Opening Remarks and Introduction
	Moderator: Ms Allison Drayton, Senior Advisor Regional Bureau for Latin America and the Caribbean
	Presentations
11:00am	Governance Challenges in Development Planning
	Ms Amina Mohammed, Special Adviser to the UN Secretary-General
	The Role of Multilaterals in strengthening good governance
	Dr Inder Ruprah, Regional Economic Advisor, Inter-American Development Bank
	Caribbean Governance: Are we missing Forecasting Skills?
	Professor Anthony Clayton, Alcan Professor, Caribbean Sustainable Development, Institute for Sustainable Development, UWI Mona
	Discussants
	Is the Politics in Caribbean Governance our Problem?, Dr Wendy Grenade, Lecturer, Department of Government, Sociology & Social Work UWI, Cave Hill
	Caribbean Governance and multidimensional security threats, New Governance Scenarios for Small States, Professor Lino Briguglio, Director, Islands and Small States Institute, University of Malta
	Have Caribbean Growth Strategies Failed?, Dr Justin Ram, Director of Economics, Caribbean Development Bank
	Questions and Answers

1:00pm	**Lunch** **Luncheon Presentations** Caribbean Youth and Regional Sustainability: Ensuring a Future for the Region Professor Rhoda Reddock, Deputy Principal, UWI, St. Augustine Mr Hamilton Moss, Vice President of Energy of the Latin American Development Bank (CAF)
2:00pm	**Session 7: Advocating Innovative Financing Solutions** **Economic Commission for Latin America and the Caribbean (ECLAC)** To advocate innovative financing solutions for the Caribbean amid high debt, reduced aid and stricter loan concessionalities. What can the Caribbean expect from the ongoing discussion on financing for development and what are the new opportunities for access to finance? What are the new and emerging opportunities for development financing domestically, regionally and internationally? How can the region identify strategies, partnerships and arrangements to create a new compact which seeks to establish a multi-stakeholder platform with governments, international development organizations, private sector and academics to arrive at practical solutions? Opening Remarks and introduction Moderator Dr Antonio Prado, Deputy Executive Secretary ECLAC Presentations Addressing financing for development issues in the Caribbean Ms Gail Hurley, Policy Specialist, Development Finance, UNDP Bureau for Policy and Programme Support New thinking on Bond Financing (diaspora and "blue" bonds) Mr Jwala Rambarran, Governor of the Central Bank of Trinidad and Tobago Discussants Mr Ransford Smith, Former Deputy Secretary-General for Economic Affairs and Development of the Commonwealth of Nations Dr Compton Bourne, Former, Executive Director Caribbean Centre for Money and Finance Questions and Answers
3:45pm	**Coffee break**

	Session 8: Global Diplomacy in the Caribbean
	Institute of International Relations, UWI, St. Augustine
	To take bold action through diplomacy and advocacy in creating a new global compact that supports development in the Caribbean.
	Diplomatic activity has to contend with a more plural and complex world that is experiencing tension resulting from concurrent processes of fragmentation and integration. In such a context, is there a role for small states? What are the economics of new space diplomacy?
	Opening Remarks and introduction
	Moderator Professor Andy Knight, Director of the Institute of International Relations, UWI, St Augustine and Professor and former Chair of the Department of Political Science at the University of Alberta
	Presentations
	Small states diplomacy: Has it vanished?
	Professor Andrew Cooper, Professor of Political Science, University of Waterloo, Canada
4:00pm	Asymmetrical Diplomacy or Diplomatic Asymmetries?: The Caribbean and Global Health Governance
	Dr Obijiofor Aginam, Head of Governance for Global Health, UNU International Institute for Global Health, Kuala Lumpur (Global Health Diplomacy)
	Strategic Diplomacy in the 21st Century: Survival Skill yet to be Learned
	Professor Jochen Prantl, Associate Professor, Australia National University
	Space Exploration and Developing Countries: A tool for diplomacy and sustainability
	Camille Wardrop Alleyne, Aerospace Engineer, National Aeronautics and Space Administration
	Discussants
	Dr Alissa Trotz, Caribbean Studies at New College and Women and Gender Studies University of Toronto
	Mr. Rajiv Ramlal, Senior Officer, Office of the Chef de Cabinet, Executive Office of the UN Secretary-General
	Questions and Answers
	Forum Closure
5:30pm	PVC Professor Clement Sankat, Principal, UWI, St. Augustine
	The Honourable Mr. Winston Dookeran, Minister of Foreign Affairs, Trinidad and Tobago

Index

www.ingramcontent.com/pod-product-compliance
Lightning Source LLC
Chambersburg PA
CBHW060136280326
41932CB00012B/1539